Conservation Politics
The Last Anti-Colonial Battle

Whilst the science of conservation biology is thriving as a discipline, ultimately global conservation is failing. Why, when the majority of people say they value nature and its protection? David Johns argues that the loss of species and healthy ecosystems is best understood as human imposition of a colonial relationship on the non-human world – one of exploitation and domination. Global institutions benefit from transforming nature into commodities, and conservation is a low priority. This book places political issues at the forefront, and tackles critical questions of conservation efficacy. It considers the role of effective influence on decision making, key policy changes to reduce the human footprint, and the centrality of culture in mobilising support. It draws on political lessons from successful social movements, including human anti-colonial struggles, to provide conservation biologists and practitioners in scientific and social science disciplines and NGOs with the tools and wider context to accelerate their work's impact.

DAVID JOHNS is both a conservation practitioner and Adjunct Professor of Political Science in the Hatfield School of Government at Portland State University, where he teaches courses on politics and the environment, US constitutional law, and politics. He has published extensively on science, politics, and conservation issues. He is a cofounder of the Wildlands Network, Yellowstone to Yukon Conservation Initiative, and Conservation Biology Institute, and is currently Chair of the Marine Conservation Institute board which created the Global Ocean Refuge System Initiative. He has worked with NGOs on conservation projects in the Russian Far East, Australia, Europe, southern Africa and throughout the Americas. He is recipient of the Denver Zoological Foundation's Conservation Award, 2007.

Bruce Babbitt, when he was Secretary of the Interior, was fond of saying to conservationists, "Don't expect me to do the right thing, make me do it." Conservationists made impressive strides after Rachel Carson's *Silent Spring*, by relying on passion and persuasion, but little progress has been made since the 1970s, as corporate opposition has coalesced into a powerful counter-movement. Meanwhile, with shrinking opportunities for habitat protection and the looming specter of climate change, the need for further progress is greater than ever. David Johns, a political scientist with a deep interest in popular movements, makes the case that conservation will only return to the forefront of the nation's agenda when citizens mobilize into a vigorous movement with the energy to elect advocates to positions of political power. His new book offers deep insights into how to achieve this goal.

John Terborgh, Ph.D.

The scientific case has been made. Poets have spoken with deep feeling. Now comes the hard part. In this well-written and very timely book, David Johns lays out the practical, political steps required to save the rest of life on Earth, and ultimately ourselves.

Edward O. Wilson, Harvard University

We the people must accept that any conservation activity of worth must be a political act. This is a simple but not a small idea. The insults foisted upon Mother Earth are so pervasive, that nothing less than the world's greatest collective action will suffice as redress. Politics is the only scheme that can organize and advance such action. David Johns writes clearly to this end from the hard ground of history and science. His book is a call to arms to use politics to promote peace, prosperity, and justice for all life. Let's hope that we the people heed the call. Every future depends on it.

Mike Phillips, Turner Endangered Species Fund,
Montana State Senator

David Johns has done it again! The author of *A New Conservation Politics* brings his wide knowledge of the conservation movement and other social movements to provide practical insights on how to make conservation more effective. This book fills a critical gap in conservation literature by explaining how to overcome the political obstacles to conservation. For those who care about the extinction crisis, he offers a path to action beyond business-as-usual. In the end conservation is too complex to leave it to scientists, and much too important to leave it to politicians. He combines both worlds into a powerful mix.

Ignacio Jiménez Pérez, The Conservation Land Trust Argentina

In the 30 years I've worked with David Johns for things wild and free, I've seen him become a leading activist on the visionary cutting edge of rewilding and also as our deepest thinker on effective activism. Witness his latest book.

Dave Foreman, author of *Rewilding North America* and
The Great Conservation Divide

Conservation Politics
The Last Anti-Colonial Battle

DAVID JOHNS
Portland State University

CAMBRIDGE
UNIVERSITY PRESS

CAMBRIDGE
UNIVERSITY PRESS

University Printing House, Cambridge CB2 8BS, United Kingdom

One Liberty Plaza, 20th Floor, New York, NY 10006, USA

477 Williamstown Road, Port Melbourne, VIC 3207, Australia

314–321, 3rd Floor, Plot 3, Splendor Forum, Jasola District Centre,
New Delhi – 110025, India

79 Anson Road, #06–04/06, Singapore 079906

Cambridge University Press is part of the University of Cambridge.

It furthers the University's mission by disseminating knowledge in the pursuit of
education, learning, and research at the highest international levels of excellence.

www.cambridge.org
Information on this title: www.cambridge.org/9781107199583
DOI: 10.1017/9781108185752

First published 2019

Printed in the United Kingdom by TJ International Ltd, Padstow Cornwall

A catalogue record for this publication is available from the British Library.

Library of Congress Cataloging-in-Publication Data
Names: Johns, David, 1951– author.
Title: Conservation politics : the last anti-colonial battle / David Johns,
    Portland State University.
Description: Cambridge, United Kingdom ; New York, NY : Cambridge
    University Press, 2019.
Identifiers: LCCN 2018046209 | ISBN 9781107199583 (hardback) |
    ISBN 9781316648933 (paperback)
Subjects: LCSH: Nature conservation–Political aspects.
Classification: LCC QH75 .J64 2019 | DDC 333.95/16–dc23
LC record available at https://lccn.loc.gov/2018046209

ISBN 978-1-107-19958-3 Hardback
ISBN 978-1-316-64893-3 Paperback

For Gunter & Chocomo. Always close to the Earth; they know what's what. And to all those on the front lines – unafraid to lead and to embrace without hesitation the fight on behalf of Earth and its life, who follow their love where it takes them regardless of the obstacles. And for Signe.

Science without politics has no impact, politics without science can be dangerous ...

Peter Piot, MD, co-discover of Ebola,
World Health Organization administrator, and United Nations
Under Secretary-General, *No Time to Lose*, 2012

[A]ll attempts to rationalize a subjugated biosphere with man in charge are as doomed to failure as the similar concept of benevolent colonialism.

James Lovelock,
Gaia: A New Look at Life on Earth, 1979

Contents

Foreword

Kristine Tompkins, Conservación Patagónica

There is a conscious decision being made today at every level of modern industrial society to convert this beautiful, living Earth into commodities for personal gain, regardless of the consequences. It seems that despite our scientific knowledge, technological sophistication, and innate survival instincts, people are racing down a path that ends with the collapse of modern society and the destruction of millions of species of our fellow travelers on Earth. Immeasurable suffering, human and non-human, is resulting. These decisions are being made by relatively few people, those my late husband, Douglas Tompkins, always called "The Faceless Ones," inspired by the poem of that name by Jack Whyte. Looking to past examples of societal collapse, Dr. Jared Diamond has said this great tragedy is because "culture always trumps common sense" – and this is surely true with our present techno-industrial culture, which ignores the wondrous beauty and diversity of life to focus on maximizing economic growth. Human and non-human suffering has been relativized by the Faceless Ones as the price of progress.

I have for many years informally studied the history of societies large and small whose collapse was so abrupt, harsh, and, for the most part, so complete that they left little trace. I fear that contemporary society is at that point. This time, given the reach of the global economy and size of the human footprint, the impacts of unraveling will be far greater. Millions of species, many never described by science, will be lost and the Earth's potential for sustaining and generating biodiversity will be greatly diminished.

This trajectory of human population growth and overdevelopment precipitating a global extinction crisis is not immutable, however. Engaged citizens around the world are working to create a better and more durable future for people and the rest of life. The organized conservation movement has for 150 years now resisted the forces that would industrialize and commodify every square meter of the Earth. That movement has already succeeded in protecting approximately 14 percent of the land and 3 percent of the oceans. No, that is not nearly enough but the ideas, institutions, and laws are in place for us to dramatically increase the amount and interconnectivity of protected areas globally.

National parks are one of those vital institutions, globally recognized and culturally valued, for protecting wild places and things. For the past quarter-century my husband and I have worked to expand national parks and other protected areas. Through our family foundations we have acquired approximately 2 million acres of conservation land and have been incrementally donating it to the national park systems of Chile and Argentina, typically using our donations to leverage additional government land into the newly designated parks. Working with many partners including four presidents of varying political parties, we have helped create eleven new national parks, in total conserving millions of acres of forest and grasslands. Our Tompkins Conservation team has complemented that parklands creation work with ecological restoration and species reintroduction work, returning natives like giant anteaters, pampas deer, and collared peccaries back to their rightful landscapes (i.e. their homes).

This work has been successful and personally gratifying. I do not recount it to tout our team's accomplishments but to stress that there are still myriad opportunities to put the brakes on human impact and to help nature heal. Our team is relatively small, our finances relatively modest compared to many philanthropists, and certainly tiny compared to the financial resources of governments – and yet working with vision and dedication much positive for wildlife and local economic vitality has been accomplished. So much more can be done if individuals will *act*.

My conservation experience has left me repeatedly astounded and heartbroken at the unwillingness of those who understand what is happening to become activists – to step forward and join in protest or try to address the disintegration of the living world. Neutrality is not an option. Too much is at stake. Ed Abby reminds us that "sentiment without action is the ruin of the soul." It is also the ruin of the world.

This is not a time of simple political or ideological disagreement. Conserving biodiversity and wild places is not just another issue. This is about life itself. No future generation of apologists will be able to put the wheels back on the bus. Nor will they be able to assuage the ethical pain of those who failed to act. Every single person has to decide what they value. All life? Or just their life?

We need a new story about the Earth that doesn't begin with staggering statistics about crashing wildlife populations, the breakdown of human societies due to unstable climate conditions, unfit water systems, and the loss of beauty as a basic value. That new story can be a positive one, using real-life examples like our work in South America, which shows how local economic vitality can be a consequence of conservation. The idea of our species living well among our wild neighbors, of helping wildlife populations recover their former abundance, of solving the climate crisis because we decided to live in a different way – and that way turns out to be more rich and rewarding – is an appealing story to tell.

In a world with unstable human communities and experiencing increasing climate chaos, leadership matters. Great leaders display the talent, vision, and capacity to make bold decisions not solely focused on human needs but on caring for all the Earth's life by protecting natural areas and taking responsibility for defending the masterpieces of their respective territories. To do otherwise is immoral.

Great leaders have the courage to do what is right, to undertake bold and spectacular and beautiful action that will withstand the test of time even in the face of great opposition. But great leaders in the political arena are rare, hence the need for organized social movements that push their political representatives toward policies that address true prosperity, which does not merely equate to humanity's economic well-being. Long-term prosperity, regardless of where you are in the world, insists that we live, if not in perfect balance with the rest of nature, at least in a truce.

There is a central truth to humanity's relationship with the natural world: we were born into it fully dependent upon it from our first breath. Our lives are not formed solely by our work to sustain our material existence, but also by the beauty of the bend of the river; we are made whole by the cry of a newborn, and the millions of small celebrations of life taking place in the cathedral of nature such as seeing a mother polar bear and her cubs. Two hundred years from now let the elephants trumpet, the giant sequoias sway in stiff winds, and our human descendants enjoy healthy lives aware of their place in this wild thing we call nature. Let them look back with satisfaction on ancestors that took on the most important of all tasks – the act of loving life on Earth. We must all be courageous leaders.

This book offers us insights into what courage means and how to use it strategically. For decades David Johns has been a leading thinker in this fight for nature's beauty and diversity, his insights on political organizing gleaned both from academic and real-world experience. In this book he forthrightly analyzes the mainstream environmental movement's weaknesses and recounts examples from positive social change movements that were successful. Grassroots organizing and movement building in the long run can build the future we seek. But to achieve it, all of us who love the Earth need to work harder and better, need to be more effective, and that means being more politically powerful. *Conservation Politics* can help teach us.

Acknowledgements

First and foremost I am grateful to all those colleagues whose day-in-day-out work on behalf of all of the Earth's life and wild places pits them against enormous odds. Despite the challenges, sometimes from those who fancy themselves conservationists, they fight on with fierceness, passion, intelligence, sometimes at great risk, and without regard for fads and trends in political correctness. I cannot begin to name them all, and even naming their organizations is a difficult task. Among those from whom I have learned much are the staff, boards, and others associated with: The Wildlands Network; Marine Conservation Institute; Oregon Natural Desert Association; Greater Hells Canyon Council; Marine Section of the Society for Conservation Biology; Tompkins Conservation and the Foundation for Deep Ecology; Paseo Pantera; *Wild Earth* magazine; Naturalia; Predator Defense; Project Coyote; Sea Shepherd Conservation Society; Rewilding Institute; Wild Country; African Wildlife Foundation; Gorongosa National Park; the Wild Foundation; Trees for Life; Wild Europe Initiative; Turner Endangered Species Fund; E. O. Wilson Biodiversity Foundation; Yellowstone to Yukon Conservation Initiative; Larch Company; Oregon Wild; Wild Earth Guardians; Sanctuary Asia; Wildlife Trust of India; and all those throughout the years I have worked with and met. Needless to say none bear responsibility for the lessons I have taken from their work.

I am also grateful to those who reviewed all or parts of the manuscript or gave permission to republish substantial portions of earlier versions of the chapters.

Jonathan Cobb, John Davis, and Signe Hagen read the entire manuscript, and their many suggestions resulted in a better-organized, more readable and, I hope, useful book. The author thanks the editors and reviewers at *Biological Conservation, Conservation*

Biology, *Wild Earth* magazine, the University of Chicago Press, and at *Capitalism Nature Socialism* for their work on original manuscripts. The author is indebted to John Peet and the late Leslie White; without their work no biological understanding of energy would be possible. The original version of what is now Chapter 7 owes much to Erica Fleischman for a careful critical reading, and to Dominique Bessee and Patty Burke, who corrected many errors. Reviewers and editors at Cambridge University Press, especially Dominic Lewis, Annie Toynbee and Noah Tate, and Ken Moxham who copyedited, worked hard to ensure this book was worth publishing. Its shortfalls remain my responsibility. I am grateful to Poala Bouley, Tom Butler, Greg Carr, Ignacia Jimenez, Mateus Metemba, Marc Stalman, and Kristine Tompkins for patiently answering my many questions about their projects. A hundred years from now my thanks will be forgotten but their legacy will live on in the wildlife that roam southern Africa and southern Latin America.

Chapter 2. Like It or Not, Politics is the Solution. An earlier version of this essay, under the same title, appeared in 23 *Conservation Biology* 2: 287–8, © 2007 Society for Conservation Biology. Permission from the Society for Conservation Biology and Wiley-Blackwell to use substantial portions of the essay is gratefully acknowledged.

Chapter 3. Ten Questions for Conservation Politics. An earlier version of this essay appeared as 110 Most Important Questions in 23 *Conservation Biology* 5: 1069, © 2009 Society for Conservation Biology. Permission from the Society for Conservation Biology and Wiley-Blackwell to use substantial portions of the essay is gratefully acknowledged. A different version appeared as chapter 8 in *New Conservation Politics*, Wiley-Blackwell, © 2009 David Johns.

Chapter 4. Adapting Society to the Wild. An earlier version of this essay appeared as Adapting Human Societies to Conservation, 24 *Conservation Biology* 3: 641–3, © 2010 Society for Conservation Biology. Permission from the Society for Conservation Biology and

Wiley-Blackwell to use substantial portions of the essay is gratefully acknowledged.

Chapter 5. Striking at the Roots: The Burgeoning Human Footprint. Permission to publish a substantial extract translated into English from Ovid's *Metamorphoses*, Book VIII, is gratefully acknowledged; A. S. Kline translation © 2000.

Chapter 6. Domination and the Intractability of Energy Problems. An earlier version of this essay appeared as Energy and Wilderness in 11 *Wild Earth* 2: 12–13 (Fall), © 2002 David Johns. The author acknowledges a deep debt to the late Leslie White and to John Peet.

Chapter 7. Turning the Tide: Lessons from Other Movements and Conservation History. An earlier version of this essay appeared as chapter 18 in Marc Bekoff, editor, *Ignoring Nature No More: The Case for Compassionate Conservation*, © 2013 University of Chicago Press. Permission to adapt this chapter is gratefully acknowledged. An earlier version of section 6 of this chapter appeared in *SCB News*, May 2008; and several elements of this chapter were discussed in Adapting Human Societies to Conservation, 24 *Conservation Biology* 3: 641–3, © 2010 Society for Conservation Biology. Permission to reprint portions of the original essay from the Society for Conservation Biology and Wiley-Blackwell is gratefully acknowledged.

Chapter 10. The Other Connectivity: Reaching Beyond the Choir. A version of this essay was published under the same title in 19 *Conservation Biology* 6: 1681–2, © 2005 Society for Conservation Biology. Permission to reprint portions of the original essay from the Society for Conservation Biology and Wiley-Blackwell is gratefully acknowledged.

Chapter 12. The Biological Sciences and Conservation. An earlier version of this essay was published as Biological Science in Conservation in Cole, David N. and Stephen F. McCool (eds.), *Proceedings: Wilderness Science in a Time of Change*. Proc. RMRS-P-000. Ogden, UT: US Department of Agriculture, Forest Service, Rocky Mountain Research Station. © 2000 David Johns.

Chapter 13. Conservation, George Orwell, and Language. A version of this essay was previously published as Caring, Killing, Euphemism and George Orwell: How Language Choice Undercuts Our Mission in 211 *Biological Conservation* 174–6. © 2017 Elsevier. Permission to reprint substantial portions of the paper is gratefully acknowledged. Permission from my co-author, Dominick DellaSala is also gratefully acknowledged.

Chapter 14. Restoring Story and Myth. Many of the ideas in this chapter were first published in Our Real Challenge: Managing Ourselves Instead of Nature, in Watson, Alan and Janet Sproull (comps.), *Seventh World Wilderness Congress Symposium: Science and Stewardship to Protect and Sustain Wilderness Values, November 2–8, 2001, Port Elizabeth, South Africa*. Proc. RMRS-P-00. Ogden, UT: US Department of Agriculture, Forest Service, Rocky Mountain Research Station, 2003. © 2003 David Johns. Many thanks to Tom Butler for permission to reproduce Lord Man: A Parable, © 2015 Tom Butler.

Chapter 15. Conservation's Moral Imperative: The Human Obligation to the Wild. A version of this chapter was presented at 50th Anniversary of the Wilderness Act, Albuquerque New Mexico, 2014. Some of the ideas in this chapter first appeared in David Johns, Joel Kovel, and Michael Löwy (2003) Has Ecosocialism Passed on the Tough Questions?, *Capitalism Nature Socialism*, 14:2, 120–8, and in a review of Joel Kovel, *The Enemy of Nature: The End of Capitalism or the End of the World?* by David Johns, *New Political Science*, 25:1, 129–43.

If one could not take delight in the gallows humor of brilliant editorial cartoonists, it would be a much bleaker world. If a picture is worth a thousand words a good editorial cartoon is worth an entire book. I am very grateful to those cartoonists who have allowed me to reprint their good work: Tom Toles, Joel Pett, Sidney Harris, Seppo Leinonen, and Dan Piraro (aka Bizarro). Like great music, their work transcends mere words.

Introduction

> It must be considered that there is nothing more difficult to carry out, nor more doubtful of success, nor more dangerous to handle, than to initiate a new order of things. For the reformer has enemies in all those who profit by the old order, and only lukewarm defenders in all those who would profit by the new order, this lukewarmness arising partly from fear of their adversaries, who have the laws in their favor; and partly from the incredulity of mankind, who do not truly believe in anything new until they have had actual experience of it.
>
> Niccolò Machiavelli, 1903 [1515]: 22

This book was written to address a longstanding crisis that grows more urgent even as it becomes normal. The human destruction of life on Earth continues to gather momentum while being recorded by scientists and others. A recent summary of the state of biodiversity finds that in the last forty years global populations of vertebrates have collectively fallen by 52 percent (WWF 2014). The loss of animals we routinely notice is only part of what is happening. Among others: dead zones, the oceans becoming a plastic soup, incessant noise and pervasive light, forests and grasslands eaten by bipedal termites.

Human institutions have adopted national and international laws (treaties) to ostensibly slow or stop the carnage; in a few cases laws call for limited recovery (the US Endangered Species Act, Convention on Biological Diversity, Convention on International Trade in Endangered Species, Marine Mammal Protection Act among others). But the trends belie the purpose of the laws. Governments and other institutions ignore such laws in the face of growing human populations and demand for consumption. Growth is the priority, the default, the ultimate arbiter of decisions (see, by comparison with the treaties and laws above, the World Trade Organization rules and subsidies for growth). Even among advocates of justice among humans there is comparatively little concern for other life; quite the contrary, some of these advocates would rather see a park undone than give back Manhattan. Yet humanity is stealing from other species as surely as colonial powers did from other humans. John Rodman (1977) eloquently explored the colonial analogy and it is a useful one. The invasion of a place, and its transformation into something that serves the invader at the expense of the existing biological community, is very much the heart of the colonial relationship. Conservation is essentially an anti-colonial struggle with one important difference – non-human species are ill-equipped to effectively resist and overcome the human onslaught, amplified as it is by technology and social organization. Humans may well fill the Petri dish and bring on their own demise, thus ending their reign of biocide. But much will be lost in the course of that, and it is not a good basis for conservation strategy. A good conservation strategy must rely on humans organized as an anti-colonial force seeking to dismantle the colonial relationship.

The language of conquest is less trumpeted today – though it is not long gone (LeGuin 1989 [1981]) – but the machinery of violent control still dominates the human enterprise. Official global rhetoric embraces protecting biodiversity and few openly damn it. After all, biodiversity is a nice thing to have, like bird feeders, and advocates of biodiversity and the wild are rarely a serious threat, so the rhetoric is not costly. Indeed, conservationists are mostly beggars, too politically weak to demand what is necessary to safeguard life on Earth. They are mostly confined to issuing calls to decision makers to do the right thing, but lack the resources or a strategy for creating a base of power that can make decision makers do the right thing in the face of strong pro-growth forces.

Many non-governmental organizations (NGOs) and scientists accept existing trends of loss even though they result in a more and more impoverished world. At a recent Society for Ecological Restoration conference, paper after paper discussed how to adapt populations of other species to ongoing human encroachment and degradation of habitat. Not one paper discussed how to take on such trends, how to stop or slow or frustrate or monkeywrench growth. Not one. Often such papers call for more study of the biology of other species. Rarely does one hear calls for the study of the one species that is the cause of almost every conservation problem, and how to halt such atrocious institutional and individual behavior. Still others, claiming the mantle of conservation, want to run up the white flag and compromise further on already anemic United Nations goals for protection (10 percent for the oceans and 17 percent for land); never mind goals set by the Wildlands Network or Half-Earth or Marine Conservation Institute, which aim for what is biologically necessary to ensure all life thrives and advocate for changing strategies in the face of obstacles rather than changing fundamental goals.

Indeed, much conservation is focused on addressing symptoms rather than causes – on playing catch-up and clean-up rather than prevention, on mitigating dams and carbon generation rather than removing dams and vastly lowering energy consumption, on so-called green consumption rather than lowering human population, on seeking to maintain minimal viable populations of species and outdoor zoos rather than reclaiming much of the Earth. While political regions add hundreds of thousands of humans, a few hundred wolves or cougars generate complaints of too many. How can 300 wolves in a region that contained thousands be considered meaningful recovery except in a blighted political landscape? Treating symptoms avoids the hard decisions and the risks that challenging the status quo inevitably carries.

Turning back extinction requires effective politics. A first step is putting political questions front and center. The primary challenge is creating and effectively utilizing a political force that can generate pro-conservation decisions from social institutions despite strong opposition; or enable taking control of decision-making institutions directly. While it is urgent to address countless emergencies in the here and now, much greater emphasis is needed on dismantling the drivers of biological destruction. Human societies must be pushed, if not forced, to adapt to the needs of the millions of other species on the planet, including creatures that are big, dangerous, and inconvenient to humans. The legislative removal of wolves in the US from protection – discussed in the first part of this book – is an example of conservation weakness.

Once conservationists recognize the necessity of focusing on politics the political questions must be framed correctly. Asking the wrong question guarantees the wrong answers or stumbling about interminably. Usually when the questions are the right ones the answers come pretty simply. The overarching question is, "how do" conservationists build and use a strong political force on behalf of life on Earth? The attributes of such a political force depend on what conservationists seek to accomplish. If their vision is mostly defensive it will operate within the status quo and that doesn't call for much that is new; perhaps some tactical innovation. A strategy intending to change what is possible – dismantling the colonial relationship and changing human societies so they are compatible with thriving populations of other species, healthy ecosystems and vast wild places – requires a very different kind of political force, one that can successfully confront and overcome structural obstacles that are much more powerful than the conservation movement currently is. It calls for a clear vision, like those laid out by the Wildlands Network, Marine Conservation Institute and the Half-Earth Initiative.

Overcoming powerful obstacles also requires a reflexive and analytical understanding of power and how to gain it and use it against those who make war on wildlife and their homes. It calls for what might best be called guerilla strategies: strategies that enable the less conventionally powerful to overcome the more conventionally powerful by using unconventional means, such as those used fighting apartheid, dictatorships, electoral oligarchies, and colonial powers the world over. It calls for understanding the drivers of biodiversity destruction that inhere in the organization of society and the ways in which various groups in society benefit and are injured by these drivers of destruction.

The book's second part seeks to bring clarity to the strategic questions, to the obstacles and the opportunities facing the movement.

The third part examines how a successful political force is to be built and succeed. The attributes of successful movements are no secret and conservationists should become well acquainted with them so they can be creatively used. The successes and failures of conservation and other struggles offer important lessons. Unfortunately, the movement for conservation of species and habitat does

FIGURE 0.1 Wildlands Network North American Wildways. The wildways are planning regions, composed of strictly protected core areas, protected corridors or linkage zones, and buffer or multiple use zones, designated to ensure all native species, ecosystems, and disturbance regimes can thrive in perpetuity. Not shown is the Gulf Wildway, which runs from Florida to the Sierra Madre Oriental, and includes important systems such as Longleaf Pine Forests of the US South.

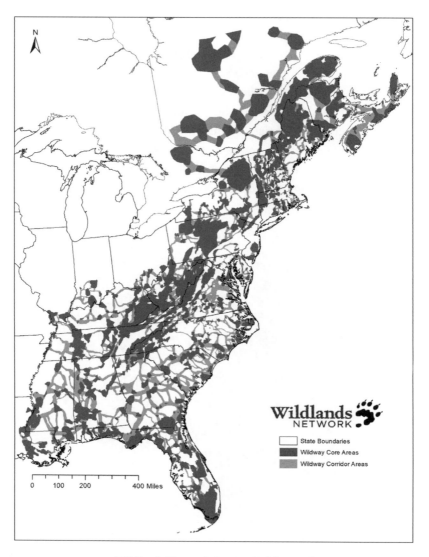

FIGURE 0.2 Wildlands Network Eastern Wildway. This map represents a
potential network of connected core habitat areas for biodiversity in
eastern North America. It is expected that safeguarding these areas and
connections will take years of land protection and restoration efforts,
including conservationists working with private landowners on a
voluntary basis. Core area boundaries are drawn broadly to include
restoration areas around existing concentrations of natural habitat.
Corridors follow available habitat pathways and modeled habitat
connectivity priorities, and in many cases would need restoration of
habitat and mitigation of road barriers to achieve functionality.

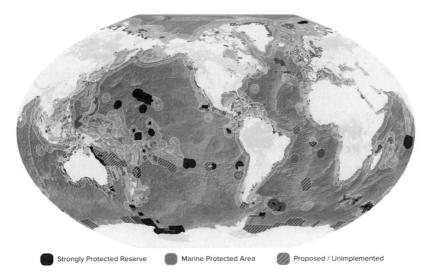

Strongly Protected Reserve   Marine Protected Area   Proposed / Unimplemented

FIGURE 0.3 Global Marine Protected Areas (MPAs). The Marine
Protection Atlas tracks areas designated by countries in waters under
their control and on the high seas as designated by international
agreement. The MPAtlas distinguishes between strongly protected MPAs
(1.8 percent of the global ocean) and areas that have more limited
protection (1.7 percent of the global ocean). The Global Ocean Refuge
System evaluates the quality of MPAs based on extensive biological
criteria.
© 2018 Marine Conservation Institute. See http://mpatlas.org. Figure and caption
reproduced with permission.

not interact with other movements to the degree protecting the
"human environment" does, so the transmission of lessons is more
limited. A deliberate effort is required to bridge movement networks.
Mobilization – generating mass-based collective action – presents
challenges that conservationists once mastered but have lost over
the last few decades with the dominance of big NGOs that find
activists inconvenient and prefer check-writers who will leave the
decisions to them. The result has been compromised goals and loss of
influence. Grassroots, mass organizing is the only thing that has ever
overcome powerful entrenched interests or created new forms of
social organization in the face of declining oligarchies.

Marine conservation faces special challenges. For most people the oceans are out of sight, out of experience, out of urgent caring. Urgent and personal are essential elements of mobilization and organizing. The global ocean is probably damaged to a much greater degree than the terrestrial parts of the Earth, but difficult to see. If that decline reaches the point of irreversibility nothing we do on land will matter. Many still look to the oceans as a source of endless food and a limitless garbage dump. Much marine conservation action lacks a strategic focus, and means to safeguard the high seas are nascent at best.

The tools of conservation organizing remain undeveloped, though this was not always so. Organizing, not just recruiting members, was once a central focus of conservation. Documentary writing and film which does not give adequate attention to the language dominates efforts to communicate. The hedged language of science is too pervasive; it is not persuasive. Findings can inform but cannot tell people why to act nor do they usually persuade decision makers.

Politics ultimately is a material fight, as those engaged in it with their eyes open well know – especially those who fight from the grassroots. Politics is also a cultural fight, and is so most of the time. Material conflict is very costly and creates lasting wounds. Better for rulers to convince people of the inevitability of the status quo or the lack of alternatives than to fill the jails and hospitals. People may rebel when conditions reach a certain point, but basic change requires a new vision and morality. It begins with cultural change among a few and spreads by way of a new mythology, new songs, new rituals, and the emergence of new institutions. All are important to mobilization, to organizing, to guiding action. They are central to building a broad-based conservation community – something essential to any successful movement.

The issues addressed in this book are not new. They are often quite thorny issues, long a matter of debate and strategizing. Every effort has been made to bring the discussion up to date, but the roots are properly apparent in these chapters. Temporal context matters: many of these chapters have previously been published as essays or presented at meetings and circulated to address contemporaneous matters. They are presented for the first time together, most of them extensively revised and integrated into a whole. I am grateful to those who hold copyright on the original versions for granting permission to partially use language in the original version in the revised version without concern for copyright.

REFERENCES

LeGuin, Ursula. 1989 [1981]. World Making. Pp. 46–8 in *Dancing at the Edge of the World*. Grove Press. New York.

Machiavelli, Niccolò. 1903 [1515]. *The Prince*. (Luigi Ricci trans.) Grant Richards. London.

Rodman, John. 1977. The Liberation of Nature? 20 *Inquiry* 83–131.

WWF. 2014. *Living Planet Report 2014: Species and Spaces, People and Places*. WWF. Gland, Switzerland.

PART I   The Problem

I   The Tragedy of Political Failure

...search out controversy and issues, rather than avoid them, for
unless there is controversy people are not concerned enough to act.

Alinsky 1971: 122

Wolves have been persecuted almost since Europeans began to settle
in North America (Lopez 1978). They were not only seen as material
threats to human life and limb, and to livestock, but as spiritual
threats. They were creatures of the dark, the wild, the forest; in some
cases, of the devil. Wolves, more than any other predator, challenged
human domination of the landscape – at least in the human mind.
Perhaps that was in part because we saw them as like us: social
animals which kill others to live. Unlike us they were still
wild: they had not domesticated themselves as we had, nor were they
dogs who had been domesticated and had in some sense bargained
away their freedom for handouts. Humans projected onto wolves
human rapaciousness, brutality, vengefulness, and violence and
attacked those split-off parts of ourselves with an energy that cannot
be explained by self-defense or protection of domestic animals.

The destruction of wolves was systematically carried out by
individuals and governments until they were gone from many parts
of North America by the twentieth century or rendered ecologically
ineffective. Wolves remained in only a few areas of the United States: –
the Boundary Waters, the borderlands of Mexico, and as visitors to the
mountains of northern Washington, Idaho, and Montana. They continued to be persecuted in Mexico, much of Canada and in Alaska
using various loopholes in the Endangered Species Act (ESA). It took
well into the twentieth century for ecologists and others to recognize
the important ecosystem role apex predators, including wolves,
played in controlling ungulates and mesopredators (e.g. Eisenberg

2010). Without the former ungulates populations swelled, preventing forests from regenerating and reshaping grasslands. Similarly populations of smaller predators greatly increased, markedly increasing the mortality of many birds.

The effort to recover wolves in the US and the health of the landscape remains bitterly controversial in many parts of the country, having at root less to do with dislike of wolf behavior than with political polarization focused on wolves and wolves as a challenge to human control. Despite this long-running conflict over wolves, many conservation scientists and NGOs were not only appalled but surprised when the US Congress delisted wolf populations in the northern US Rocky Mountains (Herring 2011). Wolves in this region were protected pursuant to the ESA, a federal law requiring that endangered species be recovered. Delisting, under the law, occurs when a species is appropriately found to be no longer endangered by the agency responsible for recovery, in this case the US Fish and Wildlife Service (USFWS). The USFWS claimed recovery and issued rules to delist, but these were successfully challenged in the courts (Alexander 2011). It was in this context, discussed fully below, that the US Congress acted to remove ESA protection from wolves in the US northern Rockies region. That delisting should be supported by legislators who had historically defended the ESA was profoundly unsettling to conservationists. At the same time, at the global level, conservation biologists were expressing a similar and growing disappointment that the world's governments were not delivering on their promises to protect biodiversity following the findings of the Millennium Ecosystem Assessment (MEA) (e.g. Perrings et al. 2010a, 2010b).

To be appalled by the US Congress's decision or most countries' failure to respond to the MEA is one thing; to be surprised is another. The surprise is symptomatic of a failure to grasp how political power works, and to recognize the limits of scientific knowledge: it alone rarely persuades decision makers – carrots and sticks do. Carrots and sticks include campaign contributions or the equivalent (Fellowes and Wolf 2004; Kamieniecki 2006; Duffy 2007);

control of media resources that help shape the frameworks and views of those groups in society that decision makers consider important (Libby 1999; Kamieniecki 2006; Duffy 2007; Layzer 2007); control of economic institutions whose cooperation is needed by political leaders (Lindblom 1977; Grover 1989; Gonzalez 2001; Kamieniecki 2006); control of information (Cogkianese 2007); and longstanding personal relationships based on shared interests or goals (Domhoff 1998; Gonzalez 2001; Furlong 2007; Dye 2013). These political resources are persuasive "arguments" because they help or hinder decision makers in gaining or keeping power and advancing their own agenda. Sometimes science can be a carrot or a stick but it is rarely enough by itself. The case of the legislative delisting of wolves in the face of favorable court decisions and broad public support for their recovery makes plain the cost of this denial of realpolitik.

On April 15, 2012 President Obama signed the Department of Defense and Full Year Continuing Appropriations Act (PL 112–10). Section 1713 of the law ordered the Secretary of Interior to reissue the 6 March 2009 rule removing wolves in Montana, Idaho, and parts of Oregon and Washington from ESA protection which prohibited harming them except in a narrow range of circumstances as determined by the USFWS. The rule was dutifully reissued on May 5, 2012 (74 Fed Reg 25590 et seq.). Section 1713 also removed the reissued rule from judicial review – a first in ESA history (Alexander 2011). It is significant that the March 2009 rule issued by the Obama Administration was the same as the rule issued by the Bush Administration on January 14, 2009.[1] It was issued by the Obama Administration without further scientific review (Bergstrom et al. 2009) despite the

---

[1] The January 14, 2009 rule was a modification of the Bush wolf delisting rule issued in March 2008. The 2008 rule was overturned as illegal in *Defenders of Wildlife v. Hall* (565 F. Supp. 2d 1160 D. Mont 2008), for failure to show it provided for genetic exchange among subpopulations as required by the USFWS recovery plan. The revised rule issued in January 2009, inter alia, proposed human transport of wolves to meet the genetic exchange requirement and increased the recovery goal from 100 wolves/10 breeding pairs in each state to 150 wolves/15 breeding pairs

Bush Administration's record of ignoring, suppressing, and distorting scientific findings (e.g. Union of Concerned Scientists 2008) in agency policy making, including the USFWS (Robinson 2005).

HOW DID THIS COME ABOUT?

In the decades before legislative delisting, conservation NGOs repeatedly and successfully challenged inadequate federal wolf recovery actions in the northern US Rockies. They relied on citizen suit provisions in the ESA, and other important laws passed in the late 1960s and early 1970s when conservation rode a wave of significant influence (Repetto 2006). By the 1980s, however, both the executive and legislative branches had become hostile to conservation, and litigation became much more critical (Bevington 2009). The hostility had roots in the transformation of US politics in the 1970s that resulted in one of the major parties (Republican) abandoning its conservation heritage while simultaneously increasing its ability to elect presidents and congresses (Mansbridge 1986; Gilgoff 2007; Lambert 2008; Critchlow 2011), and in the other major party (Democratic) recognizing conservationists had nowhere else to go, and therefore feeling it could safely ignore them. Conservationists found themselves in an unenviable and weak bargaining position.

This unhappy (for conservationists) political situation is not confined to elected officials but extends to the agencies' elected officials guide by means of substantive and appropriations legislation, and executive authority that includes the ability to appoint many agency officials. That the USFWS, which is responsible for wolf recovery and implementing the ESA generally, is highly susceptible to political influence from its own political appointees, Department of Interior political appointees, the White House, and relevant congressional subcommittees, is well documented (Thomas 2003; Robinson 2005; Union of Concerned Scientists 2008; Bevington 2009). This is so despite the Service's large cadre of excellent scientists who have seen their work at times ignored, suppressed, and distorted by higher-ups – and not just during the Bush Administration. Certainly there are scientific differences over wolf recovery within the USFWS, within and between other agency scientists, and among scientists outside the agencies. Bergstrom et al. (2009), for example, question whether recovery can be considered achieved, inter alia, without proof of genetic exchange, when genetic exchange requires human transport, when the recovery population size is less than 1 percent of the species's original population size and exhibits depleted genetic diversity, and when management plans include hunting that disrupts pack structure and makes dispersal difficult.

The USFWS took six years after listing wolves in the US northern Rockies as endangered to identify recovery areas in 1981 (Robinson 2005). During the 1980s, as Congress periodically blocked funding for wolf recovery the Service leadership dutifully followed suit, delaying release of a wolf recovery plan for two years (until August 1987) when a lawsuit threatened (Robinson 2005). Between 1992 and 2002, 70 percent of all species listed under the ESA were listed because of litigation. USFWS documents obtained in one of the first such suits show species were not listed for political reasons (Bevington 2009). Once listed, lawsuits are often needed to generate recovery plans and designation of critical habitat. The USFWS is not aggressive in pushing other agencies to cooperate with it under §7 of the Act, and NGO lawsuits were needed to obtain cooperation via court order (Thomas 2003).

During the course of litigation which led up to the congressional delisting, the courts found that the USFWS ignored its own earlier scientific findings that genetic exchange between wolf subpopulations was necessary to "long-term persistence" (recovery) of the US northern Rocky Mountain metapopulation (565 F.Supp. 2d 1160, D.Mont. 2008). The court also rejected as inadequate the Service's argument that genetic exchange might be occurring despite the lack of evidence and noted that the state management plans approved by the Service would increase the killing of wolves and thus reduce chances for exchange through dispersal. The same court found in a 2009 order that "[t]he Service had distinguished a natural population of wolves based on a

political [that is, jurisdictional] line, not the best available science."
(Case 9:09-cv-00077-DVM Document 93 Filed 09/08/2009: 9). In
Defenders of Wildlife et al. v. Salazar et al. (729 F. Supp. 2d 1207,
D. Mont. 2010) the Court again found the Service seeking a political
solution by contradicting its long-established rule that a biologically
"distinct population segment" could not be divided.

The proximate driver of White House and Senate leadership
support for delisting, notwithstanding longstanding opposition by
Democratic leaders and many Republicans to any state-by-state or
species-by-species exceptions to the ESA, was the Democratic Party
leadership's fears that Senator John Tester (Democrat, Montana)
would lose his seat in 2012 and this might further cost them control
of the Senate. They had some reasons on other issues to fear for
Tester,[2] but how did Tester's political fate come to be seen as hinging
on wolf recovery?

Some electoral context is helpful. In 2006 Tester won the
Democratic primary against an establishment candidate by twenty-
five points relying on grassroots organizing. (In about two-thirds of
US states voters in the various parties select the party's nominees for
office in an election prior to the election in which the office holder is
selected.) However, he won the general election against three-term
incumbent Conrad Burns by only 3,000 votes. Republicans had
targeted Tester for defeat in 2012 even before the District Court
decision (*Defenders of Wildlife et al. v. Salazar et al.* [729
F. Supp. 2d 1207, D. Mont. 2010]) that set up the congressional
delisting fight. In the two years leading up to the 2012 election
Tester's opponent, Representative Denny Rehberg (Republican,
Montana), sought to mobilize his political base and distinguish himself from Tester by, inter alia, fanning controversy over wolf recovery, state management of wolves and wolf hunting, and doing so
using the same populist tone Tester had relied on in 2006.

---

[2] Tester won re-election in 2012 by 28,000 votes or 4 percent, a healthy margin.

The closeness of Tester's 2006 general election win in what analysts consider a Republican-leaning state (McCain beat Obama by 2.2 percent there in 2008) apparently dominated Democratic thinking despite Montana's two Democratic senators and a Democratic governor. It is true that Tester's opponent, Rehberg, won his 2008 statewide House race with 64 percent of the vote and his 2010 race with 60 percent. But in 2008 Democratic Senator Max Baucus took 73 percent of the vote and Democratic Governor Schweitzer 65 percent, – wider margins than Tester's razor-thin win in 2006 or Rehberg's most recent win.

Rightly or wrongly fearing a close race, Democratic strategists were acknowledging through legislative delisting that Rehberg had made wolf delisting and state management of wolves a divisive issue, with Tester on the wrong end of it. Rather than fight the issue on the merits, the Democratic leadership and Tester wanted the issue to disappear.

How is it Tester and Democratic leaders felt they could not defend wolf recovery against Rehberg's attacks when there is broad popular support for wolves and wolf recovery? That there is such broad support cannot be reasonably questioned. A 2002 meta-analysis of thirty-eight studies undertaken between 1972 and 2000 shows a majority of Americans support wolves and wolf recovery (Williams et al. 2002). Some studies – it is unclear how many – allowed people to respond neutrally to wolves and about 25 percent did so. Support for wolves varied by region, urban compared to rural residence, gender, political party, and other factors. More temporally relevant to the case at hand may be a 2011 poll finding that 87 percent of Americans and 79 percent of Westerners viewed wolves as a vital part of wilderness and the US's natural heritage (Harris Interactive 2011: 5). Only 4 percent were neutral or refused to answer. Similar results were obtained in the US Southwest (Research and Polling, Inc 2008a, 2008b).

Tester, of course, had to win in Montana, not "in the Western US." But regardless of the locus of his electoral district, public opinion polls do not translate into policy in conservation or in other policy areas. Both Democratic and Republican Party political calculus recognized this while conservation reasoning did not.

- It is not opinion poll results that are persuasive but action and the resources actors have at their disposal to affect outcomes, such as money, votes, media access and a compelling story, and other resources. There is no general public, only –
  - groups that engage and groups that sit on the sidelines
  - groups that know how to make a difference and those that fumble about
  - groups that organize people to act and those that point to opinion polls.
- Most of those who care about wolves don't care enough to act on their own, indicating a weak commitment to their views; they must be mobilized to act.
  - They do not vote based on the wolf issue (a pro-wolf population and anti-wolf Congress is not a political anomaly).
  - Of those who care about an issue, it is the side that is best organized and otherwise wields relatively greater resources that usually makes its influence most strongly felt: those who can deliver more votes, more money (the 2008 US elections cost $6 billion; the 2010 elections $5 billion; the 2012 elections $7 billion), and who can successfully frame the debate (is the issue wolf recovery and ecological health or is the issue outside interference in local/state matters?) (e.g. Etzioni 1968; Rucht 1999; Shaiko 1999; Giugni 2004; Cashore and Howlett 2006).

In sum, political decision makers were responding to the fact that conservationists compared to wolf opponents (including some elected officials in the US northern Rockies) brought fewer resources to bear and did so less effectively (Herring 2011). Conservationists litigated and pointed to polls in support of their views. They did precious little organizing. Anti-wolf forces organized their supporters reminding elected officials that they can deliver money, votes, op-eds and other communication resources to frame the debate successfully in the media and for many fence-sitters. Anti-wolf forces had the carrots and sticks in this fight. Even sympathetic elected officials in these circumstances rightly felt they had more to fear from anti-wolf organizations than pro-wolf recovery and healthy-ecosystem organizations. It was not politically safe to support wolves.

WHY DID CONSERVATIONISTS LET THIS SITUATION COME ABOUT?

Most conservationists did not see the looming threat, at least with any specificity. They felt secure with broad public support for wolves and longstanding opposition by federal legislators to carving out state-by-state or species-by-species exceptions to the ESA. The legislative breach in the ESA, however, was not the first time court victories had been reversed or seriously undercut. Although the particular lesson conservationists should have had in mind is specific to the US political system – that political organizing can trump the results of science-based victories won in court under citizen lawsuit provisions – it is a mistake to rely exclusively on achieving goals through formal decision-making processes at the expense of grassroots organizing, which is the basis for the capacity to generate enough pressure on decision makers to overcome vested interests (e.g. McAdam et al. 2001; Dryzek et al. 2003).

The starkest example of that lesson was the political reaction to the January 23, 1973 US Supreme Court decision in *Roe v. Wade* (410 US 113, 1973). The decision was not one the authors of the 7–2 decision thought would be controversial because it built on a long line of earlier decisions (what the US legal profession calls precedent, a major source of legitimacy for the courts). Reproductive rights groups hailed the decision as a great victory, and their grassroots organizing in support of changing state laws on abortion faded – the court had struck the antiabortion state laws down. Rather than organizing to maintain or increase broad support for the court decision these groups moved on to other issues and to professional lobbying (Staggenborg 1991).

Those opposed to the *Roe* decision, however, *did* start organizing. Fundamentalist Protestants joined conservative Catholics who had long fought state-level liberalization of abortion laws. More importantly, cultural conservatives in the Republican Party leadership saw an opportunity to mobilize large numbers of people who were part of a demographic that had mostly withdrawn from politics after the Scopes "monkey trial" of the 1920s (Keller 2017). Organizing against *Roe*, in part by building on anti-Equal Rights Amendment (ERA) efforts and anti-feminist backlash against cultural changes brought about in the 1960s, and in part building on anger and fear generated by the 1978 Carter administration's threat to revoke tax-exempt status for Christian schools that practiced segregation, millions of new voters were mobilized by churches and Republican leaders. Mobilization of these constituencies in the 1970s relied on grassroots techniques adopted from the civil rights and other mass movements. The leaders of this effort cobbled together an anti-abortion, anti-affirmative-action, anti-ERA, anti-youth-culture, anti-communist, anti-environmentalist, anti-government coalition that played a pivotal role in generating the Moral Majority and similar NGOs (Dobson et al. 1981). It was a coalition that had no need of and little room for conservation. In alliance with conservative business interests, who were openly hostile to conservation, a very different Republican Party coalition emerged in the late 1970s, electing Ronald Reagan as president in 1980 (for historical and analytical accounts of this process see, inter alia, Mansbridge 1986; Gilgoff 2007; Lambert 2008; Critchlow 2011). Reagan alone appointed half of the federal judiciary (Federal Judicial Center 2012) and they whittled away at *Roe* and other laws, including environmental laws in subsequent decades (Staggenborg 1991; Liptak 2009).

Cultural conservatives, allied with economic conservatives and most of the resource extraction industry, elected both Bushes and gave Clinton (more of an Eisenhower Republican than anything else) a conservative Republican Congress for six of his eight years. Wealthy conservatives, including extractive industries, bankrolled some of this organizing in the early stages and much more later, realizing it was the path to an electoral majority including a White House and Congress supportive of their interests. They funded right-wing think tanks that attempted to give a gloss of intellectual legitimacy to, inter alia, the destruction of biodiversity (Beder 2001; Jacques et al. 2008).

While all of this was going on, grassroots conservation groups, facing a mostly hostile federal government since the 1980s, lobbied defensively, did some organizing but lacked the means to do it on a mass scale. Many litigated or worked at the state level (Bevington 2009). Others sought to reawaken the movement with a bolder vision and action and had some success (Foreman 2004).

The large conservation groups (Wilderness Society, National Wildlife Federation, Sierra Club, Defenders of Wildlife) devoted themselves to an almost exclusively insider strategy, relying on ordinary channels of access, and abandoned grassroots organizing with a few exceptions (Shaiko 1999; Rootes 2007 [2004]; Turner 2012). This strategy failed to take account of the fact that conservation NGOs lack the chips to play a solely insider strategy successfully. Conservationists could not match the money, deliver the votes and bring the other resources to bear that their opponents could. They won some battles but biodiversity continued to decline. They ignored a primary political lesson: relatively weaker groups can successfully counter opponents' greater resources and shift policy in the desired direction only by *combining* their insider work with an outsider strategy of mass mobilization (McAdam et al. 2001; Johns 2009).

An outsider strategy is one that creates new power from the bottom up by mobilizing important groups to go around the normal channels of influence and bring pressure via mass protest, non-cooperation, direct action, and by creating alternative societal stories (myths) and sometimes new institutions. Successful outsider strategies create leverage that can bring about major reform, such as the end of legally mandated racial segregation in the US South or the passage of major US environmental and conservation laws as in the 1970s (Banaszak 1996; McAdam et al. 2001; Piven 2006). The burst of environmental and conservation lawmaking in the late 1960s and early 1970s was also due to the growing unpopularity of the Vietnam War and the desire of a besieged president (Nixon) to support popular policies and by the failure of eventual opponents of many of these laws to foresee their consequences (Flippen 2000).

The mass mobilization at the heart of outsider strategies hinges on grassroots organizing of strategically important groups of people: they must be identified, understood, approached with compelling stories about why they should act and act in specific ways, and integrated into organizations. A strong sense of community must be built. Action must be orchestrated. Outsider strategies bring elite ridicule, outrage, condemnation, and often repression. But they are the only thing that has brought about major change. Activities include one-on-one outreach; systematic efforts to gain mass media attention including protest; other forms of direct action from civil disobedience to monkey-wrenching; street theater; music; and goals informed by science and biocentric values (creation of alternative worldviews). Historically, hundreds of small, volunteer, bottom-up organizations were run by their "membership" who planned and took action.

SOME LESSONS FROM WOLF DELISTING

Lessons from the legislative delisting of wolves in the US northern Rockies apply to most conservation issues, such as climate change.

- Science is not enough; when it comes to influencing decision makers the quality and quantity of a group's political resources is at least as important as, and usually more important than, the quality of its science.
- Controversial litigation victories (and similar types of formal victories) need broad, *deep and active* support to last; this requires ongoing organizing.
- Movements that consist mostly of NGOs that rely on check-writers and postcard writers cannot generate the mass grassroots action that provides the leverage for major change and the ability to overcome big money and its well-financed "astroturf" groups. Protest, non-cooperation, and other mass displays are critical in the contest (Tilly 2004).
- Politics is about using carrots and sticks decisively and intelligently. Success requires tending the carrot patch and accumulating and honing plenty of sticks.

These lessons are not new. They explain why US President Johnson sat down with civil rights leaders to try and defuse growing protests and put his full weight behind passage of the Civil Rights Act of 1964 and the Voting Rights Act of 1965 (Garrow 1986) and why South African President de Klerk sat down with the African National Congress to bring about the end of apartheid when they did (Wood 2000). Conservationists ignore these lessons at biodiversity's peril. Scientists may not need to lead grassroots mass mobilization efforts – though sometimes they have – but they need to understand the limits of merely presenting the science of biodiversity loss and recovery to the prime minister at lunch.

REFERENCES

Alexander, Kristina. 2011. *The Gray Wolf and the Endangered Species Act (ESA): A Brief Legal History.* US Congress, Congressional Research Service. Washington DC.

Alinsky, Saul. 1971. *Rules for Radicals.* Random House. New York.

Banaszak, Lee Ann. 1996. *Why Movements Succeed or Fail.* Princeton University Press. Princeton, NJ.

Beder, Sharon. 2001. Global Spin. Pp. 242–66 in Richard Starkey and Richard Welford (eds.). *Earthscan Reader in Business and Sustainable Development.* Earthscan. London.

Bergstrom, Bradley J., Sacha Vignieri, Steven R. Sheffield, Wes Sechrest, and Anne A. Carlson. 2009. The Northern Rocky Mountain Gray Wolf Is Not Yet Recovered. 59 *Bioscience* 11: 991–9.

Bevington, Douglas. 2009. *Rebirth of Environmentalism.* Island Press. Washington DC.

Cashore, Benjamin and Michael Howlett. 2006. Behavioral Thresholds and Institutional Rigidities as Explanations of Punctuated Equilibrium Processes in Pacific Northwest Forest Policy Dynamics. Pp. 137–61 in Robert Repetto (ed.). *Punctuated Equilibrium and the Dynamics of US Environmental Policy.* Yale University Press. New Haven, CT.

Cogkianese, G. 2007. Business Interests and Information in Environmental Rulemaking. Pp. 185–210 in M. E. Kraft and S. Kamieniecki (eds.). *Business and Environmental Policy.* MIT Press. Cambridge, MA.

Critchlow, Donald T. 2011. *The Conservative Ascendancy.* 2nd edn. University Press of Kansas. Lawrence, KS.

Dobson, Ed, Jerry Falwell, and Edward Hindson. 1981. *The Fundamentalist Phenomenon: The Resurgence of Conservative Christianity.* Doubleday. New York.

Domhoff, G. William. 1998. *Who Rules America?* 3rd edn. Mayfield Publishing. Mountain View, CA.

Dryzek, John S., David Downes, Christian Hunold, and David Schlosberg. 2003. *Green States and Social Movements.* Oxford University Press. Oxford.

Duffy, R. J. 2007. Business, Elections and the Environment. Pp. 61–90 in M. E. Kraft and S. Kamieniecki (eds.). *Business and Environmental Policy.* MIT Press. Cambridge, MA.

Dye, Thomas R. 2013. *Who's Running America?* 8th edn. Paradigm. Boulder, CO.

Eisenberg, Cristina. 2010. *The Wolf's Tooth.* Island Press. Washington DC.

Etzioni, Amatai. 1968. *The Active Society.* Free Press. New York.

Federal Judicial Center. 2012. *Judges of the United States Courts.* US Courts. Washington DC.

Fellowes, Matthew C. and Patrick J. Wolf. 2004. Funding Mechanisms and Policy Instruments: How Business Campaign Contributions Influence Congressional Votes. 57 *Political Research Quarterly* 2: 315–24 (June).

Flippen, J. Brooks. 2000. *Nixon and the Environment.* University of New Mexico Press. Albuquerque, NM.

Foreman, Dave. 2004. *Rewilding North America.* Island Press. Washington DC.

Furlong, S. R. 2007. Business and the Environment: Influencing Agency Policy Making. Pp. 155–84 in M. E. Kraft and S. Kamieniecki (eds.). *Business and Environmental Policy.* MIT Press. Cambridge, MA.

Garrow, David. 1986. *Bearing the Cross.* Morrow. New York

Gilgoff, Dan. 2007. *The Jesus Machine.* St Martin's. New York.

Giugni, Marco. 2004. *Social Protest and Policy Change.* Rowman & Littlefield. Lanham, MD.

Gonzalez, G A. 2001. *Corporate Power and the Environment.* Rowman & Littlefield. Lanham, MD.

Grover, W. F. 1989. *The President as Prisoner.* State University of New York Press. Albany, NY.

Harris Interactive. 2011. Poll on Endangered Species Act conducted for the Endangered Species Coalition. www.defenders.org/publications/endangered_species_act_poll.pdf.

Heberlein, T. A. and G. Ericsson. 2008. Public Attitudes and the Future of Wolves *Canus lupus* in Sweden. 14 *Wildlife Biology* 391–4.

Herring, Hal. 2011. Wolf Whiplash. *High Country News* (May 30)

Jacques, Peter J., Riley E. Dunlop, and Mark Freeman. 2008. The Organisation of Denial: Conservative Think Tanks and Environmental Scepticism. 17 *Environmental Politics* 3: 349–85.

Johns, David. 2009. *A New Conservation Politics: Power, Organization Building and Effectiveness.* Wiley-Blackwell. Chichester.

Kamieniecki, S. 2006. *Corporate America and Environmental Policy.* Stanford University Press. Stanford, CA.

Keller, Jonathan. 2017. The Christian Right and American Biblical Tradition. Pp. 169–81 in Jonathan Keller and Alex Zamalin (eds.). *American Political Thought, An Alternative View.* Routledge. New York.

Lambert, Frank. 2008. *Religion in American Politics.* Princeton University Press. Princeton, NJ.

Layzer, Judith. 2007. Deep Freeze: How Business Has Shaped the Global Warming Debate in Congress. Pp. 93–125 in M. E. Kraft and S. Kamieniecki (eds.). *Business and Environmental Policy.* MIT Press. Cambridge, MA.

Libby, R. T. 1999. *Eco-Wars: Political Campaigns and Social Movements.* Columbia University Press. New York.

Lindblom, Charles. 1977. *Politics and Markets.* Basic Books. New York.

Liptak, Adam. 2009. Environment Groups Find Less Support on Court. *New York Times*, July 4: A8.

Lopez, Barry Holstun. 1978. *Of Wolves and Men.* Scribners. New York.

Mansbridge, Jane. 1986. *Why We Lost the ERA.* University of Chicago Press. Chicago, IL.

McAdam, Doug, Sidney Tarrow, and Charles Tilly. *Dynamics of Contention.* 2001. Cambridge University Press. Cambridge.

Perrings, C., S. Naeem, F. Ahrestani, et al. 2010a. Ecosystem Services for 2020. 330 *Science* 323–4.

Perrings, C., S. Naeem, F. Ahrestani, et al. 2010b. Response to Faith, Biodiversity Transcends Services. 330 *Science* 1745.

Piven, Frances Fox. 2006. *Challenging Authority.* Rowman & Littlefield. Lanham, MD.

Repetto, R. 2006. Introduction. Pp. 1–23 in R. Repetto (ed.). *Punctuated Equilibrium and the Dynamics of US Environmental Policy.* Yale University Press. New Haven, CT.

Research and Polling Inc. 2008a. Wolf Recovery Survey – Arizona. www.rpinc.com/wb/media/Wolf_Recovery_Survey_Summary_Arizona.pdf. (Albuquerque, NM)

Research and Polling Inc. 2008b. Wolf Recovery Survey – New Mexico. www.rpinc.com/wb/media/Wolf_Recovery_Survey_Summary_New_Mexico.pdf. (Albuquerque, NM)

Robinson, Michael J. 2005. *Predatory Bureaucracy*. University of Colorado Press. Boulder, CO.

Rootes, C. 2007 [2004]. Environmental Movements. Pp. 608–40 in David A. Snow, Sarah A. Soulé and Hanspeter Kriesi (eds.). *The Blackwell Companion to Social Movements*. Blackwell Publishing. Oxford.

Rucht, Dieter. 1999. The Impact of Environmental Movements in Western Societies. Pp. 204–24 in Marco Giugni, Doug McAdam, and Charles Tilly (eds.). *How Social Movements Matter*. University of Minnesota Press. Minneapolis, MN.

Shaiko, Ronald G. 1999. *Voices and Echoes for the Environment*. Columbia University Press. New York.

Staggenborg, Suzanne. 1991. *The Pro-Choice Movement*. Oxford University Press. New York.

Thomas, Craig. 2003. *Bureaucratic Landscapes*. MIT Press. Cambridge, MA.

Tilly, Charles. 2004. *Social Movements 1768–2004*. Paradigm. Boulder, CO.

Turner, James Morton. 2012. *The Promise of Wilderness*. University of Washington Press. Seattle.

Union of Concerned Scientists. 2008. *Federal Science and the Public Good*. Union of Concerned Scientists. Cambridge, MA.

Williams, Christopher K., Göran Ericsson, and Thomas A. Heberlein. 2002. A Quantitative Summary of Attitudes toward Wolves and Their Reintroduction (1972–2000). 30 *Wildlife Society Bulletin* 2: 575–84.

Wood, Elizabeth J. 2000. *Forging Democracy From Below*. Cambridge University Press. Cambridge.

2　Like It or Not, Politics is the Solution

So what is to be done about such political failures as legislative delisting of wolves in the US northern Rockies outlined in the previous chapter? What is to be done about the continued loss of habitat and the death of billions of creatures from that and other causes? The horror of the onslaught, even short of extinction – the diminishment of species populations, the dismemberment of natural communities, and the disruption of natural processes – is occurring on a scale in deep time not seen for 65 million years (e.g. Kolbert 2014). Only the bubonic plague (*Yersinia pestis*), and maybe smallpox (variola major), has resulted in human deaths at this scale.

Typically the first thought of conservationists and natural scientists in the face of continued biological decline and bad policy is to do more of what they have been doing and hope for a different outcome: NGOs more strenuously tell decision makers that the majority of people support conservation, species protection and ecological health; ask their members and donors for more money and to sign a petition. Scientists propose doing more research. Neither of these has proven terribly effective at slowing existing trends, let alone in turning them around. On the rare occasion when NGOs call for action – demonstrations, sit-ins, marches – it's unusual to rouse large numbers because no groundwork has been laid. Organizing that builds commitment, trust, and a sense of efficacy, all prerequisites for action, are missing.

SCIENCE AND POLITICS

Huge strides in biological understanding have been made in the last several decades. In 1985 several scientists who believed natural science needed an organization that was focused on conservation of biodiversity rather than just game animals and other forms of consumption, founded the Society for Conservation Biology (SCB). Like medicine, the discipline was intended to focus not just on doing science, but on bringing the science to bear on the health of species and the Earth. Michael Soulé (Johns 2007: 287), one of SCB's founders, noted that prior to the mid-1980s "there was virtually no awareness of edge effects, fragmentation effects, ecological sinks, extinction vortices, inbreeding effects in natural populations, habitat destruction in the seas, endocrine disruptors, island effects, ecological cascades, and top-down regulation and structuring of ecosystems by strongly interacting species, to name only" a few areas. Soulé says that we now know enough biologically about species and ecosystems to propose effective conservation solutions in most cases. Even if this is an overstatement, why hasn't this huge growth in biological knowledge made more of a difference? And what can be done to make the big changes in human behavior necessary to reverse biological trends; to stop the violence against others and begin the healing?

During a workshop held at the global 2015 SCB meeting, a participant expressed puzzlement that although humans were the cause of every conservation problem, about 80 percent of the papers presented at the meeting were about other species. Why not more focus on the problem species? Indeed, why not? This question strongly suggests that the reason for limited conservation success lies in a failure not of biological understanding but of political understanding and action – certainly among scientists but also among many advocacy groups.

Powerful interests are arrayed against conservation and they are deeply embedded in the very organization of most societies. "Speaking truth to power" whether scientific truth or moral truth, is no antidote by itself. Virtually all societies are organized around the domination and control of nature on which depends material growth. Stuart Pimm (2001) summarized the "math" neatly: when humans take more, less is left for other species; when ecosystems are domesticated or obliterated they can no longer realize their

FIGURE 2.1 Self-Delusion, America's Renewable Resource. Joel Pett editorial cartoon used with the permission of Joel Pett and the Cartoonist Group. All rights reserved.

autonomous evolutionary potential. There is no technological fix that will allow 7+ billion humans to generate commodities from nothing, leaving the wild intact. Conmen have been hard at work on making something from nothing for as long as there have been people to con, without any real progress.

ADVOCATES AND POLITICS

Realizing a vision of a biologically healthy Earth and avoiding defeats, such as the legislative delisting of wolves discussed in the previous chapter, does not require more knowledge about wolves. There is much reliable knowledge on what they need: large areas without humans with guns and traps, without roads, and with adequate prey. What is required is a much stronger conservation movement that decision makers don't want to cross; a movement that can effectively obtain institutional and other human behaviors that are compatible with wolf needs. Scientists may not understand this very well, though some do, and advocates should. Yet they all seem wedded to strategies that don't produce the desired results. The wheel has been invented, but they resist undertaking mass mobilization and grassroots organizing and then wonder why conservation has weak support in most countries, as, e.g., evidenced by the absence of adequate pressure to force governments to take the Convention on Biodiversity 2010 goals seriously (e.g. Butchart et al. 2010), such as by addressing threats to biodiversity. Progress on the next round of goals – the so-called Aichi Biodiversity Targets to be realized by 2020 which aim to reduce overall pressure on biodiversity – are not any more impressive (Tittensor et al. 2014).

Some have counseled a retreat from even these moderate goals (Perrings et al. 2010a; Kareiva et al. 2011); they argue that if conservation is to make progress it must be based on meeting people's needs, such as providing ecosystem services and food security. Others have countered that basing conservation on direct benefits to people at best leaves out much that must be conserved to stem biological decline and recover from it; at worst such an approach – people above all else – is what got us into the current predicament (Faith 2010; Wuerthner et al. 2014).

There are relatively few who are addressing how to make the conservation movement stronger and more effective or who are tackling the roots of biological impoverishment and extinction. There are few who recognize that affecting conservation outcomes is not mostly about providing information and cognitive education, but about bringing political resources – money, votes, media, direct action – to bear in the processes of selecting leaders, making policy choices, and carrying out policy. Many value access to decision makers who do not deliver, and so embrace ineffective insider strategies such as lobbying and refuse to engage strategies that could work by upping the pressure through direct action. Most simply, it's about being able to help friends and punish opponents. Conservationists make progress when they are clear and uncompromising about their goals, flexible about means, and convince their opponents that they will never tire or go away.

Looking more at how the ESA has been enforced over the years reveals why politics must be central to conservation. Although one of the strongest laws on the books anywhere in the world protecting species and despite official claims that the US supports the rule of law seriously, all US administrations have resisted implementing the ESA to some degree, mostly due to the influence of resource interests such as oil and gas, industrial logging and ranching, mining, road building, and housing development interests. Such interests are pervasive, often betting on "both sides" so they have influence no matter who wins. When a political faction or coalition includes conservationists they also have influence, but it often cannot match more powerful interests such as those pushing growth. Conservation is usually not part of the elite coalition comprising a faction, merely the electoral coalition, which limits bargaining power (Edelman 1964; Lindblom 1977; Dryzek et al. 2003). In the US, the Clinton and Obama administrations were elected with conservation support. Neither president spent much time outside or had a personal passion for wild places and creatures, and neither government was vigorous in listing species, designating critical habitat, or setting sound recovery goals, but they both undertook significant ESA enforcement (Bevington 2009).

In contrast, George W. Bush was elected over conservation opposition and with the strong support of extractive industries. This administration repeatedly broke the law. It routinely suppressed, distorted, and ignored scientific findings and recommendations, slowed the listing process to a crawl, refused to list species that should be listed, and encouraged legal challenges from industry to the law's implementation, and then offered to settle with them in court to ensure weak enforcement (Union of Concerned Scientists 2008).

Since biodiversity and wilderness protection have become divisive issues in the US, with the major parties taking opposing views and using them to mark their distinctive positions and identity, conservationists find themselves in the most unenviable position of not being welcome in one camp and being taken for granted in the other camp. For example, although nominally a supporter of conservation policies the Obama administration did not make strong conservation appointments at the very top (Clinton did; Bush and Trump have made appointments hostile to conservation), and the USFWS has refused to follow the recommendations of scientists to list species (as with the sage grouse and wolverine), apparently to avoid conflict with various economic interests and thus invite anti-ESA blowback. Despite the requirements of the law, many agencies have not lived up to the government's pledge on scientific integrity, have sought to delist species to show the ESA is working, and have refused to stand up to unreasonably fearful landowners to recover the red wolf, and much else (e.g. Stokstad 2014). Obama's frequent affairs with extractive industries prompted many lawsuits by the Center for Biological Diversity (and legal victories), but the conservation response generally has been weak. Whether this response was by choice – an unwillingness to demand "too much," rock the boat, and not get invited back for lunch – or simply a recognition that they lack leverage, is not always clear. Both timidity and weakness are factors in political ineffectiveness.

Conservation NGOs usually lack the clout to be part of the ruling or elite coalition of a party and are limited to being part of the electoral or symbolic coalition (e.g. Edelman 1964). That is, they trade votes for promises which do not have a high probability of being delivered on: it is agreed that habitat fragmentation is bad, but road building continues apace. This contrasts with being part of a party's elite coalition, who often exercise a veto over candidates and policies and deliver money, media, and other significant resources in exchange for particular policies or actions, e.g. we will open up public lands for oil, gas, and other energy-generating activities. Being part of a coalition is only one factor in explaining decision maker actions. In the US, getting into court is relatively easy, the courts generally take seriously ESA requirements for agencies to follow the best available science, and they are willing to render decisions based on the law. This means that conservationists have sought regular recourse to the courts against both opponents and nominal friends to obtain

ESA enforcement. Indeed, the Center for Biological Diversity has protected through litigation 550 species and 470 million acres of critical habitat since 1989 (McSpadden et al. 2014). The Nature Conservancy "has helped protect approximately 21 million acres in the United States and more than 103 million globally by outright purchase or via easements since 1961" (Nature Conservancy 2016). In many if not most countries the courts do not play a major role and other strategies must be pursued: international pressure, popular resistance and non-cooperation, alternative media, or use of crises to gain leverage.

Although conflict over the behavior of institutions toward other species and wild places is often framed as being about the science – how the world works, what the needs of a species are, or the likely consequences of a human action – they are at root about what different groups regard as good or desirable. They are about disagreements over competing groups' interests, values, and morality. Are human interests the only valuable ones? Is development more important than self-willed lands and life? Because powerful groups frequently cannot openly justify their interests since they would be rejected or condemned, they seek to debate the facts: sowing doubt and creating "alternative facts" – cigarettes are good for you, profits from selling fossil fuels are more important than the damage burning them causes (Brandt 2007; Otto 2016). Outside of some court systems and perhaps select other institutions, these disagreements are settled by who can bring to bear the most political resources most strategically and skillfully (Johns 2012).

The centrality of politics – understanding the political landscape, being able to help sympathetic decision makers and oppose bad ones – is also made clear by the Yellowstone to Yukon Conservation Initiative (Y2Y). This US–Canadian effort to safeguard one of the last great refuges of many of North America's wide-ranging species and large intact ecosystems has invested heavily in biological research in order to inform decisions about protected area priorities and landscape connectivity. Despite similar amounts of scientific research and understanding conservation results have been different north and south of the border. Why?

On the Canadian side, under Prime Minister Chrétien (1993–2003), whom conservationists helped elect and maintained a close relationship with, many new parks were created or expanded in the Rockies region (and elsewhere). Although the biologically import-ant expansion of Waterton Park was not accomplished it was put on the agenda and given a boost. Parks Canada adopted many conser-vation biology principles in its land and aquatic management actions, in part because of influence from NGOs in the continent's West. Under the subsequent government of the recently tossed-out Prime Minister Harper, progress greatly slowed for many years and some activists were victims of repression. It remains to be seen how things will play out with Trudeau. His support for a huge and unnecessary dam in northwest British Columbia has been disappointing. A new government in British Columbia, which conservationists helped elect, promised to stop the big dam in question but failed to do so under pressure from provincial creditors. Also at the provincial level, the new socialist government of Alberta has shown itself to be more responsive to conservation concerns than the long-standing old regime, which had been in the pocket of industry. The new govern-ment wants to protect headwaters of waterways, integrate wildlife crossings into its roads program, and to find alternatives to the tar sands as sources of employment.

Bill Clinton was US president during a good part of Chrétien's time in office. During most of his presidency the federal legislature was controlled by the opposite party (as a non-parliamentary system the US central government may have presidents and legislatures controlled by different and opposing parties); the divided government meant conservationists were relatively welcome in the executive branch and much less welcome by the legislative branch majorities, which tried to weaken the ESA and other conservation laws and blocked even limited pro-conservation legislation. Clinton did use his executive power to promulgate the "roadless rule," which prohibited new roads on federal lands without them, leaving intact many areas within the US portion of the Y2Y region (and elsewhere) that otherwise would have been lost. In the face of a legal and political stalemate, he acted administratively to create the Northwest Forest Plan, protecting vast areas of old growth forest, and continued to support limited wolf recovery in the region. At the same time the Clinton administration gave up the fight for grazing reform because of a mistaken belief it was necessary to gain approval of the North American Free Trade Agreement from the Republican-controlled Congress. Although the Republican Party had a history of supporting conservation for much of the twentieth century, this was seriously eroded beginning in the late 1970s with the realignment of interest groups within the political parties. This realignment enabled Republicans to fashion a majority coalition of religious and economic conservatives which excluded conservation in favor of extractive interests. This realignment fundamentally altered the US political landscape.

This discussion, heavily weighted to North America, is far from exhaustive, and is only meant to give a familiar example or two concerning the centrality of political effectiveness to achieving conservation goals. Political effectiveness has been equally important in setting (bad) policy toward wolves in northern Europe (Chapron 2014) and in achieving good policy in Gorongosa National Park in Mozambique (Carroll 2016). The more effective conservation is politically, the less need there is for detailed biological information. If big, unfragmented landscapes can be protected, and connectivity re-established or maintained, it is more likely that species, communities, landscapes, and seascapes can take care of themselves.

The peninsula of Kamchatka is a case in point. It was closed under Soviet rule to most human uses, the easier to keep secret the operations of the submarine bases and airbases thought to be critical to Soviet power. There were protected areas, including strictly protected *zapovedniks*, such as the stunningly beautiful Kronotsky Volcano. There was little felt urgency to establish more protected areas or to connect them by designation in these circumstances. With the fall of the Soviet Union and the opening of the region to exploitation by big multinational corporations, the lack of protection made designation of a system of connected protected areas urgent. There was a rush to figure out where to deploy limited conservation resources against those seeking to turn the peninsula's habitat into lumber, toilet paper, metals, and food. As some MiGs sat on tarmacs, cannibalized to keep other MiGs flying, the natural landscape was succumbing as well. Almost overnight a heroic effort against great odds was started to protect places and keep them connected. But where exactly? Not everything could be protected in the face of big multinational companies, official corruption, and lack of enforcement. Better information was needed quickly to determine priorities: which species were most at risk, what were their ranges? Conservation NGOs, the Kamchatka section of the Russian Academy of Sciences, and scientists from agencies stepped in to fill the need.

RESHAPING CONSERVATION POLITICS

In 1991 a group of North American conservation scientists and conservation advocates met at a house on Russian Hill in San Francisco to discuss the global decline of species and ecosystems and how to reverse it. Protected areas were becoming islands, connectivity was being lost, and outside of protected areas forests, native grasslands, and wetlands were being transformed into tree farms, agricultural fields, subdivisions, or off-road vehicle playgrounds. Existing conservation efforts were clearly missing something if they could not stop these trends. The Wildlands Network (then the Wildlands Project) was a marriage of science, advocacy, and ecocentric values; its aim was, first, to determine what it would take to ensure all native species and ecosystems could flourish and natural processes such as fire could operate unfettered – first in North America and then globally. The answer was a continental system of connected, protected areas described using the principles of conservation biology, then a relatively young, mission-driven science, and not unlike medicine, but with ecological and species health the concern (Foreman et al. 1992; Noss 1992). The second aim was to secure this system of protected areas by official designation, cultural change, and voluntary and incentivized private lands action. It was influenced by work in Mesoamerica, the Paseo Pantera project initiated by Archie Carr, Mario Boza, Jim Barborak and others, and late 1980s work by Reed Noss (1987) and Larry Harris (Noss and Harris 1986) in Florida. Paseo Pantera (Path of the Panther) was founded on conservation biology principles but was hijacked by United Nations aid programs in 1994 (Fraser 2009) and the governments that benefited from the aid money. Since then millions have been poured into Mesoamerica, not for conservation but for endless meetings and talk – perhaps best seen as a kind of jobs program, but with funds reaching only a few.

The Wildlands Network effort brought about a major change, in the decade following the initial meeting, in the science and goals of conservation so that it is no longer in question that large, connected reserves are needed: new and big protected areas, continental-scale connectivity, and restoration and rewilding across whole ecosystems (Noss 1992; Soulé and Terborgh 1999; Johns 2003, 2016). WN and similar groups, such as Y2Y, the Rewilding Europe Initiative, southern African peace parks, Wild Country (Australia), efforts in northern India and elsewhere in Asia, and in regions of Latin America, work with many, many partners, each using their expertise to achieve shared vision.

Some governments have embraced large-scale conservation, at least rhetorically. The same is true of some other major institutions. Most efforts have relied exclusively on insider strategies, i.e. using the typical means and types of influence wielding, which means that the rules of the game limit what can be achieved. Generally those with power accept that they must foster economic growth, protect their legitimacy, rebuff challenges to their power, and not compromise on these (e.g. Dryzek et al. 2003). Conservationists that directly challenge these state and elite interests will meet fierce opposition. But the vision was developed based on the needs of species and the Earth's living system and not on politics as the art of the possible; the vision requires a politics that is focused on changing what's possible. The influence of the conservation groups seeking to realize these large-scale visions, which they estimate will require half the Earth's land mass (Noss 1992; Wilson 2016) and 30–40 percent of the Earth's oceans (Marine Conservation Institute, 2015; O'Leary et al. 2016), is not currently up to their vision. Most do not seek to organize a mass-based grassroots movement which would embrace outsider strategies such as those that have brought down repressive regimes around the world. It can be politically difficult to work with regimes while also trying to change them, but even fairly tame efforts such as Earth Day, which mobilized fully 10 percent of the entire US population in 1970, are not on the radar of NGOs. Long-term organizing runs against the grain of the desire of leaders and funders who want quick results.

A strong argument can be made that conservationists have lost ground in many places in the last several decades – perhaps the price of gaining and keeping a seat at the table. Most NGOs accept existing social systems despite their inherent destructiveness, and deny the contradiction between their embrace of constant growth and safeguarding biodiversity. They have become integrated into the state in some countries and lost autonomy (Dryzek et al. 2003); they have been absorbed into green parties, the focus of which is environmentalism, i.e. concern with the Earth as a place for humans rather than concern for all species (Carter 2007; Connelly et al. 2012); and larger NGOs have grown into hierarchical organizations that find activists problematic and prefer manageable check-writers (Shaiko 1999). The United States is illustrative. In the late 1970s and 1980s conservation was transformed by its success in passing many strong environmental and conservation laws, reducing visible pollution and the pervasiveness of some toxic substances, and bringing some species back from the edge of extinction, if only just barely. Many NGOs believed they could continue down this path by becoming lobbying groups supported by members' and foundation money. They abandoned mass mobilization based on grassroots organizing. They failed to understand that mainstream lobbying not only required playing by rules designed to serve more powerful interests, but that organizations of check-writers generate only weak member commitment and low levels of mobilization – not attributes that cause decision makers to pay attention (Shaiko 1999; Dryzek et al. 2003). Some organizations have sought to maintain the face of grassroots activism, but their actions have become highly ritualized; authorities know what to expect and real contention is absent (Meyer and Tarrow 1998; Rootes 2007 [2004]). Some NGOs have attempted to farm out organizing, but it cannot be done (Fisher 2006). Going door to door or leafleting by those working on contract and not directly engaged in the substantive work raises a bit of money from small donors but does not build relationships that bring people into an organization where they regularly participate, grow in commitment, and take the initiative from the bottom up. NGOs even in countries usually categorized as democracies by experts have become self-domesticated. They function little differently, in terms of autonomy from the status quo and authorities, than NGOs in countries, such as China, where party or other officials operate within NGOs to define acceptable activities and to otherwise steer them (Broadbent and Brockman 2011).

There are other variations on the challenge of organization. The biggest problem may not be the "iron law of oligarchy" (Michels 1962 [1915]) or self-domestication, but the unwillingness to undertake grassroots organizing. It's part of the failure to grasp how power works.

Even if all conservationists and sympathizers were well organized and shared a clear vision, it's unlikely they would be influential enough to achieve their vision given societal inertia (the centrality of growth and the tendency of societies to reproduce their institutions and forms of social organization) and the determination of powerful groups to hold on to their power no matter what. Influential allies are critical to conservation success. Here too conservationist understanding of the political landscape is often lacking. As we shall examine in the following chapters, the wheel has been invented when it comes to organizing, coalition and alliance building, and undertaking collective political action. A huge reservoir of knowledge exists based on experience and research in both insider and outsider approaches, including:

- issue campaigning
- electoral campaigning
- community organizing
- coalition building
- movement building
- creating new institutions and altering social structure
- winning asymmetric and contentious struggles against powerful opponents
- and everything that goes into these, from strategy and leadership to timing and tactics.

We will discuss the differences between insider and outsider approaches to politics – politics as the art of the possible and politics as the art of changing what's possible, and the need to combine the two – in later chapters. It's also appropriate to note a recent trend in some countries, but more longstanding in others: collaboration. This is a term applied to government-sponsored or -organized efforts, nominally voluntary, in which a variety of interests attempt to find agreement on policies governing relations with other species, lands, and waters. The term is misleading in many respects. It suggests it is possible to talk through most or all political differences, when in fact many differences are fundamental and only admit to conflict until a decisive political or legal victory is won by one coalition or another. Collaboration assumes conservation is just one human interest among many others, rather than a matter of whether human degradation of the Earth is a legitimate basis for any society.

The wider political context of collaboration defines much of what goes on around the table. Conservationists did well at the table in obtaining protection for Steens Mountain in Oregon, but it was in

part because the US Secretary of the Interior had threatened designation of a national monument (administrative legal protection pursuant to legislation) if there was no agreement, and ranchers (the main
opponents of protection) did not want a monument. Ranchers had also
recently lost an important court case in which the USFWS, which had
long killed coyotes on the Hart Mountain Antelope Refuge in an
unsuccessful attempt to stop declining antelope numbers, was
ordered to stop killing coyotes and remove domestic livestock from
the refuge. Research suggested the antelope decline was due to livestock grazing rather than predators, and conservationists went to
court to force the cows off. When antelope numbers started to recover
after cattle were removed the writing was on the wall. The statements
of the Interior Secretary and the results of the lawsuit profoundly
shifted the balance of power among the parties.

More often the political context of collaboration does not go
well for conservation. Collaboration does not mean people seek consensus and embrace a shared higher collective good. Most at the table
seek to further a particular economic interest that involves displacing
or consuming wildlife, often scarce water, and plants: they want to
log, mine, graze, or otherwise transform the land by development.
Almost invariably conservationists are outnumbered in these settings. A half dozen or more human interests are at the table – usually
resource extraction or consumptive interests – while all other species
are represented by one group, conservationists, as if biodiversity were
just another human interest. Collaborations take extensive time despite often minimal results, but to not participate leaves NGOs open to
criticism for lack of good faith or an unwillingness to engage in
democratic decision making. In another era social movement
resources were taken up by repression: activists were arrested, had
to raise bail, prepare a legal defense, and ponder serving lengthy jail
sentences. Collaboratives are in one sense another means to achieve
the same results, but in a much softer way that avoids government
appearing heavy handed.

Another important difference in political context, for all forms of political conflict and resulting decisions and not just collaboratives, is the strength of the state. Some states are quite strong and able to effectively assert both decision making and enforcement authority over the relationship between humans under their control and the rest of nature. Some strong states delegate governance of this relationship to local authorities to one degree or another to maintain central government legitimacy. Such delegation can considerably complicate matters for conservationists because local authorities may be heavily dependent on "resource" extraction and/or less able to resist powerful forces such as big companies. Weak states present a different sort of problem for conservationists. Who makes decisions, or who can veto them, may shift with the waxing and waning of social groups such as economic interests, warlords, ethnic and religious groups, or groups based in a particular geography. The ability of decision makers to deliver on their promises may also be compromised or murky.

Most of the examples discussed at any length in this book come from strong states where the main task of NGOs is to mobilize groups to influence the central state or major subdivisions, and secondarily other centers of power. In weak states the centers of power may lie outside formal governmental institutions, often with local economic elites, ethnic leaders, and international corporations and institutions.

Regardless, the major obstacles confronting conservation are political not biological. For that reason a sound grasp of power generally and specific political landscapes is essential and must inform conservation strategy in all its aspects. Biological knowledge won't, by itself, bring changes in the behavior of human institutions.

REFERENCES

Bevington, Douglas. 2009. *Rebirth of Environmentalism*. Island Press. Washington DC.

Brandt, Allan. 2007. *The Cigarette Century*. Basic Books. New York.

Broadbent, Jeffrey and Vicky Brockman (eds.). 2011. *East Asian Social Movements*. Springer. New York.

Butchart, Stuart H. M., Matt Walpole, Ben Collen, et al. 2010. Global Biodiversity: Indicators of Recent Declines. 328 *Science* 1164–8.

Carroll, Sean B. 2016. *The Serengeti Rules.* Princeton University Press. Princeton, NJ.

Carter, Neil. 2007. *Politics of the Environment.* 2nd edn. Cambridge University Press. Cambridge.

Chapron, Guillaume. 2014. Challenge the Abuse of Science in Setting Policy. 516 *Nature* 289 (December 18–25).

Connelly, James, Graham Smith, David Benson, and Clare Saunders. 2012. *Politics and the Environment.* 3rd edn. Routledge. London.

Dryzek, John S., David Downes, Christian Hunold, and David Schlosberg. 2003. *Green States and Social Movements.* Oxford University Press. Oxford.

Edelman, Murray. 1964. *The Symbolic Uses of Politics.* University of Illinois Press. Urbana, IL.

Faith, Daniel. 2010. Biodiversity Transcends Services. 330 *Science* 1744–5.

Fisher, Dana R. 2006. *Activism, Inc.* 2006. Stanford University Press. Stanford, CA.

Foreman, Dave, John Davis, David Johns, Reed Noss, and Michael Soulé. 1992. The Wildlands Project Mission Statement. *Wild Earth* Special Issue 1: 3–4.

Fraser, Carolyn. 2009. *Rewilding the World.* Metropolitan Books. New York.

Johns, David. 2003. The Wildlands Project outside North America. In Alan Watson and Janet Sproull (comps.). *Seventh World Wilderness Congress Symposium: Science and Stewardship to Protect and Sustain Wilderness Values, November 2–8, 2001, Port Elizabeth, South Africa.* Proc. RMRS-P-27. US Department of Agriculture, Forest Service, Rocky Mountain Research Station. Ogden UT.

Johns, David. 2007. Like It or Not, Politics is the Solution. 21 *Conservation Biology* 2: 287–8.

Johns, David. 2012. Rescuing Wolves: States Not Immune to Politics. 335 *Science* 795.

Johns, David. 2016. Rewilding. Reference Module in Earth Systems and Environmental Sciences, Elsevier, 08-Feb-2016. doi: 10.1016/B978-0-12-409548-9.09 202-2.

Kareiva, Peter, Robert Lalas, and Michelle Marvier. 2011. Conservation in the Anthropocene. 2 *Breakthrough Journal*: 29–37.

Kolbert, Elizabeth. 2014. *The Sixth Extinction.* Holt. New York.

Lindblom, Charles. 1977. *Politics and Markets.* Basic Books. New York.

Marine Conservation Institute. 2015. *Global Ocean Refuge System (GLORES) Strategic Business Plan.* Marine Conservation Institute. Seattle, WA.

McSpadden, Russ, Lydia Millet, Mike Stark, and Kieran Suckling (eds.). 2014. *A Wild Love: The Center for Biological Diversity's First 25 Years.* Center for Biological Diversity. Tucson, AZ.

Meyer, David and Sidney Tarrow. 1998. A Movement Society: Contentious Politics for a New Society. Pp. 1–28 in David Meyer and Sidney Tarrow (eds.). *The Social Movement Society*. Rowman & Littlefield. Lanham, MD.

Michels, Robert. 1962 [1915]. *Political Parties*. Free Press. Glencoe, IL.

Nature Conservancy, The. 2016. www.nature.org/about-us/private-lands-conserva tion/. Accessed May 25, 2016.

Noss, Reed F. 1987. Protecting Natural Areas in Fragmented Landscapes. 7 *The Natural Areas Journal* 1: 2–13.

Noss, Reed. 1992. The Wildlands Project Land Conservation Strategy. *Wild Earth* Special Issue 1: 10–25.

Noss, Reed F. and Larry D. Harris. 1986. Nodes, Networks, and MUMs: Preserving Diversity at All Scales. 10 *Environmental Management* 299–309.

O'Leary, Bethan C., Marit Winther-Janson, John M. Bainbridge, Jemma Aitken, Julie P. Hawkins, and Callum M. Roberts. 2016. Effective Coverage Targets for Ocean Protection. 9 *Conservation Letters*. http://onlinelibrary.wiley.com/ doi/10.1111/conl.12247/pdf.

Otto, Shawn. 2016. *The War on Science*. Milkweed Editions. Minneapolis, MN.

Perrings, C., S. Naeem, F. Ahrestani, et al. 2010a. Ecosystem Services for 2020. 330 *Science* 323–4.

Perrings, C., S. Naeem, F. Ahrestani, et al. 2010b. Response to Faith, Biodiversity Transcends Services. 330 *Science* 1745.

Pimm, Stuart. 2001. *The World According to Pimm*. McGraw-Hill. New York.

Rootes, Christopher. 2007 [2004]. Environmental Movements. Pp. 608–40 in David Snow, Sarah Soule, and Hanspeter Kriesi (eds.). *The Blackwell Companion to Social Movements*. Blackwell. Oxford.

Shaiko. Ronald G. 1999. *Voices and Echoes for the Environment*. Columbia University Press. New York.

Soulé, Michael and John Terborgh. 1999. *Continental Conservation*. Island Press. Washington DC.

Stokstad, Erik. 2014. Red Wolves in the Crosshairs. 345 *Science* 1548–9.

Tittensor, Derrick P., M. Walpole, S. L. Hill, et al. 2014. A Mid-Term Analysis of Progress toward International Biodiversity Targets. 346 *Science* 241–4.

Union of Concerned Scientists. 2008. *Federal Science and the Public Good*. Union of Concerned Scientists. Cambridge, MA.

Wilson, Edward O. 2016. *Half-Earth*. Liveright. New York

Wuerthner, George, Eileen Crist, and Tom Butler (eds.). 2014. *Keeping the Wild*. Island Press. Washington DC.

PART II Getting the Questions Right

Before getting the answers right it's necessary to get the questions right. Then the answers are not difficult.

First and foremost, a clear vision is necessary. What is it conservationists want? Where do they want to go? Sadly, many conservationists accept as inevitable existing trends of a growing human footprint and less and less for wildlife and wild places. Dan Ashe, former Director of the US Fish and Wildlife Service – the agency charged with protecting wildlife and administering laws such as the Endangered Species Act – said more than once during his tenure that people need to get used to less wildlife. That's because humans are taking more and more. Conservation should not be looking to bureaucrats for leadership, in any event – conservation's job is to lead. Conservation has a vision: one of a healed world with vibrant populations of all species living in functional, natural communities. This vision is partly enabled through the creation of a global system of large, strictly protected areas, connected at all appropriate scales so animals and plants can move as they have in deep time. Such a vision, by describing a positive direction, grounds strategy. It is essential. The US civil rights movement used to speak of keeping their Eyes on the Prize.

The prize is the vision and the goals that embody it. If a strategy is how a group or movement gets from here to there, the prize is the there. No clear prize in mind, no effective strategy is possible. There are several shortcomings to typical conservation strategizing: lacking a "clear prize," focusing on short-term goals that do not move in the direction of the prize, and engaging in strategic planning. Strategic planning is too often a straightjacket. It is typically based on a SWOT (strengths, weaknesses, opportunities, threats) analysis. This can be a useful exercise, but by itself it leaves organizations forever stuck in

47

the short term (current strengths and weaknesses), unable to address the long term; or allows others to define an organization's agenda (opportunities and threats). Only by focusing on the vision, the final prize, is it possible to make progress toward it. Goals should be derived from the vision: what must be achieved, step by step, to get to the vision. Even for a 100-year vision (or longer) in which the final steps are fuzzy at best, it is important to keep the vision at center to avoid being sidetracked or stuck in the short term. To heal the Earth requires politics as the art of *changing* what's possible. Biodiversity-compatible human societies will of necessity be fundamentally different than human societies are today.

All of this does not abnegate the importance of clarity about the current landscape: the "here" in the getting from here to there. What aspects of the status quo and the groups invested in it stand in the way of the policies and societal changes needed to secure biodiversity and wild places? Obstacles to conservation may be cultural, economic, or political; they may involve hostile motives or inertia. It's also important to assess likely blowback from the non-human world resulting from human actions, e.g. unstable climate. Without getting the question quite right, developing effective strategies is unlikely.

At the heart of any strategy – especially one that seeks to realize a bold vision – is mobilization. Mobilization is the process of generating organized and effective political action; of lighting people's hearts and brains on fire, feeding the fire, and putting the energy of that fire to good use.

The next several chapters will look at the questions that need answering to arrive at good conservation strategy, the central importance of bringing human societal change, including the roots of societal destructiveness in human population growth and consumption, the particular problems posed by energy-intensive society, and opportunities presented by structural and cyclical crises. Successful strategy must address all of these or it will fail life on Earth.

3   Ten Questions for Conservation Politics

In 2009 a group of pre-eminent conservation biologists (Sutherland et al. 2009), in consultation with many dozens of others, published a list of the 100 most important science questions facing the protection of biological diversity. Winnowed to 100 from an initial list of 2,291 questions, the list misses fundamental strategic questions for advancing conservation. The list is itself an example of not getting the question right. If one sets out to identify the most important *science* questions, but the main obstacles to conservation are political, the results will be less than optimally helpful. The following ten questions prompt conservationists to address how they will bring about the change needed to stop decline of other species, including their extinction, and recover a vibrant living world.

1. What are the most important goals for the conservation movement or for a conservation group?
2. Who has the power to make the decisions needed to reach the goal? Which legislature, chief executive, agency, business, landowner, or combination of these? It's not always easy to tell who is making decisions because all political systems involve obfuscation, finger pointing, and informal institutional back-scratching as well as conflict. Decision making may be formally vested in a government, but it may be religious, military, party, or business leaders that actually make the decisions. Identifying decision makers with specificity is important because knowing who decision makers are institutionally and as individuals informs how best to influence them. Individuals, ruling coalitions, and institutions all have specific and shifting vulnerabilities, strengths, and idiosyncrasies.
3. Do the decisions sought require structural change in a social system or otherwise run contrary to powerful interests? If yes, what needs to change structurally, i.e. what aspect of societal organization? What interests are opposed to the goal? At the broadest level, conservation of biodiversity

and human appropriation of more and more of the Earth are incompatible. A biologically diverse and wild Earth, free of human-caused extinction, requires far fewer people and lower overall consumption. Specific goals, however, have specific obstacles – growth, pollution, roads, development in particular places, favored by legal infrastructure that protects capital accumulation (development) over other human interests and the natural world. Taking on growth and the dominant institutions that feed on endless growth requires changes in how society is organized. Such change is not easy and most conservationists are in denial about the need to tackle such problems.

4. Can an insider approach prevail? Can conservationists and allies assemble the resources needed to successfully use normal channels of influence such as lobbying, elections, litigation, boycotts, and similar means? If resources are not adequate for this approach – enough influence cannot be obtained in this way – or structural change is required, then an outsider approach must also be pursued. Mass mobilization and protest that either disrupts or threatens to disrupt business-as-usual are the only tools that have effectively overcome powerful interests (e.g. the anti-apartheid movement, pro-democracy movements, etc.), and even they do not always work.

5. How can the conservation movement greatly strengthen itself, add to its resources, and use such resources effectively? Where is the movement weak and strong? How are gaps in resources to be filled? – sources of expertise (organizing, communications, media, administration, knowledge of opponents and the political system, and strategic direction); number of activists, members, and supporters; experience and commitment of leaders and other staff, board and activists; knowledge of target constituencies; access to decision makers and brokers; capacity to integrate and utilize those mobilized into the organization; capacity to withstand efforts at repression. Are conservation NGOs well coordinated and do they have an intelligent division of labor; does trust between them exist; are the tasks of achieving goals and organization-building well integrated; what are the functional, political and geographic gaps in work and how are they to be filled? In addition to greatly strengthening their own organization, what groups in society do conservationists need on their side to have the influence needed to obtain the desired decisions from decision makers? Are decision makers divided on relevant issues

such that sympathetic factions can be mobilized in support of the goal? At what price? What specific actions are needed from these groups and when?

6. How can the groups whose support is needed be effectively enlisted as allies to bring about the right decision from decision makers? What opposition groups can be made neutral or undermined? What are their weaknesses? To answer these questions several subsidiary questions must be addressed regarding those groups interested in an issue: What are the interests of various groups? How do they see their interests? Which messages will emotionally resonate with the target group and motivate desired action or quiescence? How can messages be tied to the group's most fundamental assumptions about the world and therefore be cognitively satisfying? Which story is the most effective vehicle for carrying the message? Who is (are) the best messenger(s)? Which channels are the most effective for reaching a particular group? What can conservationists offer in return to groups whose conservation support is solicited (quid pro quos, not shared values or goals, are the basis of much politics)? From these answers important aspects of strategy and tactics can be shaped. For example both animal activists seeking changes or an end to factory farming and dolphin conservationists found that going after food retailers – McDonald's and the big three US tuna packers along with supermarkets – brought more dramatic action than relying only on the political process. Businesses and other non-state actors are frequently more vulnerable to pressure than is government, depending on the country involved and other circumstances. At the same time business enterprises are more powerful than governments in parts of the world and can command the state with good or bad results for conservation, as bank investment decisions in development projects demonstrate.

7. What is the plan for ensuring that mobilization is sustained over the required period, i.e. following decision making and through implementation and long-term enforcement? What resources are available and what resources are needed to accomplish this? Having the capacity in place is a great advantage, but not always possible, especially when responding to an unforeseen opportunity. More important than money in most cases is skilled people: brokers with good connections, organizers, and others not easily found or replaced. The cultural aspects of mobilization are also extraordinarily important in sustaining mobilization. Do the NGOs involved in the campaign have music, song, a

strong sense of community, ritual, and other structured interactions that are interesting, exciting, and meet human needs for belonging and companionship?

8. How can opposition to conservation goals be minimized so that the relative power of the coalition in favor of the desired solution outweighs the power of opponents and how can this balance of power be sustained to ensure the decision isn't reversed or is a paper decision only? Relative, not absolute, levels of mobilization are critical. Conservationists can expect smear campaigns against them, opponents planting seeds of doubt about the importance of preventive or remedial action, and efforts to divide and conquer. Some positions on conservation issues cannot be justified so opponents try to reframe the debate: it's about freedom to choose rather than protecting wildlife. Successful efforts by conservationists to isolate the worst bullies can cause other opponents to take note. Many opponents of conservation are mistrusted to begin with and this can be useful defending against them. Exposing front groups and phony experts ("tobacco company doctors") for industry and others is also a useful tool. Reminding audiences of past exploitation and disasters visited upon them by those with no respect for the land, oceans, or living things can undercut opponent effectiveness. There are ups and downs in the course of any conflict over achieving a goal, and perseverance is critical (see Chapter 8).

9. How will progress toward success be monitored and evaluated, especially given the very long time it can take to achieve conservation goals? The advantages of a written strategy – not necessarily a strategic plan which is usually formulaic – include making gaps and inadequacies visible, teasing out assumptions that need examination, and identifying milestones and intermediate steps.

10. Question 10 is not a question but a reminder that we must not over-invest in our strategy or expectations, but instead remain observant and open to suddenly appearing opportunities such as a crisis that makes the status quo less tenable, weakens opponents, or causes decision makers to be more receptive. Legal decisions, new scientific findings that can't be ignored, or "natural" events that are destructive of human life or infrastructure and that have an obvious human causal element (e.g. massive flooding resulting from logging) can create opportunities. Movements can also force events based on the circumstances: the US Endangered Species Act would never pass today, but in 1973 taking to the

streets was more common than today, business was asleep at the switch, and most of all a president intensely disliked by the young because of the slaughter in Vietnam wanted to do something to appease these critics and conservationists. There are many similar examples across the range of movements, such as the Montgomery bus boycott as a response to the arrest of civil rights activist Rosa Parks for refusing to give up her bus seat to a white person. Among other things, unanticipated national media coverage created an extraordinary opportunity and it was seized.

Effective advance toward goals requires the skill of a whitewater boatman, adjusting to both waves and current, relying on experience and intuition. A strategy should not be abandoned lightly; but improvisation is essential. The responsibility for achieving this balance mostly falls to leaders who need to be well grounded in reality and agile. But a good push from the rank and file is sometimes necessary to stiffen the backbone of cautious leaders.

REFERENCE

Sutherland, William, W. M. Adams, R. B. Aronson, et al. 2009. One Hundred Questions of Importance to the Conservation of Global Biological Diversity. 23 *Conservation Biology* 3: 557–67.

4   Adapting Society to the Wild

If we take biodiversity conservation seriously then the causes of its destruction must be addressed directly. Nothing can be off the table. Anthropologist Roy Rappaport (1976: 65) observed that "survival is nothing if not biological ... [and] perpetuating economic or political institutions at the expense of biological well-being of man, societies, and ecosystems may be considered maladaptive."

Our planet is finite. The human footprint is growing rapidly. As our species commandeers more of the planet, extinction rates are climbing and ecosystems are unraveling (Ceballas et al. 2015). Species such as lions and elephants, who are not immediately threatened with global extinction, are seeing huge declines in their numbers and range (WWF 2016).Whole native forests in Indonesia are falling before palm plantations to feed the junk food markets and the oceans are choking with millions of tons of plastics. Growth of the human footprint[1] is in the fabric of almost all human societies today and its origins go back to the beginning of agriculture, if not earlier. What Marvin Harris (1977) called the cycle of intensification means a constant ratcheting up of the continuous conversion of the world's ecosystems and life into commodities (also Johnson and Earle, 2000), presenting conservationists with a daunting challenge which magical thinking cannot make go away.

Accomplishing structural change is difficult enough because of the great inertia associated with how a society is organized. Like biological homeostasis – the built-in capacity of organisms and

---

[1] The term footprint is used in this book not in its technical sense: the amount of the Earth's net primary product that humans take, which excludes the drawdown of non-renewable "resources," soil degradation and loss, biodiversity loss and much else – but as shorthand for the overall human impact on the Earth's life, ecosystems, and abiotic processes.

communities to maintain essential processes, from breathing and blood sugar regulation based on activity levels to healing injuries – societies tend to reproduce their social organization. Those occupying the top positions in political and economic hierarchies are also a formidable obstacle to making the fundamental change needed: making a biologically vibrant Earth a top priority in lieu of endless growth. Growth is not just the faith of elites, it is their lifeblood; from it flows power, the ability to control others, and it feeds their self-importance. (Adam Smith 1976 [1759]: 50) observed that "[t]he rich man glories in his riches because he feels they naturally draw upon him the attention of the world. At the thought of this, his heart seems to swell and dilate itself within him, and he is fonder of his wealth on this account, than for all the other advantages it procures him." And the other advantages can be substantial. "Wealth is power . . . it is the power of purchasing; a certain command over all the labour, or over all the produce of labour which is then in the market" (Smith 1976 [1776]: 31). It is also a stepping stone to political and military power. More than two centuries earlier Machiavelli (1996 [1531]) found that a small number of people are always intent on achieving great wealth or power at the expense of the rest of us (and the larger world), and it is mostly they who occupy top decision-making positions.

Few political or economic leaders, even if they care about nature, will consider solutions that might diminish their power, their ability to decide for others how things are going to be. Hence, their habitual deflection of demands to address the causes of conservation problems to debates about symptoms. If existing societal structures continue as they are, most conservation achievements may turn out to have been little more than temporary stays of execution. More than a few conservation leaders suffer from this narcissism as well, limiting their effectiveness and their willingness to undermine the societies that give them the attention they need. Thoreau (1964 [1854]) expressed Machiavelli's insight in a way more directly relevant to conservation when he wrote that a person is wealthy in proportion to what they can leave alone.

Most of those engaged in conservation, though genuine and caring, are resigned and far from bold or visionary. They are "realists," believing that the best conservationists can do is to adapt their goals to the growing human footprint. To do so should be no more morally acceptable than accommodating racism or genocide. In many parts of the world, conservationists are middle class, with much vested in the status quo; they don't want to change things too much for fear it would undermine their security or comfort. Others avoid looking too deeply into causes. They hear decision makers, including the most powerful, admit that human well-being depends on nature. Indeed, hostility toward nature and the mentality of conquest have faded. So why hasn't societal behavior changed? Why are the bad policies that have led to ecological ruin in many parts of the globe still in place? The "people" support conservation, why not their leaders? There is a predisposition to attribute good faith to leaders, perhaps for the same reason many want to believe the police don't lie – it's deeply unsettling.

FIGURE 4.1 Compromise Position on Habitat Preservation. Tom Toles for the Buffalo News

What are conservationists to do? Eminent scientist Archie Carr (1964) declared that the future of wild things depends on human conscience, but conscience has not proved reliable or effective. Existing human societies do not produce intense empathy (an essential element of conscience) with the natural world among sufficient numbers of people to overcome the societal embrace of endless growth. If destructive trends are to be halted and reversed, conservation cannot avoid confronting and mobilizing to change how society is organized any more than could those who ended apartheid.

Changing the structure of society seems utopian or hopelessly grandiose even to those working in the political realm. Maybe especially to them if they have become insiders. But just as no one focused on the biology would assess their prospects for success without reference to the ecological landscape, so no one should dismiss the potential for structural change without assessing the political and economic landscape that governs much human behavior affecting conservation.

A first step toward a different society – one that embraces life rather than routinely destroys it – is figuring out what conservation-compatible societies look like. For many in conservation this is a quagmire. It threatens to take them away from direct protection and into issues they feel inexpert in and that are overwhelming even for the experts. After all, politics about the desired social order is an arena of ugly and often violent bickering. Conservation has made some gains "rising above" such disputes, but only by failing to address the causes of loss, and thus treading water. There is no group in society other than conservationists that possesses the requisite commitment to life and the capacity to determine what biodiversity- and wildlands-compatible societies would look like. They need not and cannot craft a complete vision for such societies for all time, or all the steps needed to get there. But they must play a major role; they must say this and that human activity will or will not harm the wild; they must stand for the precautionary principle. In *Cities in the Wilderness*, former US Interior Secretary Bruce Babbitt (2005) writes about a human withdrawal from much of the landscape in an effort to heal it and ourselves. He envisions cities as island-like in a wild and rewilded landscape; Babbitt is not naïve and understands cities have big impacts beyond their boundaries, but his aim is to reorient us, to reverse the gestalt.

Serious objections can be raised against pursuing nature-compatible societal reform. First, efforts at large-scale, fundamental social change often fail and have caused great misery. There is truth in this objection, but past efforts have invariably involved enlarging human power and control over nature and other humans. Dismantling power and control does not necessarily present the same problems. Second, grand vision often comes unhinged from its earthly moorings and becomes a faith; but this is not inevitable. Third, conservationists differ over what they consider to be a good society, so including social reform in the conservation agenda will divide an already politically weak group. Yet the costs of divisiveness may well be less than what will be lost biologically without changing current destructive trends. Fourth, no vision based on material sacrifice can obtain the critical mass of support needed. Creating nature-compatible societies is not about sacrifice (Maniates and Meyer 2010); rather, it is about offering the opportunity to reconnect with other humans and with the natural world, the absence of which has left our kind emotionally damaged and alienated.

In addition to describing nature-compatible societies, conservationists can and must engage in overcoming the structural obstacles and leadership recalcitrance that stand in the way. Structural change can be advanced by making better use of divisions among societies' top decision makers when such divisions exist and helping to widen them into chasms from mere cracks. The opportunities presented by the crises that permeate modern societies offer another path to steer societies toward more ecologically compatible forms. Let's look at divisions and crises.

When top decision makers are unified they are effective at limiting policy options even in so-called democratic societies; when decision makers are divided the policy debate is often more robust and a wider range of viewpoints gain legitimacy, including grassroots viewpoints. Often arguments made by a powerful faction can be reconfigured to support policies directed at structural change. When the powerful are divided, each faction usually needs support from less powerful groups to help it prevail. This increases the ability of less powerful groups to enter the debate and extract policy concessions. When factions of the powerful must rely on other groups, the latter gain access to the powerful. The ensuing interaction provides opportunities to encourage powerful individuals to use their influence to restore and protect biological diversity and wild places. John Muir's (albeit limited) influence on US President Teddy Roosevelt is one example. Absent a mass movement supporting Muir, Gifford Pinchot's utilitarian influence and its economic backers prevailed. Humans wanted Yosemite's water and they got it; Muir's cathedral was flooded by dam waters.

It is not necessary to wait for divisions to emerge. Organizing by less powerful groups in support of far-reaching claims usually divides the powerful, if only on how to respond. A good understanding of the differing interests among the powerful allows policy objectives to be framed in ways that resonate with some factions and divide them from others. Some of the privileged will speak out, if not renouncing their privilege, at least demonstrating that their benefits are based on the exploitation of others (Ayres and Brown 2005) as with slavery and apartheid.

Division is no magic bullet for overcoming opposition; policy disputes are distinct from the desire of those with power to keep it, and this desire is a major motivation for unity among the powerful whatever their factions. Policy gains with this approach are usually limited but can be surprising. Piecemeal reform is not the enemy of fundamental change so long as the conservation community remains focused on the overarching goal. Obtaining results by dividing decision makers also depends on the conservation community's capacity to reward and punish decision makers. Abolitionist Frederick Douglass (1985 [1857]: 204) admonished that "Power concedes nothing" except to those who demand and fight. This has been true of every social reform: the fight over labor rights, women's rights, for self-determination.

Crises offer wide-ranging opportunities for those who can anticipate or quickly identify them, understand them, and act. Some crises, such as the 2008 global economic disaster led by investment bankers, are cyclical, and indeed this one was predicted by some observers (e.g. Berry 1991). Had conservation professionals and allies been prepared, public outrage and the temporary weakness of big business might have helped, for example, to restore laws requiring, as a quid pro quo for corporate charters, that those granted charters would undertake a public good and do no public harm or harm to the natural world. But reformers were not ready.

Climate change, water and energy shortages, and the rise of new power centers in the next few decades will generate crises. Scandals happen. Wars never go right. Under siege from massive and sustained antiwar protests US President Nixon supported many far-reaching environmental and conservation laws to regain voter approval (Repetto 2006). When systems or leaders lose legitimacy, aspiring leaders may have much greater autonomy from structural constraints and be more susceptible to pressure from below. Crises combine with regular events such as elections to create opportunities. Even in strongly authoritarian regimes such as China, crises create room for challenges to the leadership who are forced to adapt and sometimes expel some of their own (Zhao 2011). True, replacing a leader or two is hardly significant change, but the repression of the pro-democracy movement of 1989 did starkly reveal the fault lines, the fears of aging rulers, and forced them to adjust to maintain their collective rule.

More serious crises usually offer greater opportunities for deeper change, so the nature of each crisis must be grasped. An economic collapse or major technological innovations can change the relative power of groups in a society, generating opportunities to influence meaningful shifts in leadership, reallocation of power to new groups, or setting of new social priorities. Without decisive action and adequate resources for influence, opportunities will be lost or, worse, reactionaries will carry the day as they too often have (Moore 1967). Conservationists as a group do not enjoy great influence, but can often obtain it by alliances with those who have influence. The right alliances allow bargaining from a position of strength rather than as supplicants – the typical state of affairs when it comes to battles over biodiversity. Begging by conservationists has become a bad habit adopted in the course of consistently asymmetric struggles. Whatever the reasons, to not demand support from those we have supported, including allies and decision makers, is self-defeating. So is the failure to press boldly for action for fear of outpacing supporters or losing a seat at the table. The first problem is best addressed by deliberately bringing supporters along, the second by the conservation community's pursuit of both insider *and* outsider strategies. We lack the resources to take a solely insider approach which depends on traditional carrots and sticks – items conservationists are relatively poor in. Only with an outsider approach does it become clear that politics is not just the art of the possible; it is also the art of changing what is possible.

Taking advantage of crises and divisions among the powerful to alter societal structure and goals has paid off in many struggles (e.g. Wood 2000). Apartheid and the Berlin Wall are gone. The former because of the threat of a civil war rulers could not win and more effective international boycotts resulting from mass mobilization outside South Africa; the latter because economic failures stirred citizen dissatisfaction and protest against which new Soviet leaders were unprepared to use blunt repression. Labor and women enjoy rights in many parts of the world where they once did not. Achieving such change requires an understanding of the nature of power, avoiding the temptation to accept too little just to maintain access to decision makers, and not being afraid to push hard. The point is not to win recognition and awards from the powerful, but to stop the carnage, aid in recovery, and ensure the carnage cannot continue. Conservation is a life-and-death struggle for the species and systems under assault. To be successful conservationists will need to act as if they are the ones being shot, trapped, poisoned, snared, and having their homes bulldozed.

Recognizing that decision makers respond to pressure is not meant to suggest that we abandon cooperation or dialogue or civility. But history is clear: no meaningful reform has been achieved without some groups engaging in conflict that the powers that be have called unruly, uncivil, or far worse. The recent battle over an oil pipeline at Standing Rock North Dakota is a good example. (Although US federal approval has been reinstated, the banks have backed away.)

Conservation is a political endeavor at heart; an endeavor that calls for fundamental change in the trajectory of human societies.

REFERENCES

Ayres, Ian and Jennifer G. Brown. 2005. *Straightforward*. Princeton University Press. Princeton, NJ.

Babbitt, Bruce. 2005. *Cities in the Wilderness*. Island Press. Washington DC.

Berry, Brian J. L. 1991. *Long Wave Rhythms in Economic Development and Political Behavior*. Johns Hopkins University Press. Baltimore, MD.

Carr, Archie. 1964. *The Land and Wildlife of Africa*. Time-Life. New York

Ceballas, Gerardo Ceballos, Paul R. Ehrlich, Anthony D. Barnosky, Andrés García, Robert M. Pringle, and Todd M. Palmer. 2015. Accelerated Modern Human-induced Species Losses: Entering the Sixth Mass Extinction. 1 *Science Advances* 5: e1400253 (June 19). doi: 10.1126/sciadv.1400253.

Douglass, Frederick. 1985 [1857]. The Significance of Emancipation in the West Indies. Pp. 183–208 in John W. Blassingame (ed.). *The Frederick Douglass Papers. Series One: Speeches, Debates, and Interviews. Volume 3: 1855–63.* Yale University Press. New Haven, CT.

Harris, Marvin. 1977. *Cannibals and Kings*. Random House. New York.

Johnson, Allen W. and Timothy Earle. 2000. *The Evolution of Human Society*. 2nd edn. Stanford University Press. Stanford, CA.

Machiavelli, Niccolò. 1996 [1531]. *Discourses on Livy*. University of Chicago Press. Chicago, IL.

Maniates, Michael and John M. Meyer (eds.). 2010. *The Environmental Politics of Sacrifice*. MIT Press. Cambridge, MA.

Moore, Barrington. 1967. *The Social Origins of Dictatorship and Democracy*. Beacon. Boston, MA.

Rappaport, Roy A. 1976. Adaptations and Maladaptations in Social Systems. Pp. 39–79 in I. Hill (ed.). *The Ethical Basis of Economic Freedom*. American Viewpoint. Chapel Hill, NC.

Repetto, Robert R. (ed.). 2006. *Punctuated Equilibrium and the Dynamics of US Environmental Policy*. Yale University Press. New Haven, CT.

Smith, Adam. 1976 [1759]. *Theory of Moral Sentiments*. Clarendon Press. Oxford.

Thoreau, Henry David. 1964 [1854]. *Walden*. 2nd edn. Pp. 258–572 in Carl Bode (ed.). *The Portable Thoreau*. Viking. New York.

Wood, Elisabeth Jean. 2000. *Forging Democracy from Below*, Cambridge University Press. Cambridge.

5 Striking at the Roots: The Burgeoning Human Footprint

There are a thousand hacking at the branches of evil to one who is striking at the root.

Thoreau 1964 [1854]: 330

During the 20th Century more people were added to the world than in all previous human history ... The pattern of human population growth in the 20th Century was more bacterial than primate.

Wilson 2002: 86

God forbid that India should ever take to industrialism after the manner of the West. If an entire nation of 300 millions took to similar economic exploitation, it would strip the world bare like locusts.

Gandhi 1928: 422

Our [the US's] enormously productive economy demands that we make consumption our way of life, that we convert the buying and use of goods into rituals, that we seek our spiritual satisfaction, our ego satisfaction, in consumption ... We need things consumed, burned up, worn out, replaced, and discarded at an ever increasing rate.

Lebow 1955: 7

THE ROOTS OF ECOLOGICAL DEGRADATION AND EXTINCTION

There is no substitute for direct protection and recovery of species, lands, and oceans. There is growing consensus among top scientists who value biodiversity that ensuring other species and communities are healthy requires at least (the right) half of the Earth be set aside for them (e.g. Noss 1992; Wilson 2016). The human-dominated part of the Earth must also take into account the needs of other creatures, plants, and processes. It's highly unlikely societies will achieve this goal of 50 percent protection or maintain what is presently safeguarded unless the causes of despoliation are halted and reversed. Existing human social structures are corrosive of biodiversity: more and more humans consuming more and more of the Earth displace other species and natural communities. Achieving structural change is difficult (Johns 2009); even revolutionary upheavals usually fail at their stated goals and typically become mired in compromises with the old order, which doesn't simply disappear (Moore 1967). Human societies are not as complex as the natural world, but human understanding of social dynamics is limited and the cross-purposes of change agents are highly problematic.

The destruction of biodiversity is not the result of this or that industrial society or a particular system such as capitalism (or state capitalism, state socialism, or any other particular order) – though some are more destructive than others – but of the cycle of intensifying exploitation that started with the Neolithic (Harris 1977, 1989; Chase-Dunn and Hall 1997; Johnson and Earle 2000; Montgomery 2007; Higgs 2014). Population pressure drives increased exploitation of a place and its species, of the soil, an increasingly ravenous search for energy subsidies, from fire and slaves to fossil fuels, and conversion of habitat to human uses, depriving others of what they need to survive (Higgs 2014).

The real "revolutions" in human social structure were driven by the concatenation of population growth, emergence and growth of hierarchical structures, technologies of control, and psychological deformation (loss of connection to the wild and domestication to hierarchy [Searles 1960; Shepard 1982]). These deep seated changes are (1) the emergence of agriculture and eventually the state and (2) the industrial/fossil energy transformation. These structural transformations changed the biotic metabolism of the planet via cascade effects initiated by humans (Marx 1954 [1887], 1959 [1894]; Harris 1977; Johnson and Earle 2000; McKee 2003). The "agricultural revolution" took millennia. The modern transformation was much faster: European colonialism generated a global economic system beginning in the sixteenth century, which gained access to new territories containing gold, timber, slaves, fertile soil, and much else, fueled investment in technology, science, navies and armies, organization, and other instruments of control, and ultimately the industrial transformation and the harnessing of fossil energy sources, generating huge subsidies (Chase-Dunn and Anderson 2005; Higgs 2014). Wijkman and Rockstrom (2012: 62) estimate each American has 200 "energy slaves" at their disposal – i.e. 2,000 calories a day × 200. Certainly the last 130 years of fossil fuel use have transformed the Earth in unpredictable ways with enormous consequences for all life on Earth.

The consequences of energy subsidies have always been unforeseeable, as have those of other human decisions institutional and individual. Although humans may hold a vision of where they want to go, the unintended consequences of their actions seem more important than the intended consequences; Wright (2004) argues that humans have always navigated by trial and error whatever the claims to the contrary.

Human economic activity, which entails the transformation of living nature into commodities for trade, consumption, and profit, doubled between 1500 and 1900; doubled again between 1900 and 1950; quadrupled between 1950 and 1992; and doubled again between 1992 and 2014 (Higgs 2014). Cheap energy helped make this possible as has energy efficiency. Both have led to increased energy use (Wijkman and Rockstrom 2012). Growing energy subsidies make possible bulldozers in lieu of digging sticks and shovels. They enable the production and application on a vast scale of chemicals such as nitrogen and phosphorus to the soil (Montgomery 2007), irrigation, mechanization, and refrigeration (Pimentel et al. 1973; Jackson 1987). Soil erosion has increased twenty times on average over the geologic rate, and what is left is degraded by treating it as a chemical rather than a biological system (Montgomery 2007). Whether rich or poor, farmers mine the soil – because their plots are too small to support them or to pay off debts for equipment, proprietary seeds, or chemicals. The cheap energy which makes so much possible – cheap mining, cheap food, large-scale movement of food and waste – is cheap because costs are externalized. From climate change to the armies and navies that secure supply lines, to pollution, damage is ignored, hidden, or shunted off to others.

All the dominant economic models are problematic for biodiversity; they all rationalize or embrace endless growth, hierarchy, and large-scale society. Classical economists, Marxist economists, and others with the exception of no-growth economists (e.g. Victor 2008; Jackson 2009; Daly and Farley 2010) ignore resource depletion, ignore the long term, ignore the limits of island Earth. Mainstream economists, along with markets and other organizational arrangements, are insensitive to ecological damage because the natural world is treated as worthless until appropriated for human use (Hames 2007; Harris 2013). They also ignore the historical context of energy and other factors in economics, including the law of entropy – humans can only burn oil once, the Americas can only be plundered once (Higgs 2014). The dominant economic models informing decision makers continue to ignore the reality of nature's economy: the abstraction of dollars is the measure of all things, not calories, the soil, the richness of life (Peet 1992; Montgomery 2007; Korten 2013). Systems of national accounting consistently fail to capture many elements of nature's economy and as a result things never quite turn out as thought (Hecht 2005). Early modern economists (e.g. Smith, Ricardo) and Marx in the nineteenth century – all moral philosophers at heart – saw growth for exclusively human benefit as the proper end of economic systems and that progress depended on the negation of nature (Ophuls 2011). When ancient, giant redwood trees passed from Pacific Lumber Company to Maxxam Corporation in 1985 a decision was made by the new owners to liquidate the forest because the return on investment wasn't as high as in other sectors; it made economic sense to cut the thousand-year-old trees and invest the proceeds elsewhere (Bevington 2009).

Many critics of the human impact on the Earth and its life like to focus almost exclusively on consumption by the rich, ignoring that many poorer people think "to get rich is glorious," a phrase attributed to China's former leader Deng Xiaoping (Schell 1984). Encouragement to increase consumption, and ramping up production to meet it, has an enormous impact on the world, which is already providing more than can be annually replaced (GFN 2016). To overlook the fact that more people contribute to more demand is nonsensical, however. To say that hierarchical and inegalitarian economic systems encourage consumption is true, but that is to ignore the obvious: large and growing human populations generate inegalitarian and hierarchical social structures (Harris 1977; Boehm 1999; Johnson and Earle 2000). Individuals and groups easily generate digging sticks; but bulldozers depend on an extensive division of labor to manufacture, fuel, create a supporting infrastructure, and otherwise operate (including trained labor), and that system is hierarchically organized. Status seeking also runs deep in human societies and psyche, even in societies in which artifacts cannot be accumulated (e.g. Clark 1986). Consumption's role in soothing mortality anxiety appears to go very deep as well (Solomon et al. 2004).

Hierarchy, inequality, colonial forms of domination, and center–periphery relationships go back 12,000 years in some places, not 300 or 500 years. They even pre-date the first states of 5,000–6,000 years ago. The minor reality of the temporal depth of hierarchy and inequality is ignored by those who would like to blame everything on social forms of the last few hundred years (e.g. Kovel 2007). Abolishing these recent social forms – capitalism, state capitalism, and others – could be positive if replaced with something better, but simply abolishing them cannot solve the problem of environmental destruction. It requires addressing the real roots of hierarchy and inequality: the effort to control the natural world, as a response to population growth and growth in overall consumption. No one has explained how 7.5 billion people will organize their affairs without efforts to control and subdue the world and generating the hierarchy and inequality that are part and parcel of the machinery of control. Increasingly humans depend on economic relationships they have created but that are too complex to understand, let alone manage.

Biodiversity has been under assault at least since humans left Africa, and the assault has intensified. Growth in human numbers has a direct impact – more people take more even if not per capita (McKee 2003); but more is being taken per capita – our social structure makes that not just possible but often requires it and we strive to make taking more easier for a number of reasons. Wealth-seeking drives much politics, and politics drives the allocation of wealth to reinforce hierarchy, and also conflict among competing factions of the elite. Allocating rewards to individuals and social groups is important in maintaining loyalty and stability. We leave aside for a moment the pathological narcissism – the neediness expressed in "look at me, look at me" – that make the wealthy want more and more (Smith 1976 [1759]; Ellman and Reppen 1997; Masterson 2006), and the economic structure that demands grow or be eaten (e.g. Jackson 2009).

Overfishing, for example, is not simply a matter of trying to satisfy protein hunger and maintain political stability. Finley (2017) documents the major role that human social organization and conflict play in overfishing. Many countries overfished for geopolitical reasons. The US, Soviet Union, and some other countries sought to use fishing, and the right to fish anywhere, as a means of asserting the right of military vessels to go anywhere as well as to stake claims to fishing territories. At the same time the US helped Japan rebuild its pre-World War II fishing capacity to deprive Soviets of the same fish and aid Japan's stability. Other countries sought to increase their capacity as well, and heavy ship-building and operational subsidies became the norm. The US also allowed almost unrestricted imports of fish from Japan and Iceland to reinforce their political loyalty to the West even at the expense of its own fishing industry. The political competition clouded the ability to see crashing fish populations, as did the belief in the infinite bounty of the oceans.

At the same time as fishing was emerging as a major political issue in the latter half of the twentieth century, human population was rapidly increasing – from about 2.5 billion in 1950 (up from 1.6 billion in 1900) to 6.1 billion in 2000. Claims that industrialization of fishing would make more food available for people were not unreason-able, but this was not the main driver (Finley 2017). High-quality fish such as tuna and salmon went to rich countries, and much else went to fish sticks and fish meal, intended to feed terrestrial animals for human consumption. Human population growth fed direct demand for fish (and for cropland, electricity, housing, and much else) and it also fed hierarchy and growth.

There are countless other examples in which population per se creates demand for more of the Earth for humans while depriving or consuming other species' habitat (Crist et al. 2017). But it is invariably entangled in particular social relationships. Mazur (2010) points out that rapid population growth in Ghana did contribute to rapid defor-estation. But the 90 percent decline in the rainforest was also caused by International Monetary Fund demands that Ghana increase exports. Gold, timber, and cocoa for export all contributed to deforest-ation and vastly increased inequality within the country. Many other countries, such as Brazil, have had similar experiences.

Population growth beyond the size of human bands and hier-archy in one form or another are inextricably entwined. Once human societies reach about 400 people, hierarchy emerges because the group as a whole cannot manage its affairs directly; specialization is needed in organization and leadership. This provides opportunities for those who seek control. Size also begins to preclude the ability of the group to check those who seek power (Boehm 1999). As societies grow yet larger, hierarchy becomes more institutionalized and leaders self-aggrandizing. Hierarchical structures become an essential part of the dynamic of societies, engrained in personalities, in the systems of status, labor, and material rewards and otherwise bind people to the institutions that supply those things. The technologies and forms of social organization that extract more and more from the non-human world to supply goods are one and the same with the control mechan-isms by which the few control the many (e.g. Johnson and Earle 2000). Large-scale societies are inherently unequal and hierarchical. There are no examples of large-scale egalitarian societies, though clearly there are differences in the extent of inequality and to a greater degree in the harshness used to maintain inegalitarian social orders. There are also many examples of rebellion against hierarchy and inequality – and some that have lessened it a bit for a limited time – but none that have overcome it (Scheidel 2017). One can imagine the old Eastern European joke extending back to Uruk and before: under capitalism man exploits man; under socialism it's just the reverse. Population growth also contributes to trapping the poor – people and nations – in poverty: this was a major factor in China's one-child policy which allowed the accumulated surplus that would have been eaten by more people to be used to finance economic development.

Human population growth also correlates directly with bio-diversity decline (e.g. Scott 2008, table 5.1) via cycles of growth and intensification of extraction which generate ever more exploitative or disruptive (to living systems) institutions and technologies (Johnson and Earle 2000; Michaux 2014) and take more and more land for human food, housing, roads and similar (McKee 2003). When humans come into a place they frequently kill what they like to eat, often until extinction, and persecute and kill species they dislike, fear, or find inconvenient, wrecking ecological communities just as colonizing countries do to the places they conquer and dominate. Marine life is also commandeered as "resources" and used as a garbage dump. Deforestation is among the more obvious and ugly consequences (Williams 2003). We don't see what we do to the oceans.

Humans should not stop struggling for greater equity among humans nor an end to injustice amongst themselves. To do so would result in a deterioration of the human condition. But humans have not lived in egalitarian societies since before agriculture, and sometimes not even then (Pringle 2014). Human justice is an end in itself, but securing it does not automatically stop the destruction of other species or the Earth's living systems. Conservation is its own end and the need for conservation is generated by humans seeking control over the natural world to feed growing populations and the greed of elites gener-ated by those efforts at control (Harris 1977; Johnson and Earle 2000).

The social machinery of control over the natural world inevitably creates structures of human control over humans. The size and complexity of human institutions needed to (attempt to) control the natural world require systems of control themselves which are hierarchical as we discussed above. This relationship is invisible to most theorists and human justice advocates and helps to rationalize trying to solve human inequality by extracting more from nature and further degrading ecosystems and injuring other species. In response to claims at a World Parks Congress in 2003 that we could not afford biodiversity if human poverty was to be addressed, Bittu Sahgal (2017) of Project Tiger in India said that humans had not ended poverty by taking most of the Indian land base for humans and they weren't going to solve poverty by taking the rest. And they weren't going to get it. Putting humans on a pedestal is part of the problem, not part of the solution.

THE IMPACT OF POPULATION AND CONSUMPTION

There have been five major extinctions of life on Earth, each killing at least 75 percent of all species. The most recent, 66 million years ago (MYA), at the end of the Cretaceous, was caused by an asteroid hitting the Earth. Only one of the earlier four, at the end of the Triassic (200 MYA), had no clear cause. Other causes included an ice age (444 MYA), massive algal blooms sucking up all the marine oxygen following the "rapid" emergence of terrestrial plants (375 MYA), and vulcanism (251 MYA). The sixth great extinction is being caused by us – *Homo sapiens sapiens*. We have been at it at least since we left Africa 60,000 years ago (Barnosky 2008; McGlone 2012; Rule et al. 2012), extinguishing many large animals on our arrival such as mammoth, mastadons, and many large marsupials. Often slow-moving, slow to reproduce, and unused to humans, they were easy to kill for food and other reasons. *Homo erectus* may have caused the extinction of some of our African competitors (McKee 2003), and beyond our out-of-Africa extinctions there is evidence that hunter-gatherer societies, fully aware of which animals are scarce or plentiful, will kill rare animals if there is a high caloric return (Low 2013).

It's also true we often don't see the consequences of our actions: extinction can take a long time from the beginning of doing injury, to noticing decline, to the end (Cowlishaw 1999; McKee 2003). Denial, whether in individuals or institutions, as Finley (2017) describes with fishing, is a prominent human trait.

Short of extinction, much damage is being done by the presence of so many humans across the globe (Ceballos et al. 2015; Crist et al. 2017). Humans take 40 percent of terrestrial Net Primary Product (NPP) and 30 percent of Marine NPP. (NPP is the difference between all the energy plants produce and that which they need for their own respiration.) In the last two human generations, the populations of 10,000 vertebrate species have declined by over half on average (WWF 2014). The spectacles of elephant and shark slaughter, of polar bears facing swims absent sea ice that drown their cubs and make it difficult to find enough food, and of collapsing fish populations, are ongoing. If current trends continue, not only will biodiversity loss grow more extreme (McKee et al. 2013) but "resources" to feed growth will become unavailable. Li (2008) for example, argues that China's growth machine which has raised 300 million people out of poverty will not be able to deliver that level of consumption to the other 1.2 billion because of materials exhaustion. The pollution from the associated production is also problematic, causing climate change and disease. Despite the many problems with economic growth, it continues to be the priority for Chinese decision makers (Zheng and Cao 2014). Biodiversity loss was not even on the radar until the early 1970s, and before that Chinese ideology embraced the nineteenth-century European notion of the "conquest of nature" (Shapiro 2001). Since then China has put in place laws and policies to protect and recover biodiversity, with an emphasis on protecting and regenerating forests. Although over 2,600 nature reserves have been designated covering 14.9 percent of terrestrial China and a majority of "ecological zones," many are compromised by roads, dams, sprawl, and the presence of people (poachers, resource exploiters) (Zheng and Cao 2014). The pressure to deliver an improved standard of living is enormous and the basis on which officials are judged by higher authorities. This also generates local corruption. Many major decisions by the over-centralized bureaucracy have not been informed by science, such as campaigns against sparrows, pika, and zokor, which caused many negative ecological results (Pech et al. 2007; Xin 2008; Liu 2010; Zheng and Cao 2014). Neither China nor India appears to have learned anything from the experience of other countries: dam building is a biological disaster (Yeh 2009; e.g. Ramachandran 2016).

The violence perpetrated against non-human life – with or without extinction – is carried out by direct killing for food and other reasons (Benítez-Lopez et al. 2017); by converting and degrading habitat so it no longer supports the full community of native species or ecologically effective populations of species; by fragmenting habitat which has the same impacts; by depriving other species of food, water, and NPP because they are taken for human use or are otherwise rendered unusable (lack of access, toxicity); and by facilitating or deliberately transplanting invasive species. Ibisch et al. (2016), for example, find that the terrestrial parts of the Earth are divided into 600,000 patches because of roads and development. More than half of patches are under one square kilometer, and only 7 percent are larger than 100 square kilometers. Critics think Ibisch et al. have underestimated the fragmentation and number of roads (Hughes 2017; Wu et al. 2017). The human appropriation of more of the landscape and intensification of extraction – a process that marked the beginning of the Neolithic – continues to drive biodiversity loss today (Johnson and Earle 2000; Gossner et al. 2016). Forest loss in particular is a major contributor to species loss. Roads not only fragment habitat but bring hunters and invasive species. Energy capture and use greatly multiplies human impact in numerous ways, from extraction of metals and water to utilization of machines and appliances, e.g. rural electrification allows for greatly increased consumption (Higgs 2014). The overall disruption of the biosphere not only generates species decline and extinction but prevents recovery of species and the natural emergence of new species (Rosenzweig 2001).

Rates of species loss are up to 100 times the background rate (Ceballos et al. 2015). Anyone who claims they are serious about safeguarding biodiversity and stemming the tide of loss must address the oversized human impact which is driving extinction and diminishment. Efforts at direct protection must continue, but they are not enough. Alas, denial about the need to address population and consumption seems second only to climate change denial. There's also denial about being in denial.

At a population workshop at the 2015 International Conference on Conservation Biology, attendees gave several reasons other than denial for not addressing the human footprint:

They don't know what to do about it or where to begin with such a huge problem;
They fear conflict with peers and peer disapproval;
They fear the politically correct who advocate for individual choice regardless of social and biological consequences;
They fear funder disapproval and abandonment.

Coole (2012) finds that shaming and fatalism are effective at silencing those who might otherwise speak out; they feel badly about raising the population issue or fear it won't do any good. Critics also try to generate skepticism about population as a problem as the oil companies have done with climate. Sowing confusion is often enough to forestall action.

Overwhelmingly most discussion about human population and consumption is anthropocentric and expresses little or no concern for biodiversity unless it affects humans. Cohen (2010) states that the Earth could support twice the current population at subsistence, at least for a while, but makes no mention of biodiversity, i.e. the needs of other life. This is all too typical. There are exactly three index entries for biodiversity in a thirty-one-chapter book discussing a wide range of human population and consumption issues (Mazur 2010). It is disheartening for conservationists. This circumstance not so subtly suggests that only humans are important or are the most important species. This leaves conservationists not just having to argue on behalf of biodiversity but also to make the case it's a legitimate issue.

Shrinking the human impact is an enormous challenge that is unlike anything else humans have attempted to deliberately change. It is on a par with the agricultural and industrial "revolutions." Necessarily so. Major social revolutions seem small events and easy to manage compared to stopping and reversing the human colonial relationship with the rest of the world. Growth and domination have many millennia of inertia behind them. Even institutions critical of the destruction of biodiversity may have much vested in growth – inter alia, it funds them. Humans are notoriously easy to manipulate as well (Rice and Atkin 2001; Trent and Friedenberg 2004; Guber and Bosso 2007; Butchart et al. 2010; Coole 2012) and those on the growth side have most of the resources to shape collective behavior – it's part and parcel of inequality and hierarchy and embedded in social structure.

AN ADEQUATE CONSERVATION RESPONSE TO GROWTH'S IMPACT

What is to be done? We know that the growing human footprint is associated not just with biodiversity loss but with a host of other problems, including much human suffering: hierarchy; gross inequality based on class, gender, and ethnicity; large-scale violence over control of energy, land, water, and labor. Efforts to address these problems are ends in themselves and are long-term projects. Conservation is also an end in itself – a central moral imperative. It is not reducible to justice among humans. Indeed, virtually all conservation problems are human-caused and there is a strong propensity for humans to try and solve their intraspecies problems – scarcity, poverty, the desire for more, and the conflicts these circumstances generate – on the back of biodiversity by converting more and more of the world to human uses. It is the path of least resistance and aligns with the dominant orientation of society that growth must not be limited. Notwithstanding this widespread view, there are groups who are injured by the pursuit of economic growth and are potential conservation allies.

To forge successful alliances with such groups will require bargaining. Human groups who suffer from aspects of growth also have something vested in extant institutions, which can dull enthusiasm for fundamental change. Even many conservationists are unwilling to acknowledge the need to dismantle the drivers of biodiversity loss. If conservationists enter alliances without clarity on what must change to secure biodiversity they will get sidetracked by those who do have clarity about their goals.

The work of mobilizing political action on behalf of conservation is discussed in Chapter 7 and in *A New Conservation Politics*, which synthesizes the social movement literature from both practitioners and academic observers (Johns 2009). Below we focus on three topics: the cultural (moral) battle over population and consumption, identification of actions that can be taken to limit population and consumption, and identification of priority targets for alliances. It is almost unnecessary to say that the conservation movement alone is not strong enough to make a significant dent in humanity's trajectory.

Before discussing prospects for alliances we must examine competing claims regarding human demands on the biosphere and the needs of biodiversity.

THE MORALITY OF GROWTH

Earth Overshoot Day – the day of the year when human use of the Earth's renewable "resources" exceeds the Earth's capacity to regenerate what is used in a year – was August 8 in 2016. In 1990 the date was December 7, in 2000 November 1, and in 2010 August 21 (GFN 2016). This is just one measure of injury and doesn't take account of the consequences for biodiversity.

Reversing these trends entails significantly changing human behavior in ways that markedly reduce human impact. That will involve not only conflict over the goals of reducing the human footprint versus continued growth and the values associated with each, but over the efficacy and morality of the methods. China's development path makes clear the issues.

Development is usually considered a good, improving lives by lifting people out of poverty, though it opens the door to new diseases, pollution, resource wars and so on. China's one-child policy (1979–2015) seems to have worked from the development perspective. Authorities claim it resulted in 400 million fewer births and contributed significantly to development take-off (*People's Daily* 2011). Other consequences of this policy, such as gender imbalances, will resonate for decades. There has also been widespread accusation of coerced or forced abortions and sterilizations. Such critics ignore the high costs of earlier development which included raising capital from plundering of entire nations, slavery, and other forms of exploitation – options not available to late developing countries, and so much the better. China also exempted minority groups (about 6 percent of the population of the country) from the policy, many of whom reside in critical border areas, avoiding some criticism on that account.

Biodiversity protection was not a motive force for China, though it may have played a small role in India under Indira Gandhi's stringent birth control efforts in the 1970s. Neither was Iranian population policy motivated by biodiversity concerns, but it proved very effective, reducing fertility from 5.5 children in 1998 to 1.7 children in 2009 (Crist 2013). It was a deliberate and comprehensive policy, like China's, relying on rural health clinics, education, free contraception, media campaigns, and education of girls. It included many of the types of programs advocated by the "Cairo Alliance" (the Catholic Church, the conservative US government at the time, supported by even more conservative Protestant churches, parts of the women's movement, and some Marxist groups) but also established demographic goals, going beyond individual and family-driven birth control.

The problem for those who make safeguarding all the Earth's species a priority is that they do not enjoy the support that growth and development advocates do. They have an uphill fight. Ruling elites' power and wealth are anchored in growth, and the Earth's elites and upper middle classes have a vested interest in human domination and exploitation of the Earth. The pursuit of things, despite the very high price, is firmly anchored in many cultures (Czech 2000; Kasser 2002; Kasser and Kanner 2004; Jackson 2009; Dietz and O'Neill 2013; NGS/Globescan 2015). Billions of other humans who are victimized and hungry justifiably want more than they have. Non-human life is just grist for the grinder.

It is useful to look briefly at the value claims associated with population policy and then with economic growth. Population and consumption (broadly defined) contribute about equally to the human impact and its growth over the last half century (Jackson 2009).

Population

Laurie Mazur (2010) notes that in the 1960s and first half of the 1970s population growth was on the global agenda and the agenda of many countries. The first Earth Day, in 1970, had population as a main theme, along with overconsumption and pollution, and saw participation by 20 million people, or 10 percent of the US population. Population growth was seen as a threat to development, making it impossible to accumulate surpluses to invest, keeping families and countries in poverty (while the wealthy got richer), and threatening stability. At the time a billion people were being added every twelve to thirteen years. Population growth was also seen in some wealthy countries as threatening their quality of life, by increasing congestion, pollution, infrastructure costs, and causing loss of natural areas. There were also competing concerns in some countries (and among some ethnic groups): workers and soldiers were needed. So was an ever-growing tide of consumers. Some groups saw population control as a means to weaken them politically or as a threat to traditional gender roles – which it could be. But international family planning worked:

from the 1960s to the 1990s fertility in poorer countries went from around six children to a bit over three, and birth control use went from 10 percent to 60 percent. In China the one-child policy was in effect from 1979 to 2015 and resulted in 400 million fewer births. In India millions of sterilizations occurred under government emergency orders between 1973 and 1977. India was the first country to have a formal family planning effort, starting in 1952, but because of India's cultural diversity it was slow to take root and even today is very uneven.

Partly as a reaction to what were seen as coercive programs in China, India and elsewhere, an unusual alliance of conservative religions and churches, the administration of US President Reagan, some feminists, and some Marxists (Cairo Alliance herein, for convenience) claimed that such programs violated basic human rights (Mazur 2010) or "respect for persons" (Kissling 2010). In this view, birth control must serve humans and more particularly individual men's and women's (assuming they agreed) wishes. If this is not the case then birth control programs are coercive. It is also argued that this people first approach will in any event meet the demographic goals countries have set for themselves. The Cairo Alliance view was dominant at the 1992 Rio Earth Summit and adopted at the 1994 International Conference on Population and Development at Cairo (Kissling 2010; Weeden and Palomba 2013). Human well-being must be the priority in all politics related to population. This view has become law in many countries and is reflected in international documents.

The rise of this view, however, diminished support for family planning and population issues (Kissling 2010), including among those concerned with the environment and conservation. Seeing less to gain from more limited birth control programs, they also grew tired of accusations of being unethical. With support harder to come by – including official US funding from the 1980s onward – and with rising concern for climate, some in the Cairo Alliance have come to see the need to link family planning to climate to regain allies and funding. Religious leaders, including those associated with the Alliance, are increasingly concerned with climate and biodiversity loss but are not ready to address population directly (Collins 2014).

Alternative religious views, some very longstanding, call for compassion for all living things, and these views make it more difficult for anthropocentric claims to go unchallenged. The Earth is not just for humans, as attested by statements from many mainstream religious leaders (Gottlieb 2006; Jenkins 2008). In addition, several mainstream sects have long argued that justice and ethics require that all children be wanted and desired (Brooks and Chandler 1994; Martin-Schram 1994).

With many examples of energy and material use per capita holding steady but overall use still rising, it's become clearer that human numbers per se matter (Jackson 2009; Palmer 2013). It is also recognized that because the existing human population is so large, even declining fertility won't slow growth of sheer numbers very quickly. (Current UN estimates for global population and its growth are 7.6 billion at present, 9.772 billion in 2050, and 11.184 billion in 2100 [United Nations 2017].)

There is very little discussion of three important issues by those who agree with Ruth Macklin (1994: 193) that the "right of individuals to control their own reproductive lives without interference by the state" is sacrosanct. Advocacy of the right of persons to decide freely and responsibly regarding the number and spacing of children rarely includes much discussion of what "responsibly" means. Responsibility appears to exclude the principle that freedom "consists of doing all that which does not harm another" (Veil 1978: 320). Great harm is being done to non-human species and the Earth from human population increase (Butler 2015). And it is being done without apparent concern for the present harm, much less the long-term consequences, because the bases for reproductive decisions are usually near-term and selfish (Mills 2013). Reproduction is governed by the tyranny of small decisions.

Eugenics, prohibitions on birth control and abortion, discrimination against minorities, discrimination against women and the like are good reasons to be concerned with state intervention into reproductive decisions or the capacity of more powerful groups to control less powerful groups. Yet protections of free speech to ensure effective political participation are not absolute and why should reproductive rights – if indeed they are rights – be absolute? With speech there is a recognition of other important interests: protecting people against defamation, limiting speech that encourages imminent lawless action (more often aimed at politically weak groups than at the state or powerful actors), or the right to a fair trial, e.g. one not decided in the media. In these cases conflicts are resolved not in general or between broad, abstract categories, but on the basis of specific cases. Do the facts support authorities' reasonable fear of lawless action, for example?

The second issue involves a type of cultural coercion that is often invisible because it does not always involve what we usually think of as politics (the state and the individual; between groups in society with unequal access to the state) or economics (power differentials between groups based on control of assets, land, water, energy). Children do not choose the culture they are born into (or the families they are born into), and cultural indoctrination begins prior to the development of critical faculties. Yet it is early on that attitudes toward the natural world and reproduction are formed (e.g. Kahn and Kellert 2002). Those who think it wrong to intervene into the enculturation and socialization processes generally object selectively, depending on the issue. But if it's okay to inoculate against child marriage and encourage or require girls' access to school, then inoculating against behavior that leads to destruction of biodiversity should pass moral muster as well.

The third issue little discussed involves countervailing interests to laissez-faire human reproduction. Former French Health Minister Simone Veil (1978) acknowledges societal interests in reproduction and the state's duty to represent and further those interests. The right to found a family, implied in the US and French human rights declarations of the eighteenth century, was included in the Universal Declaration of Human Rights (United Nations 1948). Since that time, population has continued to grow rapidly and states are expected to ensure housing, education, health, and social and economic development – all costly. It is also up to states to look at the long term and big picture – to look beyond decisions made solely or mostly in the interest of individuals or families. Others in addition to the state must live with the consequences of individuals' reproductive decisions. Ultimately Veil defers to French public opinion over recent decades, namely that the state has a role: it should not intervene directly but can properly set the conditions that influence individual decisions (Veil 1978: 319).

Ecocentric or biocentric conservationists argue that humans have no right to drive other species to extinction, or to greatly diminish their numbers or wild ("self-willed") qualities (Foreman 2011). When "private" reproductive decisions – which usually don't consider consequences for other species' well-being – impose costs on those species, then human reproductive decisions stop being private. Myths, which are supposed to help guide humans and keep them focused on the longer term rather than immediate benefits that might have negative long-term consequences, do not do a good job of integrating ecological concerns and haven't for a very long time.

Defenders of the primacy of individual decision making in human reproduction argue that improvement in women's status lowers fertility, as does old-age security, an end to arranged and early-age marriages, access to and support for girls' education, access to birth control, and better public health (Dixon-Mueller 1994; Engelman 2016). Overall education also correlates with lowered fertility. Women will usually seize opportunities to reduce fertility if they can. All of these circumstances are good ends in themselves, not just because they lower fertility. But that doesn't mean fertility rates will be reduced enough to reverse growth enough to safeguard and recover biodiversity, wildlands, and the oceans.

Invariably there is an unstated assumption in discussions of human reproductive prerogatives that they are a human right. That claim involves several facets: that human reproduction is more important than the existence of an entire species; that human sub-populations are more valuable than an entire species; that conservation of biodiversity is just another human interest; that equity is only about relations among humans; and diversity only concerns relations among groups of humans. No sound arguments are made for these claims.

Although many animals have culture, not just humans, none possesses the behavioral flexibility humans have. We can stop behaving in ways that cause great injury to others. Other species cannot survive the loss of their homes.

Growth

Concern with economic growth and its drivers did not begin in 1972 with *Limits to Growth* (Meadows et al. 1972) nor with Earth Day in 1970, nor with Rachel Carson's (1962) critique of the use of chemicals to kill species that would otherwise claim a portion of crops or contribute to the human disease burden. It did not even begin with Ovid's eloquent 16 BC (2001) poem about gold, lust, foolish human cleverness, and more:

> Jupiter, realising nothing's more powerful than gold,
> turned himself to coinage to seduce a virgin.
> Without that wealth, father was harsh, she severe,
> the doors were bronze, and the tower was iron.
> But when the adulterer knowingly came as cash,
> she offered love herself and saying 'give', she gave.
> Yet when ancient Saturn ruled the heavens,
> Earth covered all her wealth in deep darkness.
> She stored the copper and silver, gold and heavy iron,
> among the shades, there were no ingots then.
> She gave better things – crops without curved ploughs,
> and fruits, and honey found in the hollow oaks.
> No one scarred the earth with a strong blade,
> no measurer of the ground marked out limits.

no dipping oars swept the churning waves:
then the longest human journey ended at the shore.
Human nature, you've been skilful, against yourself,
and ingenious, in excess, to your own harm.
. . .
We dig the earth for solid gold not food.
Soldiers possess the wealth they get by blood.
The Senate's shut to the poor – money buys honours:
here a grave judge, there a sober knight!
Let them have it all: let arena and forum serve them,
let them conduct merciless war or manage peace.

When examining claims about economic growth and its costs, the term consumption is often used as if it is one thing. We shall do so as well but with this understanding in mind: it is not just modern (the last century or so) mass consumption, but longstanding (millennia) elite consumption, and the structural imperative to increase institutional (states, businesses, etc.) wealth and power. The three categories of consumption are entwined. As we have noted, elites respond to increasing population pressure (more people $\Rightarrow$ more extraction $\Rightarrow$ more people $\Rightarrow$ more extraction and so on), and also seek more for themselves; they seek status which is often associated with acquisition of material goods; elites have factions that compete with each other for status and goods; rulers of societies compete with other rulers for status and for everything from soil and slaves to oil, water, cheap labor, and markets. It is difficult to disentangle the personal motives of leaders of states, firms, and similar from their institutional roles. Almost by definition, most are self-aggrandizing as Adam Smith observed and we noted in the previous chapter.

Machiavelli (1996 [1531]) believed that those who sought great wealth and power were different in temperament than most people and indeed a pest to ordinary people. Their drive to stand out and be noticed is not the result of a "big ego" but the result of great neediness. Their early lack of genuine love and its internalization leaves them emotionally empty and in need of constant attention from others (Ellman and Reppen 1997; Masterson 2006). Not all those driven by narcissism succeed to wealth and power but those that do command social institutions.

Mass consumption, a phenomenon largely of the last century, is a deliberate invention: an effort to foster and maintain growth following World War I (Bernays 1923, 1929, 1955; Sachs 2012; Higgs 2014). In developed countries it has become necessary to economic expansion and to avoiding or ameliorating crises of overproduction which threaten economic breakdown and social conflict, testing the ability of states to rule (Gurr 1970; O'Connor 1973). Many have documented institutional efforts to foster a mass consumption ethic – making shopping a ritual in support of beliefs that consumption gives purpose and meaning to life (Sachs 2012). The habit of consumption bears a striking similarity to addiction: feel discomfort, ignore the causes and avoid addressing them – go shopping instead (Lasch 1978).

One reason it may be so easy to manipulate people toward constant consumption is a deep-seated yearning for status, which seeks to bring specialness in mass society, a search for novelty or to cure insecurities, and to compensate for poor relationships, among other things (Gorz 1980; Kasser and Kanner 2004). These motives can be as insatiable as those driven by narcissism. Status, novelty seeking, and the like only temporarily scratch the itch – and may make it worse (Kasser 2002),

There may be a much deeper motive for consumption, which transcends class and other distinctions. Solomon et al. (2004) argue that with sedentary society humans become anxious about their own mortality – something absent in foraging society. That anxiety is broadly shared by elites and the multitudes and can be assuaged in three ways: through propagating children, through religious promises of immortality, and through consumption. Acquiring and possessing goods makes people feel they are special and different and not subject to the rules that include death. People seem to prefer consumption if it is an option. One of the earliest stories from a state-based society is the Gilgamesh Epic (Tigay 1982). An early, swaggering king of Uruk, Gilgamesh was overcome with fear of dying upon seeing the death and decay of his partner in hubris, the seduced and tamed wild man, Enkidu. After failing to be granted immortality by the gods he sets about building great monuments so he will be remembered for them for eternity. Mortality anxiety may present one of the most serious obstacles to conservation. Today we see similar striving among the wealthy: castles to private rocket ships. But it is a widely shared striving. Death is feared as an end, as annihilation, not a return.

Although the billions can do as much damage to biodiversity as the rich in total, their low per capita consumption is easier to defend morally. Much more to the point, however, is this: the "1 percent" – and this is probably a high number – are those most invested in the status quo, who make the decisions to keep what Wright (2004) has called the great pyramid scheme going despite the high cost to other humans and to biodiversity. Their collective personal interests and societal structure are, if not seamless, pretty much the same and act to limit all other actors. The 1 percent decide we invest in roads today, not trains. The rest must drive cars or be greatly inconvenienced; more important is the failure to resist or overthrow the 1 percent – perhaps because people intuit that overthrowing them is not the same thing as getting rid of the pyramid scheme. Many who fought the American Revolution sought unsuccessfully to get rid of the colonies' elites, not merely replace a British elite with a North American elite.

The moral claims for growth's goodness are well known, if not shopworn. Business spends millions on think tanks to produce research, and millions more propagating the findings that support growth's goodness and necessity (Higgs 2014). "Tobacco company doctors" are still with us. (For most of the twentieth century and well into this one, tobacco companies recruited and funded medical doctors to make the case that smoking did not cause disease and could even be healthful – despite evidence they had from their own research that smoking caused cancer, emphysema, and the like. When that became untenable they sowed doubt about the health effects of smoking.) Chemical companies aggressively attacked Rachel Carson's work on pesticides, and oil companies attacked climate change researchers and others whose research is problematic for industry (Otto 2016). Growth advocates have attacked critics of consumerism and those who have raised the issue of endless growth on a finite planet such as the Club of Rome report's authors (Meadows et al. 1972). The growth mantra: it lifts societies out of poverty; lifts all boats and reduces inequality; enables addressing environmental issues; reduces conflict among and within societies and engenders social trust (American Enterprise Institute 2013).

The reality of growth's consequences is much different. Some groups in some societies have been lifted out of poverty, and some countries have grown wealthy, but at the expense of others: the poverty of poor countries is created by more powerful countries that became wealthy through plundering conquered countries, imposing unequal terms of trade, exploiting cheap labor (or enslaving people), i.e. colonialism and other forms of imperialism (Biel 2000; Chase-Dunn and Anderson 2005; Tucker 2007). This sort of inequality goes back to the first states that sought to dominate their neighbors. Today there are more people hungry (900 million) and malnourished (about 2 billion) than were alive at the beginning of this period (500 million people) in 1650. An odd sort of progress. Inequality tends to wax and wane in history (Scheidel 2017), but the benefits of growth are concentrated (Jackson 2009; O'Connor 2014) and growth creates constant crises of overproduction, financial bubbles, and economic insecurity.

The claims of ecological modernization that as societies grow richer they can afford to address certain kinds of pollution – mostly visible water and air pollution that were caused by development in the first place – invariably ignore the problems growth does not and cannot fix: loss of intact forests; loss of habitat; more roads; loss of soil through erosion and soil exhaustion and use of toxins and chemical fertilizers; and the massive slaughter of other species so humans can consume them, take their habitat, and remake the world in their image (e.g. Theobald et al. 1997; Ewing 2017). Human societies organized around growing economies externalize costs, and ignore limits including the second law of thermodynamics (oil can only be burned once) (Jackson 2009).

The relationship of economic and political elites varies by country: in some cases they are virtually coterminous, in others the division of labor sets them apart and the state has greater autonomy. But both depend on growth for revenue, which makes it difficult for those decision makers nominally responsible for ensuring the long-term societal good which is at odds with growth insofar as the societal good depends on healthy living systems. Political and business leaders are usually under great pressure to defer to the near term and to profit. Growth is a core state interest – perhaps the most powerful (Dryzek et al. 2003). In many societies in which business is privately owned (profits are private, costs are socialized) political leaders are nonetheless held accountable for economic performance and so need the cooperation of big business (Dye 2013; Miroff et al. 2014).

The costs of growth include resource wars, not only between countries but also within countries where factions seek control of anything lootable on behalf of themselves and their principals (Klare 2002). Ironically these costs can undercut growth and impose quite high overheads. Just as privately held companies cannot fully escape the pressures exerted by the larger economy, whole countries are not allowed by the various aid programs – the International Monetary Fund, World Bank (International Bank for Reconstruction and Development), and the World Trade Organization – to opt out (Associated Press 2017; Bretton Woods Project 2017).

Most pro-growth forces do not even bother trying to make a moral case in relation to biodiversity loss. The violent destruction of other species and wildlands is ignored or considered the norm – or it is called progress and is good. Growth economies have long externalized the natural world: it has no intrinsic value, only value when humans use it (Daly and Farley 2010). Economists of all stripes treat the economic system as closed and unrelated to the rest of the world even though the world is the source of all the things humans consume and depend on and are governed by (Peet 1992; Nadeau 2006).

We noted above that some growth advocates put hope in environmental modernization and decoupling, wherein wealth can cure all problems or growth can continue without harm because material consumption or inputs into the economy do not increase with growth. Trends are currently moving in the other direction, however. Habitat loss and fragmentation are increasing (Ceballos et al 2015); mining minerals is becoming more destructive (Lindenmayer 2014; Michaux 2014); despite declines in some production inputs per capita, overall inputs continue to climb (Higgs 2014); this is true for energy and carbon emissions as well. Global automobile production is rising as is overall meat consumption. So-called smart phone production is increasing and with it the extraction of rare earths and other destructive mining (Nield 2015).

To safeguard biodiversity and reverse its decline, the impact of humans must decline – the I in the IPAT formula must shrink significantly. (I=PAT – impact of humans equals their population, affluence or average consumption per capita, and technology which can be more or less efficient and more or less disruptive and destructive of the natural world.) Population and affluence are growing at annual rates of 1.3 and 1.4 percent respectively (Jackson 2009). John Holdren (Coontz 2007), former American Association for the Advancement of Science president and science advisor to US President Obama, admitted that "I'm a great believer in science and technology, but the notion that science and technology will ride to the rescue is a pernicious one. Believing in technological miracles is usually a mistake."

Only an incredible moral argument can be made to try to rationalize the increasing negative consequences for biodiversity of high levels of consumption by humans (Rosenblatt 1999; Kasser 2002; Barnosky and Hadly 2015; Moran and Kanemoto 2017).

POLICY OPTIONS

In Chapter 3 we examined a set of strategic questions that included asking which groups can help conservationists in realizing their goals. Having clearly stated goals, then, is a prerequisite to identifying allies, which vary with goals. Allies may also vary with who the decision makers are. Often it is the state, but the state is not just the formal government; it includes theocrats, party leaders, military leaders, and those who control economic enterprises. At the international level, decision makers are usually those from more powerful countries who have an interest in an issue. Sometimes leaders cannot be influenced but must be replaced. Ultimately conservationists need new biodiversity-friendly human institutions, not just different leaders.

Whether nominal democracies, oligarchies, military-led regimes or dictatorships, states or state-like entities have three primary types of policy options: regulation, taxation, and spending (including subsidies). Although regulation is usually considered more coercive than taxation or spending, what really counts is the ability of states or their stand-ins to effectively enforce their decisions.

Before we talk about potential allies in shaping decision maker actions we need to explore specific institutional actions that will further conservation goals, because potential allies are determined largely by goals. The list below is far from exhaustive and many desired actions can only be identified along the way as the politics unfold (but see Kerr 2000).

Regulations that dampen population growth include:

- Providing easy access to cheap or free birth control and other family planning assistance, especially in the context of comprehensive health care, including in rural areas;
- Requiring adequate sex education in schools (e.g. Bongaarts 2016);
- Requiring insurance carriers to cover birth control information and devices;
- Ending insurance carriers' subsidies for infertility treatments – along with adoption encouragement (see Spending, below).
- Effective enforcement of laws against child marriage, arranged marriages, sexual abuse, and domestic violence (Males 1996; Durning and Crowther 1997; Kissling 2010).

Population growth doesn't occur evenly. Total aggregate human population is the ultimate concern along with total human consumption, but population growth in a particular place can have differential impact on biodiversity because more biodiversity is in a place, it is more sensitive to human presence, or the human presence is more pernicious because of high levels of consumption (bigger houses, more roads and cars and guns). A region's population growth is a result of natural increase (births over deaths) and net in-migration. Human migration is influenced by numerous regulations including zoning, water and land use laws, those rules affecting credit and investment, and many others (Best 2002).

Increased conversion of natural systems to commodities occurs not just because there are more people but because people want more. Homes in the US, for example, continue to grow larger (Sparshott 2016). Trophy homes in previously intact habitat are a growing threat (Langlois 2016). Zoning can discourage or prevent some of this, as can ending subsidies for development in the form of roads, water, and other amenities (Fodor 1999; Simon and Company 2001). Agriculture and grazing remain the primary culprit in land conversion, including wetland destruction and creation of dead zones. Regulations make much of this possible or protect it, as do subsidies (spending) (Diaz and Rosenberg 2008; Goudie 2013; Pimm et al. 2014; Finley 2017). "No-take" Marine Protected Areas can prevent some of the enormous harm caused by industrial fishing, both within exclusive economic zones and on the high seas (Sciberras et al. 2013), as can ending the billions in fishing subsidies provided annually (Finley 2017). Allowing fishermen to make the rules for how much they catch has failed to work in almost all cases (Bromley 2009).

Automobile mileage standards and mandatory recycling laws are examples of regulations that have reduced per capita consumption in some countries (Roodman 1997; Layzer 2016), though overall CO_2 emissions continue to rise, including from cars (Higgs 2014), and more cars are being produced than ever before – 72 million in 2016, up from 41 million in 2000 (Statista 2017). Indeed, the biological capacity of the planet has declined steadily since 1961 due to human activity (Montgomery 2007). Economic measures ignore this decline in their accounting as they do human well-being. There is no subtraction for using things up such as fossil fuels, soil productivity, or groundwater, faster than they can be recharged. Time wasted in traffic is not subtracted as a loss, nor the military costs of securing oil fields and transport.

Much more could be done with regulation to limit the human impact (e.g. Dietz and O'Neill 2013): adequate social security; embedding ecological and social good restrictions in corporate charters; limiting the size of economic entities so they are less driven by the financial sector and global interests and are tied more closely to local consequences of their actions; strict limits on wage differentials (maintaining a low ratio between CEOs' and employee pay); limits on overall material inputs for commodity production, including energy; and limits on the many consequences of production: entropy, pollution, habitat loss, and fragmentation. Strict regulation and taxation of financial markets including transactions and speculation would help limit human impact as would other actions that recognize the Earth's limits and that the economy is not a closed system.

Great ideas abound for moving human societies in the right direction. But political muscle is lacking to make it happen. And even the sympathetic are fearful. Won't a no-growth economy look like a growth economy in recession? Certainly political parties, states, and others do not want to be in the forefront. They are cautious and want to preserve their power. As we will see in Chapter 6 on energy, not only do most leaders lack vision and courage to actually lead, they see many dangers in going first as with disarmament. Most social justice and equity movements also look to growth to solve problems.

Two other major tools for reducing the human impact are available to the state and related institutions: taxation and spending (Kerr 2000). Both are usually considered to be less coercive than regulation and therefore easier to achieve because opposition is less vehement – except where anti-tax sentiment is a kind of religion. Moreover, because taxation and spending are already widely used tools for implementing population and consumption policies – usually supporting growth in both cases – conservationists need open no new doors except in naming them population and consumption policies. Taxing and spending, including ending subsidies, can do much to discourage both consumers and producers from activities destructive of the natural world, such as cyanide mining, industrial logging and fishing, raising cows and pigs, road building, and urban sprawl. These two tools can also discourage large families by fully assisting parents with one or possibly two children, but not more (Kerr 2000).

Many commodities, such as petroleum products in the United States, are priced far below their real costs because many production costs and virtually all of the consequences of consumption are externalized. High petroleum taxes, such as those imposed in Europe, can discourage consumption. Building a large house or a second house, and other indulgent consumption, can be more heavily taxed to discourage them, as with cigarette and alcohol taxes. Tax laws can require growth to pay for itself and ensure that those who profit from growth also pay the costs; presently the profits are private and the costs are socialized (Roodman 1996; Fodor 1999). Taxes can be reduced to nil on land that is kept ecologically intact or restored and placed under easement or covenant or ceded as a protected area.

Taxation of financial transactions, and even heavier taxation on gambling or speculation in financial instruments, including currencies, could not just reduce this risky behavior but push many into useful work where they would have less to spend while saving societies from at least some financial bubbles. Disallowing advertising as a business expense could go a long way in reducing consumption based on insecurity and status.

Ending massive subsidies for mining fossil fuels, many minerals such as gold, automobiles and road building, industrial fishing, logging, and ranching would not only make revenues available for better uses but would greatly ease the lethal human burden on wildlife and ecosystems.

Many subsidies simultaneously increase the cost of living, congestion, pollution, and the like. In Oregon each new house receives about $30,000 in taxpayer subsidies for utility infrastructure, despite system development charges – roads, schools, and other services – so citizens are paying to increase congestion and pollution (Fodor 1999, 1998). Each new person in Australia requires $200,000 in new infrastructure on top of a massive national backlog of $770 million (O'Connor 2014). In many countries, governments at all levels provide subsidies to attract industries that rarely deliver on promises of jobs and other improvements. Not only is tax revenue forgone, and the tax burden shifted from business to individuals, but the newcomers attracted by the promises of plentiful jobs disproportionately end up in the unemployment line (Fodor 1999, 2002; Le Roy 2005). These migrant industries are often multinational corporations, with little loyalty to communities where they operate. If ever loss of freedom and growth were linked it is evident in the shift from a community's dependence on locally owned businesses – who themselves are not necessarily civic minded – to distantly headquartered economic giants who are creatures of balance sheets. American revolutionary Thomas Jefferson (1903–4 [1814]: 119) observed that "Merchants have no country. The mere spot they stand on does not constitute so strong an attachment as that from which they draw their gain."

Rural communities – especially those historically tied to resource extraction – often resist conservation efforts. Yet economic study after study has shown that the economically healthiest communities in the US Northwest are those least dependent on resource extraction and that have protected wilderness values. This has been true for some time (Niemi 1996, 1997, 1998, 1999a, 1999b; Rasker 1997; Headwaters Economics 2016, 2017). Subsidies are better put into jobs with the greatest value added.

Government spending offers even more options to curb growth and further conservation. Industrial fishing is strip-mining the oceans (Roberts 2007; Payne et al. 2016). The fish killed for human consumption sell for about $80 billion but the fishing fleets receive about

$105 billion in revenue (Finley 2017). We are paying to destroy the ocean as a living system. Agriculture, including grazing, is the same story: government pays to degrade soil, grasslands, and water quality to produce protein with considerable negative health effects, using large quantities of water, oil, and much else while creating a dead zone in the oceans (Halwell and Nierenberg 2008). Jackson (1987) called US agriculture a process of turning oil into food by mining the soil. The energy costs are enormous (Pimentel et al. 1973; Pimentel 2009).

When Indira Gandhi became prime minister of India she identified two conditions then obtaining as the cause of most problems for the country: too many people and too many cattle (Thapar 2006). Globally roads must be added to the list of the most pernicious, along with high-tech (and highly subsidized) trawling fleets. Ending subsidies for growing populations of humans and their livestock, roads, and industrial fishing would be an excellent start at reducing damage inflicted on the wild. But despite objections to taxes by many – who might benefit from more available revenue for beneficial services if such subsidies were ended – it has been difficult to mobilize people to bring the necessary pressure. This may be due to the difference in benefits and costs: subsidies are usually concentrated, so it's easier for recipients to organize; the costs to individuals of a particular subsidy, though they add up, are relatively small, so there is a weaker motivation to organize. And subsidies usually exist as part of a system of back-scratching and so other powerful players don't complain.

Subsidies are, of course, a kind of state spending, but direct spending better allows those who can influence government to more precisely advance well-defined goals and know if they are being advanced. Government spending on campaigns to discourage high levels of reproduction, consumption, and migration and the corresponding benefits of limiting all three offer the possibility of real change if done creatively and consistently. The Population Media Center, for example, directly carries out population programs via well-researched and effective broadcast soap operas but also relies on government support, ranging from birth control to enforcement of prohibitions on child marriages.

There is a long list of options for government spending to counter population and consumption growth. Spending to ensure that all people have easy and free access to all safe forms of birth control, know about it, and are encouraged to use it could have dramatic effects. As with efforts to reduce ivory demand, it is a cultural matter of redefining status. Government can help ensure girls and women have options beyond parenthood and show that these options offer a much wider range of possibility than parenthood. It is not that poor women have more children, it is that women whose economic options are limited have more children. When women can gain social recognition for activities other than motherhood, they have fewer children (Ryerson 2013, 2014; Engelman 2016; Wang and Singhal 2016). And when women have their own resources and are not dependent on their male partner's income, they generally choose to have fewer children (Bruce 1994; Dixon-Mueller 1994).

Herman Daly and others have repeatedly reminded us that economic health does not require growth in material consumption (Daly and Cobb 1994; Daly 1996; Douthwaite 1999; Czech 2000; Nadeau 2003, 2006; Barnosky and Hadly 2015). Government spending to limit consumption or for nonconsumptive purposes such as restoration programs can help heal public and private lands. Many nations, including the US, could greatly benefit from something like the US Civilian Conservation Corps of the 1930s and '40s, which, among other things, employed the unemployed to build park infrastructure. Reorienting agencies responsible for supporting farmers to focus on the health of ecosystems instead of simply maximizing production would also aid conservation goals (Montgomery 2007).

Almost all the spending options noted above are applicable internationally, either through aid or various treaty regimes. Both the International Monetary Fund and World Bank, however, have proven themselves resistant to change. Both are owned by the rich countries and reflect their interests in growth and profits and the infrastructure that supports both. It is in the domestic political arenas of the rich countries that battles over the actions of these two institutions will be fought.

Many NGOs not only lobby states but act directly. Planned Parenthood, the Population Media Center, and others influence individual behavior and often make contraception and other health care available. They almost invariably work with governments or communities. Many NGOs work directly on girls' and women's issues such as education, making microloans, and providing other opportunities. NGOs have been important in raising awareness of the problems of consumption and recognizing the problem of inequality: the rich and middle classes consume too much and the poor lack the basics. Anti-consumption campaigns are needed but must address cultural beliefs that have been shaped for more than a century by commercial interests; indeed, even the poor are a market segment today.

Many have been encouraged to believe that consuming less is a sacrifice. This is so even though sacrifice is supposed to mean giving up something of less value for something of more value. Many see the Amish sacrificing the conveniences of technology, but the Amish see the majority working long hours for the hollowness of consumer goods, giving up leisure and family time, community, and mutual aid (Peterson 2010). Is it really a sacrifice to trade away clean air and water and the lives of other species for corporate profit? Most have lost their connection with the Earth and other species. In the Depression of the 1930s, the Kellogg company reduced the work day to six hours without reducing pay. It was not just to hire more workers but to reduce drudgery in people's lives and provide more time for other pursuits (Maniates 2010).

To address the resistance to consuming less, people first need to be made aware of what they are giving up for the status quo of chasing greater consumption. Isn't giving up time to experience closer connections so one can work more a perversion of sacrifice? (Hall 2010) A shift in the culture of sacrifice – a recognition of what is of greatest value – is needed, and such a recognition is a kind of conversion

(Rambo 1993). Bringing this conversion about will require new rituals which are vital to reinforcing new behavior amidst the old (Rappaport 1999). Jefferson (Continental Congress 1776) and Machiavelli (1996 [1531]) recognized people's fearfulness in the face of great change.

Social justice critics, such as those who call coercive any effort to influence people's decisions on reproduction, may find efforts to influence consumption similarly coercive. Power differentials are always a matter of concern. But culture change is the very stuff of human life, of animals that construct worldviews and live by them. To not engage in efforts to influence others is to cede how societies are organized and their goals to the elites who look after their own interests rather than the interests of life on Earth or even human society. It is to abdicate responsibility to protect the real human home – self-willed land and life. There is no freedom from nature. To be free from nature is to be lost (Bookchin 1980).

The cultural norms that support high reproductive rates and high levels of consumption are the results of thousands of years of domination by elites and they are lethal to biodiversity. Indeed, for most of *Homo sapiens sapiens'* time on the planet we have lived with very low birth rates (and children were highly valued rather than seen as farm labor or social security) and we consumed relatively little, perhaps because we had close relationships with each other and the world (Lancy 2008). To undo those norms is no more wrong-headed than to try to change behaviors and beliefs associated with genital mutilation, rape, child marriage, slavery, or genocide. That these behaviors are often socially sanctioned or "traditional" does not limit the harm they cause.

It is easy to call for changes by laying out proposals for action by governments and others. It's done all the time to no effect because such calls are not self-executing; action is required to change the behavior of institutions, groups, and individuals (Johns 2009 and Part II herein). Conservation is not strong enough to cause institutions to adopt many of the actions listed above, especially in the face of strong opposition. This can only be remedied by organizing people and groups into the conservation movement and thereby making it stronger, and by alliances with other groups. In the next section we will look at potential allies: those who share conservation goals, interests, or engage based on a quid pro quo.

ALLIANCES

After the Evangelical Environmental Network (EEN)'s successful 1995 defense of the US Endangered Species Act (ESA) from Representatives Newt Gingrich and Don Young's attempt to gut it, Carl Pope, then Executive Director of the Sierra Club, publicly apologized to the EEN for ignoring them and other religious groups (Barcott 2001). The anti-conservation US congress that came into office in 1995 was elected over the opposition of conservationists and environmentalists and neither group had any influence with them. But this congress was beholden to conservative Christians and among them was the EEN, an organization consisting of a thousand churches with over a million members; enough voters to swing elections in several districts. The Sierra Club could be ignored, but conservative politicos could not ignore a well-organized conservative religious group that saw the ESA as a modern Noah's Ark. They were able to stop the proposed legislation.

Pope's statement pledging future cooperation is an example of an interest-based alliance which demonstrates how important such alliances can be. Religious (Creation Care) and secular motives can generate support for the same goals. In this case the religiously motivated were essential to having influence where secular groups had none; indeed, the latter were seen as opponents by the new congressional leadership.

Alliances and coalitions provide much-needed additional political strength and the real question is why the Sierra Club and other conservationists did not ask the right question earlier: who do we need on our side to win? (Chapter 3). The Zuni campaign against a giant coal mine reached out to other tribes, white churches, secular NGOs, scientists, and civic leaders, all of whom added pressure and raised the cost of the mine to its investors and decision makers (Cox 2006). Dolphin campaigners reached out to and mobilized schoolchildren and their parents (Layzer 2006, 2012). Tompkins Conservation in Patagonia and those seeking to recover Gorongosa National Park in Mozambique reached out to local communities who could see intact wild places benefited them more than extraction (and the areas in question were not heavily settled [Carroll 2016; Jimenez 2017]). Campaigns in various countries to stop the ivory trade and elephant slaughter have relied on Buddhist leaders (Thailand), sports stars, and other cultural leaders to influence consumers (China) and ultimately the Communist Party (China), which came to see that ivory consumption generated international disapproval (WILDAID 2017). The (US) Northeast Canyons and Seamounts Marine National Monument had to demonstrate support from many constituencies to win approval, and religious groups played an important role in mobilizing support (Lorbiecki 2017). The Korean environmental movement, like the German Greens, was able to form alliances with unions, but neither were strongly conservationist and both forged alliances based on environmental and human health (Broadbent 2011; Liu 2015).

Alliances contribute to creating the critical political mass and collective resources necessary for changing institutional behavior. The more political resources – people, money, media, organizing, timing, etc. – competing groups or alliances bring to bear the more likely they are to prevail (see Johns 2009 for an in-depth discussion of mobilization of resources). Strong alliances enable greater influence in setting the agenda and defining acceptable solutions. If conservation is to succeed over the long haul, it must be able to not just play defense effectively, but take the offense on behalf of an alternative society.

In seeking alliances and answering the strategic questions set out in Chapter 3 – especially who can effectively help? – it is useful to keep in mind the five fundamental interests of ruling groups (Dryzek et al. 2003): (1) maintaining an order that benefits them (there is no "law and order" in general, only specific ones that generate different winners and losers); (2) recognition from other states of their sovereign power; (3) economic growth and (4) raising revenue – often closely tied – and (5) maintaining legitimacy among key constituencies (raw power in comparison is very expensive). Conservationists and other groups generally lose fights that seriously challenge any of these interests (Dryzek et al. 2003), but may have no choice but to go up against them if fundamental change is necessary. In the US in the 1970s, with rivers on fire, drinking water polluted, and its rulers under siege for the Vietnam War, conservation support for the ESA and other such laws backed by the Nixon regime help legitimize the government (Repetto 2006). That the ESA might be an obstacle to unfettered growth would only be recognized by elites later.

Keeping these five interests in mind helps answer with greater specificity which allies may be most helpful with influencing decision makers. Often the most important decision makers are outside the formal government structure, e.g. theocrats or high party officials or business leaders. In South Africa it was the political establishment that had become most deeply wedded to apartheid. When apartheid began to hurt important business interests as a result of effective boycotts, that sector was willing to quietly initiate talks to explore a transition (Wood 2000). It meant giving up overt political control, but not abandoning it.

We will examine only a few potential alliances; the list is too long for one chapter in a book.

Pro-democratic Allies

Pletscher and Schwartz (2000) suggest alliances be explored with libertarian groups who chafe at regulation. Many who oppose regulation have a simplistic view of the state qua state as the problem. States can be oppressive in their own right, but more often they act on behalf of powerful and narrow economic forces seeking advantage for themselves at the expense of nature and the rest of society (Lindblom 1977; Dye 2013). In the case of the US, the state has grown in response to great concentrations of wealth – initially to contain that wealth and its abuses and insure the broader public interest.

Former US president Teddy Roosevelt (1910), speaking as a politician rather than a scholar, summed it up this way:

> Our government, national and state, must be freed from the sinister influence or control of special interests. Exactly as the special interests of cotton and slavery threatened our political integrity before the Civil War, so now the great special business interests too often control and corrupt the men and methods of government for their own profit. We must drive the special interests out of politics.

Instead, wealth captured the state and was only seriously challenged in the 1930s and 1960s (Miroff et al. 2014). Democratic forms cover an oligarchy where banks are "too big to fail" or to prosecute for money-laundering (Protess and Silver-Greenberg 2012).

Other states are more directly authoritarian and, despite limited markets, economic elites are under the control of political elites. China and Japan are examples and it is noteworthy that both have strongly communitarian cultures; there is no well-organized anti-authoritarianism of the sort Pletscher and Schwartz look to in the US. And in the US, anti-regulation libertarians seem oblivious to Adam Smith's concern that all forms of power – business, religious and political – are problematic. It is equally doubtful, based on US libertarians' equation of personal freedom with corporate freedom, that they could accept state action to address growth.

Many organized groups around the globe are concerned with the threats to or denial of the influence of ordinary people. Democratic forms are often hollow, decision-making schemes are stacked, choices limited and not meaningful. If we think of democracy less as a formal structure than as the political space to create grassroots movements that can in turn influence decision makers and societal structure, then democracy is good for conservation. Creating this space does not ensure people will support conservation automatically, but it does ensure conservation has a chance – that conservationists are not all in jail.

Allying with those seeking basic protection to speak out, to assemble, and most of all to organize, makes good sense. So does allying with those seeking to check the outsize influence of business and others similarly situated, groups seeking to rein in putting profits first and demanding accountability. There are also many groups seeking to expose the many ways in which democratic forms mask oligarchy. Groups seeking to break up media monopolies and advertiser control are potential allies; US television refused to run ads for Buy Nothing Day because it is inimical to their interests (Moyer 1999).

These groups advocating for political space have their hands full and are often under siege if not under serious threat. It is in conservationists' interest to defend and seek to expand the political space for necessary speech, autonomous NGOs, and organizing. Conservationists' support cannot come free, however. They must insist that those they support recognize that equity is not just about or for people.

Population and economic growth tend to increase political and economic centralization, with public and private bureaucracies seeking more control over society because they need to impose uniformity and predictability to function (Scott 1998). When the state's legitimacy is ideologically based there is less tolerance for open speech and NGO autonomy (e.g. Zeng 2014). Stability is at stake. Political and economic hierarchies also tend to concentrate knowledge at the top, while others lose knowledge and leverage. Hierarchies generate greater reliance on experts (Worster 1985; Kairys 1990), who do not make neutral technical decisions, but value and interest, i.e. politically based, decisions. They are often experts at politics and bureaucracy, not just engineering.

China is probably the authoritarian country most important to conservation: a quarter of the world's population and hellbent on growth. It produces and consumes more and more, leaving a rapidly growing human footprint. China says it is committed to the Paris Climate Accord, which suggests some moderation in industrialization if it sticks to its promises (see Victor et al. 2017 for a reality check), but China is also gobbling up land and forests globally, i.e. the homes of other species. It is eating much higher on the food chain. Its Belt and Road Initiative is a huge threat to wildlands and wildlife. Many Chinese aspire to a US or Australian standard of living, which the US and Australia cannot maintain if conservation goals are to be taken seriously. The Chinese party–government hierarchy is susceptible to pressure of various sorts, both domestic and international. But as noted above, it is difficult for NGOs to directly challenge growth without party leaders regarding their power as being challenged (Broadbent 2011).

Ultimately biodiversity-friendly societies may depend not just on institutional changes in behavior but on enough people expelling the internalized policeman and throwing off their own domestication so they are able to demand different behavior from the state. Hierarchy is bad for the human personality – it infantilizes – and it is therefore bad for conservation. But like disarmament, who will go first is a problem.

Nimby Allies

Many potential allies fall into the category of Not In My Back Yard (Nimby). They will fight against (or for) something locally that they would never concern themselves with if it were not local. This should not be an issue for conservationists, who know too well of death by a thousand cuts. Cumulative impacts can do at least as much damage as major disasters. It is also true that small victories can have positive cumulative affects. Each cut prevented is important: each trophy home stopped; each rural community with bear-proof garbage cans is a good; as is each steer or cow not born; each piece of forest off the chopping block or restored; each human birth that doesn't occur and each car not produced; each fishing vessel retired or scrapped.

Working with Nimby groups, especially where there are opportunities to set good precedents, or important lessons and stories can be gathered and shared, contributes to conservation. Additionally working with Nimby groups can contribute to movement building, as it did with the US civil rights movement (Luders 2010). Many conservation struggles are essentially local and work in a similar fashion: horizontal sharing, transmission via national groups and meetings, and alliances among groups to obtain decisions that have broad impacts such as national legislation (e.g. Bevington 2009). Connecting Nimby groups to others seeking similar outcomes or seeking to fashion an alliance, connecting them to larger or causal issues, encouraging formation of a broader geographical network – all increase mobilization. Nimby groups or groups less deliberately locally focused can be organized into a nested hierarchy. People working on forest defense or recovery often create regional efforts, which coordinate with others in different regions, making up a Wildway, which is in turn part of a continental system (see Introduction above, Figure 2).

In many cases, groups in different regions or parts of the world come to the same conclusions about goals and strategy and they discover each other's efforts. Or an NGO reaches out to forge alliances, to find support or to offer support and resources (Keck and Sikkink 1998; Johns 2003; Bob 2005). Personal networks are often central to forging connections, as are global meetings such as International Congresses on Conservation Biology, the World Wilderness Congresses, World Parks Congresses, and similar meetings.

Religiously and Philosophically Motivated Allies

Religious institutions are already organized and have the capacity to take action on behalf of biodiversity. The EEN and the ESA, the Zuni fighting destruction of their land in New Mexico by the 18,000 acre Fence Lake open pit coal mine, and Buddhists supporting a ban on the ivory trade in Thailand are just three examples of action. Secular conservationists were allies but did not organize religious groups.

An essential link between religious and secular conservationists is that conservation is a moral fight at its core. Billions of humans increasingly look to religious leaders for moral guidance on issues related to biodiversity. Some religions provide more than moral guidance, they mobilize followers to act (Barcott 2001; McDuff 2010; Bartholomew 2012). Religious institutions are about the only sector in society that as a whole consistently tries to focus people on purposes beyond material accumulation and self-aggrandizement. There are churches that make their deity out to be a Mercedes-driving capitalist, focused on "helping those who help themselves," but most have longstanding critiques of the pursuit of wealth as meaningful. As keepers of that which is sacred – the most fundamental and unquestioned assumptions about the highest purposes in life for a group or society – they are important to almost any moral pursuit (Rappaport 1999). The EEN denied conservative Republicans their religious mantle, though most conservative churches supported the conservative Republicans.

Religious communities are usually dense networks: there are strong ties with cohorts and these are more likely to lead to group action once a project or goal becomes important. And religious adherents are connected to networks outside of their religious institution that conservationists may not have access to, such as rural or more conservative communities.

The religiously motivated often have a level of commitment that others lack because they experience their purposes as coming from a "higher" source; they are more likely to hang in for the long haul and in the face of setbacks (Aminzade and Perry 2001). Part of what sustains them, of course, is community and ritual. Both provide support – ritual stimulates commitment and community fosters reinforcement.

Religious alliances for conservation thus for have not been as successful as many have hoped. Taylor B. et al. (2016) note than in the US many of the faithful lack even basic awareness of the loss of "creation," let alone embrace creation care. Despite the emphasis in Hinduism and Buddhism on compassion for all things and though they do not persecute animals, neither has been terribly effective in halting the destruction caused by the inertia of growth. Whether habitat falls before the bulldozer, the digging stick and ax, or the machete of slash-and-burn the result is the same. Addressing the causes of biodiversity loss often competes with other, human-centered issues and pursuits and does not fare well. Even those religions that sympathize with the natural world do not support, or are opposed to, birth control. In poor countries it's not easy to draw a clear line between basic consumption and the aspiration to live like Canadians or Americans. Many religious leaders call upon their followers to change individual behavior only, while a few encourage or lead collective political action to change institutional behavior in support of conservation. In the US many leaders support politicians who oppose legal environmental restrictions on what they see as god-given property rights. So morality can come to rationalize "the smart money" (Freilich 1972). Just as religions found themselves advocating for both sides in the struggle over slavery, it is the case with conservation.

There are secular belief systems which hold sway among some groups that can be approached in the same way as religious groups, i.e. on the basis of systemic beliefs anchored in certain unquestioned and fundamental assumptions. The belief in historical progress, nationalism – both ethnic and territorial – and other worldviews that most would term philosophies may support conservation values. There is no systematic inventory to this author's knowledge.

Biophilia is an emotional tendency and like other tendencies can give rise to worldviews much in the way certain emotions give rise to specific beliefs. No doubt biophilic feelings are tied to animistic beliefs: they seem to share a sense of connection with other life. Today biophilia receives minimal cultural reinforcement and is not very strong in most people; it is best compared to a flickering candle flame about to drown in the melted wax. Seen as the affinity for other species, E. O. Wilson (1984) seeks to reawaken and cultivate biophilia as a source of motivation for conservation. Certainly the influence of Arne Naess's Deep Ecology demonstrates the power of such views; it helped to fuel many biocentric conservation activists. However, Naess himself talks little about biodiversity compared to mountains and large landscapes without human domination.

Another potential and transformational ally consists of those concerned with animal suffering at human hands, including research, hunting, confinement, and abuse. A distinction is historically made between concern with individual animals (the concern of animal welfare, animal rights) and with species (conservation), but there is increasing overlap and bases for common action. Compassionate conservation increasingly spans both concerns (Wallach et al. 2018). Together the compassionate conservation, animal welfare and animal rights constitutencies are growing while hunting and consumptive uses of wildlife are in decline. As is often the case with the material decline of groups, their influence lingers.

Cultural Allies

As surely as conservation NGOs need access to the media in all its form, they need to engage more in the production of media content, either directly producing such content or forming alliances (networking) with those who make films, generate television and radio programming, who write, record and sing songs, who draw and paint, who write, produce and act in theater, who dance and who write novels and stories. Almost all current artistic creation concerning the natural world is apolitical, does not explore causes, and mostly consists of documentaries; there is a dearth of great stories, especially that reach large audiences and that over time can change how people see and experience the world, especially in the absence of undomesticated land/seascapes and creatures. Going beyond generating empathy for places and other than human life, conservation goals and action need attention. Just as much human drama consists of conflict over the clash of goals, so stories are needed to communicate what is happening to the world and what can be done to halt the destruction and recover the Earth. Such stories do not exactly permeate the media. They should be a growing part of what gets written, sung, danced, and finds its way into film and theater.

Which comes first – passion for conservation that creates cultural demand, or efforts to generate a conservation culture that instills passion – is probably the wrong question. Conservationists should be forging relationships with artists to make conservation more and more a part of daily life. Whatever the path, it is only when passion for the wild and human covoyagers becomes part of everyday culture that behavior will change. There should be no mistake that leadership in the cultural realm is where conservation has real openings to foster change. Those who make culture lead.

Murray Edelman (1995) argues that political leaders rarely lead because it is too risky for them. To ensure that they stay in power, leaders follow powerful constituencies and pander to the mass that follow the powerful. Elites are engaged in trying to shape the cultural landscape, and spend billions on it (Higgs 2014). As with so much of life, however, unintended consequences are often more important than intended ones. Changes in understanding, perception – especially of patterns – perspective, expectations, and insight non-consciously evolve and are initially expressed in various art forms (Edelman 1995) based on the experience of artists. Economic and political elites try to manipulate what they can via funding but mostly they must adapt to these changes or try to counter them. Art offers a repertoire of frameworks that those engaged in political conflict seek to use to influence political action on specific issues.

The ability of art to influence politics cannot be seriously questioned, from the many versions of Gilgamesh, religious stories from around the world, and classical dramatists to Harriet Beecher Stowe's *Uncle Tom's Cabin*, Wu Cheng'en's *Journey to the West* (a favorite of Mao's), Wagner's *The Ring of the Nibelung* and Looney Tunes' Bugs Bunny. The simple morality tales of US films of the 1940s and 1950s influenced political expectations in the US in the 1960s and 1970s (Alberti 2015). Television helped create and reinforced expectations of a just world (Appel 2008).

Film is one of the most influential media for many reasons: it engages most of the senses, it is the right length for a single sitting, it can be experienced by tens of millions simultaneously and by hundreds of millions in a few weeks. Where films are still seen in theaters rather than on tiny screens there is a ritual aspect. And over time films of a similar type can profoundly shape a culture. *Star Wars* (the film and the series) is an extraordinary example that has permeated virtually all cultures. It brings together the morality tale of Westerns and samurai warriors, what Joseph Campbell considers the essential elements of myth, and the action typical of many genres (Brode and Deyneka 2012). Both Campbell and Akira Kurosawa influenced George Lucas who deliberately set out to fashion a myth in response to the absence of genuine myth in societies dominated by commercialism. It has been forty years since the first film in the *Star Wars* series and it continues to bring in huge audiences while also selling books and other paraphernalia because of viewers' strong identification with the story and characters. People hunger for stories of good versus evil and the triumph of good against adversity. They want heroes. Unfortunately the wild and biodiversity and their defenders are absent from these stories and society is left with a narrow, merely human world. That can be changed. But only by film makers. What would a conservation *Star Wars* look like? One in which the central characters struggle over humans accepting limits and reducing their numbers and consumption?

Enlisting all media is important. Poets, novelists, songwriters and singers, cartoonists, painters, graphic artists, performance artists, and photographers all have a role. Good journalists use story as do good documentaries. The Population Media Center (e.g. Wang and Singhal 2016) has demonstrated in its many successful efforts to reduce fertility that television and radio can be primary, but institutional support in the form of birth control devices and instructions (supplied by NGOs or governments), reinforcement from social networks, booklets, and popular songs are critical to generate and sustain momentum. To bring about the behavioral change necessary to shrink the human impact, culture must be rewoven and in that endeavor all of the threads make a difference.

Legal Allies

Although many countries lack even the pretense of the rule of law, the means of dispute resolution exist in most places. Where it can't be said there is much of a legal system or semi-autonomous courts, there usually are rules of sorts which are taken seriously because predictability is important. Whether states are strong or weak, there are also non-state institutions that have rules which engage in resolving disputes and aren't merely self-serving. Law and justice are not the same thing, of course, and knowing what outcomes people's sense of justice requires is also useful. If we take legal allies to mean those who know the rules of states, other institutions (e.g. church law, martial law, a group's customs or a people's sense of justice) and how to use them, then their help can contribute to conservation.

Where there are substantive laws supporting conservation, then the greater the degree of court autonomy and the stronger the state the better for conservation.

In the US, EU, and elsewhere, the courts have been used effectively to protect species, ecological systems and processes from economic and political actors who would otherwise overreach. In these circumstances the courts have been used not only to stop illegal actions of the powerful, and to keep political challengers out of jail, but also to secure the use of contraception and some protection against unfettered greed. In the absence of strong courts or strong enforcement pursuant to the courts, other rules may come into play. Litigation may also play a role in organizing.

Business Allies

Many business people have supported conservation, but often to shape it in ways that benefit them (Gonzales 2001, Kamieniecki 2006; Kraft and Kamieniecki 2007; Layzer 2016) and at a cost to biodiversity. The ceding of land from California to the US for Yosemite National Park was backed by Southern Pacific at a cost of 10,000 acres to the park so they could build a railroad for tourism. Redwood National Park was strongly supported by Laurence Rockefeller and Save the Redwoods League, but they limited the size to protect certain properties and at a cost of compromising the Park's biological integrity. Pinchot's "practical forestry" won out over Muir's vision due to business backing (see Gonzales 2001 for a discussion of these cases). Although many conservation issues are of no concern to business, they are very effective at framing the issues and shaping the agenda of government and public opinion (Kamieniecki 2006). Generally, business enterprises favor growth, seek profit maximization, resist social control of their actions, and try to frame the political agenda to ignore damage to or destruction of living systems their actions may cause or, if that cannot be achieved, constrain the choice of solutions to minimize costs to them (Layzer 2016). As with many potential allies, the basis for cooperation may be narrow. Sugar-water manufacturer Coke gives $2–3 million a year to the World Wildlife Fund to help protect biological hotspots while being the top consumer of aluminum and sugar in the world (Dauvergne 2016). Many businesses do great damage in one part of the world while doing good in another part. If we examine continuing biodiversity loss or compare lands converted from habitat versus those protected, the trend and ratio of bad to good is not positive (Watson et al. 2016). The Conservation Finance Center estimates that US$50 billion is spent on conservation annually in recent years (Martin 2015). Global GDP, a rough measure of the amount spent generating human impacts, from energy generation to producing cars to treating preventable disease, to growing food animals in often horrific conditions, is $65 trillion – not even remotely comparable.

In approaching businesses, conservationists must look at the overall and longer-term picture, i.e. keep their eyes on the prize. A focus on the near term makes NGOs no better than companies that focus on the quarterly balance sheets. Some businesses are directly helpful to conservation, such as those engaged in restoration work. Recreation businesses may help to protect the areas they depend on, such as national parks, but they vary in terms of the infrastructure they depend on and long-distance travel of clients which have impacts. Some try to minimize their impact and strategically seek to do good with profits. Other businesses generate toxins, destroy forests and grasslands, and oppose contraceptives.

Two factors shape the behavior of businesses: type of ownership and leadership. If an enterprise is investor-driven it is profit-driven. It will compete with other businesses to generate a higher rate of return to attract investment and grow: the only way to keep profits up in the face of technological change that replaces labor, the source of profit. One hears business leaders say they must put their duty to investors first. The law often requires the fiduciary role to be paramount, but it need not be. The law can require equal or more attention be paid to "the environment" or to workers or to the community. (Up until the 1840s in the US, states granted corporate charters only for a public good.) That the law usually does not is largely due to the influence of businesses which want a free hand if not a helping hand (Kraft and Kamieniecki 2007; Layzer 2016). Privately held companies, in contrast, do not need to live up to the expectations of investment bankers and other investors. Their owners can decide on a rate of profit that is lower (or higher). For example, Patagonia, the outdoor clothing maker, has taken a different path, focusing on limiting its impact, investing in products that last, and supporting conservation NGOs with some of its profits.

The second factor is leadership. Leaders of an enterprise make a difference. They cannot ignore the structural constraints in which they operate, but they can and sometimes do make favorable decisions within those constraints and can work to change those constraints. They can try to persuade their peers, though Doug Tompkins (founder of North Face and Espirit) said other entrepreneurs weren't quite sure about him. (Over the last twenty-five years Doug and Kris Tompkins have bought land in Chile and Argentina and are gifting it to those countries for national parks.) While most CEOs are aggressively self-aggrandizing, other entrepreneurs have launched 1% for the Planet, a group of companies that together commit major resources to effective non-profit conservation organizations, and similar efforts to support biodiversity efforts.

What can businesses actually contribute to reduction in growth? Reversing existing growth trends goes against longstanding views that are continually reinforced by what generates a return. They can use their standing, as Yvon Choinard of Patagonia has, to discourage frivolous consumption and challenge the ideology of endless growth. They can buy land for conservation and protect the oceans from pollution and overfishing. They can undercut the legitimacy of the business fraternity and its political representatives by speaking out and breaking ranks. They can support those NGOs who take on growth.

Cultivating business allies, like other allies, is often best done through business networks: business people talking to other business people, clergy to other clergy, and so on. It starts with a relationship between a business and conservationists; that business reaches out to other businesses as a peer. It is no magic bullet, however, as those supporting population and consumption limits may be seen as outsiders by others in their nominal community. As with our discussion of sacrifice earlier in this chapter, the ability to offer a new frame that makes plain the high price of the status quo and the benefits of changes is essential to communicating across the divide. Crises may also help: denial is not much of an option for businesses in coastal areas confronting sea level rise.

Labor

The venerable realpolitik principle of "the enemy of my enemy is my friend" does not always apply to the relations between labor groups and conservation groups. The relationship is frequently contentious and always complicated for many reasons: historical and global context, social position of labor and conservation, perceptions of the differences between environmentalism (threats to human health) and conservation (concern with biodiversity and wildlands), the relationship of material interests and values to action, and relative levels of mobilization (who has the most clout). All of these need to be taken into account in considering conservation strategy. All are factors conservationists must consider when they approach alliances with labor.

In Korea and Taiwan close alliances between labor and *environmental* groups have formed in recent decades, mostly around health threats to workers and to sectors of the public living near sources of pollution (Liu 2015). In these and other countries industrialization and concern with the environment have occurred simultaneously with movements arising in a self-protective response almost at the same time. Both labor and environmental groups had an interest in addressing injuries from toxic emissions and both had an interest in increased democracy and the right to organize. Labor brought their material position in the economy to bear as leverage – strikes can deprive industry of profit – and the environmental movement made appeal to values, which it sought to universalize: people should be safe from such events; it is a broad public good. Conservation of biodiversity and wildlands was not on the agenda in these heavily settled countries (Liu 2015).

In North America and Europe, industrialization pre-dated the environmental and conservation movements as *mass* movements. Early roots of environmentalism lay in the public health movement, and of course conservation has roots in Thoreau and Muir and the animism of some of the earliest migrants to the Americas (Nash 2014). For most of its history the industrial labor movement has shared with capital the view that the natural world was there to be utilized, to be transformed into commodities by human labor. The difference between capital and labor was not over the value of nature, but who should benefit from the proceeds. To "lock up resources" or protect places and non-human life from exploitation was not only to deny the purpose of nature but to deny jobs to the working class and subsistence to rural people in favor of the wealthy who had the leisure to enjoy and monopolize wildlife and beauty.

Not until the automobile became pervasive did the working class come to embrace wilderness and wildlife in non-consumptive ways (Lipin 2007). However, the US working class, as just one example, is far from monolithic. Workers in extractive industries have tended to differ with urban workers over the highest and best use of wildlife and wilderness. Workers who fear job loss from health and safety regulations may have very different views than those workers who embrace a broader public good. Indeed, workers at times tolerate poisonous and even lethal conditions to protect their jobs because they see no options. American workers and their unions tend to be more focused on wages, hours, and conditions of employment than the power relations of who defines the choices workers must make. In contrast, European unions frequently challenge social structures that leave the working class with poor choices – e.g. jobs or environment, jobs or health care, etc. (Carter 2007).

The environmental and conservation concerns of American workers are in part defined by the pervasive economic insecurity (e.g. job loss) which is used to manage them, regardless of their attitudes toward the natural world which range from consumptive use to wildlife viewing, the quest for solitude, and much else. While workers and unions may share a common interest in some things and common opponents on some issues, business can be quite adept at boxing labor in: support drilling for oil in the Arctic National Wildlife Refuge or face imminent layoffs. In the US, environmentalists and labor have formed alliances opposing the North American Free Trade Agreement and globalization, for many health and safety regulations and against rollbacks of such rules (Obach 2004). They have been at odds over the Corporate Average Fuel Economy Standard, drilling in the US Arctic Refuge, and protection of ancient forests and endangered species.

It is obvious from a quick review of the above alliances and conflicts that most issues are environmental (primarily concerned with benefit or injuries to humans) rather than biodiversity- and wildlands-related. But sometimes claims for a broader good must begin with a claim for the human public good.

In other countries – Brazil, India, China, Mexico, Australia, Japan, Kenya – the relations between (and within) labor and conservationist and environmentalist groups are complex and admit to alliances based on specific issues. One source of tension is that organized labor generally has more to offer conservation than conservation has to offer labor. Labor's position in a society's economic structure gives them material leverage. Unless and until conservationists are able to organize widespread support for the values they espouse and can mobilize people on that basis, they do not have much to trade politically (Obach 2004; Liu 2015). All fights are cultural and material, but power is ultimately material.

The ability of conservationists to establish long-term relationships with organized labor groups has many advantages. It builds the trust needed to neutralize divisive efforts by opponents. It creates greater potential for developing a shared common vision for reorganizing the economy on biodiversity-compatible bases. And it creates a much stronger defensive capability against assaults on the natural world and healthy human relationships.

Youth and Enculturation

Generational change is a primary form of change. Despite the best efforts of families, groups, schools, governments, religions and other institutions to inculcate beliefs (enculturation) and behaviors (socialization) conforming to the status quo the transfer is imperfect for many reasons: different experiences, visible hypocrisy, competing efforts to shape young people by the multitude of those seeking to do so, and ordinary slippage, among others.

Imparting worldviews to children that result in action around conservation, population, and growth issues as they mature competes with contrary and better-organized religious, economic, and political views. Despite being behind other groups in this process, conservationists can succeed in this difficult circumstance if they recognize it is not a matter of ecological education (understanding ecology), although such knowledge is important to making good decisions. Rather it is a matter of creating conditions and experiences that impart to children a felt relationship with the natural world (Hungerford and Volk 1990; Sebba 1991).

Although efforts to influence the content of human development are primarily aimed at obtaining certain behaviors in adults, it is also true that children's behavior at a number of stages is important. Marketers have long relied on "pester power" to get children to influence parental choices regarding product recycling, and much else. Adolescents help shape the larger political arena by their action or lack of action.

Basic feelings toward the natural world are shaped in the first years of life. When a child's needs are met they are comfortable with their bodies and can empathize with other bodies, including non-human ones. Empathy is a predictor of conservation action (Hungerford and Volk 1990). The experience of the non-human in early life and later nurtures and is the ground for people recognizing they are made of the same stuff and will have the same fate as all life (Searles 1960). Children, for example, seek to touch animals at three months (Myers and Saunders 2002). Animals engage or react to children and reflect back children's agency, intentions, and feelings. The presence of animals in a child's early life may even ameliorate bad parenting (Searles 1960).

If the child's needs are not met because parents or the larger world will not or cannot meet them, they may experience the world as painful, hostile, dangerous, and joyless. Lacking affirmation emotions and needs become anxiety-producing. Unable to be at home in their bodies, they may be unable to acknowledge their own impulses and to feel a link with other animals. There is little or no room for empathy to grow. There may not even be room for the self to grow and a false self may take its place (Post 1997; Masterson 2006), forever seeking attention. Turns toward fundamentalism and authoritarianism have roots in this experience of material and emotional deprivation (Norris and Inglehart 2004) and do not bode well for conservation. Belief in immortality as a defense against a hostile world and death can make killing easy because it doesn't really matter – there is an afterlife (Becker 1973; Solomon et al. 2004).

To maximize future conservation action, future activists must be produced by deliberate efforts now. Past infancy and into early school years children start to explore the world and seek competency in navigating the world. Depending on how they are nurtured they may find mastery in trying to control the world or develop *self-control in* the world, including caring for other creatures and accepting the limit of not hurting others (Chawla and Heft 2002).

There are many ways to try to ensure the latter option. Having access to the natural world for self-directed play is among the most critical (Louv 2005). It need not be real wilderness like the US Grand Canyon or Scotland's Glen Affric. It can be a tidal pool. It can be an ant nest. But it must be an unmanicured place without direct adult supervision – something more difficult to find given levels of paranoia in many societies. Caretakers want children visible at all times. For city dwellers it can be especially difficult as one urban girl on the cusp of adolescence (aged twelve) said:

> 'I wish I could walk out of that school and find myself a place where there are no whites, no black folk, no people of any kind! I mean, a place where I'd be able to sit still and get my head together; a place where I could walk and walk, and I'd be walking on grass, not cement, with glass and garbage all around; a place where there'd be the sky and the sun, and then the moon and all those stars ... If I was there, I'd be able to talk the way I want, and I'd hear myself, because there wouldn't be a lot of people listening and telling me what I said or what I should be saying.'
>
> *(Nabhan and Trimble 1994: xxiii–xxiv)*

Going up to the rooftop of her building at night offered a respite, but it was not enough, as Coles says, to satisfy her deep longing for the Earth, air, and sky, and to find her way back to herself. (But see Taylor A. F. et al. 2002.) For others, amidst chronic war and drought, it can be much worse. But electronic toys and training for consumption are enough to estrange most (Nabhan and Trimble 1994; Louv 2005).

The US Sierra Club not only leads trips for adults, but its chapters lead hundreds of trips for kids as part of their Inner City Outings Program (Louv 2005). The Portland (Oregon, US) Audubon Society (PAS) takes good advantage of the city's park system and waterways (including two major rivers) to introduce children to wildlife and let them explore. Their urban naturalist program also appeals to parents. The PAS provides information about trips families can do on their own as well as leads child-friendly group outings. Such programs only represent a drop in the bucket and people self-select for them. They are far from as pervasive as television. Sadly, scouting and similar programs are not as outdoor-oriented as they once were, but because they represent an existing organizational infrastructure with millions already involved, revitalization should be a priority.

Children also need ritual and story and action. From the Bands of Mercy (an animal welfare group founded in the UK in 1875, it grew to 4 million members in 1923) to modern campaigns around climate, pollution, and place-based conservation, children have played a big role and even led campaigns before adolescence (Ascione 2005; Loftus-Farren 2017). US congressional staff and lobbyists have commented that children often have an effect that causes the jaded to recall the promise of democracy rather than the reality of campaign contributions. This middle age of childhood is also the age at which "pester power" expresses itself effectively. Children can educate, shame, prod and cajole parents and other adults into changing their behavior.

Adolescence is a period of transition to adulthood: the period in which an identity and a role are settled on. It is also a period when unresolved issues from previous stages of development are accessible for a time and can be addressed and injuries made right. It is a time when joining groups or organizations takes on a bigger and more political role and decisions can make a lasting difference. A sense of justice is consolidated along with a sense of purpose and can motivate collective political action. Ritual, myth, and mutual support are important in this process. This age group has often played an outsize role, along with university-aged youth, in politics during periods of upheaval.

The challenges for addressing the causes of biodiversity loss are significant in this period of growth. Identity, purpose, and livelihood usually come together in this period to generate occupational and livelihood choices. Individuals and cohorts adapt to society just as societies adapt to the world in all its aspects. Not everyone can be or wants to be a conservation biologist or park ranger; but all can be activists to make change in a social order hostile to the natural world, which includes making livelihoods compatible with wildness. It can begin with working less and consuming less, playing more and engaging in action more, and making small decisions in the context of their aggregate consequences. It can be time to marry the search for livelihood with structural change, to create new roles, for example those needed in a restoration economy. The young have less invested in the status quo, are more likely to take risks and challenge the order of things, and more likely to embrace the vision of a different society. This group should be engaged with conservation in a more comprehensive way. Almost all great social movements have had a youth organization to help shape and harness the energy of this group. A path to adult group participation helps ensure meaningful activism.

Civic Leaders

Most leaders of communities dependent on "resource" extraction have failed to acknowledge that their economic reliance on the boom and bust condemns them to be at the mercy of often distant decision makers who don't care about the long term or their communities. This goes hand in hand with ignoring overwhelming evidence that communities that protect forests, waters, wildlife, and other natural attributes are economically healthier over the long term (Headwaters Institute 2016, 2017). Some communities or even nations, when led by those with courage, see parks rather than clearcuts. Some places, with varied ethnic and economic composition (not just wealthy gated communities or Vatican City), have resisted growth, especially during periods of rapid in-migration or national increase. In the US these efforts failed in part because growth was deflected to adjacent areas and spilled over. Glickfeld and Levine (1992) argue that a regional rather than town approach would have done better, demonstrating the limits of Nimby on too small a scale. US residents, of course, have a constitutional right to travel within the US.

Nonetheless civic leaders in some places are an example of nontraditional allies.

Groups such as Alternatives to Growth Oregon have also confronted social-psychological barriers when confronting growth. Support is often enthusiastic when growth is rapid but when it slows people fear economic depression. Most people lack a good understanding of how a no-growth economy is different from a growth economy in recession. Absent that understanding, they are unlikely to be easily mobilized to support what in the best of circumstances can be a challenging transition. Oregon has among the strictest land-use laws in the US and they are often cited as an example of smart growth. But like smart bombs, which aren't smart at all, smart growth doesn't ameliorate growth, it simply plans growth. Portland is on its way to becoming Los Angeles even though no collective choice to proceed in that direction has been made.

Even if growth is fast enough to make the shifting baseline apparent to most people, it is doubtful that growth's many annoyances, insults, and injuries can be channeled from road rage into growth rage. For most places, from small towns to cities, regions, and countries, a profound cultural shift is needed – a mythological shift that sees growth as bad and wrong.

Public Health Profession

Increasingly the public heath profession – a major contributor to the global population explosion by reducing human mortality from disease – has been increasing its focus on "the environment" beyond human pathogens and occupational toxics to climate change and ecological health. Though still by and large a human-centered enterprise, the importance of biodiversity health to human health is being increasingly recognized. A project in Uganda, the One Health Initiative, is based on what organizers see as a close relationship between broader biodiversity health and human health, and focuses on "the well-being of all species" and cooperation between veterinarians and other health professionals (Starkey 2016). As an organized group with an understanding of pathology and wellness, and used to trying to influence policy, they are potentially useful allies.

Veterans

Doug Peacock (1990), a Vietnam War veteran, may have been among the first to document the healing power of the natural world and wild creatures when it comes to the psychological wounds inflicted by war. For him protecting both is simple payback. Those who have been violently exploited often have a special sense of justice when it comes to abuse of those who can't easily fight back. Veterans played an important role in the US civil rights movement (Ujoma 2013) and more recently at the Standing Rock protests against a petroleum pipeline (Healy 2016). Although Vietnam and civil rights are an earlier generation – and a generation with leaders who understood the population problem, e.g. Martin Luther King – veterans in some countries see the natural world as a refuge to be defended (e.g. Duvall and Kaplan 2014). Many have directly seen the destructiveness of a huge human population and the contribution it makes to war via dependence on huge energy subsidies and the hierarchy produced by large-scale societies. Veterans also understand organization and self-discipline and make good allies on that count. *Many conservation NGOs count veterans among their activist members rather than separately organized and this is true of many potential allies noted above.*

There are other potential allies than those noted above: some regional, some focused on an aspect of population or consumption or a particular aspect of the fight, e.g. education but not action, direct protection but not human causes. Nationalism, especially anti-colonial nationalism, may be closely wedded to development and growth (US, Vietnam, India); in some few cases such as India in the earlier stages and Nicaragua, the anti-colonial struggle has sought a different path, only to be forcefully diverted by the superpowers or their subalterns. In the Caribbean, anti-colonial nationalism was effective in bringing pressure to bear on those in the parrot trade via the broader population. To sell parrots to wealthy northerners was to sell out the nation and its heritage; it was unpatriotic (Butler 1992). Many will and must be drawn to conservation as the battle plays out, as crises emerge, as institutions break down and old myths offer neither explanation nor guidance. Microtargeting is important: focusing on parts of groups which on the whole are not sympathetic, such as those in extraction-based rural communities that see the costs, and can work from within local communities. Constant tactical innovation is also required to make headway against such enormous forces as growth.

SUMMARY

Addressing the causes of biodiversity and wild place loss is the real work of conservation. Even protected areas won't last without a reversal of growth. It is also the most difficult work. It lacks many of the rewards of working directly with wildlife and places. It is long-term work. It is very difficult to unplug individuals, groups, and societies from the growth machine. There is less and less local or regional autonomy from the global economy. Only the creation of alternative institutions that actually deliver on livelihoods will entice people away, and such institutions are often targeted for destruction.

Alliance- and coalition-building takes time and energy, and sometimes the investment must be carefully weighed. It can be difficult to accurately project payoffs. Opponents are forever trying to sow discord among potential and actual allies.

Most of the potential or actual allies discussed above are organized, at least to some degree. They have resources to act. Action, whether with non-conservation allies or conservation NGOs, generally makes it easier to gain new recruits. There is no substitute for mobilizing new people into conservation NGOs. Although the culture of conquering nature still exists, there is now much less overt hostility to the natural world; indeed, there is growing awareness of the costs of separation. The main threat today is inertia: population and consumption growth on a finite planet are destroying non-human species and degrading natural systems. Understanding this dynamic, who is vested in it, and which groups object to the consequences of growth for reasons unrelated to biodiversity, is important in developing a sound political strategy. The task is urgent. *Human population growth estimates have been revised upward and may not start to slow for another century; hundreds of millions have been added to the global middle class, leading to more and more of the Earth being converted into commodities, depriving other species of their homes and their lives. These negative trends are gaining new attention despite the timidity of bigger conservation groups. Grassroots organizing can starve these trends of oxygen and we will see how in Part III.*

REFERENCES

Alberti, John. 2015. *Screen Ages.* Routledge. Abingdon, Oxon.

American Enterprise Institute (Webb, Bruce G., Edd S. Noell, and Stephen L. S. Smith). 2013. (May 28) *Is Economic Growth Moral?* www.aei.org/publication/is-economic-growth-moral/ (accessed April 11, 2017).

Aminzade, Ronald and Elizabeth J. Perry. 2001. The Sacred, Religious, and Secular in Contentious Politics: Blurring Boundaries. Pp. 155–78 in Ronald R. Aminzade, Jack A. Goldstone, Doug McAdam, et al. *Silence and Voice in the Study of Contentious Politics.* Cambridge University Press. Cambridge UK.

Appel, Markus. 2008. Fictional Narratives Cultivate Just-World Beliefs. 58 *Journal of Communication* 1: 62–83.

Ascione, Frank R. 2005. *Children and Animals, Exploring the Roots of Kindness and Cruelty.* Purdue University Press. West Lafayette, IN.

The Associated Press. 2017. Leaders of IMF and World Bank Defend Globalization. *New York Times,* April 20. www.nytimes.com/aponline/2017/04/20/us/politics/ap-us-global-finance.html?_r=0 (accessed April 22, 2017).

Barcott, Bruce. 2001. For God So Loved the World. 26 *Outside* 3: 84–126.

Barnosky, Anthony D. 2008. Megafauna Biomass Tradeoff as a Driver of Quaternary and Future Extinctions. 105 *Proceedings of the National Academy of Sciences of the United States of America* 11,543–8 (August 12).

Barnosky, Anthony D. and Elizabeth A. Hadly. 2015. *End Game.* Collins. New York.

Bartholomew, Ecumenical Patriarch. 2012. *On Earth as in Heaven.* Fordham University Press. New York.

Becker, Ernest. 1973. *The Denial of Death*. Simon & Schuster. New York.

Benítez-López, A., R. Alkemade, A. M. Schipper, et al. 2017. The Impact of Hunting on Tropical Mammal and Bird Populations. 356 *Science* 180–3 (April 14).

Bernays, Edward S. 1923. *Crystalizing Public Opinion*. Boni & Liveright. New York.

Bernays, Edward S. 1929. *Propaganda*. Liveright. New York.

Bernays, Edward S. (ed.). 1955. *The Engineering of Consent*. University of Oklahoma. Norman, OK.

Best, A. 2002. Water's for Fighting. 3 *Forest Magazine* 6: 41–5.

Bevington, Douglas. 2009. *Rebirth of Environmentalism*. Island Press. Washington DC.

Biel, Robert. 2000. *The New Imperialism*. Zed. London.

Bob, Clifford. 2005. *Marketing Rebellion*. Cambridge University Press. Cambridge.

Boehm, Christopher. 1999. *Hierarchy in the Forest*. Harvard University Press. Cambridge, MA.

Bongaarts, John. 2016. Slow Down Population Growth. 530 *Nature* 409–12 (February 25).

Bookchin, Murray. 1980. *The Ecology of Freedom*. Cheshire Books. San Francisco.

Bretton Woods Project. 2017 (April 6). World Bank Policy Lending Undermines Climate Goals. www.brettonwoodsproject.org/2017/04/world-bank-policy-lend ing-undermines-climate-goals/ (accessed April 22, 2017).

Broadbent, Jeffrey. 2011. Introduction and Conclusion. Pp. 1–29 and 481–93 in Jeffrey Broadbent and Vicky Brockman (eds.). *East Asian Social Movements*. Springer. New York.

Brode, Douglas and Leah Deyneka (eds.). 2012. *Myth, Media, and Culture in Star Wars*. Scarecrow Press. Lanham, MD.

Bromley, Daniel W. 2009. Abdicating Responsibility: The Deceits of Fisheries Policy. 34 *Fisheries* 6: 280–90.

Brooks, L. Anathea and Teresa Chandler. 1994. American Religious Groups and Population Policy. Pp. 303–9 in Laurie Mazur (ed.). *Beyond the Numbers*. Island Press, Washington DC.

Bruce, J. 1994. Population Policy Must Encompass More Than Family Planning Services. Pp. 150–7 in Laurie Mazur (ed.). *Beyond the Numbers*. Island Press. Washington DC.

Butchart, Stuart H. M., Matt Walpole, Ben Collen, et al. 2010. Global Biodiversity: Indicators of Recent Declines. 328 *Science* 1164–8 (May 28).

Butler, Paul J. 1992. Parrots, Pressures, People and Pride. Pp. 25–46 in Steven R. Bessinger and Noel F. R. Snyder (eds.). *New World Parrots Crisis: Solutions from Conservation Biology*. Smithsonian Institution Press. Washington DC.

Butler, Tom (ed.). 2015. *Overpopulation, Overdevelopment, Overshoot*. Goff Books. San Francisco.

Carroll, Sean. 2016. *Serengeti Rules*. Princeton University Press. Princeton, NJ.

Carson, Rachel. 1962. *Silent Spring*. Houghton Mifflin. Boston, MA.

Carter, Neil. 2007. *Politics of the Environment*. 2nd edn. Cambridge University Press. Cambridge.

Ceballos, Gerardo, Paul R. Ehrlich, Anthony D. Barnosky, Andrés García, Robert M. Pringle, and Todd M. Palmer. 2015. Accelerated Modern Human–induced Species Losses: Entering the Sixth Mass Extinction. http://advances .sciencemag.org/content/1/5/e1400253.full (accessed March 29, 2017).

Chase-Dunn, Christopher and E. N. Anderson (eds.). 2005. *The Historical Evolution of World Systems*. Palgrave Macmillan. New York.

Chase-Dunn, Christopher and Thomas D. Hall. 1997. *Rise and Demise*. Westview Press. Boulder, CO.

Chawla, Louise and Harry Heft. 2002. Children's Competence and the Ecology of Communities. 22 *Journal of Environmental Psychology* 201–16.

Clark, Grahame. 1986. *Symbols of Excellence*. Cambridge University Press. Cambridge.

Cohen, Joel E. 2010. Human Population Grows Up. Pp. 27–37 in Laurie Mazur (ed.) *A Pivotal Moment*. Island Press. Washington DC.

Collins, Paul. 2014. Theology Confronts Climate Change and Population. Pp. 153–8 in Jenny Goldie and Katharine Betts (eds.). *Sustainable Futures*. Csiro Publishing. Collingswood, VIC. Based on the Fenner Conference on the Future of Australia, 2013.

Continental Congress, Second (Thomas Jefferson, John Adams, Benjamin Franklin, Roger Sherman, and Robert R. Livingston). 1776. Declaration of Independence. Philadelphia PA. www.archives.gov/founding-docs/declaration-tran script (accessed May 30, 2017).

Coole, Diana. 2012. Too Many Bodies? The Return and Disavowal of the Population Question. 22 *Environmental Politics* 2: 195–215, doi: 10.1080/ 09644016.2012.730268.

Coontz, Robert. 2007. Wedging Sustainability into Public Consciousness. 315 *Science* 1068 (February 23).

Cowlishaw, Guy. 1999. Predicting the Pattern of Decline of African Primate Diversity: An Extinction Debt from Historical Deforestation. 13 *Conservation Biology* 5: 1183–93 (October).

Cox, Robert. 2006. *Environmental Education and the Public Sphere*. Sage. Thousand Oaks, CA.

Crist, Eileen. 2013. Abundant Earth and the Population Question. Pp. 141–53 in Philip Cafaro and Eileen Crist (eds.). *Life on the Brink*. University of Georgia Press. Athens, GA.

Crist, Eileen, Camilo Mora, and Robert Engelman. 2017. The Interaction of Human Population, Food Production, and Biodiversity Protection. 356 *Science* 260–4 (April 21).

Czech, Brian. 2000. *Shoveling Fuel for a Runaway Train*. University of California Press. Berkeley, CA.

Daly, H. 1996. *Beyond Growth*. Beacon Press. Boston, MA.

Daly, H. and J. B. Cobb. 1994. *For the Common Good*. 2nd edn. Beacon Press. Boston, MA.

Daly, Hermann E. and Joshua Farley. 2003. *Ecological Economics*. Island Press. Washington DC.

Daly, Hermann E. and Joshua Farley. 2010. *Ecological Economics*. 2nd edn. Island Press. Washington DC.

Dauvergne, Peter. 2016. *Environmentalism of the Rich*. MIT Press. Cambridge, MA.

Diaz, Robert J. and Rutger Rosenberg. 2008. Spreading Dead Zones and Consequences for Marine Ecosystems. 321 *Science* 926–9 (August 15).

Dietz, Rob and Dan O'Neill. 2013. *Enough is Enough*. Berrett-Koehler. San Francisco.

Dixon-Mueller, R. 1994. Women's Rights and Reproductive Choices: Rethinking Connections. Pp. 227–41 in Laurie Mazur (ed.). *Beyond the Numbers*. Island Press. Washington DC.

Douthwaite, Richard. 1999. *The Growth Illusion*. 2nd edn. New Society Publishers. Gabriola Island, BC.

Dryzek, John S., David Downes, Christian Hunold, and David Schlosberg. 2003. *Green States and Social Movements*. Oxford University Press. Oxford.

Durning, Alan Thein and Christopher D. Crowther. 1997. *Blaming the Victim*. Northwest Environmental Watch. Seattle, WA.

Duvall, Jason and Rachel Kaplan. 2014. Enhancing the Well-being of Veterans Using Extended Group-based Nature Recreation Experiences. 51 *Journal of Rehabilitation Research & Development* 5: 685–96.

Dye, Thomas R. 2013. *Who's Running America?* 8th edn. Paradigm. Boulder, CO.

Edelman, Murray. 1995. *From Art to Politics*. University of Chicago Press. Chicago, IL.

Engelman, Robert. 2016. Six Billion in Africa. 314 *Scientific American* 2: 56–63 (at 62c1).

Ewing, Jeffrey A. 2017. Hollow Ecology: Ecological Modernization Theory and the Death of Nature. 23 *Journal of World-Systems Research* 1: 126–55 (Spring).

Finley, Carmel. 2017. *All the Boats on the Ocean*. University of Chicago Press. Chicago, IL.

Fodor, E. 1998. *The Cost of Growth in Oregon*. Fodor and Associates. Eugene. OR.

Fodor, E. 1999. *Better, Not Bigger*. New Society Publishers. Gabriola Island, BC.

Fodor, E. 2002. *Assessment of Statewide Growth Subsidies in Oregon*. Fodor and Associates, Eugene. OR.

Foreman, Dave. 2011. *Man Swarm*. Raven's Eye Press. Durango, CO.

Freilich, Morris. 1972. Manufacturing Culture: Man the Scientist. Pp. 267–325 in Morris Freilich (ed.). *The Meaning of Culture*. Xerox College Publishing. Lexington, MA.

Gandhi, Mohandis. 1928. Wardha Letter II. 10 *Young India* 51: 422 (December 20). www.gandhiheritageportal.org/journals-by-gandhiji/young-india (accessed May 30, 2017).

GFN (Global Footprint Network). 2016. www.footprintnetwork.org/en/index.php/GFN/page/world_footprint/ (accessed December 24, 2016).

Glickfeld, M. and N. Levine. 1992. *Regional Growth ... Local Reaction*. Lincoln Institute of Land Policy. Cambridge, MA.

Gonzalez, George A. 2001. *Corporate Power and the Environment*. Rowman & Littlefield. Lanham, MD.

Gorz, Andre. 1980. *Ecology as Politics*. South End Press. Boston, MA.

Gossner, Martin M, Thomas M. Lewinsohn, Tiemo Kahl, et al. 2016. Land-use Intensification Causes Multitrophic Homogenization of Grassland Communities. 540 *Nature* 266–9 (December 8).

Gottlieb, Roger S. 2006. *Oxford Handbook of Religion and Ecology*. Oxford University Press. New York.

Goudie, A. 2013. *The Human Impact on the Natural Environment*. 7th edn. Wiley-Blackwell. Chichester.

Guber, Deborah Lynn and Christopher J Bosso. 2007. Framing ANWR. Pp. 35–59 in Michael E. Kraft and Sheldon Kamieniecki (eds.). 2007. *Business and Environmental Policy*. MIT Press. Cambridge, MA.

Gurr, Ted Robert. 1970. *Why Men Rebel*. Princeton University Press. Princeton, NJ.

Hall, Cheryl. 2010. Freedom, Values and Sacrifice. Pp. 61–86 in Michael Maniates and John M. Meyer (eds.). *The Environmental Politics of Sacrifice*. MIT Press. Cambridge, MA.

Halweil Brian and Danielle Nierenberg. 2008. Meat and Seafood: The Global Diet's Most Costly Ingredients. Pp. 61–74 in Linda Starke (ed.). *2008 State of the World*. Worldwatch Institute. Washington DC.

Hames, R. 2007. The Ecologically Noble Savage Debate. 36 *Annual Review of Anthropology* 177–90.

Harris, Jonathan M. 2013. Green Keynesianism. Pp. 69–82 in Robert B. Richardson (ed.). *Building a Green Economy*. Michigan State University Press. East Lansing, MI.

Harris, Marvin. 1977. *Cannibals and Kings*. Random House, New York.

Harris, M. 1989. *Our Kind*. Harper and Row. New York.

Headwaters Economics. 2016. *Protected Lands and Economics: A Summary of Research and Careful Analysis on the Economic Impact of Protected Federal Lands.* https://headwaterseconomics.org/wp-content/uploads/Protected_Lands_Economics.pdf (Fall) (accessed May 30, 2017).

Headwaters Economics. 2017. *Federal Lands in the West: Liability or Asset?* https://headwaterseconomics.org/public-lands/federal-lands-performance/ (February) (accessed May 31, 2017) .

Healy, Jack. 2016. As North Dakota Pipeline is Blocked, Veterans at Standing Rock Cheer. *New York Times*, December 6: A16.

Hecht, Joy E. 2005. *National Environmental Accounting*. RFF Press. Washington DC.

Higgs, Kerryn. 2014. *Collision Course*. MIT Press. Cambridge, MA.

Hughes, Alice C. 2017. Global Roadless Areas: Hidden Roads. 355 *Science* 1381 (March 31).

Hungerford, Harold R. and Trudi L. Volk. 1990. Changing Learner Behavior through Environmental Education. 21 *Journal of Environmental Education* 3: 8–21.

Ibisch, Pierre L., Monika T. Hoffmann, Stefan Kreft, et al. 2016. A Global Map of Roadless Areas and Their Conservation Status. 354 *Science* 1423–7 (December 16).

Jackson, Tim. 2009. *Prosperity without Growth*. Earthscan. London.

Jackson, Wes. 1987. *Altars of Unhewn Stone*. North Point Press. San Francisco, CA.

Jefferson, Thomas. 1903–4 [1814]. Letter to Horatio G. Spafford. In A. A. Lipscomb and A. E. Bergh (eds.). *The Writings of Thomas Jefferson Memorial Edition. Volume 14*. Washington DC.

Jenkins, Willis. 2008. *Ecologies of Grace*. Oxford University Press. New York.

Jimenez, Ignacio. 2017. Presentation: Tompkins Conservation Park Creation. Biodiversity Days March 2–3. Duke University, Durham, NC.

Johns, David. 2003. The Wildlands Project outside North America. Pp. 114–20 in Alan Watson and Janet Sproull (comps.). *Seventh World Wilderness Congress Symposium: Science and Stewardship to Protect and Sustain Wilderness Values, November 2–8, 2001, Port Elizabeth, South Africa*. Proc. RMRS-P-27. US Department of Agriculture, Forest Service, Rocky Mountain Research Station. Ogden, UT.

Johns, David. 2009. *A New Conservation Politics*. Wiley-Blackwell. Chichester.

Johnson, A. W. and T. Earle. 2000. *The Evolution of Human Societies*. 2nd edn. Stanford University Press. Stanford, CA.

Kahn, Peter H. and Stephen R. Kellert (eds.). 2002. *Children and Nature*. MIT Press. Cambridge, MA.

Kairys, David. 1990. Introduction. Pp. 1–8 in David Kairys (ed.). *Politics of Law*. 2nd edn. Pantheon. New York.

Kamieniecki, Sheldon. 2006. *Corporate America and Environmental Policy*. Stanford University Press. Stanford, CA.

Kasser, Tim. 2002. *The High Price of Consumer Culture*. MIT Press. Cambridge, MA.

Kasser, Tim and Allen D. Kanner. 2004. *Psychology and Consumer Culture*. American Psychological Association. Washington DC.

Keck, Margaret E. and Kathryn Sikkink. 1998. *Activists Beyond Borders*. Cornell University Press. Ithaca, NY.

Kerr, Andy. 2000. *Twenty-five Actions to End Growth in Oregon*. Alternatives to Growth Oregon. Portland, OR.

Kissling, Francis. 2010. Reconciling Difference: Population, Reproductive Rights, and the Environment. Pp. 383–91 in Laurie Mazur (ed.). *A Pivotal Moment*. Island Press. Washington DC.

Klare, Michael T. 2002. *Resource Wars*. Owl Books. New York.

Korten, David. 2013. Taking Ecological Economics Seriously. Pp. 19–30 in Robert B. Richardson (ed.). *Building a Green Economy*. Michigan State University Press. East Lansing, MI.

Kovel, Joel. 2007. *The Enemy of Nature*. 2nd edn. Zed Books. London.

Kraft, Michael E. and Sheldon Kamieniecki (eds.). *Business and Environmental Policy*. MIT Press. Cambridge, MA.

Lancy, David. 2008. *The Anthropology of Childhood*. Cambridge University Press. Cambridge.

Langlois, Krista. 2016. Where Private Land Meets Public Interest. *High Country News* (January 4). www.hcn.org/articles/where-private-land-meets-public-interest (accessed June 1, 2017).

Lasch, C. 1978. *The Culture of Narcissism*. Norton. New York.

Layzer, Judith. 2006. *The Environmental Case*. 2nd edn. CQ Press. Washington DC.

Layzer, Judith. 2012. *The Environmental Case*. 3rd edn. CQ Press. Washington DC.

Layzer, Judith. 2016. *The Environmental Case*. 4th edn. Sage/CQ. Los Angeles.

Lebow, Victor. 1955. Price Competition in 1955. 31 *Journal of Retailing* 1: 5–10, 42 & 44 (Spring).

Le Roy, Greg. 2005. *The Great American Jobs Scam*. Barrett-Koehler. San Francisco.

Li, Minqi. 2008. *The Rise of China and the Demise of the Capitalist World Economy*. Pluto Press. London.

Lindblom, C. 1977. *Politics and Markets*. Basic Books. New York.

Lindenmayer, David. 2014. The Environmental Implications of Population Growth. Pp. 7–11 in Jenny Goldie and Katharine Betts (eds.). *Sustainable Futures*. Csiro

Publishing. Collingswood, VIC. (Fenner Conference on the Future of Australia, 2013.)

Lipin, Lawrence M. 2007. *Workers and the Wild*. University of Illinois Press. Urbana, IL.

Liu, Hwa-Jen. 2015. *Leverage of the Weak*. University of Minnesota Press. Minneapolis, MN.

Liu, Jianguo. 2010. China's Road to Sustainability. 328 *Science* 50 (April 2) .

Loftus-Farren, Zoe. 2017. Youth Voices Are Powerful. 32 *Earth Island Journal* 1: 47–8.

Lorbiecki, Marybeth. 2017. Personal Communications, February 6 and July 4.

Louv, Richard. 2005. *Last Child in the Woods*. Algonquin. Chapel Hill, NC.

Low, Bobbi S. 2013. Noble Savages or Consummate Consumers? Pp. 45–67 in Robert B. Richardson (ed.). *Building a Green Economy*. Michigan State University Press. East Lansing, MI.

Luders, Joseph E. 2010. *The Civil Rights Movement and the Logic of Social Change*. Cambridge University Press. Cambridge.

Machiavelli, Niccolò. 1996 [1531]. *Discourses on Livy*. University of Chicago Press. Chicago, IL.

Macklin, Ruth. 1994. Ethical Issues in Reproductive Health. Pp. 191–8 in Laurie Mazur (ed.). *Beyond the Numbers*. Island Press. Washington DC.

Males, M. A. 1996. *Scapegoat Generation: America's War on Adolescents*. Common Courage Press. Monroe, ME.

Maniates, Michael. 2010. Struggling with Sacrifice. Pp. 293–312 in Michael Maniates and John M. Meyer (eds.). *The Environmental Politics of Sacrifice*. MIT Press. Cambridge, MA.

Martin, Chris. 2015. *Conservation Finance 101*. Conservation Finance Network. www.conservationfinancenetwork.org/conservation-finance-101 (accessed May 30, 2017).

Martin-Schram, James B. 1994. Population Policies and Christian Ethics. Pp. 310–17 in Laurie Mazur (ed.). *Beyond the Numbers*. Island Press. Washington DC.

Marx, Karl. 1954 [1887]. *Capital I*. Progress Publishers. Moscow.

Marx, Karl. 1959 [1894]. *Capital III*. Progress Publishers. Moscow.

Masterson, James (ed.). 2006. *The Personality Disorders through the Lens of Attachment Theory and Neurobiological Development of the Self*. Zeig, Tucker & Theisen. Phoenix, AZ.

Mazur, Laurie. 2010. Introduction. Pp. 1–23 in Laurie Mazur (ed.). *A Pivotal Moment*. Island Press. Washington DC.

McClone, Matt. 2012. The Hunters Did It. 335 *Science* 1452–3 (March 23).

McDuff, Mallory. 2010. *Natural Saints*. Oxford University Press. New York.

McKee, Jeffrey K. 2003. *Sparing Nature*. Rutgers University Press. New Brunswick, NJ.

Meadows, Donella H., Dennis L. Meadows, Jørgen Randers, and William W. Behrens III. 1972. *Limits to Growth*. Universe Books. New York.

Michaux, Simon. 2014. The Coming Radical Change in Mining Practice. Pp. 73–84 in Jenny Goldie and Katharine Betts (eds.). *Sustainable Futures*. Csiro Publishing. Collingswood, VIC.

Mills, Stephanie. 2013. Nulliparity and a Cruel Hoax Revisited. Pp. 154–9 in Philip Caforo and Eileen Crist (eds.). *Life on the Brink*. University of Georgia Press. Athens, GA.

Miroff, Bruce, Todd Swanstrom, Tom DeLuca, and Raymond Seidelman. 2014. *The Democratic Debate*. 6th edn. Wadsworth Publishing. Belmont, CA.

Montgomery, David R. 2007. *Dirt, The Erosion of Civilizations*. University of California Press. Berkeley, CA.

Moore, Barrington. 1967. *The Social Origins of Dictatorship and Democracy*. Beacon Press. Boston, MA.

Moran, Daniel and Keiichiro Kanemoto. 2017. Identifying Species Threat Hotspots from Global Supply Chains. 1 *Nature Ecology Evolution* 23: 1–5 (January 4).

Myers, Olin Eugene and Carol D. Saunders. 2002. Animals as Links toward Developing Caring Relationships with the Natural World. Pp. 153–78 in Peter H. Kahn and Stephen R. Kellert (eds.). *Children and Nature*. MIT Press. Cambridge, MA.

Nabhan, Gary Paul and Stephen Trimble (eds.). 1994. *The Geography of Childhood*. Beacon Press. Boston, MA.

Nadeau, Robert. 2003. *The Wealth of Nature: How Mainstream Economics Failed the Environment*. Columbia University Press. New York.

Nadeau, Robert L. 2006. *The Environmental Endgame*. Rutgers University Press. New Brunswick, NJ.

Nash, Roderick. 2014. *Wilderness and the American Mind*. 4th edn. Yale University Press. New Haven, CT.

NGS/Globescan. 2015. *Reducing Demand for Ivory*. National Geographic Press. Washington DC.

Nield, David. 2015. Our Smartphone Addiction is Costing the Earth. www.techradar.com/news/phone-and-communications/mobile-phones/our-smartphone-addiction-is-costing-the-earth-1299378 (April 4) (accessed April 18, 2017).

Niemi, E. and M. Gall. 1998. *The Economics of ICBEMP: An Initial Assessment of the Draft Environmental Impact Statement for the Interior Columbia Basin Ecosystem Management Project*. ECONorthwest. Portland, OR.

Niemi E., E. MacMullan, E. Whitlaw, and D. Taylor. 1996. *The Potential Economic Consequences of Designating Critical Habitat for the Marbled*

Murrelet, Final Report to the US Fish and Wildlife Service. ECONorthwest. Portland, OR.

Niemi, E., P. Courant, and E. Whitelaw. 1997. *The Ecosystem–Economy Relationship: Insights from Six Forested LTER sites, Report to the National Science Foundation.* ECONorthwest, Portland, OR.

Niemi, E., E. Whitlaw, and A. Johnson. 1999a. *The Sky Did Not Fall: the Pacific Northwest's Response to Logging Reductions.* ECONorthwest. Portland, OR.

Niemi, E., M. Gall, and A. Johnston. 1999b. *An Economy in Transition: The Klamath-Siskiyou Ecoregion.* ECONorthwest, Portland, OR.

Norris, Pippa and Ronald Inglehart. 2004. *Sacred and Secular.* Cambridge University Press. Cambridge.

Noss, Reed. 1992. The Wildlands Project Land Conservation Strategy. *Wild Earth* Special Issue: 10–25.

Obach, Brian K. 2004. *Labor and the Environmental Movement: The Quest for Common Ground.* MIT Press. Cambridge, MA.

O'Conner, Mark. 2014. What Population Growth Will Do to Australia's Society and Economy. Pp. 37–45 in Jenny Goldie and Katharine Betts (eds.). *Sustainable Futures.* Csiro Publishing. Collingswood, VIC. (Fenner Conference on the Future of Australia, 2013.)

O'Connor, James. 1973. *Fiscal Crisis of the State.* St Martin's. New York.

Ophuls, William. 2011. *Plato's Revenge.* MIT Press. Cambridge, MA.

Otto, Shawn. 2016. *The War on Science.* Milkweed Editions. Minneapolis, MN.

Ovid (Publius Ovidius Naso). 2001 [16 BCE]. Amores III, Elegy 8. Translated by A. S. Kline. www.poetryintranslation.com/PITBR/Latin/AmoresBkIII.htm#anchor_Toc520536664 (accessed April 8, 2017).

Palmer, Tim. 2013. Beyond Futility. Pp. 98–107 in Philip Caforo and Eileen Crist (eds.). *Life on the Brink.* University of Georgia Press. Athens, GA.

Payne, Jonathan L., Andrew M. Bush, Noel A. Heim, Matthew L. Knope, and Douglas J. McCauley. 2016. Ecological Selectivity of the Emerging Mass Extinction in the Oceans. *Science.* doi: 10.1126/science.aaf2416.

Peacock, Doug. 1990. *Grizzly Years.* Holt. New York.

Pech, Roger P., Anthony D. Arthur, Yanming Zhang, and Hui Lin. 2007. Population Dynamics and Responses to Management of Plateau Pikas *Ochotona curzonae.* 44 *Journal of Applied Ecology* 3: 615–24 (June).

Peet, John. 1992. *Energy and the Ecological Economics of Sustainability.* Island Press. Washington DC.

People's Daily. 2011. http://en.people.cn/90882/7629166.html accessed March 16, 2017).

Peterson, Anna. 2010. Ordinary and Extraordinary Sacrifices. Pp. 91–115 in Michael Maniates and John M. Meyer (eds.). *The Environmental Politics of Sacrifice.* MIT Press. Cambridge, MA.

Pimentel, David. 2009. Energy Inputs in Food Crop Production in Developing and Developed Nations. 2 *Energies* 1–24. doi: 10.3390/en20100001 (accessed May 26, 2017).

Pimentel, David, L. E. Hurd, A. C. Bellotti, et al. 1973. Food Production and the Energy Crisis. 182 *Science* 443–9 (November 2).

Pimm, Stuart, C. N. Jenkins, R. Abell, et al. 2014. Biodiversity of Species and Their Rates of Extinction, Distribution, and Protection. 344 *Science* 987 (May 30).

Pletscher, D. H. and M. K. Schwartz. 2000. The Tyranny of Population Growth. 14 *Conservation Biology* 6: 1918–20 (December).

Post, Jerrold M. 1997. Narcissism and the Quest for Political Power. Pp. 195–232 in Carolyn S. Ellman and Joseph Reppen (eds.). *Omnipotent Fantasies and the Vulnerable Self.* Jason Aronson. Lanham, MD.

Pringle, Heather. 2014. The Ancient Roots of the 1%. 344 *Science* 822–5 (May 22).

Protess, Ben and Jessica Silver-Greenberg. 2012. HSBC to Pay 1.2 Billion to Settle Charges of Money Laundering. *New York Times*, December 11: A1.

Ramachandran, Sudha. 2016. The Cost of Interlinking India's Rivers. *The Diplomat* (20 July). https://thediplomat.com/2016/07/the-cost-of-interlinking-indias-rivers/ (accessed October 20, 2017).

Rambo, Lewis R. 1993. *Understanding Religious Conversion.* Yale University Press. New Haven, CT.

Rappaport, Roy A. 1999. *Ritual and Religion in the Making of Humanity.* Cambridge University Press. Cambridge.

Rasker, R. and B. Alexander. 1997. *The New Challenge: People, Commerce and the Environment in the Yellowstone to Yukon Region.* The Wilderness Society. Washington, DC.

Repetto, Robert (ed.). 2006. *Punctuated Equilibrium and the Dynamics of US Environmental Policy.* Yale University Press. New Haven, CT.

Rice, Ronald E. and Charles K. Atkin (eds.). 2001. *Public Communication Campaigns.* 3rd edn. Sage Publications. Thousand Oaks, CA.

Roberts, Callum. 2007. *An Unnatural History of the Sea.* Island Press. Washington DC.

Roodman, D. M. 1996. *Paying the Piper: Subsidies, Politics and the Environment.* World Watch Institute. Washington DC.

Roodman, D. M. 1997. *Getting the Signals Right: Tax Reform to Protect the Environment and the Economy.* World Watch Institute. Washington DC.

Roosevelt, Theodore. The New Nationalism. Speech. Delivered August 31, 1910, at the dedication of the John Brown Memorial Park in Osawatomie, Kansas.

Pp. 211–23 in Ronald J. Pestritto and William J. Atto (eds.). *American Progressivism: A Reader*. Lexington Books. Lanham, MD.

Rosenblatt, R. (ed.). 1999. *Consuming Desires: Consumption, Culture and the Pursuit of Happiness*. Island Press, Washington DC.

Rosenzweig, Michael L. 2001. Loss of Speciation Rate Will Impoverish Future Diversity. 98 *Proceedings of the (US) National Academy of Sciences* 10: 5404–10 (May 10).

Rule, Susan, Barry W. Brook, Simon G. Haberle, Chris S. M. Turney, A. Peter Kershaw, and Christopher N. Johnson. 2012. The Aftermath of Megafaunal Extinction: Ecosystem Transformation in Pleistocene Australia. 335 *Science* 1483–6 (March 23).

Ryerson, William. 2013. *Global Innovation, Local Success*. Population Media Center. Shelburne, VT.

Ryerson, William. 2014. *The Effectiveness of Entertainment Mass Media in Changing Behavior*. Population Media Center. Shelburne, VT.

Sachs, Jonah. 2012. *Winning the Story Wars*. Harvard Business Review Press. Boston, MA.

Sahgal, Bittu. 2017. Personal Communication (October 19).

Scheidel, Walter. 2017. *The Great Leveler*. Princeton University Press. Princeton, NJ.

Schell, Orville. 1984. *To Get Rich is Glorious*. Pantheon Books. New York.

Sciberras, Marija, Stuart R. Jenkins, Michel J. Kaiser, Stephen J. Hawkins, and Andrew S. Pullin. 2013. Evaluating the Biological Effectiveness of Fully and Partially Protected Marine Areas. 2 *Environmental Evidence* 4 (www.environmentalevidencejournal.org/content/2/1/4).

Scott, James C. 1998. *Seeing Like a State*. Yale University Press. New Haven, CT.

Scott, J. Michael. 2008. *Threats to Biological Diversity: Global, Continental, Local*. US Geological Survey, Idaho Cooperative Fish and Wildlife Research Unit. University of Idaho. Moscow, ID.

Searles, Harold F. 1960. *The Non-human Environment in Normal Development and in Schizophrenia*. International Universities Press. New York.

Sebba, Rachel. 1991. The Landscapes of Childhood. 23 *Environment and Behavior* 4: 395–422 (July).

Shapiro, J. 2001. *Mao's War against Nature*. Cambridge University Press. Cambridge.

Shepard, Paul. 1982. *Nature and Madness*. Sierra Club Books. San Francisco.

Simon and Company. 2001. *Washington Friday Report*. Simon and Company, Inc. Washington DC (February 23, p. 1).

Smith, Adam. 1976 [1759]. *Theory of Moral Sentiments*. Clarendon Press. Oxford.

Smith, Adam. 1976 [1776]. *An Inquiry into the Causes of The Wealth of Nations*. Clarendon Press. Oxford.

Solomon, Sheldon, Jeffrey L. Greenberg, and Thomas A Pyszczynski. 2004. Lethal Consumption: Death-Denying Materialism. Pp. 127–46 in Tim Kasser and Allen D. Kanner. 2004. *Psychology and Consumer Culture*. American Psychological Association. Washington, DC.

Sparshott, Jeffrey. 2016. US Houses Are Still Getting Bigger. *Wall Street Journal*. http://blogs.wsj.com/economics/2016/06/02/u-s-houses-are-still-getting-bigger/ (accessed January 5, 2017).

Starky, Marian. 2016. Editor's Note. 48 *Population Connection* 4: 2. See also pp. 14–21.

Statista. Worldwide Automobile Production from 2000 to 2016. www.statista.com/statistics/262747/Worldwide-Automobile-Production-Since-2000 (accessed April 26, 2017).

Taylor, Andrea Faber, Frances E. Kuo, and William C. Sullivan. 2002. Views of Nature and Self-Discipline: Evidence from Inner City Children. 22 *Journal of Environmental Psychology* 49–63.

Taylor, Bron, Gretel Van Wieren, and Bernard Daley Zaleha. 2016. Lynn White Jr. and the Greening-of-religion Hypothesis. 30 *Conservation Biology* 5: 1000–9 (October).

Thapar, Valmik. 2006. *The Last Tiger*. Oxford University Press. New Dehli.

Theobald, David, J. R. Miller, and N. T. Hobbs. 1997. Estimating the Cumulative Effects of Development on Wildlife Habitat. 39 *Landscape and Urban Planning* 25–36.

Thoreau, Henry David. 1964 [1854]. *Walden*. 2nd edn. Pp. 258–572 in Carl Bode (ed.). *The Portable Thoreau*. Viking. New York.

Tigay, Jeffrey H. 1982. *Evolution of the Gilgamesh Epic*. University of Pennsylvania. Philadelphia, PA.

Trent, Judith S. and Robert V. Friedenberg. 2004. *Political Campaign Communication*. 5th edn. Rowman & Littlefield. Latham, MD.

Tucker, Richard P. 2007. *Insatiable Appetite*. 2nd edn (concise rev. edn). Rowman & Littlefield. Lanham, MD.

Ujoma, Akinyele Omowale. 2013. *We Will Shoot Back*. New York University Press. New York.

United Nations. 1948. *Universal Declaration of Human Rights*. www.ohchr.org/EN/UDHR/Documents/UDHR_Translations/eng.pdf (accessed May 28, 2017).

United Nations. Department of Economic and Social Affairs. 2017. World Population Prospects: The 2017 Revision. www.un.org/development/desa/publications/world-population-prospects-the-2017-revision.html (accessed September 29, 2017).

Veil, Simone. 1978. Human Rights, Ideologies, and Population Policies. 4 *Population and Development Review* 2: 313–21 (June).

Victor, David G, Keigo Akimoto, Yoichi Kaya, Mitsutsune Yamaguchi, Danny Cullenward, and Cameron Hepburn. 2017. Prove Paris Was More Than Paper Promises. 548 *Nature* 25–27 (August 3).

Victor, Peter A. 2008. *Managing without Growth*. Edward Elgar. Cheltenham.

Wallach, Arian D., Marc Bekoff, Chelsea Batavia, Michael Paul Nelson, and Daniel Ramp. 2018. Summoning Compassion to Address the Challenges of Conservation. 32 *Conservation Biology* 6: 1255–65.

Wang, Hua and Arvind Singhal. 2016. East Los High: Transmedia Edutainment to Promote the Sexual and Reproductive Health of Young Latina/o Americans. 106 *American Journal of Public Health* 6: 1002–10.

Watson, James E. M., Kendall R. Jones, Richard A. Fuller, et al. 2016 Persistent Disparities between Recent Rates of Habitat Conversion and Protection and Implications for Future Global Conservation Targets. 9 *Conservation Letters* 6: 413–21 (November/December).

Weeden, Don and Charmayne Palomba. 2013. A Post Cairo Paradigm. Pp. 255–73 in Philip Cafora and Eileen Crist (eds.). *Life on the Brink*. University of Georgia Press. Athens, GA.

Wijkman, Anders and Johan Rockstrom. 2012. *Bankrupting Nature*. 2nd edn. Routledge/Earthscan. Abingdon, Oxon.

WILDAID. 2017. Ivory. www.wildaid.org/tags/ivory?page=1 (accessed October 1, 2017).

Williams, Michael. 2003. *Deforesting the Earth*. University of Chicago Press. Chicago, IL.

Wilson, E. O. 1984. *Biophilia*. Harvard University Press, Cambridge, MA.

Wilson, E. O. 2002. The Bottleneck. 286 *Scientific American* 2: 82–91 (February).

Wilson, E. O. 2016. *Half-Earth*. Liveright. New York.

Wood, Elisabeth Jean. 2000. *Forging Democracy from Below*. Cambridge University Press. Cambridge.

Worster, Donald. 1985. *Rivers of Empire*. Pantheon, New York.

Wright, Ronald. 2004. *A Short History of Progress*. Anansi. Toronto.

Wu Ruidong, Wenli Wang, Feiling Yang, et al. 2017. Global Roadless Areas: Consider Terrain. 355 *Science* 1381 (March 31).

WWF. 2014. *Living Planet Report 2014: Species and Spaces, People and Places*. WWF. Gland, Switzerland.

WWF. 2016. *Living Planet Report 2016. Risk and Resilience in a New Era*. WWF International. Gland, Switzerland.

Xin, Hao. 2008. A Green Fever Sweeps the Quinghai-Tibetan Plateau. 321 *Science* 633–5.

Yeh, Emily T. 2009. Greening Western China: A Critical View. 40 *Geoforum* 5: 884–94 (September).

Zeng, Jinghan, 2014. Institutionalization of the Authoritarian Leadership in China: A Power Succession System with Chinese Characteristics? 20 *Contemporary Politics* 3: 294–314 (July).

Zheng, Heran and Shixiong Cao. 2014. Threats to Biodiversity by Contradictions Policy. 44 *AMBIO* 1: 23–33 (February).

6   Domination and the Intractability of Energy Problems

Energy is thus a generalized attribute of physical transformation and change, not a commodity.

John Peet (1992: 28)

It's too early to tell how far beyond promises the Paris Climate Accord will go – an accord many consider weak to begin with and some think is failing to deliver (Victor et al. 2017). At least one head of state has withdrawn under the influence of energy interests and medieval ideologues. But the climate change underway is only one of the exorbitant costs of human societies' reliance on enormous energy subsidies. Virtually all species have only the calories they burn from food to go about their lives, including getting more calories to sustain themselves. The Sun's energy converted by photosynthesis is considered the foundation of the food web, but many species exploit air and water currents, geothermal energy, and other sources of energy. Humans, however, have learned how to supplement their own direct caloric intake and expenditure by domesticating animals and exploiting their labor (caloric expenditures); humans commandeer other humans for their labor, or otherwise exploit them by paying fewer calories than their subalterns produce; humans steal from each other at large scales and small, seizing productive lands and waters and going so far as to institutionalize these transfers; but nothing compares with the recent capacity of humans to make use of energy stocks such as fossil fuels and uranium which have been eons in the making.

   The discovery and extraction of vast amounts of fossil fuel stocks and the development of technology that utilizes these stocks, dense with calories, has vastly increased the amount of energy available to some human societies. David Pimentel et al. (1973; and Pimentel 2009) estimate that for every calorie put on the table at the time of their writing, 10 calories were expended; he noted that the real amount is likely double that. A more recent estimate is that each American has on average 100 energy slaves (2,000 calories a day × 100) available at any time (Boyden 1987); by 2006 the estimate was 147 energy slaves per capita for the US (Barker 2006). For other developed countries the amount is much lower; and it is much lower still for poorer countries. Humans also commandeer, consume, or destroy about 40 percent of terrestrial net primary product, or the energy produced by plants which they do not directly consume (Vitousek et al. 1986).

Prior to 1820 most energy at the call of humans was biological and mechanical: human power, animal power, burning wood. Even then we were taking an outsize share of what plants produced and substituting our monocultures for more complex plant assemblages. In the last half of the nineteenth century, coal and then oil were extracted and burned and dams began to be used to produce electricity to do a variety of work, followed by natural gas in the twentieth century, and other sources. About 20 exajoules of energy were used by humanity in 1820 (each exajoule equals 23 quadrillion calories or the equivalent of 24 million tons of oil). By 1950 about 100 exajoules (5× 1820) were consumed; that doubled by 1965, doubled again to 400 exajoules by 1990 and will continue to grow exponentially according to the US Energy Information Administration (2013; Smil 2010).

In conjunction with public health this energy has fueled population growth (from about 1 billion in 1820 to more than 7.5 billion today). Energy-intensive technology has made it much easier to convert land to agriculture and increase the amounts grown through irrigation and adding fertilizers (Wes Jackson [1984] describes modern agriculture as the mining of soil to turn oil into food.) The magnification of the human impact has greatly increased the human ability to alter ecological systems, land forms, atmosphere, the lives of non-human animals, and much else (Goudie 2013). Ax and shovel and spear can do great damage to the natural world and to people; in the hands of enough people and given enough time, species and whole places can be destroyed. But what a difference chainsaws, bulldozers, water pumps and other energy-intensive technologies make. Energy subsidies are fundamental to the economic growth of the recent period (Ayres and Voudouris 2014).

The alterations humans have worked have taken a heavy toll on the natural world. Conservationists know all too well the biological price of the human quest for energy, from habitat destruction and fragmentation and species loss to climate change (Goudie 2013). The costs of obtaining and using massive energy subsidies have an enormous price tag for most humans as well. China's governors were recently bringing a new coal-fired power plant on line every few days even as their people choke and sicken from the smog. A dozen "post-industrial" countries started a brutal war in the mountains and deserts of southwest Asia over oil – just one in a long series – while other countries engage in a mix of diplomacy, intrigue, skirmishes, covert operations, terrorist incidents, and low-intensity wars (for the victims it's *all* terrorism) over energy sources. Western military bases stand as sentries along energy pipelines in central Asia, and Western fleets patrol the oil shipping lanes, while at home civil liberties are sacrificed to the "emergency." Chinese leaders have announced major increases in naval and military spending.

Why, given the cost in natural and human treasure, is it so difficult to get energy consumption under control and address the social and natural costs generated by obtaining energy, its transmission, and its use? That the obsession with obtaining caloric subsidies is not new but deeply rooted in the history of our species (White 1969, 1987; Johnson and Earle 2000; Wright 2004; Smil 2017), points us toward an answer. It has little to do with air conditioners, the weakness of the conservation movement, or the educated person's lack of understanding that although the human economy is measured in dollars it rests on nature's economy, which is all about calories

(Peet, 1992). Instead it has to do with the centrality of energy to maintaining political and economic hierarchy, the management by leaders of masses of people and of other societies, and the deep-seated anxiety many feel over powerlessness and mortality.

It is no accident that the words "energy" and "power" are used interchangeably in many circumstances. Virtually all human societies today are, and perhaps almost all over the last 12,000 years have been, hierarchical. Even so-called democracies are usually oligarchies. The control and allocation of energy in many forms, from high-protein foods, to irrigation works, domestic livestock, and ultimately oil, are major sources of political power (White 1969). Maintaining political control and acquiring new energy supplies are central goals of the powerful, and having energy to begin with is a great advantage. It not only takes energy to get energy, as with drilling for oil, mining for coal, but to move these calories over great distances and defend shipping lanes and pinch points (Suez, Panama). The rate of return is slipping: it now takes more energy to obtain the same amount of energy of virtually every type (Hall et al. 2014), especially the more energy-dense types such as coal and oil, which are especially import-ant to feeding economic growth rates (Ayres and Voudouris 2014), which enables the control of goods and services that buy the loyalty or acquiescence of a variety of groups to existing political and eco-nomic arrangements.

It does not matter that elites do not think in terms of calories or joules or understand the world-historical evolution of energy subsidies and power. They do understand that their power within a society and the relative power of their society compared with other societies, depends on the control of energy and using it strategically. Energy is more than just a commodity; it is pivotal to the production of all commodities. Oxen and serfs and forests with wood to burn may once have been a measure of control and wealth, but the energy margins were thin though real. The energy that has come with and makes possible industrialization, including the global division of labor, global enterprises, and the gargantuan instruments of repression, has generated a degree of hierarchy never before possible or even imagined. It's doubtful Caesar could have imagined the Central Intelligence Agency, airborne troops with global reach, flying armored chariots to a battlefield, let alone intercontinental ballistic missiles or strategic attack submarines. The grim metric of body counts is discussed below.

The essential role of energy in political power becomes much clearer when the relationship between societies is examined. Those societies that have harnessed relatively greater energy subsidies have pushed aside, conquered, absorbed, or destroyed societies that have controlled less energy or used it less effectively (White 1969, 1987). Hunting and gathering cultures – those with the lowest subsidies and the most ecologically friendly form of human social organization – have disappeared except in "peripheral" areas of the globe. Wealthy countries dominate the poorer countries *in part* because the former harnessed energy in greater amounts earlier, and have sustained the advantage over time, using it to extract wealth (and energy) from poorer countries. Domination depends on energy, and energy subsidies enable domination. Domination makes possible and requires the capture of more energy than competitors.

It should be no surprise that for about 100 years Britain and the US have coveted southwest Asian oil fields and constantly intervened in the region to secure energy supplies (Phillips 2006). With Saudi fields peaking, Iranian oil fields in "hostile" hands, and Iraqi oil fields largely untapped, the latter became a prime target for those wanting to ensure future energy supplies for themselves. The invasion of Iraq is in character with past behavior.[1] But what is largely ignored – especially in the face of the media and academic focus on US

---

[1] Following the OPEC oil embargo in 1973 the US Nixon government undertook comprehensive planning for an invasion of Middle Eastern oil countries. US President Jimmy Carter warned the Soviets after their invasion of Afghanistan in 1979 to keep out of Iran, Saudi Arabia and the rest of the oil-rich region; any threats to these countries would be considered threats against the US (Phillips 2006). In 1953, when the democratically elected Iranian prime minister nationalized the oil industry (which was owned by the British), the US engineered a coup, placing the Shah in power. The US gained not only a friendly tyrant who would ensure oil

ineptitude in the invasion and follow-up – is the central role of energy in making the invasion politically possible for Western countries. Energy fuels the weapons of war and the technology that makes the weapons of war, allowing those with the technology and energy to overcome those without it – *at least for a while.*

The vast industrial complex fueled by massive energy consumption gives a related advantage to those who possess it – it allows them to fight with relatively little loss of life for their combatants and civilians. Nixon's Vietnamization of a war five decades ago made it clear that Americans would tolerate loss of non-American lives so long as the body bags of Americans stopped coming home. With machines that run on oil, and with oil-fed factories that make the machines, the US and similar societies can fight capital-intensive wars, insulating themselves from the high political costs of domestic casualties. The use of drones is perhaps the most developed example of this. Those without access to the machinery must fight with their bodies, or try to turn the machines of their opponents against them. Three million Vietnamese were killed in the fight to throw the US out of Vietnam; 58,000 Americans died to maintain US presence. Asymmetric conflicts such as Vietnam, other anti-colonial and anti-imperial struggles, and energy wars in southwest Asia do not guarantee victory for the most powerful. Indeed, since World War II, the weaker powers won just more than half the time (Arreguin-Toft 2005). Factors such as strategy, leadership, and political circumstances are important as well.

Fossil energy is to some extent being replaced by other sources in an effort to mitigate climate warming and its consequences. Almost all renewable energy, however, only makes electricity, and electricity only comprises 20 percent of the energy used in rich

supplies to the West, but US oil companies gained direct control of a substantial portion of Iranian oil production. In the 1920s and 1930s then US Secretary of the Treasury Andrew Mellon's Gulf Oil acquired the oil concession in Kuwait, Socal and Texaco the concession from the Saudis. US and other developed-country meddling continues as China competes more strongly for calorie-dense sources of energy.

countries (Trainer 2014). Biomass can generate liquid fuels, but nowhere as energy-dense as oil and it cannot remotely replace oil because land is needed for food and other uses. The energy return on investment (EROI) for biomass is also very low compared to most oil extracted. Biomass and other energy sources cannot match the versatility of oil. All sources of energy – dams, solar panels, nuclear power plants – are made with energy and with material manufactured using energy. Most estimates of energy embedded in non-fossil energy generation are underestimates. The many other materials important to industrial–consumer economies, from rare earths to phosphate for fertilizers, also take energy to obtain, transport, and utilize, including military and economic coercion to obtain access and protect supply lines.

There is widespread awareness, if not understanding, of the importance of calories to the machinery of developed societies. But many people still seem willing to believe highly improbable cover stories concocted to justify war and the pursuit of energy and other materials, and the destruction of countless lives of creatures of many species to obtain them. Even those who see through the stories rarely act.

Given the investment in control of energy by elites and institutions, what can conservationists do? Power is rarely relinquished by individuals or societies. If humans damaged by the pursuit of energy do not rebel, what are the chances of people rebelling on behalf of nature? Relying on improvements in energy efficiency to check the overall effect of humans on the natural world is as absurd as pundits and US officials predicting that Iraqis would welcome them as liberators and that the economy could be rebuilt within a year using its own oil revenue.

The reality of energy subsidies as the core of economic growth and military power confronts conservationists with the revolutionary nature of the task ahead of them. Challenges to growth in energy demand and its drivers are likely to be seen as hostile. Past challenges to the status quo that have generated major societal transformations have resulted in strengthening hierarchy, the institutions of control, and imposed greater intensification of extraction and efforts to control and rearrange the biological and ecological world relying on more energy appropriation (e.g. White 1987 [1975]; Smil 2017). In short, transitions have enhanced power – the control of the few over the many and the control of the natural world by humans. What the biological health of the world requires is not new forms of energy or power but dramatically less energy in the hands of humans and the dismantling of control mechanisms. That hierarchy, growth in energy use, and efforts at human control of the world have grown with population only makes the matter more urgent (Harris, 1977, 1989; Boehm 1999; Johnson and Earle 2000).

Reducing energy subsidies markedly and human institutions of control represents a break with 12,000 years of growing hierarchy (Johnson and Earle 2000) and charting a new direction for society and for politics. Elite investment in energy subsidies as an instrument of control and fear of what might happen if that control seemed to be slipping are major obstacles to basic change. Indeed, the "collapse" of the Soviet Union – the loss of power by the center and the subsequent devolution of power to smaller centers, often corrupt, ineffective at governing, and overwhelmed by newly intrusive multinational corporations – is a reminder that the cause for concern is genuine. The volunteer path away from these subsidies – to avoid hitting the wall, to protect biodiversity, and to recover less hierarchical human societies – is unlikely to be linear, but will be characterized by all the back and forth of any major political struggle. We know what societies without institutionalized power look like. But they were and are small – at most a few hundred people, and usually less than fifty people. Seven and a half billion is a long way from that. The preceding chapter sought to demonstrate that reversing, not simply slowing, population growth, is urgent.

The problem of disarmament suggests a way through some of the initial difficulties. As with disarmament, no one wants to reduce energy use first or alone. The potential for destabilization makes the status quo appealing despite its high costs.

But disarmament has succeeded in some cases, such as the Strategic Arms Limitation Talks (SALT I and SALT II). It requires a shared recognition of dangers and costs; a manageable framework for reduction in arms (or energy use); verification cannot depend on trust; implementation must be slow enough to allow for some stability as adjustments are made to less energy use and changes in infrastructure; and some state or group of states must offer incentives to states especially disadvantaged. Can conservationists bring such pressure on a group of states? Or leverage these states' recognition of the need for change? Conservationists lack the political muscle at present and don't even seem to think in the terms we have been discussing. The conservation agenda will need to explicitly address overall energy use and control, not just changing out combustion motors for batteries.

There are two very problematic obstacles to constraining energy use, which we noted briefly in Chapter 5. One relates to human anxiety over mortality when we separate ourselves from the natural world with agriculture and its consequences (Berman 2000). The story of Gilgamesh and his quest for immortality through conspicuous consumption still resonates (Tigay 1982). Why it is that ongoing consumption should assuage mortality anxiety is not completely understood, but where it is an option it is preferred to religious belief in immortality and seeking immortality through children (Becker 1973; Solomon et al. 2004). Unlike in foraging societies, humans and non-humans live in different worlds with the coming of agriculture; we live in an alien cocoon populated by things (Searles 1960; Berman 1989, 2000).

Although the varieties of soothing mortality anxiety are not mutually exclusive, and although having children actually has a material basis in an immortality of sorts – felt but not understood in previous eras – consumption has a powerful appeal. Children are also part and parcel of ethnic competition and group size and become embedded in systems of social control (Norris and Inglehart 2004).

Much less psychologically theoretical is the role of energy in producing stuff and the role of disbursing stuff in helping keep social peace (often at the cost of conflict in other societies from which high surpluses are extracted). When people have something to lose, it tempers their motive to rebel significantly if not completely (Pinard 2011); though short of rebellion many options to resist exist and can nonetheless be used to undermine what people regard as unjust social relationships (Scott 1990). Acquisition of amenities can become habitual and drive self-control: play by the rules and shopping is available to you. It has proven to be the drug of choice to alleviate anxiety and discomfort – at least for those who can afford it (Lasch 1978).

Relief offered by consumption is always temporary, making it ideal for policy makers not just as a tool for ensuring social peace if not loyalty, but a means to generate production and jobs – also a tool of social discipline. Growing consumption is a perfect fit for late capitalist and other growth-driven societies. Consumption is easy to manipulate by elites even if they do not understand the deeper dynamic but simply attend to the technical aspects – how to increase consumption of cigarettes by identifying smoking with freedom (Tye 1998).

The path away from consumption ultimately lies in emotional reconnecting with other species, wild places, and the cycles of birth and death (Berman 2000). With connection and a "stable non-human environment" in childhood, anxiety diminishes – we are no longer alone and a visitor in an enormous alien universe but at home (Searles 1960). Earth-friendly religions and mythologies that make sense of and extol this connection have long assuaged or prevented mortality anxiety and can do so again (Hart 1999; Rappaport 1999). They reinforce in us a recognition that we are not aliens but share the same world with others, share the same fate, and are made of the same stuff (Searles 1960). Some religions are moving in this direction and away from distant sky-god deities or interpreting them much differently (Gottlieb 2006). Most conservation NGOs still do not admit or discuss consumption and human population growth as problems, let alone act on them. Both problems seem overwhelming and there is fear these issues will be divisive – never mind that conservation is incompatible with endless population and consumption growth. No one wants to be accused of advocating poverty or the middle ages, however false such charges. There is no substitute for direct protection of species and large biologically productive lands and waters; but protected areas and species are unlikely to survive in the face of the current trend of increases in human energy use and efforts to control the world.

These comments only suggest hints toward a solution. Halting the extinction crisis will require significant and fundamental societal change. Facing this circumstance is the first step in a reality-based strategy. We have yet to answer what societies not dependent on extinction-causing economic and political processes would look like or how we build a political movement that can bring about such changes. Such questions can't be answered until they are asked. They won't be asked until conservationists recognize what they are up against. In Chapter 3 we discussed the need to create a vision and we will discuss in Chapter 7 the attributes of successful movements and how to leverage the growing schisms in society brought about by the powerful clinging to the status quo. There are also many whose great need for certainty causes them to fear change and they are easily recruited by factions of the powerful to resist change (Lakoff 1996; Norris and Inglehart 2004).

REFERENCES

Arreguin-Toft, Ivan. 2005. *How the Weak Win Wars*. Cambridge University Press. Cambridge.

Ayres, Robert and Vlasios Voudouris. 2014. The Economic Growth Enigma: Capital, Labour and Useful Energy? 64 *Energy Policy* 16–28.

Barker, Jennifer. 2006. How Many Energy Slaves Do We Employ? www.alt energymag.com/content.php?issue_number=06.08.01&article=slaves (accessed June 18, 2016).

Becker, Ernest. 1973. *The Denial of Death*. Free Press. New York.

Berman, Morris. 1989. *Coming to Our Senses*. Simon & Schuster. New York.

Berman, Morris. 2000. *Wandering God*. State University Press of New York. Albany.

Boehm, Christopher. 1999. *Hierarchy in the Forest*. Harvard University Press. Cambridge, MA.

Boyden, Stephen. 1987. *Western Civilization in Biological Perspective: Patterns in Biohistory*. Oxford University Press. New York.

Gottlieb, Roger S. 2006. *A Greener Faith*. Oxford University Press. New York.

Hall, Charles A. S., Jessica G. Lambert, and Stephen B. Balogh. 2014. EROI of Different Fuels and the Implications for Society. 64 *Energy Policy* 141–52.

Harris, Marvin. 1977. *Cannibals and Kings*. Random House. New York.

Harris, Marvin. 1989. *Our Kind*. Random House. New York.

Hart, Keith. 1999. Foreword. Pp. xiv–xix in Roy A. Rappaport, *Ritual and Religion in the Making of Humanity*. Cambridge University Press. Cambridge.

Jackson, Wes. 1984. *Altars of Unhewn Stone*. North Point Press. San Francisco.

Johnson, Allen W. and Timothy Earle. 2000. *The Evolution of Human Society*. 2nd edn. Stanford University Press. Stanford, CA.

Lakoff, George. 1996. *Moral Politics*. University of Chicago Press. Chicago, IL.

Lasch, Christopher. 1978. *The Culture of Narcissism*. Norton. New York.

Norris, Pippa and Ronald Inglehart. 2004. *The Sacred and the Secular*. Cambridge University Press. Cambridge.

Peet, John. 1992. *Energy and the Ecological Economics of Sustainability*. Island Press. Washington DC.

Phillips, Kevin. 2006. *American Theocracy*. Viking. New York.

Pimentel, David. 2009. Energy Inputs in Food Crop Production in Developing and Developed Nations. 2 *Energies* 1–24. doi: 10.3390/en20100001 (accessed May 26, 2017).

Pimentel, David, L. E. Hurd, A. C. Bellotti, et al. 1973. Food Production and the Energy Crisis. 182 *Science* 443–9.

Pinard, Maurice. 2011. *Motivational Dimensions in Social Movements and Contentious Collective Action*. McGill-Queens University Press. Montreal.

Rappaport, Roy A. 1999. *Ritual and Religion in the Making of Humanity*. Cambridge University Press. Cambridge.

Scott, James C. 1990. *Domination and the Arts of Resistance*. Yale University Press. New Haven, CT.

Searles, Harold F. 1960. *The Non-human Environment in Normal Development and in Schizophrenia*. International Universities Press. New York.

Smil, Vaclav. 2010. *Energy Transitions*. Praeger. Westport, CT.

Smil, Vaclav. 2017. *Energy and Civilization*. MIT Press. Cambridge, MA.

Solomon, Sheldon, Jeffrey L. Greenberg, and Thomas A. Pyszczynski. 2004. Lethal Consumption: Death Denying Materialism. Pp. 127–46 in Tim Kasser and Allen

D. Kanner (eds.). *Psychology and Consumer Culture.* American Psychological Association. Washington, DC.

Tigay, Jeffrey H. 1982. *Evolution of the Gilgamesh Epic.* University of Pennsylvania Press. Philadelphia, PA.

Trainer, Ted. 2014. Some Inconvenient Theses. 64 *Energy Policy* 168–74.

Tye, Larry. 1998. *The Father of Spin.* Crown. New York.

US Energy Information Administration. 2013. International Energy Outlook 2013. www.eia.gov/todayinenergy/detail.cfm?id=12251 (accessed July 9, 2016).

Victor, David G, Keigo Akimoto, Yoichi Kaya, Mitsutsune Yamaguchi, Danny Cullenward, and Cameron Hepburn. 2017. Prove Paris Was More Than Paper Promises. 548 *Nature* 25–7 (August 3).

Vitousek, Peter M., Paul R. Ehrlich, Anne H. Ehrlich, and Pamela A. Matson. 1986. Human Appropriation of the Products of Photosynthesis. 36 *BioScience* 6: 368–73.

White, Leslie. 1969. *The Science of Culture,* 2nd edn. Farrar Strauss. New York.

White, Leslie. 1987 [1975]. The Energy Theory of Cultural Development. In *Ethnological Essays.* University of New Mexico Press. Albuquerque.

Wright, Ronald. 2004. *A Short History of Progress.* Anansi. Toronto.

PART III Taking the Offensive

How do conservationists create a political force that can effectively counter the currently overwhelming human inertia which is destroying wild creatures and their homes?

One way is to learn from other movements and from conservation's own history. The wheel has been invented. Because there is little overlap between conservation and other movements, conservationists often lack knowledge or experience with movement building. Many seem unaware of their own movement's history in various parts of the world.

Other factors confound mass-based organizing. Conservationists in developed countries are usually middle class and have much invested in the status quo on that account. There is little enticement to stand the world on its head. Martin Luther King began to wonder in

"Then a miracle occurs" by Sydney Harris. Reproduced with permission.

"I THINK YOU SHOULD BE MORE EXPLICIT HERE IN STEP TWO."

the two years before his murder whether more than a few whites would go to the mat over desegregation and civil rights (Garrow 1986). Serious conservationists are confronted with a similar question: will more than a handful of humans – including those who take great risks on behalf of other humans though they have nothing to personally gain – act decisively on behalf of other species? Some people do and will, but thus far it is a small number.

The single greatest challenge for conservation is how they are to exercise adequate leverage. Bringing about major change invariably requires disruption and shock to the status quo (Piven and Cloward 1977; Aminzade et al. 2001; Piven 2006; Tilly 2008). An organized labor movement, for example, exercises leverage by virtue of its class position: through strikes and other means they can deprive owners of the economy of labor and thus profits and other benefits of production; they can self-fund; and they are also convenient targets for repression. In contrast the conservation movement occupies no such economic position. Conservationists in many parts of the world may be middle class, but they are not *the* middle class and they are not organized as such. They typically organize around caring for the natural world; they appeal to empathy and associated values, to a broader good. Ultimately, to be effective, movements must go beyond the attributes of displaying worthiness, unity, numbers, and commitment (Tilly 2004), to exercising material force (Liu 2015) – the ability to take action to boycott, refuse cooperation with the state, and generally make business-as-usual difficult or impossible unless demands are met.

Just as the labor movement sometimes evolved beyond concerns of particular unions, segments of the working class, or the working class as a whole, to espousing and working for broad principles of justice in the face of modern assaults on justice (Polyani 1944), the conservation movement, also essentially defensive in origin, transforms ideological power into material power through action. To do so requires that conservation values be widely shared, deeply felt, and the movement be well organized (disciplined).

Liu (2015) points out in his analysis of the Taiwanese and South Korean environmental (not conservation) movements that discipline can be a heavy lift, because ideological support is inherently unstable, especially in the absence of grassroots organizing. He also notes that the vision of a "green" society, as opposed to an economically just society, is largely lacking. Vision is important to mobilization for long-term change.

Conservationists have many additional weaknesses that need to be overcome. They often fail to document their efforts so it is difficult to learn from them. Unless the conservation movement can become self-financing, it will remain constrained by the inherent caution that characterizes donated big money. Understanding the limits of science in politics and decision making is also important, as is a better grasp of human motivation. Failure to keep their "eyes on the prize" and being strategic are also problematic. Conservation as a profession creates careerism, which ties people to the status quo, though in the global south where people frequently risk their lives this is much less the case. That there is no conservation church, broad community, liturgy, literature, theater, song, and ritual is a major handicap.

Thus, conservation is rarely in a position to make demands; begging is rarely an effective strategy for safeguarding and recovering wildlife and wild places from those who would otherwise exploit them. In this part of the book we examine actions that conservationists can take to greatly increase their political effectiveness and overcome opponents.

Conservation's opponents are better organized – as the neoliberal offensive of the last few decades demonstrates on almost all fronts – better connected, have more experience at playing an insider game and usually have access to police and other coercive tools such as the military, jails, and law. These opponents have social inertia on their side – the tendency of existing social relations and structure to reproduce themselves. But inertia is dynamic and is forever creating crises that offer opportunities to conservationists to undermine the status quo.

REFERENCES

Aminzade, Ronald R., Jack A. Goldstone, Doug McAdam, et al. 2001. *Silence and Voice in the Study of Contentious Politics*. Cambridge University Press. Cambridge.

Garrow, David J. 1986. *Bearing the Cross*. Morrow. New York.

Liu, Hwa-Jen. 2015. *Leverage of the Weak*. University of Minnesota Press. Minneapolis, MN.

Piven, Frances Fox. 2006. *Challenging Authority*. Rowman & Littlefield. Lanham, MD.

Piven, Frances Fox and Richard Cloward. 1977. *Poor People's Movements*. Pantheon. New York.

Polyani, Karl. 1944. *The Great Transformation*. Farrar and Rinehart. New York.

Tilly, Charles. 2004. *Social Movements 1768–2004*. Paradigm Publishers. Boulder, CO.

Tilly, Charles. 2008. *Contentious Performances*. Cambridge University Press. Cambridge.

7 Turning the Tide: Lessons from Other Movements and Conservation History

> There is a tide in the affairs of men, which, when taken at the flood, leads on to fortune; omitted, all the voyage of their lives is bound in shallows and miseries.
>
> William Shakespeare, *Julius Caesar*, Act 4, scene 3, ll. 218–21

Movements that have succeeded in fundamentally changing the social order share certain attributes: (1) a clear and bold vision; (2) uncompromising on ends but flexible on means; (3) perseverance over the long haul; (4) good use of insider and outsider (good cop/bad cop) approaches; (5) they are situated within strong supporting communities (e.g. US civil rights movement and Black churches); (6) they are good at exploiting crises and opponent and decision-maker weaknesses; and (7) they understand power and are unafraid to use it – they are unafraid of success and its consequences.

THE BIOLOGICAL AND POLITICAL LANDSCAPE

At an international meeting on wildlands someone mused that if conservationists had led the struggle against apartheid it would likely still exist in some form. The sixth great extinction is not slowing but gaining momentum (Brashares 2010; Butchart et al. 2010; Pimm et al. 2014; Ripple et al. 2016; Watson et al. 2016a, 2016b; Brashares and Gaynor 2017; Johnson et al. 2017). The human footprint is growing, not shrinking (Ewing at al. 2009; Venter et al. 2016). Our species is drawing down or destroying "natural capital" and commandeering a huge proportion of the interest or net primary product (NPP) – 30 percent of marine NPP and 40 percent of terrestrial, NPP (Pimm 2001).

Although important species, land and water protections have been achieved and the ideology of conquest has waned, most human societies behave as conquerors. Leaders pay lip service to biodiversity, but humans are consuming the Earth, converting more and more of the living world into commodities and collateral damage. Influential people talk about balancing growth and ecological integrity as if they were equivalents – as if the Earth, its ecosystems and species were just another factor in production, rather than the basis for all life.

Any opportunity for balancing passed 12,000 years ago at the beginning of the Neolithic, when our population was about 10 million. And human-caused extinctions pre-date this period, going back to our migration out of Africa 60,000 years ago (Miller et al. 1999; Barnosky et al. 2004).

Human societies are built on growth. Capitalist, state-capitalist, state-socialist, communist, and post-forager pre-modern economies are and were organized around growing human numbers and growing consumption per capita (Cohen 1977; Harris 1977, 1979; White 1987 [1975]; Johnson and Earle 2000; Wright 2004). Heads of state and government, central bankers, business leaders, international regimes (World Bank, International Monetary Fund, World Trade Organization, Organization for Economic Cooperation and Development, . . .), labor unions, and other institutions are dedicated to material growth and envision no alternative (Kasser 2002; Jackson 2009; Dietz and O'Neill 2013). Political and business leaders – those whom conservationists call on to make wise decisions – know that their power and positions depend on maintaining growth. Indeed, when growth falters and the pyramid-scheme nature of social organization reveals itself by threatening to unravel, they rush to shore it up rather than call for alternatives (Wright 2004). Dryzek et al. (2003) see supporting growth as one of the five core state functions, along with keeping order, maintaining sovereignty, raising revenue (closely linked to growth), and maintaining legitimacy. When conservation is able to align itself with a core function, such as legitimacy in the 1970s – a period when many states suffered from low popular support – it can make significant progress; but when it opposes head-on a core function like growth, it is usually blocked. Even conservation organizations depend on the growth of donors' stock portfolios (a recent Giving USA report (2016) again shows donations tracking economic growth). Many conservation leaders resist acknowledging this dependence and the need to address the structural dynamic of growth, fearing doing so would alienate donors and because it appears unnecessary as near-term goals can be accomplished without addressing the issue; taking on growth seems quixotic.

Until conservationists understand the political landscape as well as the natural, and until they understand the bigger picture, they will be forever caught in the short term and addressing symptoms rather than causes. Politics is sometimes said to be the art of the possible, and that is partially true as discussed in Chapter 4. But it is also – and must be for conservationists – *the art of changing what's possible.*

CHANGING WHAT'S POLITICALLY POSSIBLE

For living things, "survival is nothing if not biological ... [and] perpetuating economic or political institutions at the expense of biological well-being of man, societies, and ecosystems may be considered maladaptive" (Rappaport 1976: 65). Only in the realm of magical thinking can a growing human footprint be reconciled with ending human-caused extinctions and ecosystem decline.

Changing societal structures is daunting. As with so many struggles – anti-colonial, for equality, for labor rights – many powerful interests block the road; interests unafraid to use violence (e.g. Helvarg 2004; Davenport et al. 2005; Boykoff 2007). Even many of the victimized are too frightened of change to take on the status quo. Long before psychologists noted that some people are fearful of leaving destructive personal relationships, the US Declaration of Independence noted that people also have trouble leaving bad political relationships: "all experience hath shewn that mankind are more disposed to suffer, while evils are sufferable than to right themselves by abolishing the forms to which they are accustomed." Moreover, many people's sense of well-being depends upon identifying with the social order and regarding it as legitimate; to think and feel otherwise calls one's own sense of worth into question (Jost et al. 2001). Hubris also stands in the way: the faith of eighteenth-century Humanism permeates the world's dominant cultures. David Ehrenfeld (1978: 16–17) summarized the main points of this faith:

> All problems are solvable.
>
> All problems are solvable by humans.
>
> Most problems are solvable by technology.
>
> If a problem cannot be solved by technology it can be solved
>   through changes in social organization.
>
> When times get tough humans hunker down and solve problems.
>
> Some resources are infinite; finite resources have substitutes.
>   Civilization will survive.
>
> If we don't get it right we just didn't know enough at first & we will
>   get it right.

Reality is turning out quite differently than faith would have it.

Conservationists typically resist taking on structural change because it seems to require that people make material sacrifices and this is unrealistic. But is giving up mindlessly complex social hierarchies that infantilize people a sacrifice? Emerson (1994 [1847]: 63) observed that "Things are in the saddle, and ride mankind." Is giving up such servitude a sacrifice? Is giving up the drudgery of so much labor to pay for toys that distract us from the drudgery a sacrifice? Despite the fantastical promises of material progress for all, there are about twice the number seriously hungry today than were alive at the beginning of the modern period (UN FAO 2010).

Although structural change always confronts enormous obstacles it has been accomplished many times. Decolonization, the largely successful abolition of slavery, tyrannies toppled, apartheid gone, labor rights and women's rights gained (but not completely), and many other basic economic and political changes have required the transformation of societal structure. These struggles continue. Conservationists can and must do the same if they are serious about sustaining and restoring life on Earth. Lessons from conservation's history and from the successes and failures of other movements suggest seven essential attributes of successful movements for major change.

1. Clear, Bold Vision

Movement success is more likely and less costly when the groups in a movement forge a common, overarching vision and invest in maintaining it, commit to good inter-organizational communication, and subordinate strategic thinking to that vision while checking self-aggrandizing leaders (Aminzade et al. 2001).

NGOs will always have differences in priorities, but successful movements share broad common themes such as equality in the US civil rights movement or popular elections and freedom of speech in pro-democracy movements (Staggenborg 2011). Without clear and common themes intra-movement divisions are difficult to manage, and effective shared strategies fail to get beyond paper. Nor are shared visions timeless. The experiences of NGOs differ; efforts are made to sow mistrust among them, leaders change and many of them have fragile egos and must be the center of attention. Maintaining unity of vision requires much effort and is a moving target. But the effort is cheap compared to the costs of allowing opponents to exploit differences (Meyer and Tarrow 1998; Benford and Snow 2000; Polletta and Ho 2006). Pre-democratic South African security forces cost the anti-apartheid movement much blood and treasure by successfully exploiting Inkatha Freedom Party leaders' divisive ambitions (Wood 2000).

The injuries that give birth to movements – injustice, oppression, and brutality – do not by themselves generate resistance and support for alternatives (McAdam et al. 2001; Staggenborg 2011). Cohorts of people join movements not just in response to demands to end evils being perpetrated but that also present a compelling and credible vision of an alternative – an alternative that appeals to the needs, emotions, and intellect of target audiences (Johns 2005 – see also Chapter 10; Stern 2000; Goodwin et al. 2001; Brader 2005). The vision must describe what is wrong, what a better world looks like, and outline the path forward (Wallace 1970; Rambo 1993; Harkin 2004; Ingram and Fraser 2006). The vision must be conveyed by a powerful story in which people can find themselves (Cornog 2004; Cox 2006; Polletta 2006).

Obviously wild places and animals cannot fashion a vision of protected areas, a vision for conservation-compatible human societies, or mobilize to defend themselves and their homes before human decision makers; humans do all those things. But this differs little – at least in some respects – from other movements in which the vision is fashioned by those who understand the situation of the injured, who are best able to see a more just alternative, *and who understand the dynamics of power.* Visionary leaders such as Thomas Jefferson, Nelson Mandela, Elizabeth Katy Stanton, Franz Fanon, and many others, if not the children of privilege, were not among the most victimized, and had a much wider range of experience and sense of possibilities than those they spoke for and served (Morris and Staggenborg 2004). Nonetheless conservation presents a special challenge of speaking for the needs of countless species with whom humans have imperfect empathy. A sound vision will most likely emerge from those who care most about wild places and creatures and less about the approval of other humans.

Bold vision is also a hallmark of successful movements. Movements emerge in response to the failure of existing societal structures to treat some groups fairly and justly. Structurally rooted failures can only be addressed by structural solutions – by definition, bold – not bandages. Visions of the end of racism, economic and political domination, or the lethal exploitation of the natural world, are visions of fundamental change. Boldness is also a tactical imperative – one can bargain down, but not up.

Conservation has a history of bold visionaries, from John Muir to Marjorie Stoneman Douglas, Reed Noss, Dave Foreman, Doug and Kris Tompkins, Greg Carr, and Mario Boza, to name just a very few most familiar in the developed countries. Some have understood the challenges of 12,000 years of institutional inertia. But too often conservationists' vision has been too timid and too cautious. It has not been up to encompassing the tasks required to achieve the change needed; it has shied away from causes (human institutions) and focused on symptoms, as if endless study of elephants, bears, and whales would stop their slaughter; it has not recognized that politics is a primitive enterprise based on carrots and sticks, including, e.g., the threat or exercise of violence by opponents seeking "resources" such as oil (Klare 2001; Paskal 2010); or that politics usually requires action before all the data are in. Many conservationists are from educated, middle-class, professional backgrounds that do not provide a good experiential education in contentious politics (Edelman 1988).

A bold and shared vision does not guarantee success, but it is a condition for intelligent and purposeful action. In 1963 Martin Luther King regalvanized a movement and much of a nation by giving voice to a bold vision of equality and an end to racial hatred. He also understood there was more to a bold vision than a dream; it must encompass a sound understanding of power, strategy, and organization. Eventual passage of the US Wilderness Act, partial recovery of North American brown bears, and the listing of many species under the ESA reflect such an understanding. Similarly, efforts by Sea Shepherd Conservation Society to undermine pirate whaling, driftnets, and illegal fishing reflect sound political understanding.

2. Combine Insider and Outsider Approaches (Good Cop/Bad Cop)

Insider approaches understand politics as the art of the possible and rely on normal channels of political influence. Outsider approaches are about changing what is possible and typically rely heavily on disrupting the status quo to bring pressure. Combining both approaches is necessary to achieve major or structural change. Many conservation NGOs, of course, subscribe to goals that do not require structural change, and therefore do not see outsider approaches as relevant. But for those who seek an end to human-caused extinctions, confronting structural change is a must.

Throughout much of the world, conservation politics relies overwhelmingly on insider approaches such as lobbying within established and normalized channels, on personal connections with economic and political elites, and on the largesse or personal inclinations of some leaders. Insider approaches have led to the creation of national parks and other protected areas, and limiting the trade in rare, threatened, and endangered species. But insider approaches are inherently limited, as demonstrated by parks and other protected areas not meeting biological needs of species and the lax enforcement of domestic and international conservation laws. That trade law has primacy over conservation law is highly problematic Elites may agree to conservation concessions, but seldom abandon their material interests (e.g. Gonzalez 2001; Kamieniecki 2006; Kraft and Kamieniecki 2007). In the United States and other countries the fingerprint of elites is evident in biologically irrational borders for protected areas, inadequate rare, threatened, and endangered species protection and recovery, and deference to resource extraction and livestock industries. Conservationists, though capable and skilled, typically lack the insider approach's resources (e.g. money, access, mass media) when facing powerful opponents. Opponents are often not just part of the economic elite (controlling various businesses or whole industries, and thus are economic decision makers) but have close ties to or are political decision makers (Domhoff 2009; Dye 2013). Banks, oil and gas, and grazing interests are not just on the outside exercising influence, but are inside government. Conservation opponents are often directly and, by virtue of being part of the elite, well connected to police and private repressive entities (e.g. Donner 1990; Drohan 2003; Helvarg 2004), giving them a powerful tool in political conflict. Their greater command of expert political resources (to frame issues, attack conservationists' credibility, and propagate the dubious findings of anti-conservation think tanks) is significant (e.g. Ewen 1996; Libby 1999; Helvarg 2004; Otto 2016). They spend hundreds of millions of dollars on this alone.

Insider approaches generally cannot, alone, yield fundamental change. The current climate agreement lacks mandatory emissions targets, for example. The passage and maintenance of the ESA of 1973 (following on the Endangered Species Preservation Act of 1966, P.L. 89–669) is a good, if complicated, example of the role of outsider forces at work. The Act was the result of typical legislative work but was also the result of mass unrest over many issues, including the environment of which conservation was only a part, that pushed a president and Congress to act virtually unanimously. It was also true that potential opponents of the Act were unaware of its implications and otherwise occupied (Rocheleau 2017). Once in place and its implications understood by both sides, the Act became the object of major contention. Were it not for two aspects of the US political system, it would have been much less of an issue: the US courts are strong and have taken the law and its mandate to be guided by the science seriously, and once a law is in place in the US it can be very difficult to change. Legislative change requires a "yes" at several stages in the process, while blocking change only requires a "no" at one step.

Absent ESA peculiarities, fundamental change invariably requires overcoming elites and that can only be done with outsider approaches: mass mobilization of groups new to the political system which in turn provide the credible threat of disrupting business-as-usual unless and until demands are met (McCarthy and McPhail 1998; Meyer and Tarrow 1998). The rules of any political system generally favor the elites who make them; basic changes require breaking the rules and creating new rules. No major societal change has been achieved without outsider approaches. In the US neither slavery nor Jim Crow laws were dismantled without outsider approaches. Dictatorships are not brought down nor decolonization achieved by playing by the rules. Structural change is not the product of the timid or amateurs, but of efforts led by those practiced at mass mobilization (Meyer and Tarrow 1998) and willing to take on the risks of repression (McAdam 1986). It must also be noted that fundamental change is often only possible when the extant system is already weak; change agents create new power more than they overthrow existing power (Moore 1966).

When existing structures or foes are strong, non-violent protest may be the only way to avoid crushing repression. Non-violent but disruptive protest was successfully used by groups in the US civil rights and anti-Vietnam War movements, but their success was owed in part to other groups in the movement espousing revolution. Although unrealistic, calls for revolution shifted the political center, making non-violent disruption more acceptable. On the one hand, the US American Indian Movement, though not revolutionary, engaged in armed defense of Indian communities against corrupt tribal governments backed by the US government, and it was crushed by repression (Hendricks 2006) as were many pro-democracy movements around the world (e.g. China: Zhao 2011). On the other hand, it was primarily the effective threat of civil war in South Africa – a civil war the elites knew they could not win – that ultimately brought authorities to the bargaining table (Wood 2000). Pro-democracy struggles played out in a similar way in El Salvador and Guatemala.

To be effective, groups pursuing outsider approaches must forge alliances and coalitions with those pursuing insider approaches and other groups whose support prevents opponents inside or outside the state from isolating groups pursuing outsider approaches, i.e. "radical" groups (Meyer and Tarrow 1998; Davenport 2005). It took decades of patient organizing for the US civil rights and labor movements to achieve broad support via allies and the media for their goals if not always their disruptive tactics. In extremely repressive countries, gaining international attention and support is critical (Clifford 2005). Successful outsider approaches also depend on correctly anticipating the mix of concessions and repression that disruptive action will trigger from elites (McAdam 1997 [1983]). Gauging elite responses can be difficult because decision makers are often divided, uncertain, and irrationally fearful (Goldstone and Tilly 2001; Zhao 2011).

Whether outsider approaches challenge strong centers of power or try to create new centers of power, they encounter repression because elites see a threat to their decision-making capacity and options, the more so in the case of disruptive tactics. Most regimes will go to great lengths to forestall the creation of any autonomous centers of power because they lead to permanent changes in power relations.

Some repression is inevitable. Successful movements prepare for it and minimize it by exploiting elite divisions and finding sympathizers within the elite who may limit its use, by demonstrating to those using it that it won't work or will backfire, and by gaining broad recognition that repression is unjustified and indicates elite malevolence (Goldstone and Tilly 2001; Giugni 2004; Davenport 2005; Koopmans 2005; Zwerman and Steinhoff 2005).

Combining outsider and insider approaches allows movements to simultaneously create new centers of power that work to force structural changes and openly challenge elites, and use insider connections to negotiate with elites. Outsider and insider approaches must usually be pursued by different organizations within a movement to enable decision makers to save face when they make concessions: they concede to representatives of insider approaches, and denounce outsider approaches as irresponsible, illegal, and immoral even though they are responding to their disruptive pressure.

In the face of existential threats, NGOs pursuing insider and outsider approaches sometimes go beyond quiet cooperation and organize alliances such as the Endangered Species Coalition or Wildlands Network Policy Coalition. Focusing on common ultimate goals and survival, movement NGOs will put aside differing approaches and tactics for a period of time. Such efforts usually have a limited life but can buy time in the face of repression and remind activists and supporters of what the movement is about.

Obstacles to coordination among insiders and outsiders includes insiders' protectiveness of their access to the powerful, their desire to be players above all else, and their tendency to temper their demands to avoid making powerful friends uncomfortable – though these "friends" may give them very little in return (e.g. Michels 1962 [1915]; Piven and Cloward 1977; Dryzek et al. 2003; cf. Rootes 2007 [2004]). Change is not made by movements afraid of upsetting powerful people. The primary outsider obstacle to coordination is their sense of purity: they may refuse to work with those they see as compromisers. Competition over funding may play a role in undercutting cooperation but the competition is mostly among insiders.

Another major obstacle consists of movement opponents: industries with opposing interests, the state, and countermovements. In the US the "wise-use" opposition tried to paint conservation as a vast conspiracy of international forces ganging up on rural communities – but was itself the creature of powerful industries that lacked much public sympathy. Similar efforts have been organized in Canada and Australia, and in the Amazon and parts of Africa ranchers and poachers have gone so far as to kill activists and rangers. Opponents may seek to divide NGOs from each other through a number of means: infiltration and disruption, sowing mistrust, violence and threats of violence, prosecutorial harassment and illegal police activities such as illegal surveillance, break-ins and searches, economic deprivation, and media demonization (e.g. Boykoff 2007; Davenport 2010; see Johns 2009: 319 for a summary of extensive documentation). These are precisely the activities united front efforts are aimed at defending against. The COINTELPRO program run by the US Federal Bureau of Investigation in cooperation with police departments is an example of an extensive and successful effort to divide, discredit, jail, physically injure, and otherwise undermine and destroy movement organizations.

3. Embed the Movement within a Strong Community

Movements consisting mostly of organizations whose members are check-writers supporting professional staff typically lack the passion and energy to create fundamental change (McCarthy and McPhail

1998; Meyer and Tarrow 1998). Such organizations often cannot even mobilize enough member support for insider approaches because check-writers do not follow organizational leaders (Shaiko 1999). In many countries organizations are also precluded by law from participating in processes that choose leaders – which is where lobbying begins – by their dependence on tax-deductible contributions.

In contrast, successful movements are embedded in a strong, mass community or network of communities. Community is critical for a number of reasons. The bonds of community extend beyond politics, to friendship, family, ritual, marriage, sex, love, play, music, and other cultural relationships. Such bonds create feelings of belonging and forestall attrition resulting from the uncertainty of outcomes, the often multi-generational path to realizing significant change, the oppressive asymmetry of power relationships, the potential for demobilization following major interim successes, and the vilification of movement members by defenders of the status quo (Lofland 1997 [1978]; Aminzade and Perry 2001; Goodwin et al. 2001; Staggenborg 2011). Personal relationships afforded by community buffer against isolation, fatigue, and fear; the more developed they are the more resilient the movement organizations (Taylor 1989). Tompkins Conservation, for example, has sought, in the creation of new parks in Chile and Argentina, not just to hire local individuals but to embed park infrastructure in local concepts of beauty (Jimenez 2017).

Fostering systemic change is high-risk. The bonds of community, not just bonding with a cause or with charismatic leaders, sustain political action in the face of repression (Taylor 1989). Trust and loyalty are built upon strong interpersonal ties, a commitment to a common cause, and ritual. Ritual reinforces belonging, emotional connections, identity and purpose, i.e. community (Moore and Myerhoff 1977; Kertzer 1988; Barker 2001; Goodwin and Pfaff 2001). Virtual social networks are effective at recruitment for mass events, but inadequate to support the organization building necessary to sustain over time active involvement of large numbers of people

(Cassen 2004; Tilly 2004). It is organization that "fixes" the level of mobilization – the commitment of people's time, energy, money, and other political resources to collective political action.

Movements create a core community of activists, but to be effective this small community must be embedded in a broader one – usually pre-existing communities (McAdam et al. 2001). The US civil rights movement relied on Black churches, universities, and fraternal orders (Skocpol et al. 2006); the anti-apartheid movement on the townships, labor organizations, and simultaneously on ethnic ties and transcendence of ethnicity (Wood 2000); the US labor movement on fraternal orders, mutual aid organizations, the Granges, and neighborhood ties (Foner 1975); and the US anti-war movement on liberal churches, universities, feminist women's networks, and many old left and labor networks (Wittner 1984; DeBenedetti 1990).

The conservation movement in much of the world is not embedded in a larger community. Activists and others have their personal and professional networks, but nothing like the equivalent of the US civil rights movement's Black churches. Probably the closest base may be universities where many activists were trained, but these are transitory. In larger cities where NGOs may have significant *member-ships*, some may come together once a year. Activists may find support in NGO membership, but the membership as a collective is not embedded in supportive institutions. In the 1980s Earth First! – a grassroots direct-action "non-organization" – was extraordinarily creative, generating an ecocentric culture, but it lacked the capacity and inclination, perhaps, to reach broad audiences and create that community in which it could thrive (Lee 1995). It's not clear that there exists a "natural community" for conservation in much of the world. There is no religion singularly dedicated to biodiversity. There are no broad communities (ethnic, gender, national or regional, class, linguistic) for which conservation of biodiversity is an essential interest. The closest conservation might come to that is the global cohort that spent much of their childhood outside, in non-consumptive proximity to the natural world. But they are not organized into a community except for those who went on to engage in conservation or environmentalism. There is no call across global borders, as with Islam, to turn one's attention five times a day to the natural world, reaffirm one's connection with it, and act according to one's belief. Scouting has faded in the parts of world where it once played a significant role in the lives of children. And the cohort of children who spend much of their lives outside is shrinking (Louv 2005). The bulk of conservation supporters lack conservation-centered community ties (Shaiko 1999). Conservation remains a sideshow or an afterthought, not central enough to the lives of enough people to make it a society-changing movement.

Can the conservation movement create such a community? Will some religious or secular communities make conservation a primary concern? Will crises generated by climate change reshape cultural institutions to the point that conservation can find a home? These crises could just as well generate self-interested action from fear as an interest in Earth-care. As the world urbanizes there is less contact with the natural world, and shifting baselines – the easy adaptability of humans to what is familiar – means most do not know what they have lost. The success of biodiversity depends on a community or communities that nurture the movement; a community for whom biodiversity recovery and rewilding is as urgent and personal as equality and justice. The last section of this book will discuss what conservationists can do to build community.

4. Uncompromising on Goals, Flexible Means

Movements are energized and sustained by organization, real and perceived progress toward goals, threats, leaders, relationships among movement participants, and the inspiration imparted by vision. Compromise on core goals – those essential to achieving an organization's or movement's vision – drains the energy and determination that purpose generates. As graphic commentator Toles illustrates so well, compromise directly undercuts realizing vision (Figure 4.1, page 56 herein). Opponents and decision makers do not take seriously those who compromise on important goals.

Because movements consist of diverse organizations having different goals, the same position may mean compromise for one but not for another. Nevertheless, successful movements share key elements of a vision, such as equality in the US civil rights movement, autonomous political organizations and free speech in pro-democracy movements, an end to the loss and recovery of biodiversity in the conservation movement. If these are compromised then the movement's capacity to achieve its core goals is diminished (Staggenborg 2011).

One of the greatest enticements to compromise on basic goals is partial success. When an organization attains a seat at the table with decision makers, it comes under significant internal and external pressure to compromise (Michels (1962 [1915]). Winning a seat at the table is not the same as winning substantively and can undermine the latter when movement leaders like being players to the degree that they will "go along to get along." Decision makers exert strong pressure on organizations to limit demands or tactics and many leaders self-censor (e.g. Garrow 1986). Some observers think these tendencies are not a problem for the conservation movement because it is decentralized and uncompromising organizations are constantly emerging that keep pressure on more staid organizations (Piven and Cloward 1977; Dryzek et al. 2003; cf. Rootes 2007 [2004]). Shaiko's (1999) work suggests otherwise; in his study of several US conservation organizations during the period of professionalization in the 1980s and 1990s, he found they limited activism as they sought to raise money to pay for lobbyists and other insider staff, and as they grew more dependent on donors who wanted tax deductions they limited their actions to comply with charitable laws that limit politicking. The dominating presence of larger, more conservative organizations makes it difficult for smaller, activist groups to gain attention and attract even the minimal resources they require.

Although differences among the goals of organizations within a movement create tension, they are also key to success. Organizational variety is necessary if movements are to attract those with different levels of commitment, different views about what needs to be done, and different risk tolerance. Variety also provides a pathway for people to move among organizations as commitment and political sophistication grows (Shaiko 1999). Different organizational approaches also are adapted to different targets of action, e.g. gaining legislative change and gaining cooperation of private landowners.

In any movement a few organizations pursue high-risk outsider approaches and many pursue low-risk approaches. Diversity becomes a weakness and movements falter when low-risk groups allow opponents or decision makers to divide them from the high-risk groups that play such a pivotal role in defining the political landscape; it is those pushing the edge that define the political center.

If unwillingness to compromise on goals is critical to achieving them, so is flexibility in the means employed. Many paths may lead to realizing a goal; being open to taking advantage of unexpected opportunities can make all the difference (see the discussion of crises below). Sometimes goals and strategy are confused. Some US civil rights organizations were criticized for compromising although they had not abandoned their demand for full equality, but merely pursued a strategy that first sought equality in public education, and then in other areas one by one. A step by step strategy is problematic for conservation. It's not just that extinction is forever. The loss of habitat, fragmentation of lands and waters, the isolation of subpopulations, the loss of genetic diversity, and other injuries are very difficult to heal. The inertia of human numbers and consumption causes losses that make recovery difficult not just biologically but politically. The existing situation – with conservationists relatively weak – forces what is at best a triage. The survival of many species depends on conservationists becoming much stronger and learning how to better use the lessons of asymmetric conflicts.

The fundamental differences in conservation which lead to conflicts over what constitutes compromise are related to whether conservation should accommodate existing human domination of the world or challenge it; and what constitutes conservation success – is it a biologically healthy world or a bunch of outdoor zoos that keep some charismatic species going? Some groups embrace a timid vision and can't see beyond outdoor zoos; others want to rewild the world (Wuerthner et al. 2014).

5. *Persevere*

Achieving significant change depends on opportunities and on advocates with uncompromising vision, adequate resources, capable leaders, constant tactical innovation, and perseverance among other things (Kriesi and Wisler 1999; McAdam et al. 2001). If defenders of the status quo think those who demand change will tire and fade, the former will try to wait out the latter or encourage their waning. When a movement's organizational strength and commitment of participants makes clear that it will pursue its goals indefinitely, decision makers are more likely to bargain – or resort to repression.

Sustained action, although not sufficient, has always been necessary to achieve systemic change (Giugni 2004). Perseverance depends on harnessing people's emotions (e.g. anger, outrage, affection for other participants), needs (e.g. to belong, a sense of efficacy and purpose), and deepest beliefs (what constitutes justice and the highest good) (Clayton 2000; Wood 2001).

Many movements' goals take decades and longer to achieve. Nearer-term milestones are needed – milestones under the control of conservation NGOs rather than dependent on, e.g. governmental or corporate decision makers: shortening the workday to eight hours, women's suffrage, or the end of legal segregation in education all required state action (Rucht 1999). At the same time they must be meaningful milestones, such as achieving a public show of strength. Nelson Mandela's seventieth birthday tribute, which included a pop music concert that filled Wembley Stadium in London and was broadcast to sixty-seven countries, is an example. Many of the 600 million who watched gathered outdoors in public. It enabled the anti-apartheid movement to reach new audiences and raise awareness with them as a first step (Field 2010). Edelman (1995) argues, and the success of this event demonstrates, that politically indirect art is usually more effective than the directly political. More generally, no climate change demonstration or conservation event has been able to generate the same level of enthusiasm, probably for several reasons: conservation values are not as widely or as deeply felt as anti-racism, the anti-apartheid campaign was more developed, it had a human face in Mandela, and the South African government was increasingly isolated and violent.

Outcomes are uncertain in conservation. Results, such as whether protecting an area will secure its species and ecological function, may only be clear in the distant future. The immediate costs of achieving protection may be high. That wins feel temporary and losses feel permanent takes a toll on the energy that underlies perseverance.

In the face of these difficulties one powerful countervailing factor is ritual, which presupposes a community of belief. Rituals define, declare, and celebrate dedication to purpose and achievements which may otherwise be obscure. Just as most cultures recognize people as adults at a particular age by declaring them to be adults even though adulthood is achieved gradually, so conservation ritual may celebrate growing population numbers of a species even if they have not reached recovery. A change in direction is important, such as may happen with a CITES (Convention on International Trade in Endangered Species of Wild Fauna and Flora) vote on protecting elephants or tigers or the denial of a fossil fuel pipeline permit. Ritual is also important in reaffirming commitment to action in the face of partial achievements: a vote does not mean the struggle is over, no one gets to go home, but it does represent a victory (Taylor 1989; Bevington 2009).

Perseverance partly rests on feelings of effectiveness, and effectiveness means making progress toward goals. Progress toward goals depends on many factors, but one of the most important is constant tactical innovation that keeps a movement ahead of opponents and authorities (Sellars 2004). When groups do not innovate, their actions become easy to counter or neutralize.

Leadership is also critical to perseverance. Successful movements and organizations are led by a group of people who collectively are able to inspire, organize, and implement effective strategies (Aminzade et al. 2001). No one person possesses all the attributes of a good leader. The ability of a visionary to attract, keep, and not be threatened by highly competent "lieutenants" reinforces perseverance by generating progress.

Generating hope is often identified as critical to perseverance, but hope is much like notions of democracy and justice: vague concepts with a number of meanings that can convince people they all believe in the same thing but difficult to measure progress against. Hope for many is the notion that things will turn out in the end whether one acts or not. That view is unlikely to generate needed action. For others hope is grounded in reality: it's a recognition that if "we" are strategic, act decisively, have a good grasp of the landscape, we can achieve our ends. Insurgents in El Salvador were quite aware of the difficulties before them: they had fought to a stalemate but victory was not in sight (Wood 2001). What kept them going day to day was the ability to strike back at injustice, even at great risk.

Ideology expresses vision in greater detail, but perhaps more important from the standpoint of perseverance it explains the nature of the struggle and its importance, fulfills supporters' need to make sense of things, and sustains people by sanctifying purpose, not just by providing it. Sanctification entails making a purpose fundamental and unquestioned, part of the air and water. Religion has often played an ideological role in movements, but there are secular variants as well: notions of inevitable historical development, or the notion that the universe unfolds in ways that favor justice or progress (e.g. Aminzade and Perry 2001; Skocpol et al. 2006).

In the last decade mobile telephones and the Internet have made it possible, without direct physical interaction, to organize mass events on short notice. In a few cases such events have led to important political consequences and on that count offered participants a sense of efficacy. But observers also note that most participants show little inclination for organization building or discipline, a prerequisite to creating a base of political power that can bring sustained pressure (Cassen 2004). Without such an organizational base, movements cannot persevere long enough or increase their pressure enough to bring systemic change. Overfishing continues to be a major problem and is growing worse (Finley 2017). Those who participate only in events and in between in virtual social networks do not develop the trusting personal relationships and organizational bonds that underlie community and encourage ongoing involvement (Tilly 2004). The loss of Congress in 2010 by the movement that brought Obama to power in 2008 resulted from the failure to sustain it.

6. Exploit Divisions within Elites and Crises

Divisions within decision-making elites, divisions among a movement's opponents, and crises that weaken opponents and delegitimize dominant ideologies and institutions are important opportunities for movements if they are recognized and acted on decisively. *Structural* crises provide opportunities for much greater change, and by identifying them and understanding them, activists can achieve much. Although structural crises and deep elite division may seem to appear suddenly, they are invariably a long time in the making (McAdam and Sewell 2001). A good understanding of societal dynamics can provide early warning and suggest points of maximal political leverage, as noted below. With early warning, conservationists are also better able to prepare to counter elite efforts to spin a crisis for their benefit by manipulating perception away from real causes and solutions (e.g. Ewen 1996; Brock 2006).

When national or global elites are united they usually get their way (McAdam et al. 2001; Guigni 2004). Elites share an interest and desire to maintain the social order that rewards them so disproportionately, but they also are divided into factions by differing interests. In constantly seeking advantage they often are at odds with each other; the depth of division varies with the degree their interests are in conflict. Understanding potential and actual divisions makes opportunities easier to exploit. For example, elites tend to be more divided in states that have been at the top of the international pyramid (e.g. US, UK, Germany, France) than elites in rising states (e.g. Brazil, China) because of the greater need for unity in the face of stronger powers (Chase-Dunn and Hall 1997).

When elites are divided or in the midst of crisis it can open up political space for new ideas and action, undermine repression, cause elite factions to look for support from below, giving those below temporarily greater leverage, and so on. Being able to recognize a crisis in the early stages, knowing what type of crisis it is (e.g. a leader's sex scandal or a systemic breakdown), being prepared to take advantage when the moment is right, and knowing how to push to the limit for concessions, are all important factors. Some crises are predictable, e.g. economic cycles, while others may be inevitable but unpredictable, e.g. strong storms or severe drought due to climate change or events such as the Deep Water Horizon explosion and long-term oil spill. Governments may rise and fall due to scandal, though investment bankers may be able to cling to their jobs despite disastrous decisions.

The NGO and institutional decision-making landscape is shaped in part by crises resulting from accidents, scandal, or systemic problems that develop over decades or longer but the consequences of which may appear suddenly. Crises can be generated by movement action. Division between economic and political elites was a major proximate cause for negotiations between rebels and the governments of Guatemala and South Africa (Wood 2000); these divisions were brought about by the pressure of a civil war that neither side could win.

Elite divisions do not generate desired results on their own, they must be exploited aggressively. *Nature* (2010) – not noted for politically feisty editorials – advised climate scientists that they were in a street fight, not an academic debate, over greenhouse gas emissions. The power of the energy sector and their willingness to use it is evident: although many elite factions accept and are concerned about climate change, many energy companies have resisted serious restrictions by spending millions on sowing doubt and confusion over the role of greenhouse gas emissions and likely consequences (Layzer 2007; Frumhoff and Oreskes 2015).

Progress in conservation has been marked by punctuated equilibrium in countries with routinized politics (Repetto 2006). In the early 1970s, for example, CITES was ratified by the US Senate, and the United States also passed numerous environmental laws such as the Endangered Species Act, Coastal Zone Management Act, and Clean Air Act. That Congress was supportive was not surprising given its constituent base at the time and the strength of more progressive social movements, but a number of factors beyond those made such laws important to legislators and to a president (Nixon) not known for making the environment or conservation a priority. A very unpopular war and efforts to turn back progress made in civil rights, women's rights, and in other areas pushed him to look for ways to undermine growing voter hostility, especially among the young and new voters. More generally it was a politically volatile time in the US, with high levels of mobilization: people were routinely in the streets to make demands and protest; concern over conservation, pollution, and other issues was rising, and the first Earth Day, in 1970, engaged 10 percent of the US population or about 20 million people. Human population growth and birth control were major issues in the 1970s. Not least of all, presidential involvement in criminal activity and lethal covert operations, such as the destruction of democracy and installation of a military dictator in Chile, were becoming public and the source of political conflict. The concatenation of these events and related issues, which revealed an America very different from how Americans liked to think of themselves, weakened the ability of the president and his supporters to resist passage of these laws in the face of the need to counter low systemic legitimacy pervasive at the time (Crozier et al. 1975; Wolfe 1977). Indeed, the great appeal of conservation was to legitimacy: these laws' mandates are the right thing to do (Dryzek et al. 2003). Importantly, opposition to these laws was also moderated by the failure of elites and potential opponents to recognize their consequences.

Of course political opportunities, whatever the tide, do not transform themselves into good legislation, block bad legislation, generate better leaders or major cultural shifts, or create new power relations. Opportunities must be recognized, understood, and acted on with skill, resolve, and adequate resources.

As noted, in countries with routinized politics, of which bureaucratic inertia and byzantine legislative processes are usually components, policy and institutional change are usually incremental. Failed leadership or policies are usually not enough to precipitate change failing attractive alternatives with sufficient backing (Wallace 1956, 1970; Ingram and Fraser 2006). Low personal or institutional legitimacy may hamper leaders, but by itself does not foster rebellion. Rebellion is risky and risks can keep people docile.

But low legitimacy *is* an opportunity, and social scientists have long noted the clustering or pulses of change in societies with routinized politics: periods of new legislation, the emergence of new dominant cultural paradigms, or altered social relationships (e.g. Goldstein 1988; Berry 1991; Fischer 1996; Berry et al. 1998). The many factors that generate opportunities in addition to legitimacy also cluster: crises of various sorts, the mobilization of new groups and the relative decline of others, new knowledge that leads to reconceptualization of problems and solutions (e.g. Kriesi 2004; Baumgartner 2006), or simpler events, such as the outcome of litigation. In the US, for example, endangered species cases have often had significant ripple effects (Gunter 2002; Davis 2006; Shepard 2006). Although these factors play different roles in different regime types – so-called democracies and other soft oligarchic systems, one-party states, theocracies, military regimes, and so on (Koopmans 2005) – political-economic cycles may explain much of this clustering and therefore deserve attention because they are at the root of many opportunities.

Economist Nicholas Kondratieff described cycles in prices and cycles in technology and infrastructure investment at intervals of approximately 55 years between troughs or peaks (e.g. Berry 1991;

Berry et al. 1998). Nested within one of these 55-year cycles (termed K-waves after Kondratieff by Schumpeter [1939]) are two growth cycles, the first approximating the rising price phase of the price–investment cycle (20–25 years) and the second synchronic with the decline (25–30 years). Picture the two humps of *Camelus bactrianus* superimposed on the one hump of *Camelus dromedarius*. When price troughs and growth troughs coincide, economic conditions are typically termed a depression or recession. However, like oceanic tides, K-waves are not synchronous across all economies but vary with political interventions, the size of the economy relative to others and the global economy, and the degree of integration into the global economy.

Political shifts from conservative to liberal rule (not reducible to which political party holds power) typically follow on recessions and associated increased inequality. High inflation combined with a growth trough (stagflation) typically marks a shift from liberal to conservative rule (Berry 1991; Berry et al. 1998). There is nothing mechanical or magical about the relationship between economic circumstances and political changes. Rather, the former contribute to mobilization of specific groups in society which seek outcomes such as improved social welfare or unrestricted economic growth. Managing legitimacy presents different challenges in different economic circumstances: labor and wealth are mobilized to greater or lesser relative degrees. To turn opportunity into political reality requires mobilization and strategic collective political action. Conservationists are not exempt from this rule. If they are to take advantage of economic cycles to change leaders, policies, and even systemic arrangements, they must organize and act.

Differences in political systems can magnify or diminish opportunities presented by cycles: in parliamentary systems with proportional representation center-left governments are more likely than in district-by-district winner-take-all electoral systems (Döring and Manow 2015). This has benefited green parties, which tend to be more environmentalist than conservationist, but there may be somewhat more leverage with them than typical left parties (Carter 2007). More authoritarian regimes may limit incremental change out of fear or too close ties to reactionary groups (their supporters won't permit any change), causing an unnecessary increase in social tension; but such systems have managed those tensions through economic development and full-labor projects, and by interfering with the development of nascent group autonomy as China and Singapore have done (Broadbent and Brockman 2011). The ethnic homogeneity of a society also affects how tensions are managed or can be managed – generally ethnically homogeneous societies are easier to rule.

Leaders also make a difference. In the first two years of his administration US President Obama enjoyed a majority in both houses of the national legislature. Many groups in society, including those who generally ignore politics, were angry over the financial crisis of 2008 which wiped out pensions and other investments, and caused bank failures and big job losses. None of the Wall Street gamblers were held accountable. Rather than use his majority and popular anger to push for major economic reform – such as breaking up institutions "too big to fail" – and campaign finance reform, Obama embraced Wall Street bankers and appointed joined-at-the-hip regulators as his close economic advisors (just as Bush II did) (Kirk and Wiser 2012). The banks are now bigger. The anger initially aimed at Bush was transferred to the cautious Obama, who lost his congressional majority after two years. Many of those from the social strata that had been economically losing ground since the 1970s were so angry in 2016 that they were blinded and helped elect a billionaire for president who had stiffed his own employees (Murray 2016).

In the current period in much of the world, as recovery from the 2008 investment bank gambling disaster continues, new groups become available for grassroots political action based on grievances with conservative rule and the economic disadvantages imposed by the crisis it caused. These new groups also sense increased opportunities and availability of resources for political change. These factors in turn foster demands that alter the political agenda. Taking advantage of the potential for grassroots action requires deep-going organizing – something in short supply in much of the developed world. In the US many of the aggrieved seem to be working against their own interests. In other countries where there has been organizing and even uprisings, the reaction of elites has been harsh: conservation activism in places such as Egypt, Iran, and other countries can find it tough going when basic rights are easily violated by police and other instruments of state power. Even in the ostensibly democratic European Union, Greece confronted ruthless pressure when it tried to stand up to the austerity of autocrats.

During the latter part of the downturn phase of the price–investment–technology cycle (1981–2008), as profits come under pressure from market saturation and volatility, the intensity of technological research and development (computerization, telecommunications, and speculation in "economic technologies" like subprime mortgages, derivatives, credit default swaps) increases. Old technologies and infrastructure are wearing out. Some of these new technologies and associated infrastructure will attract major investment and become widely adopted, fueling the next upswing in prices and growth (Berry 1991). To the degree this is still the same old growth, it is not positive for biodiversity or the natural world. But to the degree the technology and infrastructure is more nature-friendly (less damaging) than alternatives, it can have a less damaging result into the future. Conservationists have affected this infrastructure transition to some degree, especially in the energy area. But they have overstated, perhaps out of felt political necessity, the impacts: wind and solar are not magic bullets and still rely on hard infrastructure. Indeed, some self-styled progressives regard mega-dams as green despite the ecological costs of concrete, habitat destruction, and fragmentation. Conservationists have also played important roles in shaping the technologies and practices of fishing, such as opposing bottom trawling, and other technologies (Macekura 2015).

The old does not die easily. The fossil fuel industry is trying to throw up roadblocks to non-fossil energy, though the train has already shifted tracks. Once a cluster of innovations is "chosen," constraints imposed by these choices shut out alternatives over time. The train must follow the tracks although attempts can be made to derail it. In addition to those defending the past are groups that play contradictory roles without considering the long term: innovators trying to create new industries for the sake of it; investment bankers and fund managers seeking higher returns; governments responding to pressure or campaign contributions. Venture capitalists play an important gate-keeping role according to Berry (1991) and are under-appreciated by conservationists. They are important not just because they make important decisions but because they are inclined to look at a broader range of factors in making decisions, including their own passions; they are thus sometimes susceptible to influence by a value-driven rather than strictly profit-driven agenda. But there is no evidence that NGOs have taken much advantage of the cyclical opportunities described here.

Periods of growth generate the search for new "inputs": energy, what economists call "raw materials" and cheap labor. This search by firms and countries results in expansion of human activity into new areas to mine (rare earths for cell phones), log, clear intact forests for conversion to monoculture (such as palm plantations). Such expansion can generate fierce competition over "resources," resulting in internal wars (often proxy wars between great powers), wars among states and even global or hegemonic wars over the resource extraction and trade system (e.g. Goldstein 1988; Klare 2002; Paskal 2010).

Some researchers have found that multiple cycles of growth and competition over resources weaken dominant powers relative to countries whose power is increasing; the former's reach shrinks in their regions of influence and globally, inevitably resulting in challenges (Goldstein 1988; Thompson 2000, 2009; Vasquez 2009). Global wars can result when the challenger seeks not just to replace the dominant power but to establish a new order (Kugler and Tammen

2009). Germany's challenge to Britain over the first half of the twentieth century resulted in its ruin (and resurrection as a regional power),
decline of Britain as a global hegemon, and its replacement by the US
as the globally dominant power. There were two great unanticipated
consequences of this conflict: anti-colonial movements around the
world took advantage of the need of the Allies for their cooperation in
World War II and gained important concessions from the war's victors
(e.g. Rosenberg 2006); within the United States the civil rights movement won similar concessions, transforming both US culture and
internal power relationships. The Soviet challenge to US influence
in a still very unequal world also gave these movements leverage.

What about conservation? The periods of modern history dominated by the unbridled pursuit of growth by Britain and the US have
resulted in the destruction of biodiversity and whole ecosystems on a
heretofore unprecedented scale. Both countries, however, have a
countervailing tradition of valuing nature that has produced species
and wildlands protection. As power shifts – with or without major
war – from North America and perhaps the European Union to China
and India, conservationists must grapple with a world order where
influence is wielded by growth even less constrained by conservation
values. Moreover, China so far does not tolerate autonomous NGOs
that might act to check the destruction of species (Jin 2011; Zhao
2011). Only recently has it started to come to terms with devastating
pollution from growth and with ensuing protests.

As China challenges the US-dominated global order in the
South China Sea and elsewhere, it is likely the beginning of a hegemonic conflict. The level of interdependence may militate against
direct and open conflict. And challenges to the dominant order may
come from elsewhere. What is clear is that climate change will produce a range of crises, from local to regional and continental to global,
which will wreck havoc with species and ecosystems but also provide
conservationists with major opportunities for political leverage.
Whether conservationists can take advantage is another matter.
They must be able to present compelling alternatives to the status

quo – both mythically and materially. People do not let go of the old just because it has stopped working (Wallace 1956). At both the cultural and material level, conservationists face a very problematic societal dynamic.

Rapid economic growth in regions that have been less developed can also generate intense conflicts as a result of increased competition over rising demand and changes in global relationships. These may or may not undermine existing dominance structures in the world system and its rules, as the cumulative impacts of decolonization did over several decades.

For conservationists this sort of influence is not the end game. The extinction crisis will not be mitigated by humanity shopping its way to the goal. Nor by technological breakthroughs (Ehrenfeld 1978; Holdren 2007).

There thus remains the more fundamental question, which conservation is wary of grappling with. Why more and more energy, whether solar or fossil fuel? Why more and more growth? When is enough enough? Certainly elites will not present this fundamental question to society; the limit to growth is off limits. Few conservation leaders present the question, though we saw in Chapter 5 that some thought leaders do (McKee 2003; Cafaro and Crist 2013; Dietz and O'Neill 2013; Goldie and Betts 2013; Higgs 2014).

Accidents and "natural disasters" also present opportunities for political leverage and cultural change. In 2015 a US military lab shipped live anthrax to eighteen other facilities in the US and South Korea. No one was affected, but it's probably only a matter of time before such leaks occur. In 1971 the Soviet Union suffered many deaths when weaponized smallpox was accidentally released, but tight control of news prevented a crisis. When the Chernobyl nuclear power plant melted down in 1986 the Soviets were not able to contain the news, and both domestic and international responses undermined the credibility of the leadership. Seven years earlier a meltdown at the Three Mile Island power plant shut down the commercial US nuclear power industry. Although there were no fatalities it was not possible for power companies to obtain insurance even with government subsidies. The government that permitted the plant to be built in an area subject to earthquakes and tsunamis, continues to pay a political price. The future of nuclear power in Japan may be in doubt. Many times, of course, mishaps don't come to a head, so they stay secret for long periods and do not produce a crisis. In May 1967 a solar storm caused the US Air Force to think the Soviets were jamming the ballistic early warning radar and they nearly sent planes aloft toward the USSR (Nature News in Brief 2016). Such events contribute to unease and over time can corrode confidence in the status quo.

The irony is that many chronic problems may be invisible, despite the high costs to humans and other species. Many millions die from pollution, including the burning of fossil fuels, every year (Smith 2014; Landrigan et al. 2017). In the US alone the health costs of burning fossil fuels are estimated to be $120 billion (Wald 2009). It has been difficult to generate political traction around these costs; perhaps industry has learned how to manage criticism after pesticide restrictions resulted from the early 1960s response to Rachel Carson's work (1962). The incompetent US government preparation for and response to Hurricane Katrina's impact on New Orleans seriously damaged the Bush administration's credibility and probably influenced the 2008 presidential and congressional elections but did not offer systemic opportunities.

Conservationists ultimately face a temporally much deeper dynamic. It emerged 12,000 years ago with the "Neolithic Revolution." Agriculture gave rise to the growth-focused hierarchical institutions so familiar today (Johnson and Earle 2000). The course of human history has overwhelmingly been one of building institutions of control: control over the natural world and control over people. We examined in Chapter 6 the central role of energy in this. But the point is that dismantling power has not been tried before on a large scale.

That is the challenge conservationists face if the biological and ecological world is to heal. People are going to leave alone at least half of the world.

At the beginning of this chapter we looked to David Ehrenfeld (1978) to summarize the dominant belief in progress, including progress as growth, and the human ability to solve all problems. Despite strong evidence to the contrary – that the world is too complex for us to understand, let alone to effectively manage and that our solutions invariably create new problems that are much more difficult to address – the faith remains strong. Sometimes a faith is strengthened in the face of contrary reality and a lack of alternatives – it can generate fundamentalism (Norris and Inglehart 2004). The situation is complicated by who holds power and their ability to foreclose material options and cultural options – dying groups shape the future more than rising ones because of this circumstance (Moore 1966).

The conservation movement seems mostly unaware of the depth of the forces destroying biodiversity or doesn't want to acknowledge, let alone address them. A forest is saved here, but logging increases elsewhere. World leaders such as former president Lula de Silva of Brazil proclaim a new path forward that stresses conservation goals, but do not deliver (Hochstetler and Keck 2007). Societies which are situated between the richest and poorest have often been a major source of societal innovation (Chase-Dunn and Hall 1997). Historically this innovation has contributed to intensifying exploitation of the natural world to strengthen their position in the world system by breaking free from longstanding domination by other countries. It is possible some of these countries might take another path?

Choices ripple through time and can have significant cumulative consequences. Every child not born today means fewer children having children in the future. The more oil that stays in the ground today and the more forests that remain intact, the less climate will be disrupted in the more distant future.

7. Understand Power

Former US Secretary of the Interior Bruce Babbitt said, "Don't expect me to do the right thing, make me do it."[1] Prevailing in the choice of policy or leaders has little to do with reasoned arguments and facts, though they may provide public justification for actions. Instead, political outcomes depend on the ability of contesting parties to effectively mobilize more money, votes, media, and other resources than their opponents. Decision makers must care about an issue before information about it matters. Although some issues are near to their heart, one of the nearest is remaining a decision maker (or getting to be one) (Johns 2009). Even sympathetic decision makers need to feel systematic pressure because it allows them to resist counter-pressure and gives them cover.

Successful movements and organizations understand who holds power, how decisions are made, who can directly influence the outcomes, and how to mobilize those groups or individuals (Johns 2009). They understand that the process of influencing decision makers starts with influencing decisions about who makes decisions. They understand that reaching goals depends on the willingness to use to the fullest and intelligently their capacity to reward and punish. Timidity or indecisiveness is ineffective.

Just as anti-colonial and pro-democracy movements have sometimes found themselves needing to change basic relationships on a very large scale in order to achieve their goals (China, Eastern Europe, South Africa) so conservationists may confront something similar: the need to challenge the human colonization of the natural world. The subjugation of other species and living systems to human will and whims is antagonistic to the wild, to the self-willed. In this sense conservation is unavoidably revolutionary; and this makes many uncomfortable.

---

[1] At the High Desert Conference on 11 September 2004 I asked Babbitt if this story was true. He said "Close enough."

Perhaps no one understood power and expressed his understanding of it more elegantly and fearlessly than abolitionist and former slave Frederick Douglass (1985 [1857]: 204):

> ... Power concedes nothing without a demand. It never did and it never will. *Find out just what any people will quietly submit to and you have found out the exact measure of injustice and wrong that will be imposed* ... and these will continue till they are resisted with words or blows or with both. ... [italics added]

> If there is no struggle there is no progress. Those who profess to favor freedom but deprecate agitation are men who ... want rain without thunder and lightning. They want the ocean without the awful roar of its many waters.

To say no – no longer, no more – to domination in its many forms puts one in opposition to those who seek to continue domination and who wield considerable power. One becomes a target.

To be successful in these circumstances rests in large part on mobilizing the unmobilized. On creating new political power by bringing people into conservation NGOs where they can act collectively in a coordinated and sustained fashion. Power also rests on forging short- or long-term alliances and coalitions around shared values or outcomes or a quid pro quo. The outcome of a political conflict depends on relative levels of mobilization of the competing parties, so undercutting opponents can have the same effect as mobilizing one's own resources.

Success also hinges on which fights to take on and choosing the field of conflict to the degree possible. In the 1960s and early 1970s contentious politics – outsider approaches – marked many struggles in the US over civil rights, war, the draft, class inequality, and other issues. The response of opponents and the state to these challenges was repression: infiltration of spies and provocateurs, violence and threats of violence, intimidation and abuse of the legal system to tie up movement resources in bail and by putting movement leaders in jail (e.g. Helvarg 2004; Isikoff, 2005; Dwyer 2006, 2007; Liptak 2006a,

FIGURE 7.1 'Stakeholders' by Seppo Leinonen. Reproduced with permission.

2006b, 2008; Tierney 2006; Boykoff, 2007; Piven at al 2009; Haas, 2010). These tools are still used, e.g. the Battle of Seattle (protests over globalization and the World Trade Organization ministerial meeting) or the 2004 Republican Convention in New York City.

Increasingly there are efforts to bog down conservation in time sinks of endless process. Process in which every conceivable human interest is given weight and more weight than the existence of entire species. It is a recipe for continued destruction of life on Earth.

With Douglass's view of power in mind, changing the basic colonial relationship to the natural world will require an unreserved focus on weakening the grip of the institutions of domination at every opportunity, without hesitation or compromise. The task of conservation is not to bargain away the lives of other species or to be "reasonable" in the view of the powerful. It is to replace the powerful and their institutions with relationships that respect, value, and care for life.

REFERENCES

Aminzade, Ronald R. and Elizabeth J. Perry. 2001. The Sacred, Religious and Secular in Contentious Politics. Pp. 155–78 in Ronald R. Aminzade, Jack A. Goldstone, Doug McAdam, et al. *Silence and Voice in the Study of Contentious Politics*. Cambridge University Press. Cambridge.

Aminzade, Ronald R., Jack A. Goldstone, and Elizabeth Perry. 2001. Leadership Dynamics and Dynamics of Contention. Pp. 126–54 in Ronald R. Aminzade, Jack A. Goldstone, Doug McAdam, et al. *Silence and Voice in the Study of Contentious Politics*. Cambridge University Press. Cambridge.

Barker, Colin. 2001. Fear, Laughter, and Collective Power: The Making of Solidarity at the Lenin Shipyard in Gdansk, Poland, August 1980. Pp. 175–94 in Jeff Goodwin, James M. Jasper, and Francesca Polletta (eds.). *Passionate Politics*. University of Chicago Press. Chicago, IL.

Barnosky, Anthony D., Paul L. Koch, Robert S. Feranac, Scott L. Wing, and Alan B Shabel. 2004. Assessing the Causes of Late Pleistocene Extinctions on the Continents. 306 *Science* 70–5 (October 1).

Baumgartner, Frank R. 2006. Punctuated Equilibrium Theory and Environmental Policy. Pp. 24–46 in Robert Repetto (ed.). 2006. *Punctuated Equilibrium and the Dynamics of US Environmental Policy*. Yale University Press. New Haven, CT.

Benford, Robert D. and David A. Snow. 2000. "Framing Processes and Social Movements." 26 *Annual Review of Sociology* 611–39.

Berry, B. J. L. 1991. *Long Wave Rhythms in Economic Development and Political Behavior*. Johns Hopkins University Press. Baltimore, MD.

Berry, B. J. L., E. Elliot, E. J. Harpham, and H. Kim. 1998. *The Rhythms of American Politics*. University Press of America. Lanham, MD.

Bevington, Doug. 2009. *The Rebirth of Environmentalism*. Island Press. Washington DC.

Boykoff, Jules. 2007. *Beyond Bullets*. AK Press. Oakland, CA.

Brader, Ted. 2005. *Campaigning for Hearts and Minds*. University of Chicago Press. Chicago, IL.

Brashares, Justin S. 2010. "Filtering Wildlife." 329 *Science* 402–3 (July 23).

Brashares, Justin S. and Kaitlyn M. Gaynor. 2017. Eating Ecosystems. 356 *Science* 136–7 (April 14).

Broadbent, Jeffrey and Vicky Brockman (eds.). 2011. *East Asian Social Movements*. Springer. New York.

Brock, William A. 2006. Tipping Points, Abrupt Opinion Changes, and Punctuated Policy Change. Pp. 47–77 in Robert Repetto (ed.). 2006. *Punctuated Equilibrium and the Dynamics of US Environmental Policy*. Yale University Press. New Haven, CT.

Butchart, Stuart H. M., Matt Walpole, Ben Collen, et al. 2010. Global Biodiversity: Indicators of Recent Declines. 328 *Science* 1164–8 (May 28).

Cafaro, Philip and Eileen Crist (eds.). 2013. *Life on the Brink*. University of Georgia Press. Athens, GA.

Carson, Rachel. 1962. *Silent Spring*. Houghton Mifflin. Boston, MA.

Carter, Neil. 2007. *Politics of the Environment*. 2nd edn. Cambridge University Press. Cambridge.

Cassen, Bernard. 2004. Inventing ATTAC. Pp. 152–74 in Tom Mertes (ed.) *A Movement of Movements*. Verso. London.

Chase-Dunn, Christopher and Thomas D. Hall. 1997. *Rise and Demise*. Westview Press. Boulder, CO.

Clayton, Susan. 2000. Models of Justice in the Environmental Debate. 56 *Journal of Social Issues* 3: 459–74 (Fall).

Clifford, Bob. 2005. *Marketing of Rebellion*. Cambridge University Press. Cambridge.

Cohen, Mark Nathan. 1977. *The Food Crisis in Prehistory*. Yale University Press. New Haven, CT.

Cornog, Evan. 2004. *The Power and the Story*. Penguin Press. New York.

Cox, Robert. 2006. *Environmental Communication and the Public Sphere*. Sage. Thousand Oaks, CA.

Crozier, Michel, Samuel Huntington and Joji Watanuki, J. 1975. *The Crisis of Democracy. Report on the Governability of Democracies to the Trilateral Commission*. New York University Press. New York.

Davenport, Christian. 2005. Introduction. Repression and Mobilization: Insights from Political Science and Sociology. Pp. vii–xli in Christian Davenport, Hank Johnson, and Carol Mueller (eds.). *Repression and Mobilization*. University of Minnesota Press. Minneapolis, MN.

Davenport, Christian. 2010. *Media Bias, Perspective, and State Repression*. Cambridge University Press. New York.

Davenport, Christian, Hank Johnson, and Carol Mueller (eds.). 2005. *Repression and Mobilization*. University of Minnesota Press. Minneapolis, MN.

Davis, Charles. 2006. The Politics of Grazing on Federal Lands: A Policy Change Perspective. Pp. 232–52 in Robert Repetto (ed.). *Punctuated Equilibrium and the Dynamics of US Environmental Policy*. Yale University Press. New Haven, CT.

DeBenedetti, Charles. 1990. *An American Ordeal*. Syracuse University Press. Syracuse, NY.

Dietz, Rob and Dan O'Neill. 2013. *Enough is Enough*. Berrett-Koehler. San Francisco.

Domhoff, G. William. 2009. *Who Rules America?* 6th edn. McGraw Hill. Boston, MA.

Donner, Frank. 1990. *Protectors of Privilege*. University of California Press. Berkeley.

Döring, Holger and Philip Manow. 2015. Is Proportional Representation More Favourable to the Left? Electoral Rules and Their Impact on Elections,

Parliaments and the Formation of Cabinets. *British Journal of Political Science*. Published online: August 24, 2015. http://dx.doi.org/10.1017/S0007123415000290 (accessed July 3, 2016).

Douglass, Frederick. [1857] (1985). "The Significance of Emancipation in the West Indies." Speech, Canandaigua, New York, August 3, 1857; collected in pamphlet by author. Pp. 183–208 in John W. Blassingame (ed.) *The Frederick Douglass Papers. Series One: Speeches, Debates, and Interviews. Volume 3: 1855–63.* Yale University Press. New Haven, CT.

Drohan, Madelaine. 2003. *Making a Killing*. Random House Canada. Toronto.

Dryzek, John S., David Downes, Christian Hunold, and David Schlosberg. 2003. *Green States and Social Movements*. Oxford University Press. Oxford.

Dwyer, Jim. 2006. Police Files Say Arrest Tactics Calmed Protest. *New York Times*, March 17.

Dwyer, Jim. 2007. At the Protest, A Civics Lesson Gets a Twist. *New York Times*, April 25.

Dye, Thomas R. 2013. *Who's Running America?* 8th edn. Paradigm. Boulder, CO.

Edelman, Murray. 1988. *Constructing the Political Spectacle*. University of Chicago Press. Chicago, IL.

Edelman, Murray. 1995. *From Art to Politics*. University of Chicago Press. Chicago, IL.

Ehrenfeld, David. 1978. *Arrogance of Humanism*. Oxford University Press. New York.

Emerson, Ralph Waldo. 1994 [1847]. Ode, Inscribed to W. H. Channing. Pp. 61–4 in *Emerson: Collected Poems and Translations*. Library of America. New York.

Ewen, Stuart. 1996. *PR! A Social History of Spin*. Basic Books. New York.

Ewing, B., S. Goldfinger, A. Oursler, A. Reed, D. Moore, and M. Wackernagel. 2009. *The Ecological Footprint Atlas 2009*. Global Footprint Network. Oakland, CA.

Field, Connie (dir). 2010. *Have You Heard From Johannesburg?* Clarity Films.

Finley, Carmel. 2017. *All the Boats on the Ocean*. University of Chicago Press. Chicago, IL.

Fischer, David Hackett. 1996. *The Great Wave*. Oxford University Press. Oxford.

Foner, Philip S. 1975. *History of the Labor Movement in the United States. Volume 1*. International Press. New York.

Frumhoff, Peter C. and Naomi Oreskes. 2015. Fossil Fuel Firms Still Bankrolling Climate Denial Lobby Groups. The *Guardian* (March 25). www.theguardian.com/environment/2015/mar/25/fossil-fuel-firms-are-still-bankrolling-climate-denial-lobby-groups (accessed August 11, 2016).

Gandhi, Mohandas. 1928. Wardha Letter. 10 Young India 51: 422 (December 20).

Garrow, David. 1986. *Bearing the Cross*. Morrow. New York.

Giugni, Marco. 2004. *Social Protest and Policy Change*. Rowman & Littlefield. Lanham, MD.

Giving USA/Center on Philanthropy. 2016. *Giving USA 2016 Highlights*. Giving USA. Lilly Family School of Philanthropy. Indianapolis IN. http://givingusa.org/ (accessed July 10, 2016).

Goldie, Jenny and Katharine Betts (eds.). 2013. *Sustainable Futures*. Csiro Publishing. Collingswood, VIC. Based on the Fenner Conference on the Future of Australia, 2013.

Goldstein, Joshua S. 1988. *Long Cycles*. Yale University Press. New Haven, CT.

Goldstone, Jack A. and Charles Tilly. 2001. Threat (and Opportunity): Popular Action and State Response in the Dynamics of Contentious Action. Pp. 179–94 in Ronald R. Aminzade, Jack A. Goldstone, Doug McAdam, et al. *Silence and Voice in the Study of Contentious Politics*. Cambridge University Press. Cambridge.

Gonzalez, George A. 2001. *Corporate Power and the Environment*. Rowman & Littlefield. Lanham, MD.

Goodwin, Jeff and Steven Pfaff. 2001. Emotion Work in High-Risk Social Movements: Managing Fear in the US and East German Civil Rights Movements. Pp. 282–302 in Jeff Goodwin, James M. Jasper, and Francesca Polletta (eds.). *Passionate Politics*. University of Chicago Press. Chicago, IL.

Goodwin, Jeff, James M. Jasper, and Francesca Polletta. 2001. Introduction. Pp. 1–24 in Jeff Goodwin, James M. Jasper, and Francesca Polletta (eds.). *Passionate Politics*. University of Chicago Press. Chicago, IL.

Gunter, Tara Rae. 2002. *The Steens Mountain Divide: Beyond Compromise in the Oregon High Desert*. Master's Thesis. University of Montana. Missoula, MT.

Haas, Jeffrey. 2010. *The Assassination of Fred Hampton*. Lawrence Hill Books. Chicago, IL.

Harkin, Michael E. (ed.). 2004. *Reassessing Revitalization Movements*. University of Nebraska Press. Lincoln, NE.

Harris, Marvin. 1977. *Cannibals and Kings*. Random House. New York.

Harris, Marvin. 1979. *Cultural Materialism*. Random House. New York.

Helvarg, David. 2004. *War on the Greens*. 2nd edn. Johnson. Boulder, CO.

Hendricks, Steve. 2006. *Unquiet Grave*. Thunder's Mouth Press. New York.

Higgs, Kerryn. 2014. *Collision Course*. MIT Press. Cambridge, MA.

Hochstetler, Kathryn and Margaret E. Keck. 2007. *Greening Brazil*. Duke University Press. Durham, NC.

Holdren, John. 2007. Opening Address to the 2007 Annual Meeting of the American Association for the Advancement of Science. Quoted in Coontz, Robert. 2007. Wedging Sustainability into Public Consciousness. 315 *Science* 1068 (February 23).

Ingram, Helen and Leah Fraser. 2006. Path Dependency and Adroit Innovation: The Case of California Water. Pp. 78–109 in Robert Repetto (ed.). *Punctuated Equilibrium and the Dynamics of US Environmental Policy.* Yale University Press. New Haven, CT.

Isikoff, Michael. 2005. Profiling: How the FBI Tracks Eco-Terror Suspects. 146 *Newsweek* 21 (November 21).

Jackson, Tim. 2009. *Prosperity without Growth.* Earthscan. London.

Jimenez, Ignacio. 2017. Personal communication. March 2.

Jin, Jun. 2011. Institutionalized Official Hostility and Protest Leader Logic: A Long-Term Chinese Peasants Collective Protest at Dahe Dam in the 1980s. Pp. 413–35 in Jeffrey Broadbent and Vicky Brockman (eds.). *East Asian Social Movements.* Springer. New York.

Johns, David. 2005. The Other Connectivity: Reaching Beyond the Choir. 19 *Conservation Biology* 6: 1681–2 (December).

Johns, David. 2009. *A New Conservation Politics.* Wiley-Blackwell. Oxford.

Johnson, Allen W. and Tim Earle. 2000. *The Evolution of Human Societies.* 2nd edn. Stanford University Press. Stanford, CA.

Johnson, Christopher N., Andrew Balmford, Barry W. Brook, et al. 2017. Biodiversity Losses and Conservation Responses in the Anthropocene. 356 *Science* 270–5 (April 21).

Jost, John T., Diana Burgess, and Cristina O. Mosso. 2001. Conflicts of Legitimation among Self, Group, and System. Pp. 363–88 in John T. Jost and Brenda Major (eds.). *The Psychology of Legitimacy.* Cambridge University Press. Cambridge.

Kamieniecki, Sheldon. 2006. *Corporate America and Environmental Policy.* Stanford University Press. Stanford, CA.

Kasser, Tim. 2002. *The High Price of Consumer Culture.* MIT Press. Cambridge, MA.

Kertzer, David I. 1988. *Ritual, Politics and Power.* Yale University Press. New Haven, CT.

Kirk, Michael and Michael Wiser. 2012. *Money Power and Wall Street Part 3.* Frontline/WGBH. Boston, MA (first broadcast May 1, 2012).

Klare, Michael T. 2001. *Resource Wars.* Metropolitan Books. New York. (Rev. edn. 2002. Owl Books. New York.)

Koopmans, Ruud. 2005. Repression and the Public Sphere. Pp. 159–88 in Christian Davenport, Hank Johnson, and Carol Mueller (eds.). *Repression and Mobilization.* University of Minnesota Press. Minneapolis, MN.

Kraft, Michael E. and Sheldon Kamieniecki (eds.). 2007. *Business and Environmental Policy.* MIT Press. Cambridge, MA.

Kriesi, H. 2004. Political Context and Opportunity. Pp. 67–90 in D. A. Snow, S. A. Soule, and H. Kriesi (eds.). *The Blackwell Companion to Social Movements*. Blackwell. Malden, MA.

Kriesi, Hanspeter and Dominique Wisler. 1999. The Impact of Social Movements on Political Institutions. Pp. 42–65 in Marco Giugni, Doug McAdam, and Charles Tilly (eds.). *How Social Movements Matter*. University of Minnesota. Minneapolis, MN.

Kugler, Jacek and Ronald L. Tammen. 2009. Implications of Asia's Rise to Global Status. Pp. 161–86 in William R. Thompson (ed.). *Systemic Transitions*. Palgrave Macmillan. New York.

Landrigan Philip J., Richard Fuller, Nereus J. R. Acosta, et al. 2017. The *Lancet* Commission on pollution and health. http://dx.doi.org/10.1016/S0140-6736(17) 32345-0 (October 19) (accessed December 6, 2017).

Layzer, Judith. 2007. Deep Freeze: How Business Has Shaped the Global Warming Debate in Congress. Pp. 93–125 in M. E. Kraft and S. Kamieniecki (eds.). *Business and Environmental Policy*. MIT Press. Cambridge, MA.

Lee, Martha F. 1995. *Earth First! Environmental Apocalypse*. Syracuse University Press. Syracuse, NY.

Libby, Ronald T. 1999 *Eco-Wars: Political Campaigns and Social Movements*. Columbia University Press. New York.

Liptak, Adam. 2006a. In Leak Cases, New Pressure on Journalists. *New York Times*, April 30.

Liptak, Adam. 2006b. Gonzales Says Prosecutions of Journalists are Possible. *New York Times*, May 22.

Liptak, Adam. 2008. A Corporate View of Mafia Tactics: Protesting, Lobbying and Citing Upton Sinclair. *New York Times*, February 5.

Lofland, John. 1997 [1978]. Becoming a World Saver Revisited. Pp. 284–9 in Doug McAdam and David A. Snow (eds.). *Social Movements: Readings on Their Emergence, Mobilization, and Dynamics*. Roxbury Publishing. Los Angeles.

Louv, Richard. 2005. *Last Child in the Woods*. Algonquin Books. Chapel Hill, NC.

Macekura, Stephen J. 2015. *Of Limits and Growth*. Cambridge University Press. New York City.

McAdam, Doug. 1986. Recruitment to High Risk Activism. 92 *American Journal of Sociology* 1: 64–90 (July).

McAdam, Doug. 1997 [1983]. Tactical Innovation and the Pace of Insurgency. Pp. 340–56 in Doug McAdam and David A. Snow (eds.). *Social Movements: Readings on Their Emergence, Mobilization, and Dynamics*. Roxbury Publishing. Los Angeles.

McAdam, Doug A. and William H. Sewell. 2001. It's About Time: Temporality in the Study of Social Movements and Revolutions. Pp. 89–125 in Ronald R. Aminzade, Jack A. Goldstone, Doug McAdam, et al. *Silence and Voice in the Study of Contentious Politics.* Cambridge University Press. Cambridge.

McAdam, Doug, Sidney Tarrow, and Charles Tilly. *Dynamics of Contention.* 2001. Cambridge University Press. Cambridge.

McCarthy, John D. and Clark McPhail. 1998. The Institutionalization of Protest in the United States. Pp. 83–110 in David S. Meyer and Sidney Tarrow (eds.). *The Social Movement Society.* Rowman & Littlefield. Lanham, MD.

McKee, Jeffrey K. 2003. *Sparing Nature.* Rutgers University Press. New Brunswick, NJ.

Meyer, David S. and Sidney Tarrow. 1998. A Movement Society: Contentious Politics for a New Society. Pp. 1–28 in David S. Meyer and Sidney Tarrow (eds.). *The Social Movement Society.* Rowman & Littlefield. Lanham, MD.

Michels, Robert. 1962 [1915] *Political Parties.* Free Press. Glencoe, IL.

Miller, Gifford H., John W. Magee, Beverly J. Johnson, et al. 1999. Pleistocene Extinction of *Genyornis newtoni:* Human Impact on Australian Megafauna. 283 *Science* 205–8 (January 8).

Moore, Barrington. 1966. *The Social Origins of Dictatorship and Democracy.* Beacon Press. Boston, MA.

Moore, Sally Falk and Barbara G. Myerhoff (eds.) 1977. *Secular Ritual.* Assen. Van Gorcum.

Morris, Aldon D. and Suzanne Staggenborg. 2004. Leadership in Social Movements. Pp. 171–96 in David A. Snow, Sarah A. Soule and Hanspeter Kriesi (eds.). 2004. *The Blackwell Companion to Social Movements.* Blackwell Publishing. Oxford.

Murray, Charles. 2016. Trump's America. *Wall Street Journal,* February 13–14: C1–2.

Nature Editors (unsigned). 2010. Closing the Climategate. 468 *Nature* 345 (November 18).

Nature News in Brief. 2016. Solar-storm War Risk. 536 *Nature* 254 (August 18).

Norris, Pippa and Ronald Inglehart. 2004. *The Sacred and the Secular.* Cambridge University Press. Cambridge.

Otto, Shawn. 2016. *The War on Science.* Milkweed Editions. Minneapolis, MN.

Paskal, Cleo. 2010. *Global Warring.* Palgrave Macmillan. New York.

Pimm, Stuart. 2001. *The World According to Pimm.* McGraw-Hill. New York.

Pimm, Stuart, C. N. Jenkins, R. Abell, et al. 2014. The Biodiversity of Species and Their Rates of Extinction, Distribution, and Protection. 344 *Science* 987 (May 30). doi: 10.1126/ science.1246752-1-11 (accessed June 8, 2014).

Piven, Francis Fox and Richard Cloward. 1977. *Poor People's Movements.* Pantheon. New York City.

Piven, Francis Fox, Lorraine C. Minnite, and Margaret Groarke. 2009. *Keeping Down the Black Vote*. New Press. New York.

Polletta, Francesca. 2006. *It Was Like a Fever*. University of Chicago Press. Chicago, IL.

Polletta, Francesco and M. Kai Ho. 2006. "Frames and Their Consequences." Pp. 187–209 in Robert E. Goodin and Charles Tilly (eds.). *Oxford Handbook of Contextual Political Analysis*. Oxford University Press. New York.

Rambo, Lewis R. 1993. *Understanding Religious Conversion*. Yale University Press. New Haven, CT.

Rappaport, Roy A. 1976. Adaptations and Maladaptations in Social Systems. Pp. 39–79 in I. Hill (ed.). *The Ethical Basis of Economic Freedom*. American Viewpoint. Chapel Hill, NC.

Repetto, Robert. 2006. Introduction. Pp. 1–23 in Robert Repetto (ed.). 2006. *Punctuated Equilibrium and the Dynamics of US Environmental Policy*. Yale University Press. New Haven, CT.

Ripple, William J., Katharine Abernethy, Matthew G. Betts, et al. 2016. Bushmeat Hunting and Extinction Risk to the World's Mammals. *Royal Society Open Science* 3: 160498. http://dx.doi.org/10.1098/rsos.160498 (accessed November 1, 2016).

Rocheleau, Bruce. 2017. *Wildlife Politics*. Cambridge University Press. Cambridge.

Rootes, Christopher. 2007 [2004]. Environmental Movements. Pp. 608–40 in David Snow, Sarah Soule, and Hanspeter Kriesi (eds.). *The Blackwell Companion to Social Movements*. Blackwell. Oxford.

Rosenberg, Jonathan. 2006. *How Far the Promised Land?* Princeton University Press. Princeton, NJ.

Rucht, Dieter. 1999. The Impact of Environmental Movements in Western Societies. Pp. 204–24 in Marco Giugni, Doug McAdam, and Charles Tilly (eds.). *How Social Movements Matter*. University of Minnesota. Minneapolis, MN.

Schumpeter, Joseph. 1939. *Business Cycles: A Theoretical, Historical, and Statistical Analysis of the Capitalist Process*. McGraw-Hill. London.

Sellars, John. 2004. Raising a Ruckus. Pp. 174–91 in Tom Mertes (ed.). *A Movement of Movements*. Verso. London.

Shaiko, Ronald G. 1999. *Voices and Echoes for the Environment*. Columbia University Press. New York.

Shepard, Harold S. 2006. The Future of Livestock Grazing and the Endangered Species Act. 21 *Journal of Environmental Law and Litigation* 383–444.

Skocpol, Theda, Arianne Liazos, and Marshall Ganz (eds.). 2006. *What a Mighty Power We Can Be*. Princeton University Press. Princeton, NJ.

Smith, Geoffrey. 2014. The cost of China's dependence on coal – 670,000 deaths a year. *Fortune* (November 5). http://fortune.com/2014/11/05/the-cost-of-chinas-dependence-on-coal-670000-deaths-a-year/.

Staggenborg, Suzanne. 2011. *Social Movements*. Oxford University Press. New York.

Stern, Paul. 2000. Toward a Coherent Theory of Environmentally Significant Behavior. 56 *Journal of Social Issues* 3: 407–24 (Fall).

Taylor, Verta. 1989. Social Movement Continuity: The Women's Movement in Abeyance. 54 *American Sociological Review* 5: 761–75 (October).

Thompson, William R. 2000. K-waves, Leadership Cycles, and Global War. Pp. 83–104 in T. D. Hall (ed.). *A World Systems Reader*. Rowman & Littlefield. Lanham, MD.

Thompson, William R. 2009. Structural Preludes to Systemic Transitions since 1494. Pp. 55–73 in William R. Thompson (ed.). *Systemic Transitions*. Palgrave Macmillan. New York.

Tilly, Charles. 2004. *Social Movements 1768–2004*. Paradigm Publishers. Boulder, CO.

UNFAO (United Nations Food and Agricultural Organization). 2010. Press Release of September 14. Rome.

Vasquez, John A. 2009. When and How Global Leadership Transitions Will Result in War. Pp. 131–60 in William R. Thompson (ed.). *Systemic Transitions*. Palgrave Macmillan. New York.

Venter, Oscar, Eric W. Sanderson, Ainhoa Magrach, et al. 2016. Sixteen Years of Change in the Global Terrestrial Human Footprint and Implications for Biodiversity Conservation. *Nature Communications* 7: 12558. doi: 10.1038/ncomms12558 (accessed August 23, 2016).

Wald, Matthew L. 2009. Fossil Fuels' Hidden Cost Is in Billions, Study Says. *New York Times*, October 20: A16.

Wallace, Anthony F. C. 1956. Revitalization Movements. 58 *American Anthropologist* 264–81 (April).

Wallace, A. F. C. 1970. *Culture and Personality*. 2nd edn. Random House. New York.

Watson, James E. M., Danielle F. Shanahan, et al. 2016a. Catastrophic Declines in Wilderness Areas Undermine Global Environment Targets. 26 *Current Biology* 1–6 (November 7).

Watson, James E. M., Kendall R. Jones, Richard A. Fuller, et al. 2016b. Persistent Disparities between Recent Rates of Habitat Conversion and Protection and Implications for Future Global Conservation Targets. *Conservation Letters* doi: 10.1111/conl.12295 (August 12; accessed December 6, 2016).

White, Leslie. 1987 [1975]. The Energy Theory of Cultural Development. In *Ethnological Essays*. University of New Mexico Press. Albuquerque.

Wittner, Lawrence. 1984. *Rebels against War*. Temple University Press. Philadelphia, PA.

Wolfe, Alan. 1977. *The Limits of Legitimacy*. Free Press. New York City.

Wood, Elisabeth Jean. 2000. *Forging Democracy from Below*. Cambridge University Press. Cambridge.

Wood, Elisabeth Jean. 2001. The Emotional Benefits of Insurgency in El Salvador. Pp. 267–281 in Jeff Goodwin, James M. Jasper, and Francesca Polletta (eds.). 2001. *Passionate Politics*. University of Chicago Press. Chicago, IL.

Wright, Ronald. 2004. *A Short History of Progress*. Carroll and Graf. New York.

Wuerthner, George, Eileen Crist, and Tom Butler (eds.). *Keeping the Wild*. Island Press. Washington DC.

Zhao, Dingxin. 2011. State Legitimacy and Dynamics of the 1989 Pro-democracy Movement in Beijing. Pp. 385–411 in Jeffrey Broadbent and Vicky Brockman (eds.). *East Asian Social Movements*. Springer. New York.

Zwerman, Gilda and Patricia Steinhoff. 2005. When Activists Ask for Trouble. Pp. 85–107 in Christian Davenport, Hank Johnson, and Carol Mueller (eds.). *Repression and Mobilization*. University of Minnesota Press. Minneapolis, MN.

8 Lessons from Large-Scale Conservation

A large body of research in conservation biology has shown that maintaining ecological structure, diversity and resilience demands strict, large-scale protection of entire ecosystems. There is evidence that roughly 50 percent of the land in a region needs to be protected in systems of linked core areas if the goal of preventing further anthropogenic extinctions is to be achieved.

Soule and Terborgh 1999: 3

In 1992 the Wildlands Network set out to design and create a continental system of connected protected areas (PAs) reaching across North America from Alaska and Greenland to Panama that would achieve the following conservation goals: (1) protect and recover all native species in natural patterns of abundance, including top predators and wide-ranging species, (2) protect all ecosystem types and ecological processes in a healthy state, (3) ensure the unencumbered operation of natural processes including disturbance regimes such as fire, and (4) ensure resilience in the face of anthropogenic change, such as global climate change (Noss 1992). Noss argued that large-scale conservation was essential to achieving these goals, and by the end of the century top conservation biologists (Soule and Terborgh 1999) concurred and even timid NGOs were coming around. E. O. Wilson, although his work emphasized "the little things that run the world" rather than wide-ranging species, went on record in support of large-scale conservation (Wildlands Project 1994) and has since become an eloquent champion of large-scale conservation and setting aside half of the Earth (Wilson 2016). Pringle (2017) has made a strong case for large-scale terrestrial conservation. Callum Roberts (2007) has argued for a minimum of 30 percent strict (no-take) protection for the global ocean to safeguard and recover almost all species and to mitigate acidification. Big MPAs work better than smaller ones (Davies et al. 2017).

Large-scale is used imprecisely and has no fixed meaning, but usually includes work at a regional scale (the Pacific Northwest, the Eastern Tropical Pacific, Southeast Asia) or a major part of such a region, an entire watershed (Columbia or Amazon Rivers), or whole ecosystem (short grass prairie, coral reefs). Conservation may involve government actions such as designating parks or other types of protected areas, or protection by private individuals or collectives (e.g. an *ejido* or communal land) with legal guarantees. Land may also go from private protected status to public, as with the 13 million acres assembled by Tompkins Conservation in Chile and Argentina which are or will be made Parks.

Ecological restoration, covered in the next chapter, works at the same scales. It is not always easy to draw a clear line between conservation and restoration. For purposes of Chapters 8 and 9, we can take conservation to describe the encompassing purpose and restoration to be a primary tool of conservation. Jordan and Lubick (2011) make clear, however, that restoration's motives and purposes may differ: not all restoration aims at conservation. Ecocentric restoration is akin to conservation of whole systems whereas "meliorative restoration" is to restore only some elements: those desired by humans for some particular purpose, e.g. to increase "game" numbers. Both usually seek to be informed by science. They have separate professional societies that overlap to some degree in membership and journal content. The science aspects have different foundational texts (Cairns 1975, 1980; Soule 1985).

Even conservation of largely intact areas requires some restoration – of extirpated species, of disturbances such as fire, dam removal – what Dave Foreman (Wildlands Project [Network] 2000) referred to as "healing the wounds." Many areas require much more extensive restoration than others, having been degraded by agriculture of various types, logging, bottom trawling, pollution, human housing, oil and gas extraction, and fragmentation by roads, rail, and intensive shipping lanes. Restoration includes repatriation of species, re-establishment of ecological processes, rewilding; it might include rehabilitation (see Chapter 9). The goal is generally to recreate what an area would be like had humans not intervened into the land- or seascape. Such recovery might take decades or centuries, and with global changes in climate might show the effects of human damage for a much longer period. Restoration may not result in protected area status, but achieving conservation goals may not be possible without that.

This chapter does not debate the goals of conservation but assumes goals such as those set out by the Global Ocean Refuge System, the Wildlands Network, and the Half-Earth Initiative. Here we focus on the politics of becoming more effective at getting conservation done by examining what works to achieve large-scale protection. In the last chapter we looked at the attributes of successful movements: a clear, bold vision to guide and inspire; strategic use of insider and outsider approaches (good cop/bad cop); embedding advocacy NGOs in a strong community; being flexible on means but uncompromising on goals; perseverance in the face of both victories (which are never final) and losses; exploiting divisions within elites and system crises; and staying grounded on an unsentimental understanding of power.

1. *Vision and Ideology*. Vision such as that noted in the previous paragraph (and in the first section of the previous chapter) is critical: it defines where a movement is going, is a means of gauging its progress, and lets participants know when they have arrived. It's not possible to have a meaningful strategy without a vision. Goals come from vision, not from formulaic reviews of what others are up to in the here and now – typical strengths, weaknesses, opportunities, threats (SWOT) analysis. Eyes on the prize. A bold vision is what inspires, what speaks to the deep motivational factors in people's lives. Often it is closely linked with a mythology which defines the most important purposes in the lives of a broader human population. Bold vision is ultimately

radical, as in going to the root of. A bold vision makes participants feel like they are part of something that will make a difference, though it can also frighten people.

For all these reasons, as the last chapter argues, vision is a major element in effective movements. For large-scale conservation, vision has additional important roles to play. Evolution operates at a number of geographic scales and levels, which vision-derived goals must concretely address: species distribution and life cycle needs, ecological processes including disturbance regimes and trophic relations (at what point do protected areas fail to provide for species and processes?), the drivers of injury such as habitat loss and fragmentation, species persecution. What, concretely, needs to be achieved and in what location? Which half of the Earth needs to be set aside and what limits are necessary elsewhere to protect that half from deterioration from, e.g. global pollution?

Global forces are important in conservation, but operating on a global scale has inherent difficulties. Political empires and giant corporations regularly try to do so but it requires simplifying the world and reducing it to a very few characteristics (Berry 1993): those aspects of life that are important for profit and to maintaining power (Scott 1998). The living world is more complex than counting profits and clinging to power – much too complex for humans to manage. A global vision, however, is necessary for nesting continental and regional goals and making sure the pieces fit together. Greenhouse gas emissions are generated from a myriad of sources all over the world. A global agreement to reduce them is necessary, but these agreements are made by states, and states and their subdivisions will carry out the agreements (or not). If wildlife connectivity is like making bridges across political boundaries and other obstacles, both ends of the bridge must meet if it is to be effective, and good habitat needs to be at either end of the bridge.

As the previous paragraph suggests, a comprehensive vision must address questions of scale politically, not just biologically. Nation-states are central to conservation decision making. They are the actors in international regimes, and, depending on the regime and the issue, some states are overwhelmingly central, e.g. the consumer countries and source countries of trafficked species. Decision making occurs at sub-state levels as well. Although China appears as a centralized and authoritarian state, it is more complex than that: provincial and central authorities are often in conflict. Many other countries – Brazil, Canada, and the US for example – have strong state and provincial governments with significant powers. They can serve as a source of innovation and can also resist central authority. Mobilizing conservation influence on decision makers is therefore also a matter of scale. The factors that shape mobilization are frequently local and not at the level injuries originate or desired decisions can be made. In the year 2000 there were 6,000 national and regional environmental NGOs and 20,000 local ones in the US, suggesting the importance of local concerns to people (Carmichael et al. 2012). Mihaylov and Perkins (2015) suggest the same is true globally. The creation of networks among local groups is one way conservationists have scaled up to have national and transnational influence. The US civil rights movement, for example, consisted of local desegregation fights that generated regional and national alliances that shared goals and demands, generated national action and supported national organizations which demanded changes in central government actions (Garrow 1986; Luders 2010). The central government action sought and in many cases obtained in turn altered political subdivision behavior. It also affected US foreign policy and the politics of other countries. Generally people do not feel the same urgency and passion about places distant from them as they do about what is close to home – one of the reasons the concatenation of many locals is important. Over time, as people interact and see linkages between their own lives and communities and those of others, the national and even transnational can become local, urgent and personal (Keck and Sikkink 1998; Bob 2005; Araiza 2014). It should also be noted that opportunities vary at different scales. The US civil rights movement and conservation movement have both taken advantage of this.

Segregation could not have been ended at the state level in the South; it had to be ended at the federal level, where the balance of power was different than in states where segregation obtained. Similarly, many protected areas have been established over the objection of locals intent on exploitation of the land. In both cases activists were condemned as "outsiders." Ending apartheid in South Africa required outside pressure, and many anti-colonial struggles have depended on outside support (e.g. Kaplan and Kaplan 1973).

Conservation confronts a serious weakness in that large companies and many states seek out places to exploit where laws are weak and opposition to their activities is weak. The explosion of palm plantations in Indonesia and elsewhere is a good example, as is continued illegal logging in the Amazon, the Congo Basin, Southeast Asia, and the Russian Far East.

Scale also has a temporal aspect. Conservation is about the very long term. It's not just that no victory is final because those who want the lands and oceans to exploit are constantly at it and conservationists must be prepared to check their efforts over time. It's that the ecological processes that make the wild what it is are the result of the long term and they must be protected over the long term to function. "Healing the wounds" is also long term as we shall see in the next chapter. Damage, such as destruction of the sea floor, ocean acidification, and habitat fragmentation, can have long-term consequences. Preventing such damage requires long-term protection and guardians committed to the long term. At the height of the cold war, Helen Caldicott (2017) suggested that a part of successful disarmament over the long haul would require creation of a kind of priesthood to oversee nuclear materials through their long half-lives and guard them from misuse. In her view, only religious orders had demonstrated the capacity for very long-term institutional commitment to a project.

By way of analogy, the struggle to end human slavery was a long-term fight and the end of legal slavery didn't by itself create equality. Much more work was needed, given the deeply embedded social habits, injuries, and consequent behavior.

The need to contain the human tendency to destroy biodiversity and wildness directly or as a byproduct of growth is an indefinite task involving cultural change and enforceable material constraints. All human societies engage in socialization/enculturation and coercion. In complex societies the state plays a major role and there is political conflict over trying to influence state actions and private actions on this issue. Conservation, even as it seeks to dismantle hierarchy, needs institutions other than its own to aid in the task of socialization and enculturation.

For readers trained in the social sciences much of what is being discussed in this section may sound less like vision and more like ideology. Ideology is the term applied to a worldview associated with an organization(s). It includes a vision of how the world should be (and why – it gives purpose and meaning and is linked to myth [see Chapter 14]); it also offers an analysis of how it is and provides a strategy to bring about change from the *is* to the *ought*. Usually an ideology identifies those who should be supporters of the cause and offers them justifications for joining – it provides a sense of meaning and purpose and other elements of identity. Ideology is generally more detailed than vision; it aims to guide action and thus is often more controversial and subject to debate. Conservation as a movement and conservation NGOs need a guide to action to be effective. A group of leaders focused on the vision, speaking for it, refining it as needed, addressing how events should be regarded within the framework of the vision, is important for effective action, but invariably will generate differences in views.

A final word on vision: notwithstanding its central importance, it is usually not enough to move people to action. What moves people to action is an intolerable present (Gilly 2003). The great challenge for conservation is that *other* species are subject to the intolerable and they cannot directly rebel. It is up to people to rebel on their behalf.

2. *Science.* Scientific findings do not provide values, and conservation is value-driven. Rather, science seeks to understand how the

world works by systematic observation and sometimes experimentation. Modeling also plays a role but it is just that – a model of the real thing, not the same as the real thing, just as a map is not the territory it seeks to portray.

Without a good understanding of the world as it is – and science has its limits – it is difficult to develop a sound strategy. Matters are complicated by bad models (we have all experienced the frustration of bad maps) and by the contamination of science by ideologies that make faulty assumptions about reality. An existing worldview is not easily abandoned, as Galileo found out, and as Soviet geneticists found out in the 1930s.

Despite this recurring problem of entanglement of the roles of science and ideology, ideology (and myth) are essential. They provide meaning, which humans need to guide their lives.

3. *Contention and Innovation.* Creating and sustaining a global system of protected areas that ensures all species and ecosystems are able to realize their evolutionary potential will not be easy. Certainly, in some parts of the world it can be easier than in others, e.g. where there is the concatenation of high biodiversity, low human population, low levels of human exploitation – especially industrial exploitation such as mining, energy extraction, industrial agriculture, and logging – the presence of well-resourced and organized conservation champions, weak opposition, and governments that are open to conservation. Such places include Gorongosa in Mozambique (Carroll 2016) and other areas of southern Africa (Kavango Zambezi Transfrontier Conservation Area 2017); Costa Rica (Pringle 2017); parts of the Rocky Mountains in the US and Canada (Fraser 2009); the oceans northwest of the Hawaiian Islands and surrounding Kiribati and Palau (MPAtlas 2017).

But at the global level there is a head-on conflict between what the millions of Earth's species need to thrive and what humans want. It will be a fight and indeed those who have studied how groups of humans have brought about fundamental change in the face of strong opposition observe that "transgressive action" is necessary (McAdam et al. 2001). Transgressive (or contentious) action is collective action outside the normal channels of politics. Elizabeth Wood (2000), writing about South Africa and El Salvador, observed that those seeking democracy needed to take a transgressive or outsider approach but didn't need to win the battle, they just needed to make the price of the status quo intolerable to decision makers and elites. It is a potentially risky and costly strategy, not much used by conservationists who tend to have much vested in the status quo, but it has been used in the "forest wars" in North America, in the Amazon and elsewhere. Earth First! in the 1980s used equipment sabotage (now called terrorism to evoke fear and justify violent police behavior and clamping down on civil liberties) to raise the cost of logging and other activities and to delay them while other approaches were pursued (Bevington 2009). Contentious action was critical in the eventual creation of the Northwest Forest Plan, which protected hundreds of thousands of acres of Ancient Forest.

Contentious action involves ongoing tactical innovation including civil disobedience, street theater, public displays to gain media attention, and other actions. Depending on the political context, action can vary enormously, from the Amazonian, Pacific Northwest, and Congo Basin rainforests to urban centers. Innovation is important because blockades, tree-sitting, and public displays lose their appeal to the media and authorities learn how to counter them. Such actions are also potentially destabilizing and if authorities are confronted with new circumstances and don't know what to do they can react out of fear. Success for those seeking change depends significantly on how authorities decide to balance concessions and repression and whether those who control the police and military will limit or forgo the use of force (McAdam and Sewell 2001). Gorbachev could have sent in tanks as his predecessors did, instead of tolerating East European demonstrations in the late 1980s and early 1990s.

If the use of force by authorities is blunt and clumsy it can strengthen the resolve of those seeking change, reinforcing their sense of identity and emotional investment in the goals and each other (Amin-zade and McAdam 2001). It can also help win support from others if it garners timely media attention (McAdam et al. 2001; Bob 2005). If repression is used intelligently it can effectively divide challenging groups, discourage the availability of resources to them, and limit aware-ness of their struggle by making media coverage difficult, dangerous, or impossible (Goldstone and Tilly 2001; McAdam et al. 2001).

There can be little question that conservationists, like those engaged in most anti-colonial struggles, confront an asymmetrical con-flict: their opponents are much stronger and usually control the state. But conservationists appear not to have studied such conflicts, though some have discovered independently the lessons of fighting from a position of political weakness: in addition to constant tactical innov-ation they seek, over time, to constantly increase pressure on decision makers and the dominant social order, to undermine the legitimacy of harming the Earth and its life and claim the moral high ground, exploit-ing every opportunity and making opportunities through action which generates crises that divide elites; effective activists also carefully target groups for recruitment or alliances based on their potential for aiding the struggle, coordinate effectively with insiders who can offer some protection, challenge the status quo in multiple venues to over-whelm their ability to respond, and are prepared for repression (Wood 2000; Arreguin-Toft 2005; Arquilla 2011; Clynes 2016).

These tools can wear down conservation opponents, make it difficult for them to strike back because of movement diffuseness, and when they do strike they may suffer from a loss of legitimacy among key social groups domestically and internationally provided conserva-tionists are able to frame the struggle in the media. A key factor in undercutting the legitimacy of conservation opponents and breaking elite consensus is to build the legitimacy or moral claim of conser-vation: the goodness and even sacredness of caring for the Earth and other species rather than slaughtering them. Not all conservationists seem comfortable making a strong moral case, but as with the struggle against slavery, it is essential for two reasons. First, it partially makes up for material weakness, motivating people to overcome obstacles and creating stronger bonds (Aminzade et al. 2001). Second, conservation, as noted, is a cultural fight. It is necessary to change extant cultures and make them much more nature-friendly. To the degree conservationists can invent or co-opt traditions or holidays or celebrations, they can bring others along. Reclaiming the Winter Solstice as a celebration of natural renewal, Buy Nothing Day, anti-Columbus Day celebrations, commemorating ecological disasters caused by opponents, and appeals to kinship – in the case of conservation, with other species – and the associated values are examples (Hobsbawm 1983; Poletta 2004).

Because the threats to life are global, conservation must be able to respond in some fashion; otherwise a forest or part of the ocean will be protected only to see exploitation moved to another area. Not all parts of the world have active conservationists and where they exist they are often relatively weak. There is much competition among such conservation groups to gain support from wealthier NGOs with access to media and the ability to bring pressure on recalcitrant governments from the outside. But getting noticed is just the beginning. Three Gorges Dam in China got international attention, but not Tehri Dam in India. Reasons include how goals are presented, framing of the struggle, tactics, values, ability to evoke emotion, nature of contacts, leveraging of larger events, and charismatic leadership among others (Keck and Sikkink 1998; Arreguin-Toft 2005; Bob 2005). Three Gorges Dam was built despite the high profile social and ecological costs. Certainly elements of the Chinese state and other institutions saw the dam as an expression of Chinese progress and power and an essential state interest.

Contentious struggles often arise in poorer countries, especially where states are weak and the opportunity for plunder by powerful actors exists; where large development projects are being backed by rich countries or international regimes, and big companies and local elites stand to benefit. Contentious politics may also arise where land scarcity relative to a burgeoning population and degradation are serious problems and factions seeking power and profit are less restrained by agreed-on rules or accepted institutions (Klare 2002, 2012; Hironaka 2005; Welzer 2012). Where such politics exists it is seldom about conservation per se, though the wildlife trade is a source of funding for rebels, criminal enterprises, and officials on the take. It is almost certain however, that as the loss of biodiversity escalates and wild places decline conservationists will be tested in their sincerity about what is most important to them. They already have experience with guerilla tactics in bureaucratic and electoral politics. Often local resistance arises to these projects, but backing others does not guarantee good conservation success because people everywhere tend to want more and their populations tend to grow (e.g. Clynes 2016; Terborgh and Perez 2017). Gaining a modicum of human justice does not generally result in equity for other species.

The challenges facing conservation have grown and not just because of the inertia of growth – more people and more consumption. Opponents are often faceless, as Kris Tompkins notes in her preface to this book. Jeff Goodwin (2003) has noted that a global hydra has replaced the clearly identified despot that is easy to hate. Yet systems, not just despots, can be opposed and overcome.

Those opposed to conservation frequently initiate contention. Systematic poaching is one example of such contention and is used to fund not just poacher livelihoods but political action and movements as well as criminal enterprises. In the last several decades US anti-conservation groups and right-wing groups have ignored conservation laws, illegally using publicly owned lands, refusing to pay fees, and threatening low-ranking officials. In the Amazon and sub-Saharan Africa, poachers have killed rangers and sub-state groups have ignored land-use laws to graze domestic livestock, log, or kill protected species. It is generally accepted under international law that a group may resist aggression when it involves "grievous bodily harm and indignity" (Gross 2016: 32). Other species suffer much grievous bodily harm at the hands of many human groups. May other humans act in defense of those species against the perpetrators? The burden of proof might well be on those who say no to this sort of defense.

4. *Funding*. Cesar Chavez (2002: 66), a leader of the unionizing efforts among US farmworkers, had this to say about creating a stronger movement: "There never is enough money to organize anyone. If you put it on the basis of money you're not going to succeed."

Yet every conservationist knows – even volunteer conservationists – that conservation costs money. Money to buy land. Money to restore land. Money to hire rangers. Money to run organizations. Money for conservationists to live in societies they did not create. Money to influence decision makers. Conservation's opponents will always have more money. And the amount of money spent on transforming the natural world into commodities is far more than conservationists will ever have to protect places and species. No amount of comparatively less damaging "green" consumption can stop the damage. Drastically shrinking the amount of transformation, starving the transforming machine is needed. Conservationists, like many who want basic change, are caught in a trap: having to survive in a system they must alter but at the same time contribute to. How to carry on the activities of conservation without feeding the machine or only minimally feeding it, and without reinforcing the power of elites is difficult. Much more powerful movements than conservation have stayed stuck in the trap. Other resources can be mobilized in lieu of money. Grassroots organizing has produced campaign victories in the face of well-heeled opposition, such as the US Northwest Forest Plan and and aspects of the Headwaters campaign (Bevington 2009) or the dolphin-safe tuna campaign (Layzer 2012).

If this were all conservation were up against, it would be daunting enough. Unfortunately conservation NGOs are beggars, dependent on the largess of foundations and individuals who usually have their own agendas. This effectively means that conservation NGOs lack the autonomy they need to do what they think is necessary. They are also forced to spend money on overhead: competing for money, meeting donor requirements, and meeting auditing and government requirements. Moreover donors are constrained by the laws governing them – though big funders as a whole are instrumental in creating these laws (INCITE! 2007; Obach 2010): limits on the kind of politics they may engage in, the need for a listed charitable purpose so donations may qualify as tax credits, and so on. Few governments are going to make rules that allow or encourage support for organizations that fundamentally challenge growth and similar status quo interests. Even NGOs that take legal forms that allow some straightforward politicking face limits imposed by donor preferences.

Laws governing charities and donors have the effect of domesticating participation and action, allowing elites to channel both. Indeed, these laws cause NGOs and foundations to self-censor so as not to come close to the line and risk losing their tax status (Obach 2010). Unsurprisingly governments are not even-handed in their enforcement; right-wing groups in the US and Canada have much less to worry about than conservation groups or liberal groups (INCITE! 2007). By their funding decisions foundations have played a major role in the US in moving groups away from grassroots movement building and funding by constituents to professional organizations with career staff who become cautious lest they are seen as radicals and lose funding. Accountability shifts from constituents to donors. Ford Foundation funding played a role in undermining black radicalism in the US in favor of black capitalism; and in shifting the African National Congress from anti- to pro-capitalist (INCITE! 2007). In the end it shifts activists from causes to ameliorating symptoms.

There are foundations and big donors who are committed to an uncompromising conservation politics. But they are rare. If "the revolution will not be televised" neither will it be funded through typical channels. Conservationists must return to grassroots organizing and funding if they are to control their own agenda and avoid being steered by others who would constrain them. Conservation needs dedicated streams of income under their own control (Moodie 2013).

Conservation success depends on using available political resources – time, money, intelligence, organizing and communications skills, strategic insight, sound leadership – in pursuit of clear goals. Depending on financial breakthroughs which usually do not materialize only causes delay.

5. *Recruitment, Coalitions, and Networks.* Conservation organizations may gain strength by growing the resources they command in order to take action (resources without action or the threat of action are wasted). NGOs may mobilize more people, acquiring their time, skills, and talent, and through forging connections with other groups. Effective movements do need check-writers but what they mostly need is to incorporate people into organizational activities over the long haul; collective political action is what changes policy and systems. Without incorporation into organization, mobilization fades. Similarly alliances require investment, structure, and action or they will fade.

Too often NGOs seek check-writers and perhaps letter-writers already sympathetic to their cause. Neither of these activities build commitment that lends itself to activism – to protest and other actions that generate sustained pressure on decision makers (Shaiko 1999; Cassen 2004; Tilly 2004; Johns 2009). Rarely do NGOs seek to identify and recruit those who are most likely to be activists by virtue of their history or association with activist organizations. More importantly, conservation NGOs are not organized in a way that has a place for activism. Some encourage hands-on conservation activities such as clean-up activities, removing fences and the like, but not collective political action, even though the former can make people ripe for the latter. Earth Day is a source of contention between those who want to make it about individual community service, which treats symptoms, and those who see it as an opportunity to mobilize people to change institutions and policy (Poletta 2004). Activism is not only an outcome of mobilization, it is a means to mobilization in two ways. It changes participants and makes future activism by them more likely (Aminzade and McAdam 2001); activism also is an important means of communicating to others about the purposes and worthiness of conservation and makes observers want to join. The excitement is contagious. Action reaches beyond existing social networks engaged in conservation, especially if there is media coverage, and does the work of a broker, connecting between networks.

Many who enjoy wildlife and being outdoors who are not organized. They want to watch birds or even wolves, and are oblivious to what is happening to the creatures they watch and their habitat. Many such people do not join organizations, let alone political organizations. Such groups, organized or unorganized, should be primary targets for mobilization into conservation organizations or as allies. Cohorts can be mobilized into existing conservation NGOs or organizers can encourage formation of new NGOs based on the experience of such similarly situated individuals.

The other major means of movement building is creating coalitions. Relationships based on common goals, motives, or ideology – including use of similar language and frames – are generally stronger and more lasting than those in defense against common opponents (Van Dyke and McCammon 2010). Opponents, including police, are good at exploiting personal and ideological differences as well as lack of trust among coalition partners (Boykoff 2007). This is one reason virtual coalitions are weaker than coalitions forged by real contact over time. Quid pro quo alliances amongst politically seasoned groups can prove quite strong and even durable despite differences.

Networks are one form coalitions take and are common among conservation NGOs. They involve, or aim to involve, long-term cooperation among groups around a common vision and across an agreed-upon geography or political territory. They are most effective when the shared vision is clear, when participants' roles are clear as well as the role of any coordinating body, and when mechanisms for scaling up and down are understood. Networks can also be slow to act, participants may not adhere to agreed-upon priorities and may disagree over what is a local matter and what is a network matter. Unless the initiators of a network bring new resources to the table and keep bringing them, there may be little enticement for participants to spend the energy necessary to support a network despite other benefits.

To be useful, networks require a center or hub that performs a number of functions: keeper of the vision – the picture on the front of the jigsaw puzzle box if you will, main propagator of the vision, cybernetic center (which does not exclude horizontal communications), organizer, investor of resources, monitor, assessor and evaluator of overall work progress, and a mobilizing agent of political resources. The hub also makes recommendations to the network for action and encourages, nudges, cajoles, and otherwise persuades participants to undertake specific implementation activities when other motivation is lacking.

Networks are one organizational tool, often playing an important role in linking "good cops with bad." Some proportional representation parliamentary systems might provide opportunities for a conservation party. Small parties can exercise outsized leverage in such systems. Generally green parties have minimized their conservation advocacy, though they can be an important insider ally (Wolf 2006). Not enough cultural change has occurred in most societies to create the soil for parties mostly focused on conservation or having conservation as a basis of an overarching worldview. But parties are important in societal transformation – they play a leading role in taking people through the stages of attempted reform to resistance and alternative institution building to finally replacing outmoded and hostile institutions with new ones. Parties are also tools for outreach, organizing and creating opportunities – elections can be great theater – as well as a means for authorities to co-opt their transformational efforts (Michels 1962 [1915]; Dryzek et al. 2003; Wolf 2006). Movements (as networks of NGOs) are not immune any more than parties to creeping or abrupt co-optation, division, and sell-out leaders, as the struggle over oil extraction in Ecuador demonstrates. In 2007 President Correa of Ecuador offered to keep oil in the ground in Yasuni Park if Ecuador and local people were paid US$6.3 billion to partially replace lost revenue (Clynes 2016). When the world – partly influenced by heavy oil company lobbying – responded poorly to President Correa's offer it was withdrawn in 2013. Many Indian groups petitioned to hold a referendum on blocking oil extraction, payment or no payment to Ecuador and local Indian groups; these groups were sabotaged by Correa's government. Other Indian groups made side deals with oil companies, using some of the income to buy guns to kill or capture wildlife for trade to outsiders (Clynes 2016). Eventually the Chinese made a deal with Ecuador to help them with their financial difficulties resulting in part from this botched deal, accepting payment only in below-cost oil. Yasuni Park, which many regard as among the most biologically diverse forests in the world, is slowly being undermined.

Networks, whether regional, national, continental or global, are not magical. They have many weaknesses as well as strengths. Among their strengths:

- overhead is less than that of a single large organization; they can generate greater mobilization through cooperation and pooling of resources;
- more easily avoid the problem of organizational confusion that comes from having a broad multiplicity of goals within a single organization;
- allow for cooperation among groups at a variety of levels: participants may cooperate closely or at arm's length, and as publicly or privately as needed to suit their strategy and the political landscape; the same organization usually cannot play good and bad cop;
- make a more difficult target to hit;
- maximize flexibility because participants can adapt more quickly to changing circumstances than if they were merged or subsumed into a single centralized structure and because a variety of approaches and centers of creativity exist;
- allow for the handling of issues and problems at the level most likely to be effective; this can prevent a problem from causing perturbations throughout the system.

Network weaknesses include:

- because participants have a high degree of autonomy the priorities of the network are not always reflected in participants' work;

- notwithstanding formal agreements discipline is difficult to impose;
- the constraints on political activity imposed on NGOs by tax exempt and deductibility status can limit the activity of others because the former may be afraid to play with the more politically active, thereby isolating the latter;
- network divisions may undermine quick, decisive action;
- the open nature of networks lends itself to inconsistent participation and demands to revisit old decisions; the larger the region and absent funding for travel, meetings tend be weighted toward participants closer to the venue, influencing agendas and decisions;
- unequal resources or commitment to the initiative by participants results in unequal influence and can give rise to resentment;
- the autonomy of participants can lend itself to blowback on the entire network;
- collective action organizations and those focused on individual action are difficult to bridge.

International conservation NGO networks face specific problems which are difficult to overcome, and these are worth mentioning. At the heart of these networks are transactions that involve use of northern resources for projects in the global south. These might include funding for projects in the south, providing staff and training, organizing boycotts of companies engaged in or facilitating logging or wildlife trafficking, bringing direct pressure on the World Bank to block funding for bad projects, and to raise awareness of political repression and misrepresentation by governments and international institutions (Keck and Sikkink 1998). Personal connections and trust can be quite important in this cooperation (Tarrow 2005).

International networks must confront many obstacles, however. One is the difference in goals among network members. Conservation groups may form networks to stop deforestation by industrial logging; but some network partners may want logging if the proceeds stay local (Keck and Sikkink 1998). A second obstacle is the difference in national politics (Obach 2010). The context for NGO operations differs from country to country. China resists autonomous NGOs. Many countries, such as Russia, have made receiving funding from outside Russia, or even close relations with "outside" NGOs, a basis for repression. International NGOs do not enjoy the same protection and clear rules that business (often conservation opponents) enjoys under the World Trade Organization (Obach 2010). A third factor is differences among countries in the repertoire of collective action (e.g. Tilly 2006). The degree to which mass demonstrations, contention, and calls for fundamental change are considered hostile varies. Leaders in some countries can react preemptively or violently but not others, making the transfer of methods problematic. There is a ritualistic aspect to politics including protest; if the rules are not understood, action can create costly responses.

Another challenge facing international networks is development masquerading as conservation. Oates (1999) recounts the many projects taken off course in West Africa. One of the most tragic stories is the destruction of Paseo Pantera, one of the earliest if not the earliest major connectivity and protected area efforts in the Americas. Initiated in the late 1980s by Archie Carr, Mario Boza and others, it sought to link existing and proposed parks from Panama to Mexico. If military dictatorships and civil wars were not significant enough obstacles to the pledge made by the seven central American governments, development interests including the Global Environmental Facility proved the kiss of death. In 1997 the Paseo Pantera Project became the Mesoamerican Biological Corridor and tens of millions of dollars flowed into the region for development rather than conservation purposes. Governments and some big conservation NGOs went along with this transformation (Fraser 2009). Geographically big is good for conservation; big institutions are usually a problem, however.

Whether recruiting activist members or building coalitions, a sound strategy is key to success. In Chapter 3 we set out the steps in developing such a strategy.

6. *Enforcement.* Enforcement of protection for places and species works, and conservationists need to be willing to use it and demand that governments use it. Against entities that constantly seek

to exploit the natural world. Such enforcement must be consistent, credible, and backed with sanctions that exceed any benefits of encroachment. If the drivers of exploitation are not ultimately addressed, enforcement will be expensive and challenging.

States and enforcement agencies are sometimes corrupt, weak, significantly under-resourced, lack political support, or are at odds with other agencies. All of these factors can exacerbate enforcement problems (e.g. Thapar 2003; Thomas 2003). Conservationists find themselves policing the police in many circumstances. Over the long term effective mechanisms for strengthening enforcement are needed, from ongoing political pressure to *instilling new traditions and values compatible with conservation* in enforcement agencies. New sources of funding for such agencies, not based on extraction, exploitation, and consumptive uses, can help with changing attitudes.

Encroachment into protected areas and destruction of life is not just carried out by states and businesses but also by the politically weak (e.g. Terborgh and Peres, 2017). Although some expect conservationists to defer to human interests over those of other species, that is not the task of conservation. Nor does conservation have the political or other resources to solve intrahuman problems. Much stronger institutions have failed in that task. The conservation movement must keep its focus on the truly unrepresented – wild species and places – and not allow efforts to remedy human inequality and injustice at the expense of other species and their homes. Human colonialism and subjugation of nature cannot solve the problem of human-on-human subjugation. Humans have already taken too much at the expense of other species.

"Tradition" cannot justify the subjugation of the natural world any more than it can justify slavery or patriarchy. As a practical matter conservationists must deal with other political forces, whether it involves fighting or cooperation. In the case of places such as Gorongosa, local communities have been integrated into the enforcement and administrative apparatus and so local livelihoods benefit from protection of places and species. In many communities in the US Pacific Northwest and US intermountain Southwest, despite the economic benefits to communities of PAs, extractive industries have successfully made many hostile to protection. As noted in the previous chapter, there are instances where conservationists and locals may oppose industry but have very different goals concerning the lives of other species and their habitat. It is always better to have local support for enforcement, but not at the cost of biodiversity.

One of the most contentious issues in conservation involves moving people to make way for other species. Displacement of people by war and other social conflicts is quite common in human history, as is movement in response to climate, soil exhaustion, and economic forces. And certainly human displacement of other species has been a norm for at least 60,000 years. Although hunter-gatherers seem to defer to human groups who first occupied a place as having priority of usufruct (Flannery and Marcus 2017), and although they recognize places and other creatures as ensouled, it has not stopped them displacing other species and even causing extinctions, not just for food but to obtain status goods. Requiring people to move to create or restore protected areas is another matter, however; critics put conservationists in the same category as miners, loggers, and other industrial interests as violators of human rights. Equity for other species is not recognized by these critics.

The creation or restoration of places and non-human species can involve moving people or limiting consumptive or extractive activities in particular areas. Most human societies do not respond well to limits placed on them by those considered outsiders. Companies don't like governments telling them what to do. If communities are given incentives they may agree to such limits. If the limitations can be sacralized or otherwise internalized so much the better. Some societies are communitarian and if there is strong peer pressure, that can work to change behavior for the benefit of conservation. If, on the other hand it is necessary to rely on power rather than authority then conservationists must be prepared to both build support for the use of power and sustain the use of that power until goals are achieved and resistance diminished. It is no different than the use of power in other situations, such as enforcing desegregation or an end to child marriage.

Conservationists should aim to minimize bickering with non-conservation groups over protecting places and species when possible. Such divisions can work in the interests of the more powerful. For decades in the US poor whites refused to ally with poor blacks, while those who benefited from racism cleaned up materially. A common opponent, however, can't justify failure to pursue wild places and species protection.

Conflict can in part be minimized by seizing opportunities. Although growth in human population and consumption usually translates into more appropriation of lands and waters, in some parts of the world economic forces are causing abandonment of extractive uses. Without water and fuel subsidies domestic livestock production in arid areas is not economical or otherwise attractive (Hansen 2003). Similarly, an end to subsidies for industrial fishing fleets, which have increased in capacity even as fish populations have declined from overfishing, could allow Marine Protected Areas to catch up (Global Ocean Commission 2015). Abandonment of coal mining areas as demand falls, or flood plains, or drought-stricken areas is not new. The world is full of ghost towns.

The matter of humans making way for other species is part and parcel of reordering society more generally into biodiversity-compatible forms. It also reverses past injustice toward other species. We will discuss this more in the next chapter on restoration.

7. *New and Existing PAs, and Champions.* Only about 1.8 percent of the global ocean is strictly protected and only about 6 percent of the terrestrial Earth is similarly protected (Jenkins and Joppa 2009; MPAtlas 2017). There is no current, independent reliable estimate of terrestrial strictly protected areas as there is for MPAs. Governments self-report and NGOs try to keep them honest. The

6 percent for terrestrial PAs comes from applying the marine ratio to the 12.9% of the terrestrial Earth protected (UNEP-WCMC and IUCN 2016). It's a long way to safeguarding half of the planet and its native species. Many PAs have dysfunctional boundaries, are too small, or are islands. Some PAs are being rendered inadequate by climate change or require much enhanced connectivity. A survey of less developed countries found that between 1900 and 2010 there were 543 cases of downsizing or downgrading of PAs covering over half a million square kilometers (Mascia et al. 2014; PADDDtracker 2017).

There is some evidence that it is easier to expand and/or restore existing PAs than create new ones (Pringle 2017). Pringle offers evidence for terrestrial PAs and in the author's experience this is also true of MPAs in territorial waters. The universe of high seas MPAs is too small to say much about. Connectivity seems to be less threatening to potential opponents and decision makers, while offering some of the benefits of larger and more PAs.

The designation of protected areas is greatly increased where dedicated champions exist with adequate resources and supportive political leaders (Oates 1999; Weber and Vedder 2001; Fraser 2009; Perez 2017; Pringle 2017). Supportive political leaders have played important roles in Canada (Jean Chrétien), Mozambique (Joaquim Chassono), Chile (Michele Bachelet), Costa Rica (Oscar Arias), Argentina (Mauricio Macri), and elsewhere. Supportive political leaders are especially important to transboundary efforts; these help ensure larger, more biologically effective PAs (Fraser 2009). In the absence of such leaders, building the political force necessary to push less enthusiastic ones, give them cover, or replace them is a major task and very much an uphill fight. But it can be done.

Re-establishing connections among wild areas and among PAs effectively enlarges PAs and can evoke less opposition than new PAs, especially where waterways are involved. Connectivity cannot, however, overcome the failings of PAs lacking important habitat for native species, with badly drawn boundaries, excessive edge effects, lack of contiguousness, or that operate as a sink for species they should support (Soule and Terborgh 1999, e.g. the US see Jenkins et al. 2015).

In the case of terrestrial protection, private lands not only play a key role in securing important habitat, but can offer an alternative to political stalemate. The Ted Turner ranches in the US and Tompkins Conservation acquisitions in South America are examples.

8. *Bargaining.* It is almost too obvious to say that those challenging the status quo bargain down rather than up. Not so obvious are some implications of this. Besides conservationists asking for more than they want, a grasp of both the political and biological landscape is important. How much do opponents know about what conservationists consider most valuable? By withholding what conservationists most want, concessions can be obtained from them. If opponents know little then conservationists can include non-critical areas to trade away. How willing are conservationists and opponents to engage in contentious action? Some places are not threatened in the near term, and in other cases landscapes are being abandoned because economies are changing. Such factors inform strategy. So does the waxing and waning of influence of opponents or issues.

Trade associations, agencies, governments, and other entities are seldom monolithic. Where are the points of fracture? Who can influence this or that faction at a critical point in the process? When conservation opponents were faced with the possibility of a national monument in eastern Oregon's high desert country they made the mistake of trying to broker a deal. They achieved some of their goals – including a name for the resulting protected area that would not attract tourists – but at the cost of having to make concessions to conservationists and others (Gunter 2001). Having influential voices or groups speak out at critical moments in negotiations can make a difference – especially if they appear independent. Sometimes children speaking up for wildlife and places can make it difficult to be in opposition, especially for public officials on issues covered by the media.

9. *Waiting Too Long.* Safeguarding places and species means acting in time – a daunting challenge for a movement chronically short of resources and not very good at politics. The state of the Vaquita, Giant Otter, Amur Leopard, Mekong River Dolphin and Bornean Orangutan, to name a few, are dire. Failure to act in response to declines until numbers are critically low is courting disaster and it raises costs – both political and otherwise. The sixth great extinction will be very well documented, but the point is to halt it. Protecting large areas of the Earth is a proximate solution, but such protection must be timely and doesn't automatically mean species with low numbers are secure. A chance perturbation can extinguish a population.

10. *Patron–Client Relations.* In those parts of the world where people live at or near subsistence, it can take little to push them to break the rules about exploiting wildlife and taking protected land for agriculture. Richard Henry Tawney (1932: 77), wrote of China that "There are districts in which the position of the rural population is that of a man standing permanently up to the neck in water, so that even a ripple is sufficient to drown him." In such circumstances it is to be expected that people will take advantage of nature when that ripple comes, especially if the safety net provided by society fails, as it often does in hard times, or the social rules break down with global intrusions (Scott 1976). To the degree that conservationists can step into the role of creating a safety net on condition that rules regarding the natural world be followed, they have been able to prevent problems, as shown in Costa Rica, Gorongosa, and Terai Arc (Dinerstein 2003; Carroll 2016; Pringle 2017).

11. *Ignorance.* There are many cases and lessons not adequately documented. Activists who know them best do not write about them. Writers and researchers often don't know the activists. This chapter is a plea to activists to document their experiences. Some should be public. Other experiences need to be recounted and circulated more quietly so opponents do not have access to them. Conservation lacks a good insider communications tool.

The state of conservation politics is in perpetual flux. If there is a constant it is that conservation remains a sideshow and afterthought for most decision makers because they are not feeling the pressure from conservationists, who remain politically weak. If the points made in this chapter aid conservationists even a little they have done their job:

- a conservation vision that is able to guide action is necessary; to do so effectively it must address the extant reality, where conservation should go at a variety of scales, and provide a conservation identity and story;
- science can only do so much; it does not provide values; it can only offer an understanding of the world; it is usually necessary to act before all the science is in;
- achieving conservation goals will necessarily be contentious, and conservationists cannot shy away from that; constant innovation is necessary;
- typical charitable funding is restrictive of conservation action; self-funding can transcend such restrictions; only grassroots activism can create new possibilities;
- recruitment into conservation NGOs should focus on people who are inclined to activism and ensure an organizational home for them; recruitment also should mobilize those not usually targeted for mobilization – new groups that add resources to conservation; coalition building should focus on groups who have a record of action and possess political influence;
- enforcement of place and species protection works; support for strong enforcement and direct action in its absence is essential;
- protecting half the Earth requires champions all over the globe to ensure creation of PAs and their efficacy; often expanding or connecting PAs is politically easier than creating new ones, but the former is not always an option;
- effective bargaining takes understanding the political as well as biological landscape;
- missing biological and political decision points forecloses the ability to safeguard and recover species; early intervention and preventing decline to the precipice is called for;
- conservationists need to better document their work, lessons learned, and find a means of circulating it without opponents having easy access.

REFERENCES

Aminzade, Ronald R. and David McAdam. 2001. Emotions and Contentious Politics. Pp. 14–50 in Ronald R. Aminzade, Jack A. Goldstone, Doug McAdam, et al. *Silence and Voice in the Study of Contentious Politics*. Cambridge University Press. Cambridge.

Aminzade, Ronald R., Jack A. Goldstone, Doug McAdam, et al. 2001. *Silence and Voice in the Study of Contentious Politics*. Cambridge University Press. Cambridge.

Araiza, Lauren. 2014. *To March for Others*. Pennsylvania State University Press. Philadelphia, PA.

Arquilla, John. 2011. *Insurgents, Raiders and Bandits*. Ivan R. Dee. Lanham, MD.

Arreguin-Toft, Ivan. 2005. *How the Weak Win Wars*. Cambridge University Press. Cambridge.

Berry, Wendell. 1993. *Sex, Economy, Freedom and Community*. Pantheon. New York.

Bevington, Doug. 2009. *The Rebirth of Environmentalism*. Island Press. Washington DC.

Bob, Clifford. 2005. *Marketing Rebellion*. Cambridge University Press. Cambridge.

Boykoff, Jules. 2007. *Beyond Bullets*. AK Press. Oakland, CA.

Cairns, John (ed.). 1975. *The Recovery and Restoration of Damaged Ecosystems*. University Press of Virginia. Charlottesville, VA.

Cairns, John (ed.). 1980. *The Recovery Process in Damaged Ecosystems*. Ann Arbor Science Publishers. Ann Arbor, MI.

Caldicott, Helen. 2017. Personal communication. June 12.

Carmichael, J. T., Jenkins, J. C., Brulle, R. J. 2012. Building Environmentalism: The Founding of Environmental Movement Organizations in the United States, 1900–2000. 53 *Sociological Quarterly*: 422–53.

Carroll, Sean B. 2016. *The Serengeti Rules*. Princeton University Press. Princeton, NJ.

Cassen, Bernard. 2004. Inventing ATTAC. Pp. 152–74 in Tom Mertes (ed.). *A Movement of Movements*. Verso. London.

Chavez, Cesar. In Richard J. Jensen and John C. Hammerback (eds.). 2002. *The Words of Cesar Chavez*. Texas A&M University Press. College Station, TX.

Clynes, Tom. 2016. A Pipeline Runs Through It. 118 *Audubon* 6: 18–27 (Winter).

Davies, T. E., Sarah M. Maxwell, K. Kaschmer and N. C. Ban. 2017. Large Marine Protected Areas Represent Biodiversity Now and Under Climate Change. 7 *Scientific Reports* 9569. doi: 10.1038/s41598-017-08758-5 (accessed August 30, 2017).

Dinerstein, Eric. 2003. *Return of the Unicorns*. Columbia University Press. New York.

Dryzek, John S., David Downes, Christian Hunold, and David Schlosberg. 2003. *Green States and Social Movements*. Oxford University Press. Oxford.

Finley, Carmel. 2017. *All the Boats on the Ocean*. University of Chicago Press. Chicago, IL.

Flannery, Kent and Joyce Marcus. 2017. *The Creation of Inequality*. Harvard University Press. Cambridge, MA.

Fraser, Caroline. 2009. *Rewilding the World*. Metropolitan/Henry Holt. New York.

Garrow, David. 1986. *Bearing the Cross*. Morrow. New York.

Gilly, Adolfo. 2003. Globalization, Violence and Revolutions: Nine Theses. Pp. 107–24 in John Foran (ed.). *The Future of Revolution*. Zed Books. London.

Global Ocean Commission. 2015. *From Decline to Recovery, A Rescue Package for the Global Ocean Report Summary*. www.some.ox.ac.uk/wp-content/uploads/2016/03/GOC_Summary_2015_AUG-1.pdf (accessed December 27, 2017).

Goldstone, Jack A. and Charles Tilly. 2001. Threat (and Opportunity): Popular Action and State Response in the Dynamics of Contentious Action. Pp. 179–94 in Ronald R. Aminzade, Jack A. Goldstone, Doug McAdam, et al. *Silence and Voice in the Study of Contentious Politics*. Cambridge University Press. Cambridge.

Goodwin, Jeff. 2003. Comment in Second Thematic Discussion, The Shaping of Revolutions by Culture and Agency and by Race, Class and Gender. Pp. 195–214 in John Foran (ed.). *The Future of Revolutions*. Zed Books. London.

Gross, Michael L. 2016. *The Ethics of Insurgency*. Cambridge University Press. Cambridge.

Gunter, Teresa. 2001. *The Steens Mountain Divide: Beyond Compromise in Oregon's High Desert*. MS Thesis, University of Montana. Missoula.

Hansen, Brian. 2003. Crisis On the Plains. 13 *CQ Researcher* 417–48 (May 9). http://library.cqpress.com/cqresearcher/document.php?id=cqresrre2003050900 (accessed December 29, 2017).

Hironaka, Ann. 2005. *Neverending Wars*. Cambridge University Press. Cambridge.

Hobsbawm. Eric. 1983. Mass Producing Traditions: Europe, 1870–1914. Pp. 263–307 in Eric Hobsbawm and Terence Ranger (eds.). *The Invention of Tradition*. Cambridge University Press. Cambridge.

INCITE!. 2007. *The Revolution Will Not Be Funded*. South End Press. Boston, MA.

Jenkins, Clinton N. and Lucas Joppa. 2009. Expansion of the Global Terrestrial Protected Area System. 142 *Biological Conservation* 10: 2166–74 (October).

Jenkins, Clinton N., Kyle S. Van Houtanb, Stuart L. Pimm, and Joseph O. Sexton. 2015. US Protected Lands Mismatch Biodiversity Priorities. *Proceedings of the National Academy of Sciences. Early Edition*. www.pnas.org/cgi/doi/10.1073/pnas.1418034112 (accessed April 6, 2015).

Johns, David. 2009. *New Conservation Politics*. Wiley-Blackwell. Chichester.

Jordan III, William R. and George M. Lubick. 2011. *Making Nature Whole*. Island Press. Washington DC.

Kaplan, Lawrence and Carol Kaplan (eds.). 1973. *Revolutions, A Comparative Study*. Random House. New York.

Kavango Zambezi (KAZA) Transfrontier Conservation Area. *Tourism Without Borders*. www.kavangozambezi.org/index.php/en (accessed December 14, 2017).

Keck, Margaret E. and Kathryn Sikkink. 1998. *Activists beyond Borders*. Cornell University Press. Ithaca, NY.

Klare, Michael T. 2002. *Resource Wars*. Owl Books. New York.

Klare, Michael T. 2012. *The Race for What's Left*. Metropolitan Books. New York.

Layzer, Judith. 2012. *The Environmental Case*. 3rd edn. CQ Press. Washington DC.

Luders, Joseph E. 2010. *The Civil Rights Movement and the Logic of Social Change*. Cambridge University Press. Cambridge.

Mascia, Michael B., S. Pailler, R. Krithivasan, et al. 2014. Protected Area Downgrading, Down-sizing, and Degazettement (PADDD) in Africa, Asia, and Latin America and the Caribbean, 1900–2010. 169 *Biological Conservation*: 355–61.

McAdam, Doug A. and William H. Sewell. 2001. It's About Time: Temporality in the Study of Social Movements and Revolutions. Pp. 89–125 in Ronald R. Aminzade, Jack A. Goldstone, Doug McAdam, et al. *Silence and Voice in the Study of Contentious Politics*. Cambridge University Press. Cambridge.

McAdam, Doug, Sidney Tarrow, and Charles Tilly. 2001. *Dynamics of Contention*. Cambridge University Press. Cambridge.

Michels, Robert. 1962 [1915]. *Political Parties*. Free Press. Glencoe, IL.

Mihaylov, Nikolay and Douglas Perkins. 2015. Local Environmental Grassroots Activism: Contributions from Environmental Psychology, Sociology and Politics. 5 *Behavioral Science* 121–53.

Moodie, Allison. 2013. The NGO-business Hybrid: More Than the Sum of its Parts? *The Guardian*. www.theguardian.com/sustainable-business/ngo-hybrid-sustainable-business-structures (November 21) (accessed June 11, 2016).

MPAtlas. 2017. *Very Large-Scale MPAs*. http://mpatlas.org/protection-dashboard/very-large-mpas/ (accessed December 12, 2017).

Noss, Reed. 1992. The Wildlands Project Land Conservation Strategy. *Wild Earth* Special Issue 1: 10–25.

Oates, John F. 1999. *Myth and Reality in the Rain Forest*. University of California Press. Berkeley, CA.

Obach, Brian. 2010. Political Opportunity and Social Movement Coalitions. Pp. 197–218 in Nella Van Dyke and Holly J. McCammon (eds.). *Strategic Alliances*. University of Minnesota Press. Minneapolis, MN.

PADDDtracker. www.padddtracker.org/ (accessed June 8, 2017).

Perez, Ignacio Jimenez. 2017. Personal communication. March 2.

Poletta, Francesca. 2004. Can You Celebrate Dissent? Pp. 151–77 in Amitai Etzioni and Jared Bloom (eds.). *We Are What We Celebrate*. New York University Press. New York.

Pringle, Robert M. 2017. Upgrading Protected Areas to Conserve Wild Biodiversity. 546 *Nature* 91–9.

Scott, James C. 1976. *Moral Economy of the Peasant*. Yale University Press. New Haven, CT.

Scott, James C. 1998. *Seeing Like a State*. Yale University Press. New Haven, CT.

Shaiko, Ronald G. 1999. *Voices and Echoes for the Environment*. Columbia University Press. New York.

Soule, Michael. 1985. What is Conservation Biology? 35 *BioScience* 11: 727–34.

Soule, Michael and John Terborgh. 1999. *Continental Conservation*. Island Press. Washington DC.

Tarrow, Sidney. 2005. *The New Transnational Activism*. Cambridge University Press. Cambridge.

Tawney, Richard Henry. 1932. *Land and Labor in China*. George Allen & Unwin. London.

Terborgh, John and Carlos A. Peres. 2017. Do Community-Managed Forests Work? A Biodiversity Perspective. 6 *Land* 22–8. doi: 10.3390/land6020022.

Thapar, Valmik. 2003. *Battling for Survival*. Oxford University Press. New Delhi.

Thomas, Craig. 2003. *Bureaucratic Landscapes*. MIT Press. Cambridge, MA.

Tilly, Charles. 2004. *Social Movements 1768–2004*. Paradigm. Boulder, CO.

Tilly, Charles. 2006. *Regimes and Repertoires*. University of Chicago Press. Chicago, IL.

UNEP-WCMC and IUCN. 2016. *Protected Planet Report 2016*. UNEP-WCMC and IUCN. Cambridge and Gland, Switzerland.

Van Dyke, Nella and Holly J. McCammon (eds.). 2010. *Strategic Alliances*. University of Minnesota Press. Minneapolis, MN.

Weber, Bill and Amy Vedder. 2001. *In the Kingdom of the Gorillas*. Simon & Schuster. New York.

Welzer, Harald. 2012 (German edn. 2008) *Climate Wars*. Polity Press. London.

Wildlands Network. 1994. *The Wildlands Project* (pamphlet). Wildlands Network. McMinnville, OR.

Wildlands Project [Network] (Dave Foreman, Kathy Daly, Barbara Dugleby, Rosann Hanson, Robert Howard, Jack Humphrey, Leanne Klyza-Linck, Rurik List and Kim Vacariu). 2000. *Sky Islands Wildlands Network Conservation Plan*. The Wildlands Project. Tucson, AZ.

Wilson, Edward O. 2016. *Half-Earth*. Liveright. New York.

Wolf, Frieder Otto. 2006. Party-building for Eco-socialists: Lessons from the Failed Project of the German Greens. Pp. 310–26 in Leo Panitch and Colin Leys (eds.). *Socialist Register 2007. Coming to Terms With Nature*. Merlin Press/Leftword Books. London/New Delhi.

Wood, Elisabeth Jean. 2000. *Forging Democracy from Below*. Cambridge University Press. Cambridge.

9　Doing Large-Scale Restoration

> More than 90 percent of the land in the lower 48 states (of the US) has been logged, plowed, mined, overgrazed, paved or otherwise modified from presettlement condition. Fire suppression has altered the composition of plant communities ... Top predators have been extirpated or reduced to scattered populations ... Rivers have ... been dammed, channeled, diked ... and aquatic organisms are under siege ...
>
> ... Land use must be prescribed on a very large spatial scale. Management practices must be reformed. Top carnivores must be restored ... Disturbed and degraded habitats must be made more natural ...
>
> Soule and Terborgh 1999: 202

If conservation is to achieve its goal of recovering species across the Earth in natural patterns of abundance it will take strict protection of half the landscape (Noss 1992; Wilson 2016) and at least 30 percent of the global ocean (Roberts 2007). That means restoration on a very large scale. There is agreement that bigger PAs are better for a variety of biological reasons and also because the larger the protected area the more realistic the goal of ecological self-regulation and less reliance on human management with all its uncertainties (Noss and Cooperrider 1994; Soule and Terborgh 1999; Wilson 2014).

Complicating our discussion of restoration is the wide variety of ways the term is used. Simberloff et al. (1999) note that restoration is used to describe "rehabilitation" projects, revegetation projects and "recovery" projects (at 65), which fall far short of restoring all the pieces Aldo Leopold referred to. Indeed, the goals of such projects are often unclear or even lacking – which species are being restored to which state?

Jordan and Lubick (2011) distinguish between two broad categories of restoration. Ecological restoration, which entails recreation of an ecosystem with all its parts and processes to a state prior to human interference or damage, and meliorative restoration which pretty much includes all other efforts to "improve" a landscape for some human benefit. Ecological restoration, they note, requires an understanding of human influence on a place and coming to terms with human responsibility and the consequences of human action. It requires a clear understanding of goals – what is being attempted? There are many challenges. The exact genomic constitution of species from past times cannot easily be re-established (Simberloff et al. 1999). How they would have evolved absent human interference is difficult to determine. Ecosystems are dynamic. Communities and processes change.

Typically restoration has been at small scales, from a farm field to a few hundred or a few thousand hectares – rarely larger than that, though the Neal Smith National Wildlife Refuge in Iowa is 40,000 hectares. It can be argued, of course, that the reintroduction of wolves and fire to Yellowstone National Park and the Greater Yellowstone Ecosystem is restoration on an even grander scale (~900,000 ha and 7.3 million ha respectively).

Ecological restoration, if it is to provide for the protection of all native species and ecosystems, disturbance regimes, and evolutionary potential, especially in the face of climate change, requires large-scale action (Simberloff et al. 1999). Ecological restoration is not about minimum viable populations, but takes account of wide-ranging species in not just ecologically effective populations but populations approximating past levels across their historic range and very large-scale disturbances such as the Yellowstone fire of 1988 (~395,000 ha).

Because restoration addresses places and species that have suffered such a wide degree of injury and in such a wide variety of political circumstances, it is difficult to approach it in the same way as conservation in the previous chapter. It makes more sense to examine several projects on a case-by-case basis: how was it gone about, what worked, what didn't, was the scale adequate? We will start with meliorative projects because they are useful in their variety and for comparison with ecocentric restoration.

MELIORATIVE RESTORATION

In North America a series of watershed or basin projects are analyzed in some detail (Doyle and Drew 2008), ranging from the Everglades, Chesapeake Bay, Upper Mississippi, Platte River, and San Francisco Bay. These efforts are invariably a response to water crises (mostly) and threats to endangered species (often present). Except for the Everglades, where Congress mandated a water-sharing goal between humans and wildlife, the projects focused on a process that brings various human groups together to divide the water among human interests. Most funding is provided by the US federal government, making possible new infrastructure. This support has been far from consistent, however, so projects wax and wane.

All of the authors in Doyle and Drew (2008) refer to the projects they write about as rehabilitation efforts, not restoration projects. That's because there is no effort to return to a baseline in which the system resembles what it once did in terms of species, disturbance, or even water flows and vegetation. The Everglades comes closest to being ecocentric restoration but even it falls short. Indeed, the goal for all projects except the Everglades is a process described by the buzzword "collaboration." There is, in almost all cases, not enough water left to heal the landscape, only to support some level of minimal ecosystem function. Too much habitat conversion, too many people, too many invasive species and too much other change makes ecological restoration impossible without social change. Thus, these efforts are meliorative in Jordan and Lubick's (2011) language.

The Klamath Basin Project in southern Oregon and northern California falls into the category of meliorative. Although politicians in the region have shared with each other a great deal of self-congratulation for the agreement that emerged from the interest group process, it mostly left out wildlife. After almost 100 years of over-allocating water in the region, the conflict between farmers enticed into the region by the US Bureau of Reclamation, downstream commercial fishermen, Native fishermen, and several species of fish protected by the Endangered Species Act, came to a head. The hard physical realities of water, fish, and people led to protest, litigation, and ill feeling over broken promises, including the shut-off of irrigation water at one point.

From 2005 to 2010, irrigators, fishermen, two states and federal agencies sought to find a solution to the conflict over water allocation and water subsidies. The agreement they finally reached aimed to restore salmon to the basin, by removing four hydroelectric dams on the Klamath River, restoring riparian areas, providing farmers with irrigation water as fish numbers permitted, and establishing a tree farm for the Klamath Tribe. Shortly after a federal deadline expired, Congress, in spring of 2016, adopted funding legislation to implement the agreement. It seemed like a solution everyone could live with.

Patrick Higgins (Lochner 2012: minute 48 et seq.), an independent fish biologist who has long worked to restore the river, had a different view than the self-congratulating politicos:

> I don't think we are going to restore salmon under the Klamath Basin Restoration Agreement because it doesn't push the river back toward its normal range of variability. So this is not a deal that looks at the ecological needs of the Klamath. This is a social deal where people have come together and found out where they can agree. Unfortunately where they have agreed doesn't overlap with the needs of the ecosystem. Those should drive the deal.

There is no question that dam removal is a major accomplishment (still in progress). So is improving riparian habitat and limited recovery of fish populations. The question Higgins raises, however, is critical – is this 12,000 square mile (3 million hectare) project really ecological restoration? Or is it about the recovery of a few of the pieces humans agree they want back? The Klamath is a remote area and not heavily populated, but it has been heavily degraded; the agreement is oriented to human wants; it is meliorative. There were no fish at the table, just those who catch or eat fish. "Stakeholders" do not include other species, and thus outcomes of stakeholder processes are invariably biased. Recovery of some of the pieces can improve naturalness but not generate a healed world. It is also likely that as human pressures increase in the region, conditions will slip back to what they were under unfettered human domination by the most powerful interests. Without clear limits on what humans can take and without commitment of places to other species, ecological restoration is not possible.

Former US Secretary of the Interior Babbitt, no stranger to large-scale meliorative restoration projects, quickly learned to call them water projects. Ordinary people, legislators and agencies tended to embrace water projects but not conservation or restoration projects. Big water projects such as returning the Everglades to something more natural were typical of the federal government in terms of size, but such projects usually brought subsidies such as dams and draining wetlands, not restoration (Babbitt 2005). The Everglades would bring in enormous amounts of federal money to repair the damage to the region and in that sense it was a subsidy. The Everglades Project was also backed *by long-term organizing by supporters*. Dubious real estate deals that peddled land to newcomers which subsequently flooded and caused threats to public health tipped the region into crisis. Huge growth also generated water impoundment and delivery problems.

During much of the 1990s and into this century Florida also worked to recover the Florida Panther and Black Bear in addition to other wildlife by buying up habitat and linking it together. The fast-growing state also sought to use zoning, building permits, and allocation of highway funding to ensure development was as compatible as possible with wildlife movement. Some restoration progress was made before hostile state governors and legislatures starved the program.

Babbitt (2005) notes precedent for large-scale meliorative restoration in the US Dust Bowl program that bought up failed farms and turned them into federal grasslands. In more recent decades the Conservation Reserve Program pays farmers to take land out of production and to plant grass to limit erosion, but there is no requirement to plant native grasses or welcome other native species. Clear restoration objectives for lands withdrawn from production are needed if ecological benefits are to be achieved.

TOWARD ECOLOGICAL RESTORATION

The Caledonian Forest Scotland was once heavily forested, but over the millennia and more rapidly in recent centuries it has been stripped by humans for agriculture, pasture, firewood, and industry. Ninety-nine percent of the forest is gone, as are wolves, brown bears, lynx, and many other creatures. Grazing, industrial forestry, and loss of predators have prevented forest recovery, and political forces have resisted the return of former inhabitants. Indeed, deer routinely crop growing trees down to the heather – they grow older but never mature.

Today the Forres-based group Trees for Life uses the term rewilding when talking about their goal of bringing back a large proportion of the former Caledonian Forest and all of its inhabitants. Initially rewilding referred to recovery of apex predators and wide-ranging species across large areas of their former range to simultaneously re-establish tropic processes, but it is increasingly used interchangeably with ecological restoration (Johns 2016). Recognizing that the relationship among the parts is complicated and much has been degraded for a very long time, Trees for Life started with vegetation. Beginning with remnant forests in places such as Glen Afric, they are replanting Scots pine and other native species. This generally requires extensive fencing to exclude deer from the planted areas or reducing deer numbers through hunting. It would be prohibitively expensive to fence and replant without the hundreds and hundreds of volunteers attracted to the project over the years in addition to donors. Doing the work directly also avoids reliance on the vagaries of politics and government budgets and substantial effort to influence government. Although reforestation with native species is not controversial, reducing deer numbers can be – especially with landowners who sell stag hunts.

Now, almost thirty years into restoring the Caledonian Forest, many areas are showing strong signs of recovery: insects, birds, small mammals, and mesopredators are back or numbers are up. Re-establishment of sea eagle, red kite, and osprey are important steps, as is a trial reintroduction of beavers. Many of the foregoing species are highly interactive, which will further restore the land-scape. In the last few years Trees for Life has also purchased the 10,000-acre Dundreggan estate, which is being restored and serves as a nursery to support replanting and other operations.

The next steps, however, are likely to be controversial, and not just with landlords who own much of Scotland outside the cities and towns. Although Scotland has the great biological benefit of being sparsely populated north of Edinburgh and Glasgow, carnivores are unpopular with those who run the 7 million sheep in Scotland. The reintroduction of many species will require government action of some sort, and that means building adequate political support to generate the needed influence. On the plus side is Scottish national-ism and a population that is less enamored of controlling the natural world. Also on the plus side is the Wild Europe Initiative (WEI) with its experience and potential political influence in repatriating key-stone species on mainland. WEI seeks creation of 100,000-hectare natural areas with a minimum total of 1 million hectares across Europe, but is in its early stages. Reserves of 100,000 hectares are not in Scotland's near future. Large PAs will move Europe *toward* ecological restoration and could be large enough for much self-regulation.

Other factors in addition to size of PAs influence restoration success and the time it takes, which can be hundreds of years:

productivity of land and waters, existing species and community diversity, infrastructure that requires removal, access to water and wetlands, alien species present, climate shifts, source populations of extirpated species, and the presence of a variety of human activities. Apex carnivores do exist in several refugia in Europe and can colonize from there if appropriate habitat is made available (with prey and free of persecution); but the range expansion of many keystone species is contentious. The UK departure from the European Union likely means less direct influence for WEI in Britain, but it can set an example and if Scotland eventually leaves the UK works directly with the WEI. The European Parliament (2009) "welcomed the establishment of the Wild Europe Initiative (WEI)," a cooperative effort of the European Commission, Council of Europe and many NGOs including Pan Parks, Europark, Bird Life International, WWF, UNESCO, and others (WEI 2013: 1).

Terai Arc The Terai Arc region lies in the lower elevations of the Himalayas in southern Nepal and northeast India. An area of temperate forest, it was lightly populated by humans until the 1950s, when malaria eradication opened the area to agriculture, industrial logging, grazing, and other consequences of human occupation such as firewood collection (Fraser 2009). Populations of tiger, rhinoceros, and elephant dropped markedly as a consequence of increased human numbers and exploitation, and intact areas started shrinking, linked to each other by thinner and thinner threads (Dinerstein 2003; Fraser 2009). In 1955 a new king ascended to the throne of Nepal and sought to stop the biological decline of large animals by turning hunting reserves and other areas into strictly protected parks and charging the army with enforcement.

Decline slowed, but only slightly in the face of continued increases in human numbers. Unwilling or unable to address growth in human population directly, the Nepalese government created community conservancies. Pioneered in Namibia, community conservancies are created by a legal framework in which parks are strictly protected and buffer zones are established around parks that communities can use to grow fodder and trees for their use within legally specified limits. Membership in these conservancies is specified in order to discourage in-migration, members of the community elect a board to make decisions, receive and disburse the revenue shared by the park from ecotourism, or they may actually operate tourist concessions themselves. Members of these communities often work for the protected area. It took time for these organizations to take root and take off, but they did. Deforestation declined. Cattle generally stay outside the parks but also out of buffer areas favored by tigers, rhinoceroses, and elephants. Riparian reforestation protects from flooding and there are other benefits to locals. Tourism and revenue have also increased.

This effort was part of something bigger: a comprehensive conservation vision to recover the region's wildlife. Unlike the experience of John Oates (1999) in West Africa where projects were primarily about development, Terai Arc was and is about conservation, albeit conservation that has direct benefit for local human populations.

Terai Arc was founded in 1987 as a one-acre tree nursery to aid in reforestation. By 1990 the reforestation efforts were focused on buffers around parks and on maintaining and recovering linkages between first the parks in Nepal and then the eleven parks in Nepal and India that constituted the Green Necklace. The Necklace aimed at maintaining and strengthening the metapopulations of rhinoceroses, elephants, tigers, and other keystone species (Dinerstein 2003). In 1993 the Nepalese government formally backed this vision of Terai Arc and increased cooperative work with the Indian government, bringing the community conservancies along with legal, enforcement, economic incentives that included the limited capacity to manage their own affairs. In 2000 the Nepalese prime minister re-endorsed Terai Arc, which by this time included a plan to increase the size of some parks, enhance connectivity, and transplant some rhinoceros to areas from which they had been extirpated. In all a 19,000 square mile

(4.2 million-hectare) area would be returned "to the creatures that once flourished here" (Dinerstein 2003: 254).

The contrast between Oates's West Africa and Terai Arc is striking. The conservation as development approach that John Oates (1999) describes is a failure in his view. It resulted in agricultural conversion of forest, logging, and where forests were left they were empty of wildlife; the development aspects of projects usually failed as well. Mostly the assumptions of those who took this development approach were nonsense: that communities, unlike national governments, are not corrupt and have strong ties to where they live and will care for it (Oates 1999). Oates argues, much as Dinerstein, that a well-drafted legal structure supporting conservation goals and enforcement is essential, committed conservationists are needed on the ground indefinitely (not plantation managers or development people, for example), conservationists lack the resources to alter larger social and economic forces in the near term, and there must be a concrete conservation plan for a defined geographic area.

Terai Arc constitutes successful restoration of a region that had small reserves, diminished or locally extirpated megafauna populations, and degraded connectivity. The goal of restoring forests and wildlife was clear, as was the science: re-establish succession, predation, and the capacity of large carnivores and wide-ranging animals to move across the landscape (Noss 1992; Dinerstein 2003). Sharing economic benefits of restoration or rewilding with locals is a means to an end and takes place within a clear legal framework that limits economic activity and makes primary strict protection of parks and other areas where mandated. As a result, tiger and rhinoceros numbers are up in both parks and buffer areas. Ecotourist revenue is up and with it local revenue. Locals can now invest in better-quality cattle that are worth feeding, so they are not out offering themselves as poor-quality tiger food or otherwise competing for browse with native herbivore populations (Dinerstein 2003).

To make it work politically there are also several elements that must be in place according to Dinerstein (2003):

- A clear, large-scale vision and plan for the region to be restored;
- Bold leadership, committed for the duration;
- A legal framework in place that offers strict protection to designated areas, including core areas and areas important for wildlife movement, and to species' life needs;
- A legal framework that defines authority, strong economic incentives, fair allocation of earnings among locals, and limits on activities of local people in parks, in park buffers, and in other areas impacting parks and wildlife; this framework may also include government investments in local economic activities for basic forage and the like, until such time as ecotourism generates revenue;
- A legal framework for relocating people as needed, providing fair compensation;
- Secure land tenure vested in part in communities to minimize in-migration and maintain community stability;
- Healthy populations of all native species and functional ecological processes such as succession, disturbance regimes, and predation among others; charismatic species must in part be accessible to tourists to support revenue for the park and local populations;
- Stable private ecotourism on which to build community tourism, or a benevolent entrepreneur to invest in ecotourism;
- Good relations between locals and officials;
- Effective anti-poaching laws and enforcement;
- Utilization of resilient habitat for human economic activities because this habitat is best able to resist degradation;
- Economic benefits and a safety net must be part of conservation planning such that it takes immediate and longer-term pressure off of parks; so the safety net does not draw an influx of new people; who is local must be defined from the beginning;
- Evaluation of how well conservation goals are being met at all biological and political levels.

The applicability or primacy of particular lessons varies depending on the degree of degradation of habitat and species loss, availability of relatively unoccupied land for restoration or terrestrial and marine obstacles to restoration, the size of existing protected areas, the existing legal framework, effective and sympathetic political leadership, and the presence or availability of investors in restoration.

Patagonia (Jimenez 2017; Butler 2018; Tompkins 2018). Tompkins Conservation, in partnership with the governments of Chile and Argentina, and in cooperation with other NGOs and phil-anthropists has helped to conserve 13 million acres in the two coun-tries. The primary approach was to purchase high-quality conservation lands – about 2 million acres over the years – aggregate the land and then use the donation of this land to the public to leverage governments in the region to expand their park systems by creating new parks or expanding existing parks. The resulting national parks include Monte León, Impenetrable, Patagonia and Iberá National Parks (Iberá is north of the Patagonia region, in marshland) in Argentina, and Yendegaia, Patagonia, Kaweskar, Melimoyu and Pumalin National Parks in Chile.

The lands were secured with private funds guided by what was determined to be needed to assemble and maintain complete ecosys-tems and meet the life needs of all native species including top predators. Beauty was also an essential part of the work: the wild beauty of the land and the beauty of park infrastructure which expressed deeply rooted cultural traditions.

Although much of the landscape was intact and industrial activ-ities absent, restoration plays a central role in many facets of the work. Repatriation of extirpated species and reconnection of habitat broken by roads and other human artifacts is part of the work under-way. This rewilding has been most ambitious in the Iberá marshlands, where Tompkins Conservation has reintroduced giant anteaters, pompas deer, collared peccaries, tapirs, green-winged macaws, and is presently working to breed jaguars for eventual return to the wild. Alliances with local and national groups focused on particular issues, such as opposition to river-killing dams in Patagonia, has raised awareness among an increasingly urban population, mobilized support for new parks and made them a source of national pride and, increasingly, national identity.

Powerful negative stories arose from resistance to the land purchases and parks over the years, including associated restoration: they will keep Chile or Argentina subjugated to rich foreigners, they will cut Chile in half, water will be stolen from farmers and herders, predators will slaughter livestock, halting dams will deprive the region of prosperity, and so on. Stories about the benefits of conservation, restoration, and natural preservation are important. They need to be conveyed by local leaders and must always give credit to locals for achievements. Local variations of the grand narrative are also important.

Stories must also undermine the conservation–development dualism by being based on the ability of parks to provide livelihood to locals from ecotourism and from activities in buffer areas that are compatible with the parks. Ecotourism depends in turn on restoration and on park infrastructure that simultaneously is locally resonant and compatible with biodiversity. Eighty percent of Tompkins Conservation employees come from local communities around parks and land purchase areas. Tompkins Conservation seeks to ensure that nearby "human communities flourish with their economic vitality linked to the vibrant, good health of the natural world" (Tompkins Conservation 2017).

The Patagonian experience recognizes that both conservation and restoration are primarily political: taking advantage of opportunities in sparsely settled areas to bring back species and processes, investing in local leadership and leadership autonomy, careful timing of land acquisition, species reintroductions and other actions and demonstration of the benefits, and the importance of personal relationships at all levels.

What cannot be easily replicated is the financial resources to buy land quietly on a very large scale. Having significant financial resources in the hands of those with clear vision means less initial reliance on mobilizing a mass movement to influence decision makers. Nonetheless, organizing support is of ongoing importance.

Gorongosa The restoration of Gorongosa National Park is called by Carroll (2016) a resurrection. Not a typical scientific term but an accurate one. Founded in 1960 by the Portuguese colonial authorities in a less developed and less populated area of Mozambique, Gorongosa was considered to hold the possibility of setting a high standard for parks: big enough to maintain healthy populations of its rich wildlife assemblage and free of the political, demographic, and criminal pressure of other parks in southern Africa.

After a war of independence which ended in 1975, the park's wildlife remained healthy. Compared to human numbers, other large mammal numbers in the park area seem small, but compared to many other reserves the wildlife numbers were large: 14,000 Cape buffalo, 5,500 wildebeest, 3,500 waterbuck, 3,000 each hippos and zebras, and 2,200 elephants (Carroll 2016: 184). Two years after independence those unhappy with the new government launched their own war to displace it, a war supported by apartheid South Africa and its allies. The war lasted from 1977 to 1992 and killed a million people. It was violent for wildlife as well. Humans are an ignorant and lethal species, as Wilson (2014: 136–7) observed, in ways that other species are not. The park was attacked directly as a symbol of the government, but both sides killed large animals for food. By the time the fighting ended, most big mammal species' numbers were sharply reduced – some to a few dozen, though elephants may have numbered 200 and waterbuck more than 300. Poachers pursued them. Nile crocodiles were the only big animal species that remained in good shape.

In the meantime Nelson Mandela in South Africa had concluded that ecotourism could be an immediate major driver of income growth throughout southern Africa's rural areas provided much of the money stayed there. Mozambican president Joaquim Chissano was persuaded by Mandela and both believed that strong human ties to the natural world contributed to peace (Wilson 2014; Carroll 2016;

Mutemba 2017). Chissano attended the Rio Earth Summit in 1992 and came away feeling reinforced in these notions. His cabinet and military leadership were directed to meditate twice daily on peace and nature. Mandela and Chissano prioritized development but also cared about their natural heritage. (When wildlife or its representatives win a revolution then justice for all species may be the priority, not just justice for humans.)

It was not until over a decade later that Greg Carr met the Mozambican ambassador to the UN and was invited to meet Chissano. To summarize a more complicated story, Carr, also mostly concerned with development and human rights, was struck with the great beauty of Gorongosa and with the possibility of protecting and restoring wildlife as a conservation-compatible means of doing it all. Carr also had the capacity, like Doug and Kris Tompkins, of making it happen. With a country's president committed to restoring the park as a functional biological and ecotourism entity and a recently conservation-educated entrepreneur willing to bring money to the table, two major drivers were in place, drivers that in other cases would need to be built by a conservation movement.

In 2004 Carr committed US$500,000 to get restoration underway and a year later pledged US$40 million over thirty years (Carroll 2016). He also pulled together various experts to survey the park for wildlife and identify first steps toward restoration. A plan for the park was developed in Cambridge, Massachusetts, and in Mozambique during 2005–7 which led to an agreement between the Carr Foundation and the Mozambican government to co-manage the park.

As was clear from our brief discussions of Patagonia and Terai Arc, Gorongosa is integrating several elements to ensure biological and political integrity and resilience: restoring species and biological processes, organizing ecotourism from the beginning, protecting the park from continued injury from poaching and other exploitative activities, ensuring that the benefits of the park accrue to locals through employment and in other ways, and to the nation through pride in their natural heritage and sustainable foreign exchange earnings.

Based on knowledge of how the park worked in the 1960s and '70s and on the intervening findings of conservation biology, park managers started with restoration of herbivores. They had been slaughtered during the civil war. The absence of herbivores had allowed the grasslands to become seriously degraded and disturbed. And without herbivores healthy predator populations cannot be supported. In many degraded ecosystems the predators are the first to go because they are persecuted; herbivore populations explode and vegetation succession is halted and trees do not regenerate. Here the herbivores were the first to go because they were food.

The number of herbivore species reintroduced seems small, as do the number of each species: 210 Cape buffalo were introduced from Kruger National Park (South Africa) and Limpopo National Park (Mozambique) from 2006 to 2011; it took several years to gather fourteen of the zebra subspecies original to Gorongosa, where they were placed along with the buffalo in a 15,000-acre sanctuary; in 2007 180 wildebeest were introduced into the sanctuary; six elephants and five hippos were added to the park in 2008; and in 2013 thirty-five eland. It is expensive and traumatic for animals to be transported and it was fortuitous that most of the 8,000 animals to be transported were to come from Zimbabwe, which subsequently closed its borders to such activity (Stalmans 2016). The park thus relied on the few big animal additions just noted and the few remaining herbivore populations in the park. These populations proved very resilient and herbivore numbers grew rapidly so there are currently 78,000 large animals (Mutemba 2017), including 700 elephants, up from 200. The grasslands are returning to health, as are herbivore populations. Carnivore populations are catching up. There are about 100 lions in the park, and cubs have high survival. Leopard, brown and spotted hyena are now in the park, and wild dogs are recovering (Carroll 2016; Bouley 2018). It is the large animals, of course, that will fuel ecotourism. Opportunism as well as planning are important to restoration.

Research is currently underway on smaller animals, trophic relations and the like at Gorongosa. The park invites research projects from around the world and gives access to professional training for Mozambicans, including locals.

To ensure that repatriated and existing wildlife thrive, another initial step was to hire and train rangers to patrol the sanctuary and eventually the entire park. Overwhelmingly local people, they understood the poaching situation and its bushmeat motivation. A primary task was to prevent poaching and snares, which not only kill but cripple. The rangers, understanding both poachers and the wildlife, were able to achieve significant success. Guides were also hired very early on to lay the groundwork for tourism among locals, Mozambicans and southern Africans more generally; tourists from more distant places were beginning to return.

From the beginning the park was considered as more than the strict park boundaries. It was seen as a mosaic of strictly protected areas and buffers managed primarily for wildlife but able to accommodate conservation-compatible forestry, hunting, and agriculture such as coffee and cashew to support the 250,000 people that lived around the park (hereinafter Greater Gorongosa) (Carr 2018). Taking advantage of these lightly settled areas (the buffers) allowed for the movement of species across a wider area, including to the coast and north along the rift valley, a traditional movement corridor. In 2010 Mount Gorongosa was incorporated into the park proper to protect the source of water for the Greater Gorongosa area and for some buffer areas. Deforestation was undermining the ability of the catchment to do its job. The 3 million hectare (7.4 million acre) effort envisions connectivity north up the rift valley, perhaps one day to Tanzania although agriculture is growing more intensive and is an obstacle.

In 2008 Mateus Mutemba was hired to manage the park and he proved to be one of those leaders who can assemble an inspired, capable, and committed team around him, including Marc Stalmans, Director of Scientific Services, and Pedro Muagura, Director of

Conservation. Equally important to making the park a biological success is new tourist infrastructure that walks a fine line between offering the services visitors need and want – hotel rooms, restaurants, and transport – and not opening up the region to population growth and extraction. Roads or improved roads into largely intact areas are usually the beginning of the end for wildlife, especially absent strong enforcement (Ibisch et al. 2016).

The park management also seeks to build political resilience into the park in numerous ways. The park's 500 employees are overwhelmingly from local communities. Training programs and opportunities for education and advancement are part of this effort. Twenty percent of park revenue is committed as a matter of policy to local communities, in addition to employee salaries and wages. "Human development" programs are administered directly by the park, including support for ninety-three primary schools, health care for 100,000 people, and agricultural inputs for 4,000 farm families. It very much resembles the better and reciprocal aspects of patron–client relationships of older agricultural societies (Scott 1976), which fostered strong social bonds. The Carr Foundation funding for Gorongosa directly supports much of this well-being work.

The park vision and action plan also takes a very long-term view of political resilience expressed in its Girls' Club program. School-based (seventeen schools currently), these clubs meet daily after classes to work on reading skills, learn about natural history, health, nutrition, and birth control, watch films, become acquainted with female role models, and serve as interns in the community. They encourage girls to stay in school, the alternative to which is usually early marriage to an older man, pregnancy, and an end to other opportunities. Older girls or young women rotate leadership of each club under the guidance of individuals in the Gorongosa Women's Club.

Although the area around Gorongosa is not heavily populated, and although many head to the cities after adolescence, population is growing. Since the Earth is finite, stabilizing population is good for conservation. Many involved in the Gorongosa Restoration Project describe it as a development project that benefits conservation. It is taken for granted by many that conservation must pay to survive in an increasingly crowded world. Others will say both are important: the twin goals, at least to a point (no one is proposing rural Mozambicans live like Canadians or Americans), are compatible. Still others say that making conservation work is the priority and bickering won't help – look to results. It is fair to say that there are differences in motivation within and between large-scale restoration projects. Interestingly, though Mandela, Chassono, Carr, and others are not ecocentric, the outcome for conservation in Gorongosa looks like ecological restoration.

When restoration projects have strong support among the highest levels of government it contributes greatly to success. Having engaged, wealthy, and committed benefactors helps; or the equivalent in those able to find funding mechanisms.

Marine Restoration Humans know less about what the oceans were once like than the land (Costello 2014). Though sea water flows in human veins, it is an alien place compared to the land. Even human societies that rely on fish, sea mammals, and other ocean life do not live in the oceans. Thus humans are better able to follow the consequences of human behavior on the terrestrial Earth in much greater detail than in the oceans. The evidence is more accessible (see Chapter 11 for a discussion of the special challenges of marine conservation).

Jeremy Jackson and colleagues led the way with two 2001 studies exploring the impact of fishing on ocean health and particularly species recovery following more recent human and natural disturbances (Jackson et al. 2001; Jackson and Johnson 2001). Pinnegar and Engelhard (2008) have documented the devastating effects of industrial fishing since it began at different times and in different places, but they also persuasively argue that human fishing has had negative impacts on fish populations for millennia, especially on slow-growing fish. Harpoons 90,000 years old have been found in the Congo and they cite evidence for fishing of reefs 35,000 to 40,000 years ago.

Efforts to reconstruct the human effects on the ocean are more systematically relying on tools new to this effort, though not new in themselves: archaeology, genetics, the records of explorers and historians, literature and other anecdotal records. The result is a better understanding of the oceans and the *consequences* of human behavior for species and ecosystems (Pinnegar and Engelhard 2008). Climate change has also prompted more intensive study of coral reefs, estuaries, mangroves, and other species-rich areas (Roberts et al. 2017). Costello (2014) urges conservationists to get to remaining lightly fished parts of the oceans and document what remaining healthy areas look like and how they work, with the caveat that large-scale human-degraded marine processes have already negatively affected these areas.

The damage to the ocean takes many forms. Warming and acidification are well underway, sea ice and glacier melting is releasing freshwater and stored toxins as is runoff from arctic ice fields. Dead zones continue to track the human footprint in the northern hemisphere; urban and agricultural run off are the primary contributors (Diaz and Rosenberg 2008). Only reduction in fertilizer use seems to make a difference and most of the trends are going the other way. The decade lag time between use and consequences does not contribute to human learning. The size of dead zones is also affected by variations in river flow. Edgar et al. (2014) estimate that two-thirds of coastal biomass is gone due to overfishing, pollution, and other factors. By one estimate 90 percent of the bigger fish in the ocean are gone, which includes most of the predators, disrupting trophic relationships (Myers and Worm 2003). Industrial whaling and fishing; factory ships that take everything to make fish sticks, dog food, and plant fertilizer; bottom trawling, dredging, and other fishing gear have fundamentally altered the whole biotic structure of the ocean (Costello 2014). The roots of this are temporally much deeper than the industrial period, however. Pre-industrial human groups, spreading across the globe with slowly growing populations can have significant affects as noted above (Pinnegar and Engelhard 2008).

The introduction of exotics can also alter the oceans as it does the rivers and lakes of the world. An oil spill can contaminate sediments for decades and storms can agitate the toxins. Ship damage to reefs can take a long time to recover and even small incidents can undermine longstanding equilibria.

These human inflicted wounds mean that almost all ocean conservation is ocean restoration. This includes hands-on restoration such as reconstructing corals or oyster beds, cleaning birds' feathers and mammals' fur, but more usually involves management actions to stop injuries and other steps to encourage regeneration. A very small part of the ocean has been strictly protected: about 1.8 percent is in no-take (strictly protected) reserves (MPAtlas 2017). Still, some bio-geographic regions, ecosystems, and other types of places – sea-mounts, corals, mangroves – are in much better health than others. Acidification, pollution, and noise affect areas differently depending on sources of the problem, ocean currents, and other factors. The Global Ocean Refuge System (GLORES) program of the Marine Conservation Institute, for example, seeks to strictly protect at least 30 percent of the oceans and thereby marine biological diversity and ecological processes (GLORES 2017). It must be the right 30 percent of course, and to that end experts from all over the world are engaged in identifying and mapping those areas. The process includes trying to project the consequence of continued warming, acidification, ice loss, and other factors. Even if the causes were halted the momentum of past behavior will continue to create problems for some time.

MPAs work to conserve species and places (e.g. Sciberras et al. 2013; Costello 2014; Gill et al. 2017), but without more resources they are inadequate. Worm (2017) observes that by itself building a hospital does little – it requires expert staff, supplies, infrastructure and much else. In a review of 443 MPAs, Gill et al. (2017) found that 65 percent had inadequate staff and 91 percent had inadequate budgets. Seventy-one percent of 218 MPAs examined for changes in fish populations showed increases and these were highly correlated with adequate staffing and funding. Such a relationship is not surprising and defines the challenge for conservationists: how to get and sustain adequate support. In the US political process, for instance, conservationists may win the high profile battle and get designation, only to see backdoor deals ensuring inadequate funding to make reserve opponents happy.

Other important factors in MPA efficacy include size (Gill et al. 2017; Edgar et al. 2014, who examined 87 MPAs); no-take regulations (no fishing or other killing or removal of sea life, mining, oil extraction, or war games) (Edgar et al. 2014); strict enforcement (Gill et al. 2017) which Edgar takes to include not just consistent and comprehensive policing but also community cooperation, compliance, and support; and MPA age, which has two aspects: the older an MPA the more recovery time will have elapsed, and the longer an MPA has existed the longer it is likely to exist. For Edgar (2014), if an MPA has existed ten years then recovery should show signs of taking off, with recovery perpetuating more recovery; the larger the MPAs the more regenerative capacity of the ocean is harnessed (Gill et al. 2017); in most cases 100 square kilometers is a floor (Edgar et al. 2014), but depending on the ecological community and life needs of species – especially top predators – and healthy population size, it could be larger; chlorophyll concentration (Gill et al. 2017); and isolation from human activity (Edgar et al. 2014). With three or less of these criteria present, MPAs have little value. Only 4.6 percent have the five factors that Edgar et al. (2014) list, and another 5.7 percent have four. He notes that networks of connected reserves might compensate for some missing factors, as with terrestrial reserves which permit metapopulation interaction, dispersal, and greater genetic variability.

IN SUM

The lessons for the global ocean are not terribly different than for the land: *A clear and bold vision is needed, delineating what is needed at a variety of scales in strictly protected ("no-take") reserves to ensure all native species and ecological processes are safe-guarded and can recover – their location, boundaries, linkages creating networks of MPAs, specific outcomes and the management regimes most likely to achieve that. Buffer zones that allow reserve-compatible activities also must be mapped or those who see the oceans only as money, food, garbage dump or a place for naval advantage will take all they can.*

Urgent action is needed on behalf of the ocean and its life. We know that people react viscerally and negatively to clear cuts. They are ugly. This has helped the forest conservation cause. We also know that most don't know a healthy or diseased grassland when they see it and this has made it difficult to address one of the biggest disasters on the planet – livestock. People do not even see the oceans; unless bad things are washing up on the beaches or plastic is floating on the surface they are out-of-sight and out-of-mind. There are cultural predispositions that make people regard the oceans as indestructible or limitless, but neither is true (Patton 2007). Building political support for the oceans is way behind the terrestrial world. For more than two decades warnings by conservationists have said a twenty-year window exists to right things; they have not been righted. Degradation grows, making recovery more and more difficult. It is yet more difficult with the oceans because the losses are much greater and the damage is less completely understood or easy to see.

Marine protected areas are created by states. They can be created by one state in its exclusive economic zone through the political processes of that state. The high seas are nominally governed by the United Nations Convention on the Law of the Sea (UNCLOS) and the United Nations Convention on Biodiversity (CBD). The current process for creating high seas MPAs is very cumbersome and complicated. Negotiations are underway pursuant to UNCLOS to make it more straightforward. Expediting this process deserves increased pressure. As with most international regimes, which includes UNCLOS, decisions will be shaped by particular states that have the interest, will, and resources to lead other states toward particular outcomes. Outcomes will depend, then, on the domestic politics of these states, not just on the typically plodding interactions among states over time (the "PrepComs," or preparatory meetings). Identifying these states and moving them in the desired direction is strategically critical. The importance of vision in defining demands on states and other decision makers is plain.

Because of the experiential and psychological distance of the oceans from actual and potential supporters, a focus on the long term is incumbent on those organizing on behalf of the oceans. Attention must be paid not just to enforcement in perpetuity, to evaluation of changes and trends, and to adjustments needed, e.g. in MPA boundaries in response to ocean temperature change, but to maintaining strong political pressure for MPA effectiveness. The clout of narrow marine interests – fishing, oil, mining, and other extractive interests – will not let up. They will take any advantage to block reserves, keep them small, keep rules weak, or make them go away. The Trump administration is not the only government to undo or shrink PAs or weaken safeguards.

In Chapter 11, successful methods of mobilizing people on behalf of marine conservation are discussed. Appeals to protect wildlife and their homes, rather than protecting places per se, have proven most effective. Particular wildlife species, from sea otters and orcas to octopuses, can serve as umbrellas for places and other species. Appeals to justice, as with anti-whaling and anti-shark-finning campaigns, have been effective. Coastal areas can have strong appeal to significant groups, but most of the ocean is not close to shore and most of its life is under the surface of the water. Divers are too limited a constituency and even they only go so deep. Over two generations ago Jacques Cousteau made the oceans accessible to large numbers of people via prime-time television and created awareness. But awareness is only the beginning of mobilization.

NGOs are essential to mobilization and especially to sustaining it. If they are doing their job they concentrate political resources (time, money, skills) and use them to change institutional behavior. They provide a home for activism and a place for activists to evolve and mature. NGOs also evolve. The Surfrider organization has gone beyond cleaning up coasts enjoyed by surfers and become a major force in defense of the oceans.

If we lose the oceans, most life on Earth is gone. Period. As with terrestrial conservation problems, the source of injury to marine life and ecosystems is human: plastics, fertilizer, oil and chemical pollution, noise from ships, sonar, seismic activities, fishing, persecution, acidification. Many humans have what Phil Slater (1970) called the toilet syndrome: flush away whatever you want to get rid of and don't think about where the pipe comes out. Patton (2007) and Mack (2011) note as well that the oceans have long been regarded in most cultures as a method of material and ritual cleansing. That broadly shared attitude needs to be dismantled and in its place new cultural attitudes and traditions created à la Hobsbawn and Ranger (1984) and Etzioni and Bloom (2004).

Creating marine and terrestrial PAs that can sustain all native species and ecosystems including disturbance regimes and succession is essential to the future of the fabric of life on Earth. Ecocentric restoration, regeneration, rewilding – whatever it is called – is necessary at a variety of scales and especially at those scales typically ignored: the continental or ocean basin (or gyre) scale, and whole biogeographic and ecosystem scales.

Utilizing species that make good umbrellas for the large scale and evoke strong emotional resonance with target audiences is effective and therefore essential. Mobilization will only occur if organizing encourages and enhances personal connections with these species and fosters a sense of urgency. Species that bridge the marine and terrestrial such as salmon have a special role to play. Wide-ranging animals such as antelope, salmon or whales, and top carnivores such as brown bears, wolves, or sharks are important for setting lower limits on protected area size and ensuring that top-down as well as other eco-regulatory processes remain robust.

Many invasive species are often not considered invasive if one or another human group considers them not to be. Domestic cattle, cows, sheep, cheatgrass, and many fish species are among them and they cause no end of mischief to native species and ecosystems. Their removal or containment are required despite complaints from these groups, who often claim special favors.

On land roads are among the most serious problems: they fragment the landscape, directly kill many animals, allow access by humans who bring garbage, lethal toys, disease, mining, logging, sprawl, dams, and other water diversions and other industrial activities and disruption. They contribute to creation of mortality sinks and generate huge increases in conflicts between humans and other species. There are similar problems in the oceans. Shipping has grown enormously and with it direct damage via strikes and engine noise to whales and other species; noise from sonar and seismic activity has permanently injured many creatures; poison spills and garbage dumping ends up not just on coastlines but in huge patches of junk at the center of high seas gyres where it is ingested by everything from zooplankton (and taken up the food chain) to fish and seabirds.

In the end the goal of restoration is something like what Bruce Babbitt imagines in *Cities in the Wilderness* (2005). It is to restore the land- and seascape to a self-regulating state, help heal the wounds, and remove human behavior that continues to inflict wounds. It will take a very long time to fix some things. As all of our mothers said, an ounce of prevention is worth a pound of cure. But here we are, in need of pounds and pounds if not tons of cure because we did not listen. It is difficult work. But there is no real choice if we care.

REFERENCES

Babbitt, Bruce. 2005. *Cities in the Wilderness*. Island Press. Washington DC.
Bouley, Paola. 2018. Personal communication. January 31.
Butler, Tom. 2018. Personal communication. February 17.
Carr, Greg. 2018. Personal communication. January 29.
Carroll, Sean B. 2016. *The Serengeti Rules*. Princeton University Press. Princeton, NJ.
Costello, Mark J. 2014. Long Live Marine Reserves. 176 *Biological Conservation* 289–96 (August).

Diaz, Robert J. and Rutger Rosenberg. 2008. Spreading Dead Zones and Consequences for Marine Ecosystems. 321 *Science* 926–9 (August 15).

Dinerstein, Eric. 2003. *The Return of the Unicorns.* Columbia University Press. New York.

Doyle, Mary and Cynthia A. Drew (eds.). 2008. *Large-Scale Ecosystem Restoration.* Island Press. Washington DC.

Edgar, Graham J., Rick D. Stuart-Smith, Trevor J. Willis, et al. 2014. Global Conservation Outcomes Depend on Marine Protected Areas with Five Key Features. 506 *Nature* 216–20 (February 13).

Etzioni, Amitai and Jared Bloom (eds.). 2004. *We Are What We Celebrate.* New York University Press. New York.

European Parliament. 2009. Resolution on Wilderness in Europe. P6_TA(2009) 0034. Adopted February 3, 2009; final version posted October 13, 2009. www.europarl.europa.eu/sides/getDoc.do?pubRef=-//EP//NONSGML+TA+P6-TA-2009-0034+0+DOC+PDF+V0//EN (accessed September 3, 2015).

Fraser, Caroline. 2009. *Rewilding the World.* Metropolitan/Henry Holt. New York.

Gill, David A., Michael B. Mascia, Gabby N. Ahmadia, et al. 2017. Capacity Shortfalls Hinder the Performance of Marine Protected Areas Globally. 543 *Nature* 665–9 (March 30).

GLORES (Global Ocean Refuge System). 2017. https://globaloceanrefuge.org/ (accessed June 24, 2017).

Hobsbawm, Eric and Terence Ranger. 1984 [1983]. *The Invention of Tradition.* Cambridge University Press. Cambridge.

Ibisch, Pierre L., Monika T. Hoffmann, Stefan Kreft, et al. 2016. A Global Map of Roadless Areas and Their Conservation Status. 354 *Science* 1423–7 (December 16).

Jackson, Jeremy and Kenneth G. Johnson. 2001. Measuring Past Biodiversity. 293 *Science* 2401–3 (September 28).

Jackson, Jeremy, Michael X. Kirby, Wolfgang H. Berger, et al. 2001. Historical Overfishing and the Recent Collapse of Coastal Ecosystems. 293 *Science* 629–38 (July 27).

Jimenez, Ignacio. 2017. Presentation: Tompkins Conservation Park Creation. Biodiversity Days March 2–3. Duke University, Durham, NC.

Johns, David. 2016. Rewilding. *Reference Module in Earth Systems and Environmental Sciences*, Elsevier, 08-Feb-2016. doi: 10.1016/B978-0-12-409548-9.09202-2.

Jordan, III, William R. and George M. Lubick. 2011. *Making Nature Whole.* Island Press. Washington DC.

Lochner, Stephanie. 2012. *The Klamath Basin: A Restoration for the Ages*. KVIE Television. Sacramento, CA.

Mack, John. 2011. *The Sea*. Reaktion. London.

MPAtlas. 2017. Global MPAs. www.mpatlas.org/map/mpas/ (accessed June 26, 2017).

Mutemba, Mateus. 2017. Personal communication. March 23.

Myers, Ransom A. and Boris Worm. 2003. Rapid Worldwide Depletion of Predatory Fish Communities. 423 *Nature* 280–3 (May 15).

Noss, Reed. 1992. The Wildlands Project Land Conservation Strategy. *Wild Earth* Special Issue 1: 10–25.

Noss, Reed and Allen Cooperrider. 1994. *Saving Nature's Legacy*. Island Press. Washington DC.

Oates, John F. 1999. *Myth and Reality in the Rain Forest*. University of California Press. Berkeley, CA.

Patton, Kimberley C. 2007. *The Sea Can Wash Away All Evils*. Columbia University Press. New York.

Pinnegar, John K. and Georg H. Engelhard. 2008. The 'Shifting Baseline' Phenomenon: A Global Perspective. 18 *Reviews in Fish Biology and Fisheries*. doi: 10.1007/s11160-007-9058-6 (accessed June 26, 2017).

Roberts, Callum. 2007. *The Unnatural History of the Sea*. Island Press. Washington DC.

Roberts, Callum M., Bethan C. O'Leary, Douglas J. McCauley, et al. 2017. Marine Reserves Can Mitigate and Promote Adaptation to Climate Change. *Proceedings of the (US) National Academy of Sciences*. www.pnas.org/cgi/doi/10.1073/pnas.1701262114 (accessed June 9, 2017).

Sciberras, Marija, Stuart R. Jenkins, Michel J. Kaiser, Stephen J. Hawkins and Andrew S. Pullin. 2013. Evaluating the Biological Effectiveness of Fully and Partially Protected Marine Areas. 2 *Environmental Evidence* 4. www.environmentalevidencejournal.org/content/2/1/4.

Scott, James. 1976. *The Moral Economy of the Peasant*. Yale University Press. New Haven, CT.

Simberloff, Daniel, Dan Doak, Martha Groom, et al. 1999. Regional and Continental Restoration. Pp. 65–98 in Michael E. Soulé and John Terborgh (eds). *Continental Conservation*. Island Press. Washington DC.

Slater, Phillip. 1970. *The Pursuit of Loneliness*. Beacon Press. Boston, MA.

Soule, Michael and John Terborgh. 1999. *Continental Conservation*. Island Press. Washington DC.

Stalmans, Marc. 2016. Personal communications. March 26 and April 21.

Stalmans, Marc. 2018. Personal communication. January 31.

Tompkins, Kris. 2018. Personal communication. February 6.

Tompkins Conservation. 2017. *Creating Parklands / Restoration and Rewilding, Ecological Agriculture / Activism*. Tompkins Conservation. San Francisco.

Wild Europe Initiative (WEI). 2013. *A Working Definition of European Wilderness and Wild Areas*. Wild Europe Initiative. London.

Wilson, Edward O. 2014. *A Window on Eternity*. Simon & Schuster. New York.

Wilson, Edward O. 2016. *Half-Earth*. Liveright. New York.

Worm, Boris. 2017. How to Heal an Ocean. 543 *Science* 630–1 (March 30).

10 The Other Connectivity: Reaching Beyond the Choir

The breakdown of pre-modern institutions produced "... the first of those self-disciplined agents of social and political reconstruction who have appeared so frequently in modern history. [They are] the destroyers of the old order for whom there is no need to feel nostalgic ... [They are] above all, ... extraordinarily bold, inventive, and ruthless politicians ..."

Walzer 1965: vii

Some years ago the astronomer Timothy Ferris was asked why Americans were so enthralled with space exploration, especially in light of its expense and the many problems society confronts. His answer was that many of us want to know whether we are alone in the universe. It was a curiosity he shared.

Of course we are not alone. We are surrounded by life. How could an astute, thoughtful observer like Ferris miss this small fact? I cannot say for sure, not having had the opportunity to ask him. But I think the answer is this. We miss the obvious – that life fills the Earth – if we are emotionally separated from it and are not deeply connected to it. It is emotional connection which generates meaning, which makes this or that aspect of reality important. A lack of connection is what proximately accounts for the anemic social reaction by so many to the accelerating loss of wildlife and wild places (Searles 1960, 1979). We saw at the beginning of this book how precipitous the losses are as a consequence of the growing human footprint (WWF 2014).

To change this situation is going to require the mobilization of important sectors of society that have up to now not *acted* on behalf of conservation. Catalyzing the action of millions and forging more effective alliances with other powerful political players depends on reaching others at a deep level – conservation must be felt as urgent and personal. To be effective this outreach must be done in the context of organizing, of bringing people into a group, and having a role for them. It is organizing that generates collective political action which in turn changes institutional behavior. In short, the most pressing matters facing conservation are not biological or ecological, but political.

There are many aspects to organizing or mobilization – the process by which people come to devote their time, money, skills, networks, and other resources to collective political action. These include identifying the audiences to be mobilized, understanding what moves them, developing a strategy not only for initial mobilization, but sustaining it by integrating people into an organization, and deciding what actions are needed and when to gain desired results from decision makers. Here I focus on one element of mobilization: how to bring it about; how to effectively connect with target audiences so the likelihood of mobilization is maximized. The principles are general, the examples are North American.

Often conservationists fail to appreciate how different the audiences they want to reach are from themselves and each other; they talk to the world as if they were talking to themselves. Too often they offer answers to people who are not yet asking the questions. Good strategy seldom emerges from such confusion.

Conservationists need to remember that most of those who will have to be mobilized are not scientists, may be smart but are not always well educated, very frequently are not interested in politics, and if they are engaged in politics they may not give much thought to biodiversity and conservation as pressing matters of justice and equity, or conservation is far from their top priority. In North America most people prefer to get their news by watching – 80 percent via television – and of those who read to obtain news only about 20 percent look to a newspaper online or in hardcopy (Mitchell et al. 2016). Although it varies considerably by age, overall most read and watch television online. The better educated rely on television the least (Saad 2013). Although media ownership has become highly concentrated (Dye 2014), media outlets are more numerous and fragmented, aiming at specialized audiences. Those Americans who do read print are not reading the *New York Times* or *Washington Post*, but *USA Today* and local papers.

If healing the many wounds humans have inflicted requires mass political action to bring the pressure needed to change behavior, then touching people's emotions, need-states, and values linked to the sacred and a sense of efficacy will be important. All three are necessary for action.

Emotion and motivate come from the same root – to move. Conservationists need only reflect on themselves to realize the power of emotion. They feel *love* for Nature. They *fear* they are losing it. They are *angry* at those destroying it. Emotions are what connect people to the world; they are the primary means of adapting to it. To be effective conservation must arouse strong emotion in those it seeks to mobilize. Information and facts alone cannot do that.

Even when aiming at emotion, it's easy to forget that many of those who must be mobilized are not moved by what moves conservationists. We all have the same emotions (within a range of variation) but they are aroused by different things (Searles 1960, 1979; Erikson 1968; Evans 2001; Pfaff 2007). We need to understand what arouses the group of people we are talking to and touch that. Some years ago, in an effort to halt the decimation of parrots by smugglers in the Caribbean, conservationists tried a new approach. Instead of appealing for the protection of the birds based on love or respect for nature per se, they appealed to nationalism and patriotism (both involve emotions of pride, bonds with others, a desire to avoid humiliation of the group). Appeal to people saying that capturing and selling parrots to rich countries was a betrayal of their national heritage and perpetuated neocolonial relationships evoked a strong response including peer pressure and a sharp decline in parrot trading (Butler 1992).

Need-states are also powerful motivators (Bernays 1928, 1955; Edelman 1964, 1988, 1995; Dinnerstein 1976; Damasio 1994, 1999; Rappaport 1999; Solomon et al. 2003). Humans need healthy food, clean water and air, need to belong, to be valued, to love and be loved, to be creative, to believe in something bigger than themselves. They have a need to make sense of the world and a propensity to see a pattern in things and to posit a purpose (Keleman 1999). People need the wild. One of the problems with need-states is that they are easily co-opted, deformed, or we are distracted from them and settle instead for socially accepted worldviews (Ellul 1972) or approved compensations. People don't belong, so they shop. They lack love, so they seek power and control. Conservationists must become better at penetrating these deformations and compensatory distractions and tap into genuine needs. When that happens tremendous energy is unlocked, as other social movements have demonstrated in the past. It's not easy. People are often afraid of the needs they have buried or ignored. They are afraid of change. Thomas Jefferson wrote in the US Declaration of Independence that people often tolerate the oppressive because it is familiar (Continental Congress 1776). People can have bad political relationship, not just bad personal relationships. Fortunately toleration has its limits.

Values are also powerful motivators (Rappaport 1999; Clayton and Opotow 2003; Pfaff 2007), notwithstanding the findings of neurobiologists such as Antonio Damasio (1994, 1999) who say that about 95 percent of our emotional and cognitive processing is non-conscious. Not *un*conscious in the sense of that which is repressed, but non-conscious as when someone decides they are hungry for sushi and starts heading to the restaurant before they make a conscious decision to go there. Or when someone walks into a room and their hormones start raging and they begin making their way toward the attractive someone across the room that triggered the hormone rush before they have conscious intent to do so. Even though much thinking has its roots in emotion, humans all need to explain the world to themselves and to believe their explanation is correct and proper. That's morality. Humans invest much emotion in their values and understanding of the world (Tavris and Aronson 2007). At the root of the sense of propriety and values are basic, unquestioned (and usually untestable) assumptions. These constitute our sense of the sacred, which can be religious or secular (Rappaport 1999).

Thus, if some hold Genesis to be literally true there's little point in arguing that they should protect nature in order to protect the "theater of evolution." To quarrel about motivations is unlikely to generate cooperative or effective political action. All movements have been coalitions of groups with a variety of motivations. If the creator says creation is good and that leads to action to safeguard biodiversity, then conservationists who are secular should seek common ground based on goals rather than motivations. The poorest forty countries, many with high biodiversity, have populations 90 percent of which say "religion is an important part of (their) daily life" (Crabtree 2010). Both this Gallup poll and extensive analysis of polling about religious belief and economic data over decades confirm that material neediness in childhood tends to generate a desire for religious certainty in adulthood (Norris and Inglehart 2004). The relationship is not simple, however. The US population, for example, reports being highly religious (65 percent), a rate much closer to poorer countries rather than developed ones. One explanation is that the great inequality in the US and lack of a strong safety net creates material insecurity.

Understanding a group's sense of the sacred and framing appeals in those terms is not enough to generate action. To act people require a sense of efficacy – that they can make a difference (Forgas and Cromer 2004; Tavris and Aronson 2007). Generally conservationists cannot create this – it tends to be a personality trait shaped over time, beginning early in life. But because conservation problems can seem so overwhelming to those who must be mobilized, demonstrating how problems can be addressed by strategic action is important.

How do conservationists touch people at the level of emotion, need-states, and values? There are long-term strategies like making sure kids get into the woods, grow up passionate about life and unafraid of their emotions. But this chapter focuses on the nearer term. There are three primary tools to evoke the link between conservation and emotion, needs and values: story, ritual, and organization.

Not all scientists or advocates are comfortable with using all tools, but it is important to know they are there.

We are storytellers in our very souls (e.g. Lakoff 1996; Sachs 2012). We understand the world through story. We place our lives in the context of story. We enjoy stories. Many conservationists are master storytellers. But we need to do more of it. And we need to develop stories that resonate with the specific audiences we are trying to reach. Talking to ourselves is important in maintaining our own sense of identity, but we need to talk to all those others whose support is vital to conservation success. That means the stories we use must be familiar to those we are trying to reach; they must be able to identify with the characters, their circumstances, and passions and frustrations (Sachs 2012). Stories will be much stronger if they can be nested in the mythology the target group embraces, the grand narrative which conveys the group's highest purposes and meaning (Rappaport 1999).

Conservation stories that become narrative films (not just documentaries watched by the same 1 percent of the population) or find their way into music, dance, theatre, and other performance media help create a broader culture and community which embraces biodiversity, a phenomenon important to generating and reinforcing action (on the great power of film see Nichols 1981). Science journals are important for scientists. Public intellectuals reach relatively small, if sometimes influential, audiences. But almost everyone listens to the radio and watches television or rents videos. Millions still go to the movies and attend concerts.

Ritual – patterned collective behavior that codifies invariant meaning, often by "keeping together in time" (d'Aquila and Laughlin 1979; Scott 1990; McNeill 1995) – helps establish collective identity and promotes bonding among people and to a cause. Rites of passage are important rituals – joining a group, a first demonstration or arrest, celebrating a victory, or mutual support in a defeat – marking important, shared transitions and tying together present with past (origins, the founding) and with a desired future (Moore and Myerhoff 1977).

Ritual invests certain actions with legitimacy; or an entire order. It also invests challenges to an order with legitimacy (Kertzer 1988; Hughes 2003) and affirms what must be defended at all costs (the holy) (Rappaport 1999). Holidays, the change of seasons, life events such as birthdays, weddings, and deaths are important to groups and all can be linked to biodiversity in one way or another (Etzioni and Bloom 2004). Indeed, for conservation to become central to people's lives, it must be linked closely with these events and rituals.

Conservationists have some rituals – giving awards, holding banquets, occasionally outdoor celebrations – but come up short in utilizing existing rituals or in fashioning new, mass-based rituals that will attract others to the conservation movement (Hobsbawm and Ranger 1984; Etzioni and Bloom 2004). Ritual is important for two reasons. First, it involves a public performance and usually involves emotionally charged symbols, which can include public monuments or spaces and holidays. What people proclaim publicly obligates them more strongly than a private pledge: they feel obligated (Rappaport 1999). Second, ritual is collective. When people act together to proclaim a belief or in support of a cause, it creates a bond and people are more likely to act again together. Collective action can generate tremendous energy. When the US Declaration of Independence was published in newspapers the general response was tepid. When the Declaration was read publicly and followed by burning King George in effigy the crowds were moved to action (Kertzer 1988).

Finally, conservation requires huge organizational changes. When outreach causes new audiences to ask what they can do they are almost invariably told to write checks, sign petitions, and send postcards. It's difficult to imagine a more perfect recipe for failure, for rapid disengagement. To make use of the resources mobilization brings to the movement and to cultivate those resources, people must become part of an organization in which they can participate. They must have an active role in it. Without an ongoing organizational role people do not build bonds to cause or to others (Giugni et al. 2001; McAdam et al. 2001; Tilly 2002; Diani and McAdam 2003). They do not learn and gain political sophistication. They do not learn how to fight, to deal with repression, to reach out to others and speak with enthusiasm from experience. Without organization they do not act . . . and act again. To ensure that people will act when we truly need them, they must be continuously involved in work and *play*. Action need not always result in some accomplishment but it keeps people engaged, sustaining mutual support.

People desire to be involved with NGOs in different ways. They vary in the time they have, the level of activity they want, their willingness to take risks, their comfort with different kinds of activity. There will always be a place for groups that take insider or outsider approaches. When many North American conservation groups transformed themselves from activist organizations to organizations of check-writers supporting professional staff they lost enormous dynamism and political clout (Shaiko 1999; Turner 2012). Politicians know most of the big groups can't deliver. To be asked for a big check and to sign a petition to stop the slaughter of elephants in Africa accomplishes nothing except to help pay the bills for an office in Washington DC, which may or may not be doing anything effective. It does not stop the slaughter of elephants; indeed it is a betrayal of elephants to the degree people are kept from engaging in meaningful activity such as bringing pressure on ivory-consuming societies, supporting rangers and other enforcement, supporting strong laws. Policy change requires real pressure, real carrots and sticks. NGOs which depend on charitable contributions are often severely restricted from accumulating and using those carrots and sticks.

It is not adequate to understand the biology of conservation problems, which are usually related to consequences of causes that are rooted in human societies. The drivers must be understood, named, confronted, and dealt with. Without a sound understanding of our own species, what moves us, and how to harness what moves us in the service of conservation, the conservation movement will continue to stumble. Decisive action against the causes of harm against biodiversity is indispensable. Conservation is up against institutions with enormous resources and that routinely use violence. Conservationists can't match the resources of those so terribly destructive of life on Earth, nor do they wish to match their violence. They must be smarter and more strategic. The politically weak can and do prevail (Arreguin-Toft 2005).

The battle conservationists fight is not just to realize the dreams of conservationists – the lives of countless creatures are at stake.

REFERENCES

Arreguin-Toft, Ivan. 2005. *How the Weak Win Wars*. Cambridge University Press. Cambridge.

Bernays, Edward L. 1928. *Propaganda*. Liveright. New York.

Bernays, Edward L. (ed.) 1955. *The Engineering of Consent*. University of Oklahoma Press. Norman, OK.

Butler, Paul J. 1992. Parrots, Pressures, People and Pride. Pp. 25–46 in Steven R. Beissinger and Noel F. R. Snyder (eds.). *New World Parrots in Crisis*. Smithsonian Institution. Washington DC.

Clayton, Susan and Susan Opotow (eds.). 2003. *Identity and the Natural Environment*. MIT Press. Cambridge, MA.

Continental Congress, Second (Thomas Jefferson, John Adams, Benjamin Franklin, Roger Sherman, and Robert R. Livingston). 1776. Declaration of Independence. Philadelphia, PA. www.archives.gov/founding-docs/declaration-transcript (accessed May 30, 2017).

Crabtree, Steve. 2010. *Religiosity Highest in World's Poorest Nations*. www.gallup.com/poll/142727/religiosity-highest-world-poorest-nations.aspx (accessed August 14, 2016).

D'Aquila, Eugene and Charles D. Laughlin. 1979. The Neurobiology of Myth and Ritual. In Eugene d'Aquila, Charles D. Laughlin and John McManus (eds.). *The Spectrum of Ritual: A Biogenetic Structural Analysis*. Columbia University Press. New York.

Damasio, Antonio. 1994. *Descartes' Error*. Grosset/Putnam. New York.

Damasio, Antonio. 1999. *The Feeling of What Happens*. Harcourt, Brace. New York.

Diani, Mario and Doug McAdam (eds.). 2003. *Social Movements and Networks*. Oxford University Press. Oxford.

Dinnerstein, Dorothy. 1976. *The Mermaid and the Minotaur*. Harper and Row. New York.

Dye, Thomas R. 2014. *Who's Running America?* 8th edn. Paradigm Publishers. Boulder, CO.

Edelman, Murray. 1964. *The Symbolic Uses of Politics.* University of Illinois. Urbana, IL.

Edelman, Murray. 1988. *Constructing the Political Spectacle.* University of Chicago Press. Chicago, IL.

Edelman, Murray. 1995. *From Art to Politics.* University of Chicago Press. Chicago, IL.

Ellul, Jacques. 1972. *Propaganda.* Knopf. New York.

Erikson, Erik H. 1968. *Identity, Youth and Crisis.* Norton. New York.

Etzioni, Amitai and Jared Bloom (eds.). 2004. *We Are What We Celebrate.* New York University Press. New York.

Evans, Dylan. 2001. *Emotion, the Science of Sentiment.* Oxford University Press. Oxford.

Forgas, Joseph and Michelle Cromer. 2004. On Being Sad and Evasive: Affective Influences on Verbal Communication Strategies in Conflict Situations. 40 *Journal of Experimental Social Psychology* 511–18.

Giugni, Marco, Doug McAdam and Charles Tilly (eds.) 2001. *How Social Movements Matter.* University of Minnesota Press. Minneapolis, MN.

Hobsbawm, Eric and Terence Ranger. 1984 [1983]. *The Invention of Tradition.* Cambridge University Press. Cambridge.

Hughes, Richard T. 2003. *Myths America Lives By.* University of Illinois Press. Urbana.

Keleman, Deborah. 1999. Beliefs about Purpose: On the Origins of Teleological Thought, in Corballis, Michael C. and Stephen E. G. Lea (eds.). *The Descent of Mind.* Oxford University Press. Oxford.

Kertzer, David I. 1988. *Ritual, Politics, and Power.* Yale University Press. New Haven, CT.

Lakoff, George. 1996. *Moral Politics.* University of Chicago Press. Chicago, IL.

McAdam, Doug, Sidney Tarrow, and Charles Tilly. 2001. *Dynamics of Contention.* Cambridge University Press. Cambridge.

McNeill, William H. 1995. *Keeping Together in Time.* Harvard University Press. Cambridge, MA.

Mitchell, Amy, Jeffrey Gottfried, Michael Barthel. and Elisa Shearer. 2016. *The Modern News Consumer.* Pew Research Center. Washington DC.

Moore, Sally Falk and Barbara G. Myerhoff (eds.). 1977. *Secular Ritual.* VanGorcum. Assen.

Nichols, Bill. 1981. *Ideology and the Image.* Indiana University Press. Bloomington.

Norris, Pippa and Ronald Inglehart. 2004. *The Sacred and the Secular.* Cambridge University Press. Cambridge.

Pfaff, Donald W. 2007. *The Neuroscience of Fair Play.* Dana Press. New York.

Rappaport, Roy A. 1999. *Ritual and Religion in the Making of Humanity.* Cambridge University Press. Cambridge.

Saad, Lydia. 2013. TV is America's Main Source of News. www.gallup.com/poll/163412/americans-main-source-news.aspx (accessed August 14, 2016).

Sachs, Jonah. 2012. *Winning the Story Wars.* Harvard Business Review Press. Boston, MA.

Scott, James C. 1990. *Domination and the Arts of Resistance.* Yale University Press. New Haven, CT.

Searles, Harold F. 1960. *The Non-human Environment in Normal Development and Schizophrenia.* International Universities Press. New York.

Searles, Harold F. 1979. *Unconscious Processes in Relation to the Environmental Crisis in Countertransference.* International Universities Press. New York.

Shaiko, Ronald G. 1999. *Voices and Echoes for the Environment.* Columbia University Press. New York.

Solomon, Sheldon, Jeffrey L. Greenberg. and Thomas A. Pyszczynski. 2003. Lethal Consumption: Death Denying Materialism. Pp. 127–46 in Kasser, Tim and Allen D. Kanner (eds.). *Psychology and Consumer Culture.* American Psychological Association. Washington DC.

Tavris, Carol and Elliot Aronson. 2007. *Mistakes Were Made (but not by me).* Harcourt. New York.

Tilly, Charles. 2002. *Stories, Identities and Political Change.* Rowman & Littlefield. Lanham, MD.

Turner, James Morton. 2012. *The Promise of Wilderness.* University of Washington Press. Seattle.

Walzer, Michael. 1965. *Revolution of the Saints.* Harvard University Press. Cambridge, MA.

II   The Special Challenge of Marine Conservation

That the oceans and marine species are in serious decline cannot be seriously disputed (Roberts 2007; Brewer and Peltzer 2009; Halpern et al. 2012; Finley 2017).

The evidence is also strong that strictly protected (no-take) areas in the right location, of sufficient size, that incorporate considerations of ocean dynamism, and with good enforcement are very effective at protecting and recovering a wide range of marine species and processes (Lester and Halpern 2008; Lester et al. 2009; Devillers et al. 2014; Edgar et al. 2014).

One proposal, advanced by the Marine Conservation Institute (MCI) and partners, calls for *at least* 30 percent (the right 30 percent) of the oceans to be strictly protected. Others have suggested that at least 40 percent of all biogeographical regions need protection to

FIGURE 11.1 Fishing's hidden history lesson.
Bizarro © Dan Piraro 2009. Distributed by King Features Syndicate, Inc. Image used with permission.

ensure biological recovery (Roberts et al. 2006). Something like the Institute's Global Ocean Refuge System (GLORES) won't address every problem, but it will address many, and is an essential and primary element in healing the world ocean and its life.

Achieving at least 30 percent protection will run up against powerful interests: industrialized fishing, some sport and subsistence fishing, mining, oil and gas extraction, and increased militarization. Given unequal political resources, a strictly insider strategy such as lobbying and connections with the powerful is unlikely to be enough in itself. Conservationists can't match opponents' resources most of the time. And a mechanism for designating MPAs on the high seas, other than treaty by treaty, does not yet exist, though negotiations are underway via the Law of the Sea Treaty. Outsider approaches which can change what's possible, coordinated with insider approaches relying on typical carrots and sticks, are required: mass mobilization to create new political power in addition to ratcheting up mobilization of existing constituencies is critical in overcoming entrenched interests (Johns 2009; Kraft 2011). In that sense, marine conservation will not be much different than terrestrial conservation. But there are some obstacles unique to mass mobilization around marine conservation, and activists must find a path to overcome them.

Two major obstacles to generating enough caring to spark action exist. The first is the:

> Invisibility of the oceans, ocean life, and the injury humans do to them. Bottom trawling, for example, unlike a terrestrial clear cut, lies beneath the ocean's reflective surface. Missing fish are likewise invisible. In many of the dominant cultures the sea is an undifferentiated mass; there are no "places" except along coastlines.

The second:

> Many cultures have strong and longstanding beliefs that the oceans are not only ancient, but indestructible, self-renewing and beyond

harm. As Euripides put it – the sea can wash away all evils – all that is dirty, dangerous or contaminating, both symbolically and materially. (Patton 2007; Mack 2011)

How, then, do conservationists make the oceans visible and evoke the strong emotional connection necessary for groups to act on their behalf rather than allow their societies to harm them? How is ocean protection and recovery to be made urgent and personal to critical, influential audiences? It is not simply a matter of awareness, as Lotze et al. (2017) suggest. It is positive that people know the ocean is threatened by human activities and that protection in the face of these threats is a good thing. But this awareness shows no signs of generating the sort of collective political action that moves decision makers, especially in the face of significant opposition.

The cliché that facts don't persuade but stories do is a cliché for a reason. It's true. Most people understand and navigate the world through story (see Chapters 10 and 14). Stories are pleasurable. Most readers would rather be watching a good movie than reading this or an even more sleep-inducing journal article. Stories not only convey information about how the world works, giving it structure and thereby making reality manageable. They also convey what is good and bad, right and wrong. The stories we call myths are bearers of individual and group meaning and purpose. They answer the *why* questions (Campbell 1959; Nichols 1981; Fulford 1999; Rappaport 1999; Gottschall 2012).

A primary task for marine conservationists is to displace the stories that portray the ocean as invisible and indestructible. To achieve this depends not just on different stories but more *compelling* stories. Along with the rest of conservation a new overarching myth is needed to replace those of domination, ownership, separation, and exploitation. The same myth can work for all groups, but some aspects must be tailored to specific audiences' needs, emotional predispositions, and cognitive understandings (Johns 2003). As always, those groups who can make a difference should be prioritized for mobilization. The organizations into which people are mobilized – and organization is what sustains mobilization – must also address each of these with their ideologies.

Unlike the terrestrial realm – where we live – the marine realm does not offer *most* audiences the opportunity for intimate connection, though certainly people living on coasts appreciate those places. Live marine webcams can make places more routinely accessible (e.g. Levine and Mijung 2014). But the oceans' places, beneath the reflective surface and often masked by murky water (humans are visual, while sound is more important in the sea), generally do not or cannot evoke strong emotion via identification and empathy. However charismatic marine species can achieve this.

Campaigns to protect and recover charismatic species offer some important lessons for protecting biodiversity generally and for protecting places that are their homes – and the homes of many other species. It's kind of like selling a house by furnishing it with puppies. Unless the buyer is a cat person and then the seller must scramble to redecorate. Research on protecting places by protecting certain species is far from comprehensive, so the focus is on cases.

Cetacean conservation has been relatively successful and has relied heavily on stories emphasizing these "attractive" species' attributes of sociality and family relationships, the uniqueness of individuals (Flipper, Willy), playfulness, and pre-existing human feelings of empathy and justice, built over decades of popular familiarity disseminated via television and other media (e.g. Layzer 2011).

It helps that whales and dolphins are generally not seen as threats and their economic value as food or for other consumptive uses is no longer great or widespread. The result is that when they are seen to suffer at human hands it is possible to tap into widespread outrage. Sam LaBudde's undercover film of dolphins being abused, drowned in nets, and crushed alive in fishing tackle was enough to make the big three tuna marketers agree to sell only dolphin-safe tuna to avoid becoming the objects of that outrage (Layzer 2011; Robbins et al. 2013). MPAs have been established for cetaceans which benefit other species; though yellowfin tuna would probably not be impressed.

Regional and local campaigns to protect and recover "cute, cuddly" sea otters resulted in place-based protection along the North American Pacific coast and other places along the Pacific Rim, in part because of the regulatory role otters play in ecosystems. The Convention on International Trade in Endangered Species (CITES) and the US Endangered Species Act (ESA) are also important levers for protection in this case. Sea otters also reveal the limits of some MPAs: they are susceptible to larger disturbances in trophic cascades and to pollution from which MPAs offer little protection.

Sea turtles are not cuddly but they are charismatic enough to generate campaigns on their behalf lasting decades and overcoming major counter-mobilization. Stories focus on their venerable ancient-ness, their longevity, and their marathon migrations. They appear stoic and determined, and harmless to humans.

Turtle deaths resulting from shrimp fishery bycatch proved the easy part of the problem: use of turtle excluder devices was directly required by law and required before shrimp could be imported into the US. Campaigns against coastal development including light pollution, egg poaching and consumption, high seas bycatch, and dredging are much more difficult and complex matters – they are multi-jurisdictional and come up against modern societies' addiction to endless growth (Spotila 2011; Layzer 2011). Nonetheless MPAs have proven important for turtle protection (Science Daily 2012) as have other place-based and regulatory protections. Ongoing vigilance is required to sustain these, and more comprehensive protections are needed.

Some fish species have inspired campaigns for both place-based protection and a variety of gear and catch regulations and benefit from both. But the strength of the fishing industry, though not monolithic, has generally resulted in weak measures falling far short of recovery and science-based recommendations for achieving recovery (e.g. Roberts 2007; Finley 2017). The industry is well connected politically in much of the world. Many states see fishing not only as a source of protein and fertilizer, but as a means of staking claims to parts of the high seas and as a jobs program, though it is not cheap in this last regard (Finley 2017). Subsidies run to about US$25 billion and fleet capacity is about 2.5 times what a sustainable catch would be. Conservationists have not been strong enough to bring adequate countervailing pressure for stronger regulation, place-based protection or consistent and strong enforcement.

Salmon, however, have become an icon in parts of the world, motivating mass support for restoration and conservation and even removal of smaller dams and extensive stream restoration. The salmon's long journey is a story which resonates with people and there is a certain romanticism associated with Native American–salmon relationships. Native American groups are often in a position to shame others and force action via treaty rights. That salmon interests overlap with water quality is helpful. Litigation or the threat of litigation under the US Clean Water Act and ESA are important levers in the US. Thus far, however, the salmon's story has not translated into adequate stream buffers in many places, nor removal of bigger dams, nor adequate regulation of farmed salmon (Lichatowich 1999; Augerot 2005). Indeed, salmon have become another example of humans trying to balance the books on the backs of other species, in this case California sea lions and double-crested cormorants. In the latter case, thousands are slaughtered because they have the audacity to eat salmon, though they are not the cause of salmon being endangered. Humans are the problem, but to take action against them is politically more difficult.

Sharks present an interesting case. They are feared – unreasonably so, statistics suggest – and in contrast to Flipper, much popular media has demonized them. They are sometimes seen as competitors by fishermen. And in many cultures they are food, and shark fins considered a delicacy, leading to mass killing for that purpose only. Evidence suggests that MPAs benefit sharks, especially as nurseries, but because sharks are so geographically wide-ranging much of the focus has been on regulation preventing the taking of fins, bycatch, and deliberate overfishing. Significant NGO pressure has led to US legislation (Shark Conservation Act of 2010) and increased protection of several shark species by CITES in 2013. The main markets for shark fin soup are in Asia, and campaigns by WildAid and others have resulted in significant declines in consumption in China as well as statements by several Asian governments that they will no longer serve shark fin soup at official functions (WildAid 2016). Declines in shark finning are no doubt real, but may be closer to 25 percent than 50 percent (Eriksson and Clarke 2015). Shark fin soup, the consumption of which took off with the rise of a large Chinese middle class in recent decades, may partly be declining due to slower economic growth, not just successful conservation campaigns. Public service announcements on Chinese television featuring celebrities have been effective along with making agreements with hotel and restaurant chains. Prior to the launch of the campaign many did not know actual shark parts were used in the soup or thought that fins grew back. However, restaurants in Hong Kong and other institutional consumers show little sign of limiting their shark offerings, sparking protests (Lee 2016). Cathay Pacific Airlines succumbed to protests and banned all shipments of shark fins, abandoning a "sustainable shark fin only" policy. They join twenty or so other airlines. Of the estimated 100 million sharks killed each year, most are not killed for their fins but their meat and as bycatch.

Whether conservationists' goals are protection of all marine species and communities via MPAs, or a narrower suite of species via catch or gear regulation, putting a face and sometimes a name on marine lives as characters in a dramatic story can help build and sustain much-needed political action. It can bring people into organizations where their time, skills, and other support translates into effective political pressure.

The real challenge for successful marine biodiversity protection, as in other areas of conservation, is not to manage nature or non-human species but for humans to manage themselves. The shift to effectively managing humans and their technologies is still a ways off. At a recent marine biodiversity conference, fish were rarely mentioned. Instead the much more frequently used word was "fisheries," with its implication that fish are primarily food and belong to humans for that purpose.

As with terrestrial conservation, politics is not just about winning hearts and minds, it's about sustained organized action. Action on behalf of the oceans, however, is about places and life that many people may never see in person. Many live in places where the great oceans can never be heard nor will the wind carry the deeply evocative smell of salt water. But through stories of animals that humans can empathize with, support for marine conservation can be mobilized.

REFERENCES

Augerot, Xanthippe. 2005. *Pacific Atlas of Salmon*. University of California Press. Berkeley.

Brewer, Peter G. and Edward T. Peltzer. 2009. Limits to Marine Life. 324 *Science* 347–8 (April 17).

Campbell, Joseph. 1959. *The Masks of God. Volume 1: Primitive Mythology*. Viking. New York.

Devillers, Rodolphe, Robert L. Pressey, Alana Grech, et al. 2014. Reinventing Residual Reserves in the Sea: Are We Favouring Ease of Establishment over Need for Protection? 25 *Aquatic Conservation: Marine and Freshwater Ecosystems* 4: 480–503 (August).

Edgar, G. J., R. D. Stuart-Smith, T. J. Willis, et al. 2014. Global Conservation Outcomes Depend on Marine Protected Areas with Five Key Features. 506 *Nature* 216–20. doi: 10.1038/nature13022.

Eriksson, Hampus and Shelley Clarke. 2015. Chinese Market Responses to Overexploitation of Sharks and Sea Cucumbers. 184 *Biological Conservation* 163–73 (April).

Finley, Carmel. 2017. *All the Boats on the Ocean*. University of Chicago Press. Chicago, IL.

Fulford, Robert. 1999. *The Triumph of Narrative*. Anansi Press. Toronto.

Gottschall, Jonathan. 2012. *The Story Telling Animal*. Houghton Mifflin Harcourt. Boston, MA.

Halpern, Benjamin S., Catherine Longo, Darren Hardy, et al. 2012. An Index to Assess the Health and Benefits of the Global Ocean. 488 *Nature* 615–20 (August 30).

Johns, David. 2003. The Real Challenge: Managing Ourselves Instead of Nature. In Alan Watson, and Janet Sproull (comps.). *Seventh World Wilderness Congress Symposium: Science and Stewardship to Protect and Sustain Wilderness Values, November 2–8, 2001, Port Elizabeth, South Africa*. Proc. RMRSP-00. US Department of Agriculture, Forest Service, Rocky Mountain Research Station. Ogden, UT.

Johns, David. 2009. *A New Conservation Politics*. Wiley. Oxford.

Kraft, Michael E. 2011. *Environmental Policy and Politics*. 5th edn. Pearson Longman. New York.

Layzer, Judith. 2011. *The Environmental Case*. 3rd edn. CQ Press. Washington DC.

Lee, Danny. 2016. Food for Thought: Hong Kong Shark Fin Protesters Take Campaign Directly to Diners. South China *Morning Post*. February 5, 2016. www.scmp.com/news/hong-kong/education-community/article/1909879/food-thought-hong-kong-shark-fin-protesters-take (September 12, 2016).

Lester, S. E. and B. S. Halpern. 2008. Biological Responses in Marine No-take Reserves versus Partially Protected Areas. *Marine Ecology Progress Series* 367: 49–56.

Lester, S. E., B. S. Halpern, K. Grorud-Colvert, et al. 2009. Biological Effect within No-Take Marine Reserves: A Global Synthesis. *Marine Ecology Progress Series* 384: 33–46.

Levine, Mike and K. Mijung. 2014. *Marine Connections through Web Streaming Interfaces*. Presentation at 3rd International Marine Conservation Congress, Glasgow, August 17.

Lichatowich, Jim. 1999. *Salmon without Rivers*. Island Press. Washington DC.

Lotze, Heike, Haley Guest, Jennifer O'Leary, Arthur Tuda, and Douglas Wallace. 2017. Public Perceptions of Marine Threats and Protection from around the World. *Ocean and Coastal Management*. https://doi.org/10.1016/j.ocecoaman.2017.11.004 (accessed January 12, 2018).

Mack, John. 2011. *The Sea*. Reaktion. London.

Nichols, Bill. 1981. *Ideology and the Image*. University of Indiana Press. Bloomington, IN.

Patton, Kimberly C. 2007. *The Sea Can Wash Away All Evils*. Columbia University Press. New York.

Rappaport. Roy A. 1999. *Ritual and Religion in the Making of Humanity*. Cambridge University Press. Cambridge.

Robbins, Paul, John Hintz, and Sarah A. Moore. 2013. *Environment and Society: A Critical Introduction.* 2nd edn. Wiley. Oxford UK.

Roberts, Callum. 2007. *The Unnatural History of the Sea.* Island Press. Washington DC.

Roberts, Callum, L. Mason, and J. P. Hawkins. 2006. *Roadmap to Recovery: A Global Network of Marine Reserves.* Greenpeace International. Amsterdam.

Science Daily. 2012. Marine Protected Areas are Keeping Turtles Safe. www.sciencedaily.com/releases/2012/03/120319095043.htm (accessed August 8, 2014).

Spotila, James R. 2011. *Saving Sea Turtles.* Johns Hopkins University Press. Baltimore, MD.

WildAid. 2016. wildaid.org/sharks (accessed September 13, 2016).

12 The Biological Sciences and Conservation

Albert Einstein was asked one day by a friend "Do you believe that absolutely everything can be expressed scientifically?" "Yes, it would be possible," he replied, "but it would make no sense. It would be description without meaning – as if you described a Beethoven symphony as a variation in wave pressure."

Clark 1971: 192

Continental or ocean-scale reserve systems offer one of the best bases for slowing and then reversing the loss of biodiversity and wild places. Wide-ranging species and large-scale processes require large reserves that are connected to each other; evolution has long operated at this level, among others (Soule and Terborgh 1999). Establishing reserve systems requires sound science to determine where reserves should be, how big, and how they should be managed and connected (Noss 1992, 1994; Soulé and Terborgh 1999; Roberts 2007; Roberts et al. 2017). Likewise, without effective advocacy and uncompromising values, there can be no reserve systems. The Wildlands Network

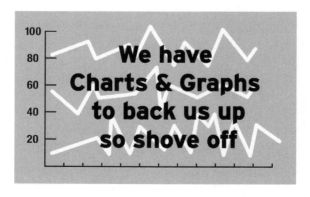

FIGURE 12.1 "We have charts & graphs to back us up so shove off."

and its partners in North America and other NGOs around the world, and the Marine Conservation Institute, have melded science and advocacy in the service of conservation and have made a difference. In the early 1990s large-scale conservation and even connectivity were controversial, though for different reasons. Most NGOs, especially larger ones, fled from large-scale conservation like urban crowds from Godzilla. By the time of *Continental Conservation*'s publication (Soulé and Terborgh 1999) it was difficult to deny where the science was pointing. Scientists around the globe were influenced by the North American work but also coming to the same conclusions independently and critics were looking foolish.

If the marriage of science and advocacy is necessary it is not without tensions. Scientists and advocates have differences in methods of work, different understandings of the origins and place of values in conservation, and differing expectations about the efficacy of biological information in achieving conservation. Despite these differences, successful relationships can be forged where the differences are acknowledged and directly addressed in conservation planning and implementation.

That the natural world is more complex and sublime than a symphony, even one of Beethoven's, suggests that while science is central to conservation, it also has limitations. These limitations are understood differently by scientists and advocates, often confounding cooperation between the two even when they recognize science's centrality. This chapter examines the experience of some NGOs, most in English-speaking countries and focused on terrestrial conservation, that have looked to natural science to guide their work. (The term "science" throughout this chapter means the biological sciences, especially conservation biology. This is the default view of most in conservation; other sciences – political science, sociology, psychology, etc. – play an important role but are usually not referred to as "science.")

By the early 1990s both advocates and scientists had come to realize that existing protected areas – given the historic criteria for their selection and their increasing islandization – were proving inadequate to stem the loss of biodiversity in the face of burgeoning human numbers and consumption (Foreman et al. 1992). One response to this situation was the creation of the Wildlands Network (at that time The Wildlands Project) in 1991 by prominent conservation biologists such as Michael Soulé and Reed Noss and activists such as Dave Foreman, Doug Tompkins, and others. The Wildlands Network set out to design and designate a continental system of connected protected areas (PAs) reaching across North America from Alaska and Greenland to Panama that would achieve the following conservation goals: (1) protect and recover all native species in natural patterns of abundance, including top predators and wide-ranging species, (2) protect all ecosystem types and ecological processes in a healthy state, (3) ensure the unencumbered operation of natural processes including disturbance regimes such as fire, and (4) ensure resilience in the face of anthropogenic change, such as climate change, pollution or edge effects (Noss 1992).

For a PA system to achieve these goals it must be guided by the best science. Just as conservation biology, ecology and island biogeography help to identify the causes for the decline of species populations and the unraveling of ecosystems, so they contribute significantly to crafting solutions. The biological sciences, in the view of the Wildlands Network, could answer questions such as: What areas need to be protected? How much needs to be protected? How should protected areas be connected to maintain genetic flows, seasonal migration, dispersal, repatriation of locally extirpated species, and range shifts? What management regimes should govern protected areas and connections?

The Marine Conservation Institute, partly inspired by the Wildlands Network, was founded in 1996, to take the same big picture and science-based approaches to the oceans. The Institute initially sought to bring scientists together because they recognized the oceans were in much greater peril than thought by policy makers and documenting this state of affairs was a first step. But closely in tandem with that was translating scientific findings into policy prescriptions. Not surprisingly, large, strictly protected areas were a high priority: reserves

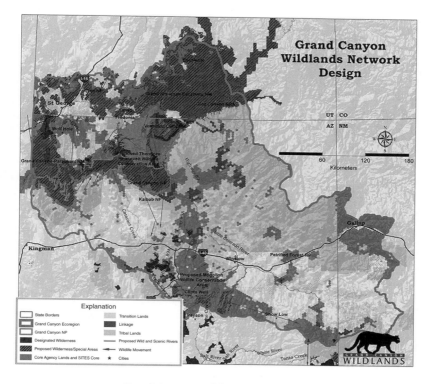

FIGURE 12.2 Grand Canyon Wildlands Network Design. Map shows
Wildlands Network design for the Grand Canyon ecoregion. This is an
example of a detailed, science-based regional plan that provides a
common vision for groups working in an area. Plans seek to ensure in
perpetuity healthy populations of all native species – including carnivores
and wide-ranging species, functional ecosystems of all types, and natural
disturbance regimes – while supporting resilience in the face of climate
and other change.

such as Papahānaumokuākea Marine National Monument (Hawaiian
Islands). So was banning bottom trawling, especially on seamounts,
and destructive fishing gear.

This marriage of science and advocacy has been and continues to
be successful in most respects. Several large-scale Wildlands Network
Designs have been completed and recently an Eastern North American

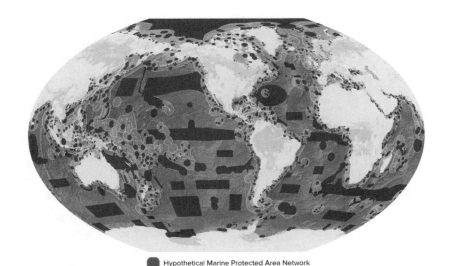

Hypothetical Marine Protected Area Network

FIGURE 12.3 Draft vision for protecting marine diversity. Estimates vary, but strictly protecting at least 30 percent of the ocean should ensure marine biodiversity can thrive, though human-caused threats remain a serious problem. Conservationists rely on scientific findings and expert judgment to determine which 30 percent of the ocean needs such protection. Threats from outside protected areas, including terrestrial pollution and injury, must also be addressed.
© 2018 Marine Conservation Institute.

reserve system has been proposed (Wildlands Network 2017). The Global Ocean Refuge System aims to protect at least 30 percent of the global ocean by 2030 and looks in part to the Ecologically and Biologically Significant Marine Area work vetted by the Convention on Biological Diversity (Marine Conservation Institute 2017; Convention on Biological Diversity/EBSA 2017). The Marine Conservation Institute also houses the MPAtlas (www.marine-conservation.org/MPAtlas), which is a globally respected authority on the status of existing MPAs.

All marriages have problems, however, and simple-in-concept doesn't mean simple-in-practice. Scientists and advocates come to this relationship with differing expectations, backgrounds, training, and experience, even if they share a love of the natural world and a desire to protect it (Foreman et al. 1992; Society for Conservation Biology 1999).

We will explore the nature and sources of friction between scientists and advocates and what can be done to address them. The findings are mostly based on the experience of the author with North American projects, but also projects in Europe, Africa, Latin America, the Russian Far East, and the oceans. Although anecdotes from around the world confirm basic similarities, the roles scientists and advocates play vary among countries, e.g. Mexico (Riding 1985). The basic finding: *If the tensions between scientists and advocates are ignored, conservation progress can be confusing and slow. If the differences and tension are addressed directly it is much easier to achieve clarity of vision and purpose, and conservation work is thereby more effective and timely.* Given the human onslaught against the natural world, time is critical.

METHODS OF WORK

Scientists and advocates have different methods of work. Mission-oriented sciences like conservation biology are not essentially different from "pure" science: they aim to adhere to generally accepted standards of investigation and analysis (Schrader-Frechette 1996). Biologists, like other scientists, generally aim to avoid false positives, or type-I errors, such as finding that wolves prefer to snack on Little Red Riding Hood and her granny more than deer. Avoidance of finding an effect when there isn't one is considered a conservative approach – best serving the development of a reliable body of knowledge. But for advocates, and increasingly for many conservation biologists, being conservative means something else. Because species loss is irreversible, extinction rates are accelerating, populations of many species have massively declined (WWF 2016), and because much ecosystem damage is not easy to heal, it is better to assume there is an effect and place the burden on developers, road builders, and others who seek to alter the world to prove their actions will have no adverse biological effect. This precautionary approach provides safety for species and ecosystems.

Such errors aside, it's almost too obvious to say that knowledge is always incomplete. There are frequently opportunities (or situations in which it is necessary) to act before additional information can be obtained. Inaction resulting in losses is not an option for those serious about their responsibility to biodiversity. In such cases biological work continues, so conservationists can identify shortcomings and adjust course in the future as necessary.

Other important differences between activists and biologists are expressed in their statements made about each other. Advocates grumble about scientists' chronic skepticism, and sometimes see their pointed questions as hostile or an example of how they poke at each other for a living. Some advocates are wary of science generally, with its history of dualism (assumption of a wide chasm between human and non-human life), reductionism (ignoring the complexity of a whole and explaining how something works with reference to its parts in isolation), or mechanism (treating living things as machines); and its ties to business and government institutions that have destroyed or degraded much of the natural world. Many agree with David Ehrenfeld's (1978) critique of the Enlightenment assumption that human reason can adequately understand the world well enough to successfully manage it. That technology which allows humans to kill and consume infinitely more fish will provide humans with plenty of protein without damage to marine life, that the Green Revolution will solve the problem of hunger, or that modern agriculture is compatible with maintaining soil fertility, are good examples. Science as an institution (and scientists) does carry baggage that has historically been antithetical to conservation (Berman 1983; Merchant 1983). It is well to remember that conservation is fundamentally about values, not just understanding how the world works. Advocates, much more than scientists, are willing to act, and used to acting, with partial information – for advocates it is the political process not the scientific process that sets the timetable. Much scientific work seems needlessly complex or time-consuming to advocates. And at times it is intimidating.

Biologists and ecologists also have their complaints. Aside from a (healthy) dislike for politics in general, many fear that their work will not be understood in its complexity and nuance or used properly. They fear a different sort of reductionism as their findings are transformed into "soundbites" for audiences, though they very much want the results of their work to have a positive impact on policy. Biologists have complained of being treated as "hired guns" by advocates, rather than as full partners in conservation. They also fear that by being associated with advocates their scientific credibility will be hurt with peers, funders, employers, and other institutions.

Some sources of tension between scientists and advocates result from larger social forces such as extraction interests which in turn fund, for example, universities (Oregon State University School of Forestry, which receives funds from the timber industry, colluded with industry to block an article [Donato et al. 2006] on forest regeneration unfavorable to the industry [Demsky 2006]). Funders or tenure committees may punish scientists for activism, the press *does* demand soundbites and hides behind balance rather than ferreting out reality, and decision makers operate on their own schedule and respond to who has the carrots and sticks – the truth is secondary, if that. Conservation must deal with these factors.

The relationship between scientists and advocates is under their control, though it requires a deliberate effort to resolve or manage tensions. If the tensions are not addressed they quietly sap energy from the main task of safeguarding and recovering biodiversity. Trust is built over time. Issues seemingly resolved often resurface and need to be addressed again – because of new participants or because of the difficulty in overcoming long-held beliefs or habits.

The framework for managing and resolving tensions rests upon the shared goals of the work: safeguarding and recovering biodiversity and ecological integrity. The distractions of infighting are too costly to tolerate. Though mutual criticism is uncomfortable, it can help identify weaknesses in strategy to move conservation toward it goals.

VALUES

For conservation scientists and most other conservationists biodiversity, evolution, and ecological processes are good. Public and private policy should reflect and value this goodness. Einstein did not hesitate to acknowledge that science is driven by the notion that knowledge is good – a judgment or value he regarded as outside the ability of science to falsify (i.e. to test) (Barry and Oelschaeger 1996). Since both science and conservation are driven (proximately, if not ultimately) by values, some advocates look to science to generate or provide justification for the values underlying conservation – to tell them not only what lands or waters are needed to ensure, e.g., the survival of grizzlies, but that grizzlies are good.

Science does not generate values, although the knowledge it generates may influence values. Certainly many discoveries in cosmology (Galileo) and evolutionary biology (Darwin) have had an enormous influence on how humans think and feel about the world they inhabit, including what they consider important and valuable. Knowing we share more than 98 percent of our DNA with chimps may influence our values, but such knowledge does not directly require us to love chimps as family. (The author is 6 percent Neanderthal and Denisovan and is thankful to be able to claim some distance from ecocidal *H. sapiens sapiens*.) Values are products of the human heart and mind and the many social, cultural, and biological forces that shape them. People may share an understanding of how the world works but have different goals because their interests, predisposition, and capacity for empathy and compassion differ. Increasingly, because some values are difficult to defend (profits before biological health), there are those such as some energy companies that challenge the scientific consensus on the reality of climate, much as tobacco companies denied the relationship between smoking and cancer.

That science does not generate values doesn't mean science stands apart from values. Scientists have values and predispositions and these are part of what draws them to a life in science in the first place. Values shape the questions scientists ask. Values also shape research and the direction of science, including the values and *interests* of those who pay for it (mostly government and business), faculty tenure and promotion committees, peers who review the work of a particular scientist, and other elements of society such as the media. The multitude of individuals, networks, universities, research labs, journals, and other entities which are involved in science will often espouse values that are in conflict with each other.

It is unavoidable and appropriate that values influence the questions being asked. It is also appropriate that these values be made explicit and be discussed (Conservation Biology 1996). Too often this is not the case, but some conservation biologists have been addressing these issues for some time (Conservation Biology 1997, 1998; Wuerthner et al. 2014). As a mission-oriented science, conservation biology has been compared to medicine. Both have an explicit mission which they consider an overarching good: in the case of medicine, to heal or prevent disease and injury to humans, and in the case of conservation biology to safeguard and restore biodiversity and ecological systems and processes (Soulé 1986; Ehrenfeld 1989; Primack and Sher 2016; Society for Conservation Biology 2016). While both disciplines debate values – and the role of their practitioners as advocates in the political process – they are explicit about being mission oriented, value driven, and acknowledge that these values are not the product of science per se. The values underlying medicine are ubiquitous – so widely shared in most cultures, human health is invisible. The health of nature is not so widely shared, and this is very visible and seen by many to be at odds with human material interests.

Whether a particular discipline is mission oriented or not, science generally aims to minimize how motivating values and other factors might bias results. Values rightly shape the questions. But they must not compromise the answers to the questions posed. So the design of research, the process of investigation and testing hypotheses, the analysis of results, and conclusions are subject to various forms of review or testing. These include peer review, replication, or the ability of findings to predict future outcomes in the world. It is this aspect of science that must be assessed for bias.

The distinction between motivating values and scientific method is not the end of the matter. Some scientists believe that to exert influence or to maintain credibility, scientists need and should do no more than state the case for their findings. Concerns about credibility are not easily resolved in the general or the abstract, but case by case. It is clear that some scientists, especially those with public stature, can authoritatively speak out about what moves them as well as about their findings, without compromising their credibility, e.g. Ed Wilson, Sylvia Earle, John Terborgh, Reed Noss, or Michael Soulé. There is also strong evidence that facts are not persuasive with decision makers or other audiences, whereas values are, especially when embedded in effective stories and backed by those who wield carrots and sticks (Sachs 2012).

The task of persuasion is something scientists are rarely trained for or comfortable with, though some prove to be excellent by virtue of their personality and storytelling abilities – and with practice. Persuasion and other aspects of advocacy will continue to fall mostly on activists who also lack formal training but are more likely to have learned from experience and necessity. The challenges are formidable:

- unlike the value of human health, which is ubiquitous, conservation of biodiversity remains a matter of contention. The natural world is largely seen (or treated by institutions) as a resource for humans, not as having independent value.
- policy-making is largely framed as choices among values. The material interests of human groups are often framed in terms of values and euphemisms. Making a buck by destroying a forest sounds much grubbier than the freedom of people to "harvest renewable resources." Most of the serious questions are not on the policy agenda: population, unending consumption, and so on.
- shaping the agenda and even participating in the debates is expensive and conservation cannot match the money industry invests in sponsored think tanks or in propagating the findings of think tanks. This has always meant conservationists have had to be smarter: tell better stories, obtain free media (news, narrative film, museum exhibits), and rely on those with stature such as high profile scientists and others.

Human culture at its heart is about the tension between what is and what ought to be. Culture, most of the time in most places, is the main arena of politics and for elites its manipulation is a much less costly way of containing disputes than repression. So it is not surprising that periodically there are industry-funded attacks on the values that support effective conservation. The Sage Brush Rebellion – the protest by extractive industries in the US against threats to cut off their subsidies – in the 1970s, 1980s, and with variations into the 1990s, and starting again in the late 2000s and into the teens, marked efforts to make conservation even more subservient to growth and corporate interests (for a summary and critique of this literature see Wuerthner et al. 2014; Burks 1994). Conservation scientists and others actively responded to these attacks without loss of credibility. Their role was indispensable in setting the biological record straight and defending strong conservation values.

Attacks on conservation values are frequently accompanied by broader disinformation campaigns. The backlash against conservation, especially from those who profit from the destruction of the natural world and their sycophants, goes beyond attacks on conservation values, described just above; it seeks in addition to advance a view of the world which is concocted rather than based on research. Paul and Anne Ehrlich (1997), in *The Betrayal of Science and Reason*, have termed this a "brownlash." "[T]he brownlash has produced what amounts to a body of anti-science – a twisting of the findings of empirical science – to bolster a predetermined worldview and to support a political agenda."

In the US and some other countries, this has been carried to new levels. It's not simply the oil companies replaying the tobacco company script of denial of the harm being done and then sowing confusion and doubt (Otto 2016). Some politicians, business people and popular media have abandoned any sense that there is a reality that might constrain what they want: they simply declare reality to be thus and so as it suits them, like the Queen of Hearts in *Alice in Wonderland*.

Fortunately there are still those with regard for the truth. In collusion with the timber industry the dean of Oregon State University's School of Forestry sought to suppress publication of an article in *Science* magazine suggesting natural regeneration worked better than industrial techniques (Demsky 2006; Donato et al. 2006; Stokstad 2006). *Science* went ahead with publication. These campaigns against scientifically established understandings of how the world works tap into a deep mistrust of intellectuals and science among some segments of the US population (Hofstadter 1963, 1965).

"Alternative realities" does not leave us in some relativistic swamp, however (Soulé and Lease 1994). There is a real distinction between good science and the "anti-science" of the brownlash. Good science is peer reviewed, makes clear its methodology and the data supporting its conclusions, relies on generally accepted methodologies, does not use data selectively to support a conclusion, does not rely on fabricated "data", and is generally acknowledged to be good science even by those in the scientific community who may disagree with its conclusions. It seeks to prevent bias from influencing findings (Ehrlich and Ehrlich 1997).

Personal attacks are also typical of purveyors of "anti-science" (Flattau 1998) because the attackers' substantive case is poor. Examples of anti-science include claims that biodiversity is not threatened, extractive industries are benign, risks from toxic substances are grossly exaggerated, ozone depletion is a hoax (Ehrlich and Ehrlich 1997), cigarettes are harmless (Brandt 2007), nuclear war is survivable (Otto 2016); Ray's (1993) defense of nuclear industry practices; marketing economist Julian Simon's attempt to explain a dolphin die-off on the Atlantic coast without regard to marine biology (Flattau 1998); and efforts by non-climatologists to dispute the findings of climatologists on global warming (Otto 2016). In the last case the (US) National Academy of Sciences took the unusual step of formally and publicly disassociating itself from an unpublished article made to look like a reprint from the Academy's journal, claiming that greenhouse gases were a "wonderful and unexpected gift from the Industrial Revolution" (Stevens 1998).

The goal of anti-science campaigns is to grow constituencies that will politically oppose regulation of industry by scapegoating those who generate findings on which the laws are based. They are the ones imposing unnecessary costs on society, dragging down the economy and destroying jobs. Anti-science campaigns are largely undertaken in the popular media, sometimes based on "studies" and publications of industry-funded think tanks. To their credit many scientists have taken on these challenges in the popular media rather than just in scientific journals read by very few: Paul and Anne Ehrlich, Thomas Lovejoy, Norman Myers, Reed Noss, Peter Raven, Carl Safina, Michael Soulé, and E. O. Wilson among others. These scientists and many others have argued persuasively that scientists must speak out publicly about the crisis of biodiversity, and what must be done to avert it (Lovejoy 1989; Noss 1993, 1994; Wilson 2016). Scientists enjoy significant prestige with both media and many segments of the population, but it means little if it is not used.

No amount of knowledge is a substitute for biophilic feelings and values. Communicating with important constituencies about values is essential in making the case for conservation. But it is not enough. If the public lacks a good general understanding of how science works or what its findings are, then lies and half-truths can flourish.

To reach the widest audiences, scientific findings need to be incorporated into the stories we all live by. We are storytelling animals and most of us understand the world best through metaphor, the currency of art more than science. Many scientists who write for a larger audience, such as Stephen Jay Gould (1974–2001) in *Natural History*, Lewis Thomas (1974) and E. O. Wilson (2006, 2012, 2014), spin a good story and deserve emulation. Science has a major role to play in combating disinformation. The role of scientists in directly influencing decision makers is a limited one, however, and we now turn to that.

BIOLOGY AND ADVOCACY

Biologists have been disappointed that "speaking truth to power" doesn't have much impact on policy, but many still cling to it and want to go no further. Some funders also subscribe to this view. Advocates have been disappointed that biological findings haven't improved their success rate with most elected or appointed decision makers. If science can't help improve policy, just what is its value in conservation? Many senior scientists recognize the important role of science in politics and policy (Society for Conservation Biology Annual Business Meeting 1995), such as former UN Under Secretary-General Peter Piot (2012), quoted at the beginning of this book.

Much depends on how scientists engage with politics. In the previous two sections of this chapter I've suggested a primary role for scientists: informing conservationist advocates of what needs to be done to safeguard biodiversity. Advocates in turn have to translate science and values into policy prescriptions and also create the political clout to make policy reality. Scientists have a direct role in this as well, but unless linked to those who can bring substantial rewards and punishments mere facts get little attention. One exception may be in the legal and administrative processes in countries where the facts are taken seriously (e.g. Strauss et al. 2011).

Science Informing Activism

Science can help tell us what we need to do to save the things conservation values: species, communities, ecosystems, disturbance regimes. Conservationists must be clear on the overarching goals and be prepared to effectively advocate for the actions scientists say are necessary to achieve more specific goals: how much of the ocean must be set aside and where, for example. It's up to activists, campaigners, and social scientists with experience to figure how to mobilize the political resources needed and apply them strategically to achieve the goals. One of the most challenging aspects of this fight is to blunt and dismantle the causes of biological and ecological degradation. Existing institutions will ultimately need to be replaced with ones compatible with a living, healthy Earth. Overcoming the psychology and culture of hierarchy of necessity goes hand in hand with institutional change (Searles 1960; Shepard 1973, 1982).

Most conservationists – activists and scientists alike – do not believe that the machinery destroying the natural world can be constrained anytime soon. There are now 7.5-plus billion humans and they are asking the Earth to support another 83 million people a year. The causes of biological decline – factories, mines, dams, freeways, fishing fleets, subdivisions, shopping malls, and agriculture – are clear and must be addressed. But if other species and ecosystems are to survive, interim action will require vast areas of the Earth to be set aside now, off limits to industrial and agricultural activity, where whole systems can continue or come out of hiding.

The biological sciences help answer where to set aside and how much: What places will best ensure functioning ecosystems and healthy populations of all native species into perpetuity? What places will allow the recovery of top predators and allow disturbance regimes and succession to operate unencumbered? Where and how do we recover lost habitat? Where and how do we safeguard existing connectivity and re-establish it? What sorts of human uses are compatible in multiple-use or transition zones lying between human settlements and protected areas? Conservation biology, island biogeography, and ecology have helped to recognize and define the problems associated with species and ecosystem decline. They are also in a position, along with restoration ecology and other disciplines, to help define the solutions with specificity.

The foregoing comprise the single most important use of science in conservation. Without such guidance we would not know how to go about conservation. Even with such guidance the precautionary principle must be incorporated into our reserve designs and campaigns for protection.

Science Informing Judicial and Administrative Processes

In some countries, laws require that those who carry them out rely on "the best available science" and require courts and other adjudicative bodies to give effect to this requirement. Where courts are semi-autonomous (e.g. the US, most of the European Union, Australia) scientific findings are usually heeded by the courts even in the face of administrative or executive opposition. Under the US Endangered Species Act, for example, scientific findings and the testimony of scientists have been important in numerous lawsuits to bring agencies and others to task for failing to list a species, failing to develop adequate recovery plans, or failure to set aside habitat and to properly administer recovery plans and habitat. Findings and testimony are critical in establishing whether or not agencies or others are complying with the law.

Science is important in other settings. In complex societies legislation is often general, setting broad goals and standards, and relying on those carrying out the laws to set more detailed standards. Here too there may be requirements to rely on best science in making rules pursuant to law. Science is no magic bullet, however. Those carrying out the law are subject to pressure in rulemaking and they are not required to heed the "best" scientists or the majority of scientists. Adjudicative bodies often give great deference to executive agencies and their expertise.

Pressure on agencies comes not just from industry and other interests, but from the very legislators and legislatures responsible for the substantive law. Sometimes the make-up of legislatures is markedly different from when laws were passed. Such laws may be difficult to repeal because of popular support or procedural obstacles, but it is often easy to cut funds for agencies that "misbehave" (Wilkinson 1998). In the case of quasi-judicial action, rather than quasi-legislative, the courts may be less shy about overturning agency decisions (Strauss et al. 2011).

SCIENCE AND DECISION MAKERS

The ability to persuade decision makers can also be seen as the ability to make your problems their problems. Can scientists and scientific findings help with this? Yes, but their role in influencing law and policy makers is decidedly mixed.

For scientific information to have influence with decision makers one or more factors must be present (Bryner 1993; Bimber 1997; Repetto 2006; Kraft 2011; Dye 2014): (1) Decision makers must care about the issue. They must share some of the underlying values or at least the goals of conservationists. If a decision maker does not care about protecting grizzly bears, the best scientific information about what habitat the bears need will not be persuasive. If, on the other hand, decision makers do care, then having that information can play a role in shaping proposed solutions. (2) Decision makers may care about conservation goals because constituent groups that can help or hurt their chances of getting or keeping office care – and will act on that caring. Groups that are historically part of a decision maker's coalition of support will generally fare better with influence, but swing groups are also important. (3) Decision makers, whether supportive or opposed, undertake a calculus – are my chips worth spending on this issue? This involves an assessment of the relative resources supporting and opposing groups possess, their record of effectiveness, and related circumstances. Scientific findings may enter into this calculus. (4) Because decision makers juggle so many issues they may wait to the last moment to make a decision. Decisions may be made based on hunches and rapid assessments. In such circumstances decision makers often turn to sources they trust and that have been reliable in the past. If such sources defer to science then it may be influential with the subject decision maker. (5) Other factors may create space for scientific influence. One conservation proposal may be anathema to a decision maker, but another proposal may be worse. In such cases scientific findings may influence how the proposals are weighed. Science can provide something for a decision maker to hang their hat on. (6) Decision makers sometimes look for issues they can champion as their own. If scientific findings can provide a hook or are backed by supportive groups with influence they will have influence.

In short, science has influence when decision makers are receptive due to shared values or goals with those offering the information, or when science has power on its side and decision makers have to pay attention. Because of gross disparities in power those who possess it can distort the factual playing field. Power, like gravity, can bend perception (light): cigarettes are not a health hazard nor do greenhouse gases cause climate instability, and so on. Scientists and scientific findings can be important in debunking these deliberate distortions but it can take a very long time. The science prevailed on cigarettes when the medical establishment, insurers, child protection groups, anti-addiction groups, and others were organized into an effective coalition (Brandt 2007).

There are categories of decision makers where the dynamics are quite different. Decision makers who are private landowners or communal landowners (e.g. *ejidos* in Mexico) and have a personal commitment to the health of the land may find science important to informing and shaping how they use it less destructively. In contrast, those who see the land as only a commodity or an opportunity for profit are generally receptive only to information which makes land economically valuable. They are interested not in ecological sustainability but at best in continued productivity as measured in dollars.

More broadly across business sector decision making, receptivity to biological information varies with circumstances. Publicly traded companies have essentially sold their soul to institutional investors who expect a certain return and create problems for management when expectations are not met. Privately held companies, though requiring some profit to keep the ship afloat, have more flexibility. Profit is not their only concern, as companies such as Patagonia demonstrate with their commitment to other values (Paumgarten 2016). Retail businesses are more susceptible to boycotts because their brand is on the line (such as tuna canners in the Dolphin Safe campaign [Layzer 2011]), and this is particularly true where food safety is an issue. It's easier to pressure retailers than to pressure factory farms directly (Hamerschlag et al. 2015); efforts to directly pressure Tyson to stop using or reduce use of antibiotics in food animals failed, but pressure on the McDonald's restaurant chain succeeded and they in turn established requirements for suppliers (Velasco 2015). A threatened boycott and ongoing protests caused Home Deport to stop carrying certain tropical hardwoods and temperate old growth softwoods (Carlton 2000).

It is not the scientific evidence that persuades, but estimates of pain and gain. Bad press with the public, falling sales or falling stock prices, threats of litigation, civil disobedience – all of these can be persuasive (Careless 1997; Bevington 2009; Johns 2009). Science can help inform conservation arguments and debunk bad information.

SUMMARY

Conservation is an uphill battle most of the time. Commitment and passion are not enough to safeguard biodiversity and rewild much of the planet. Certainly a passionate commitment to the beauty, spontaneity, and creativity of the evolutionary process is necessary. But passion must be informed and intelligent. Science has a primary role in informing commitment: in understanding the needs of other species and combating disinformation. The biological sciences are a key resource in the fight for wild places and species. They are important in the courts, often with agencies, and sometimes with other decision makers.

Differences among scientists and advocates are real. Differing methods of work, in understanding the role of values, and how science works in the political process, can be a source of friction. The less energy conservationists have to put into correcting misunderstandings among themselves, the more effective they will be in shaping the larger agenda. Too much is as stake for divorce to be an option.

REFERENCES

Barry, Dwight and Max Oelschaeger. 1996. A Science for Survival. 10 *Conservation Biology* 3: 905–11 (June).

Berman, Morris. 1983. *Reenchantment of the World*. Cornell University Press. Ithaca, NY.

Bevington, Doug. 2009. *The Rebirth of Environmentalism*. Island Press. Washington DC.

Bimber, Bruce. 1997. *The Politics of Expertise in Congress*. SUNY Press. Albany, NY.

Brandt, Allan. 2007. *The Cigarette Century*. Basic Books. New York.

Bryner, Gary C. 1993. *Blue Skies, Green Politics*. Congressional Quarterly Press. Washington, DC.

Burks, David Clark. 1994. *Place of the Wild*. Island Press. Washington DC.

Careless, Ric. 1997. *To Save the Wild Earth*. Raincoast Books. Vancouver.

Carlton, Jim. 2000. How Home Depot and Activists Joined to Cut Logging Abuse. *Wall Street Journal* (September 26). www.wsj.com/articles/SB96993154428491509 (accessed January 14, 2018).

Clark, Ronald. 1971. *Einstein: The Life and Times*. World Publishing. Cleveland, OH.

Conservation Biology. 1996. Special Section on the Role of Advocacy. 10 *Conservation Biology* 3: 904–20 (June).

Conservation Biology. 1997, 1998. For example, the indices for both of these years (11:1468, 12:1431) show eight articles dealing with values and science or advocacy and science.

Convention on Biological Diversity. 2017. Ecologically and Biologically Significant Areas. www.cbd.int/ebsa/ (accessed January 14, 2018).

Demsky, Ian. 2006. In Bed With Big Wood: Emails Show OSU and Timber Sitting in a Tree, K-I-S-S-I-N-G. Willamette Week. April 18. www.wweek.com/portland/article-5526-in-bed-with-big-wood.html (accessed November 10, 2016).

Donato, D. C., J. B. Fontaine, J. L. Campbell, W. D. Robinson, J. B. Kauffman, and B. E. Law. 2006. Post-Wildfire Logging Hinders Regeneration and Increases Fire Risk. 311 *Science* 352 (January 20).

Dye, Thomas R. 2014. *Who's Running America*. 8th edn. Routledge. New York.

Ehrenfeld, David. 1978. *The Arrogance of Humanism*. Oxford University Press. New York.

Ehrenfeld, David. 1989. Conservation Biology in R. Paehlke (ed.). *Conservation and Environmentalism: An Encyclopedia*. Garland Publishing. New York.

Ehrlich, Paul and Anne Ehrlich. 1997. *Betrayal of Science and Reason*. Island Press. Washington DC.

Flattau, Edward. 1998. *Tracking the Charlatans*. Global Horizons Press. Washington DC.

Foreman, Dave, Michael Soulé, David Johns, and John Davis. 1992. The Wildlands Project Mission Statement. *Wild Earth* Special Issue on The Wildlands Project: 3–4.

Gould, Stephen Jay. 1974–2001. This View of Life [column]. *Natural History* magazine. American Museum of Natural History. New York.

Hamerschlag, Keri, Sasha Stashwick, Steve Roach, et al. 2015. *Chain Reaction*. Friends of the Earth, NRDC, Keep Antibiotics Working, Consumers Union, Center for Food Safety, FACT. http://consumersunion.org/wp-content/uploads/2015/09/ChainReactionReport_final.pdf (accessed December 1, 2016).

Hofstadter, Richard. 1963. *Anti-Intellectualism in American Life*. Knopf. New York.

Hofstadter, Richard. 1965. *The Paranoid Style in American Politics and Other Essays*. Knopf. New York.

Johns, David. 2009. *A New Conservation Politics*. Wiley-Blackwell. Chichester.

Kraft, Michael E. 2011. *Environmental Policy and Politics*. 5th edn. Pearson Longman. New York.

Layzer, Judith. 2011. *The Environmental Case*. 3rd edn. CQ Press. Washington DC.

Lovejoy, Thomas. 1989. The Obligations of a Biologist. 3 *Conservation Biology* 4: 329–30 (December).

Marine Conservation Institute. 2017. Global Ocean Refuge System (GLORES). www.marine-conservation.org/GLORES. (accessed January 14, 2018).

Marine Conservation Institute. 2017. MPAtlas. www.marine-conservation.org/MPAtlas. (accessed January 14, 2018).

Merchant, Carolyn. 1983. *The Death of Nature*. Harper and Row. New York.

Noss, Reed. 1992. A Wildlands Land Conservation Strategy. *Wild Earth* Special Issue on the Wildlands Project: 10–25.

Noss, Reed. 1993. Whither Conservation Biology? 7 *Conservation Biology* 2: 215–17 (June).

Noss, Reed. 1994. *Saving Nature's Legacy*. Island Press. Washington DC.

Otto, Shawn. 2016. *The War on Science*. Milkweed Editions. Minneapolis, MN.

Paumgarten, Nick. 2016. Wild Man. 92 *New Yorker* 29: 62–73 (September 19).

Piot, Peter. 2012. *No Time to Lose*. Norton. New York.

Primack, Richard and Anna Sher. 2016. *An Introduction to Conservation Biology*. Sinauer Associates. Sunderland, MA.

Ray, Dixie Lee. 1993. *Environmental Overkill: Whatever Happened to Common Sense?* Regency Gateway. Washington DC.

Repetto, Robert (ed.). 2006. *Punctuated Equilibrium and the Dynamics of US Environmental History*. Yale University Press. New Haven, CT.

Riding, Alan. 1985. *Distant Neighbors*. Knopf. New York.

Roberts, Callum. 2007. *An Unnatural History of the Sea*. Island Press. Washington DC.

Roberts, Callum M., Bethan C. O'Leary, Douglas J. McCauley, et al. 2017. Marine Reserves Can Mitigate and Promote Adaptation to Climate Change. *Proceedings of the (US) National Academy of Sciences*. www.pnas.org/cgi/doi/10.1073/pnas.1701262114 (accessed June 9, 2017).

Sachs, Jonah. 2012. *Winning the Story Wars*. Harvard Business Review Press. Cambridge, MA.

Schrader-Frechette, Kristin. 1996. Throwing out the Bathwater of Positivism, Keeping the Baby of Objectivity. 10 *Conservation Biology* 3: 912–14.

Searles, Harold F. 1960. *The Nonhuman Environment in Normal Development and in Schizophrenia*. International Universities Press. New York.

Shepard, Paul. 1973. *The Sacred Game and the Tender Carnivore*. Scribners. New York.

Shepard, Paul. 1982. *Nature and Madness*. Sierra Club. San Francisco.

Society for Conservation Biology. 1999. Goals and Objectives of the Society for Conservation Biology. 13 *Conservation Biology* 6: unpaginated (December).

Society for Conservation Biology Annual Business Meeting. 20 June 1995. University of Maryland. College Park, MD. A special session of the SCB business meeting spent several hours discussing advocacy and ways in which conservation biologists could be more persuasive with the public and policy makers. Two themes emerged from scientists' statements. Academic scientists stated the need for support and credit from their departments for addressing public audiences in the popular media. Generally scientists said they felt most inclined to speak out knowing that there were others that could follow through on the policy process.

Society for Conservation Biology. 2016. Strategic Plan 2016–2020. http://conbio .org/images/content_about_scb/SCB_Strategic_Plan_2016-2020_Final.pdf (accessed October 7, 2016). See also inside back cover for SCB Goals. 30 *Conservation Biology* 5 (October).

Soulé, Michael, 1986. Conservation Biology and the 'Real World' in Soulé (ed.): *Conservation Biology: The Science of Scarcity and Diversity*. Sinauer Associates. Sunderland, MA.

Soulé, Michael and Gary Lease (eds.). 1994. *Reinventing Nature? Responses to Postmodern Deconstruction*. Island Press. Covelo, CA.

Soulé, Michael and John Terborgh. 1999. *Continental Conservation*. Island Press. Washington DC.

Stevens, William K. 1998. "Science Academy Disputes Attack on Global Warming." *New York Times*, April 22. www.nytimes.com/1998/04/22/us/sci ence-academy-disputes-attack-on-global-warming.html (accessed January 14, 2018).

Stokstad, Erik. 2006. University Bids to Salvage Reputation after Flap Over Logging Paper. 312 *Science* 1288 (June 2).

Strauss, Peter S., Todd Rakoff, Cynthia Farina, and Gillian Metzer. 2011. *Administrative Law: Cases and Comments*. 11th edn. Foundation Press. Mineola, MN.

Thomas, Lewis. 1974. *The Lives of a Cell*. Viking. New York.

Velasco, Schuyler. 2015. Why Tyson Antibiotic-free Chicken is a Bigger Deal than GMO-free Chipotle. *Christian Science Monitor*. (April 28). www.cs monitor.com/Business/The-Bite/2015/0428/Why-Tyson-antibiotic-free-chicken-is-a-bigger-deal-than-GMO-free-Chipotle (accessed January 14, 2018).

Wildlands Network. 2017. wildlandsnetwork.org/wildways/eastern/reconnecting-the-eastern-wildway/half-east-map/ (accessed January 18, 2018).

Wilkinson, Todd. 1998. *Science under Siege: The Politicians' War on Nature and Truth*. Johnson Books. Boulder, CO.

Wilson, E O. 2006. *The Creation*. Norton. New York.

Wilson, E O. 2012. *The Social Conquest of the Earth*. Liveright. New York.

Wilson, E O. 2014. *A Window on Eternity*. Simon & Schuster. New York.

Wilson, E O. 2016. *Half Earth*. Liveright. New York.

Wuerthner, George, Eileen Crist, and Tom Butler. 2014. *Keeping the Wild*. Island Press. Washington DC.

WWF (World Wildlife Fund). 2014. *Living Planet Report 2014: Species and Spaces, People and Places*. WWF. Gland, Switzerland.

WWF. 2016. *Living Planet Report 2016: Risk and Resilience in a New Era*, ed. Natasja Oerlemans, Holly Strand, Annemarie Winkelhagen, Mike Barrett, and Monique Grooten. WWF. Gland, Switzerland.

PART IV Culture Change

Humans are cultural animals. Much of our behavior is not genetically specified but plastic, regulated by learned systems of beliefs, values, understandings of the world, meanings and purposes, and emotions shaped by experience and predispositions. Most politics is fought out in the cultural realm – e.g. it is much cheaper for elites to socialize people to accept inequality as natural or the result of hard work or "character," than to use force to maintain unequal relationships. Though force is always in waiting. It is easier to try and short-circuit reactions to inequality, exploitation, and injustice before they move from anger to action, and to keep those victimized from developing a vision of a more just world, an understanding of who they are as a group, who their opponents are, forming a good grasp of the political landscape, a strategy, and creating an effective organization. When those things exist and lead to serious challenges to the status quo it gets more expensive to counteract, efforts to do so may fall short, and elites have to make real concessions.

Moving society in a different direction than its current course begins with cultural change among those discontented with the status quo; who feel their sense of justice is violated. The discontent may begin with material changes affecting them – longstanding arrangements may be altered by the intrusion of the global economy, by war, by climate change, or by an elite simply breaking the rules they have lived by and increasing the level of exploitation (e.g. Scott 1976). All of these sorts of changes can displace people, forcing migration or making life more difficult or even intolerable. In the case of conservation the acceleration of the loss of species and wilderness may be experienced as a crisis which awakens a group and leads to action.

Sadly, the decline of wild things and places is usually not experienced as deeply as a societal cataclysm.

Crisis is not the only spur to culture change among groups in a society. Culture change is mostly incremental. It may be caused by long-term processes in society such as urbanization, industrialization, and fundamental changes in technology and energy availability (mechanization of agriculture, refrigeration, cheap air transport, near-instantaneous global communication). As people move to cities they are more distant from wild places and this may aid conservation to some degree: it is easier to see the violence and destruction being perpetrated. In contrast, those whose jobs depend on the violence – converting forest to farm land or subdivisions and native grasslands to pasture, building oil and gas extraction facilities, building new roads across the landscape, building dams, persecuting wildlife regarded as pests, mining the oceans for fish – may regard it as normal and not see it as violence. It's been going on for a long time, after all. Certainly those to whom great wealth accrues as a result of transforming the natural world embrace these activities. The cultural benefits of urbanization to conservation generated by perspective and distance from rural society – i.e. the ability to see animals and places in non-reductionist and non-utilitarian ways rather than as food or obstacles – usually require efforts by cultural leaders to sensitize people to this new perspective. Often artists lead the way, through film, theater, music, and literature that evoke empathy or a past (experienced in childhood) that is lost (Edelman 1995; Kahn and Kellert 2002). Religious leaders also play a role in this. And of course NGOs seek to awaken and reinforce this new perspective or worldview. The difficulty is that distance may only generate shallow rather than intense emotion. Or people may just turn away from the slaughterhouse, which is much easier than trying to shut it down or even becoming a vegetarian.

Culture change also occurs generationally (Nabhan and Trimble 1994; Kahn and Kellert 2002; Kals and Ittner 2003; Myers 2007). Whatever efforts parents and other institutions make to shape people, they cannot control all experience or the reaction to it. The young can see hypocrisy and other shortcomings; their formative experiences are almost invariably different from those of earlier generations and their would-be teachers, creating slippage; and of course there are differences of class, ethnicity, gender, and the idiosyncratic which shape experience. In short, the world for which they are raised is no longer there when they begin to join it. It need not be radically different to generate stress or insight.

The schisms that exist in any society and among groups in different societies or between societies are both material and cultural, and present political opportunities. All types of change – crises, incremental, generational – present opportunities for conservationists to intervene and try to guide that change to undercut the institutions of domination and exploitation of the wild and shrink the human footprint. These conflicts also create openings to begin to build alternative institutions. Alternative institution building is critical to movement building. Many anti-colonial struggles built support by replacing old institutions that were failing and no longer provided ideological and material services, with new ones that provided both: a more compelling worldview, a sense of community, and a safety net not dependent on domination of the world and its consequent alienation. Other movements have also provided services as part of fostering change, e.g. the Black Panther Party provided breakfast for school children and medical clinics.

Conflict defines groups and usually reinforces identity and a sense of mission. In the course of conflict what must be done to realize goals becomes clearer. In particular it becomes clearer to what degree conservation NGOs can use target groups' existing worldviews to mobilize them and to what degree worldviews must be changed to bring about action in support of conservation goals. In most cases those seeking to mobilize groups focus on the group's existing worldview and don't seek to change it. Conversion is difficult (Rambo 1993) and generally takes a very long time to move large numbers, or results from a serious personal or social crisis (Wallace 1956, 1970). For conservation conversion will be necessary because such a major reorientation of society is necessary. But most mobilization in the nearer term will not require it.

In the following chapters we will look first at some changes conservationists need to make in how they speak to themselves and the larger world in order to stop unintentionally undermining the conservation mission. We will also look at the need to begin building a new mythology that places safeguarding and restoring wild places and creatures at center stage among societies' purposes. Finally we will examine the moral imperative of conservation and its irreducibility to narrowly human concerns.

Conservation has made headway in changing many cultures; most now formally acknowledge the importance of other species and not just for utilitarian reasons. But without a much fuller and more deeply embedded biophilia combined with a culture of activism, institutional change will continue to seriously lag extinction and biological decline.

The institutions of domination and growth must be exposed, criticized, alternatives offered and built.

REFERENCES

Edelman, Murray. 1995. *From Art to Politics.* University of Chicago Press. Chicago, IL.

Kahn, Peter H. and Stephen R. Kellert (eds.). 2002. *Children and Nature.* MIT Press. Cambridge, MA.

Kals, Elisabeth and Heidi Ittner. 2003. Children's Environmental Identity: Indicators and Behavior Impact. Pp. 135–57 in Susan Clayton and Susan Opotow (eds.). *Identity and the Natural Environment.* MIT Press. Cambridge, MA.

Myers, Gene. 2007. *The Significance of Children and Animals.* 2nd edn. Purdue University Press. West Lafayette, IN.

Nabhan, Gary and Stephen Trimble. 1994. *The Geography of Childhood.* Beacon Press. Boston, MA.

Rambo, Lewis R. 1993. *Understanding Conversion.* Yale University Press. New Haven, CT.

Scott, James C. 1976. *The Moral Economy of the Peasant.* Yale University Press. New Haven, CT.

Wallace, Anthony F. C. 1956. Revitalization Movements. 58 *American Anthropologist* 264–81 (April).

Wallace, Anthony F. C. 1970. *Culture and Personality.* 2nd edn. Random House. New York.

13 Conservation, George Orwell, and Language

What does George Orwell have to do with conservation? As a mission- and *morality*-driven cause, conservationists have quite a lot to learn from Orwell. He understood the power of words to convey values, meaning, and purpose and how to manipulate them to stir or quell emotion, to describe or misrepresent reality. His novels such as *Animal Farm* (1946) and *1984* (1949) and critical essays such as "Politics and the English Language" (1968 [1946]) make plain how language can be used to manipulate how people react to issues. There is much natural scientists and advocates can learn from his insight that "political speech and writing are largely the defense of the indefensible ... Thus political language has to consist largely of euphemism, question begging, and sheer cloudy vagueness" (1968 [1946]: 136). Before conservationists can change the larger culture of human societies, greater clarity within conservation is important.

Most papers presented at conservation biology meetings and published in its journals have to do with understanding how biodiversity is impacted by human activities. Less often do presentations and papers consider the purposes, values, and motivations of conservation biology. But these aspects are equally important; they address why conservation biologists do what they do.

For example, according to its mission statement, the Society for Conservation Biology "advances the science and *practice* of conserving Earth's biological diversity" and "envisions a world where people understand, *value*, and conserve the diversity of life on Earth" (italics added).

To achieve the vision and fulfill the mission depends on motivating others to care and to act on behalf of biodiversity. In turn that means being clear about our moral purpose:

- Biodiversity is good (Soulé 1985)
- Humans are obligated to safeguard biodiversity

Science of itself cannot motivate people to address the extinction and climate crises. It takes the values just noted. It takes passion. Contrary to what some think, science does not require practitioners to be passionless or meek, only that they do not cook the books. Being unbiased does not require lack of caring; indeed, to not care is to be alienated. To express caring and evoke it in others begins with the choice of language used to communicate the importance of biodiversity to others.

The widespread use of euphemisms by many conservationist scientists, conservation journals, and conservation biology course materials undermines efforts to evoke caring in others for life on Earth and even to care for the conservation community. A euphemism is "The act or example of substituting a mild, indirect, or vague term for a harsh, blunt, or offensive one" that is more accurate (*The American Heritage College Dictionary*, 3rd edn, 1993: 473). In more words the *Oxford English Dictionary* says the same thing: "That figure of speech which consists in the substitution of a word or expression of comparatively favourable or less unpleasant associations instead of the harsher or more offensive one that would more precisely designate what is intended" (Compact OED 1971, I: 903). Euphemisms, then, use language choice to describe activities in acceptable words that audiences would otherwise find objectionable. Euphemisms mislead by obscuring reality. They sanitize and disguise, and thus are *not neutral* terms. As one example: "We harvested a sample of 100 fish for analysis of stomach contents," rather than "we caught and killed 100 fish for analysis of stomach contents."

Other ways of speaking can mislead for different reasons, including metaphors – a "figure of speech in which a name or descriptive term is transferred to some object different from, but analogous to, that to which it is properly applicable" (Compact OED 1971, I: 1781). Using economic metaphors, for example, to describe the natural world – natural assets, stocks, maximum sustainable yield, forest harvest, natural capital and debt – is reductionist: it suggests the natural world is part of the human economy rather than the other way around and that the former operates like the latter in a literal and mechanistic way; it also strongly implies that only those aspects of the natural world that have economic value have value (Coffey 2016).

Metaphors can also create strong, vivid images that impart insight via their analogies. But analogies are just that – not meant to be literal, wholly accurate terms. In contrast, euphemisms purport to be accurate descriptions when in fact they misrepresent what they describe. Both may mislead – some metaphors may be bad metaphors, i.e. not good analogies. But all euphemisms, intent aside, candy-coat and undercut caring by creating emotional distance from that which conservationists seek to evoke caring for. A metaphor might circumvent caring but if so it is more likely because of the listener's error in taking it literally rather than rejecting it as a bad analogy. For example, the metaphor "forest health" alludes to actions taken to maintain the function of a forest much like actions may be taken to maintain human function in the face of disease. Cutting old growth trees, however, is an inaccurate analogy with treating disease; such logging is part of the disease.

Similarly, language that is vague and unnecessarily abstract can be problematic: so-called buzzwords, which appear to offer easy insight and information and in the course of that become commonly used. "Sustainable" or "sustainability" are widely used, including in policy statements, but they are rarely defined. Just what is proposed to be sustained? Human societies? The human species? The Earth's ecological systems and their full complement of species? The difference is significant: one species or all species? And the course of action for the latter is quite different than for the former.

Students of narrative recognize that stories are useful to humans because they simplify reality and thereby help make life manageable. But what about when precise if complex understanding is part of the goal, as with science? Goldstein (1999) argues that scientists too often fall victim to the temptation to simplify in the face of the tremendous complexity of the biological world. They seek shortcuts in understanding the natural world, the damage done to it by humans, and in figuring out ways to heal it. In doing so they use terms that seem to offer insight – buzzwords – that in fact mislead others and even themselves. He argues, for instance, that "ecosystem management" is too broad a concept to be evaluated (1999: 249): ecosystems are dynamic and goals such as maintaining predation (authors' example) mean little apart from understanding specific native predator populations. Ehrenfeld (1979) and others raise important related questions, such as whether humans are capable of understanding, let alone managing, such complexity. Buzzwords give false impressions of precision and are misleading if also the product of good faith efforts at problem solving.

How do we know if a word or phrase is a euphemism? Here's a self-test. Apply the term or phrase to some entity or group you care about and gauge your reaction. If you are uncomfortable it is probably a euphemism. If it makes you feel dishonest it almost certainly is a euphemism. Would you "sacrifice" or "cull" colleagues or members of your family so that some knowledge might be gained?

Beyond a self-test, ask if the words or phrase convey an accurate description of what is happening, or obscure it; does it preclude a negative emotional response to an activity through use of vague and pleasant language? We are all familiar with the use of euphemism in human politics – terms such as "collateral damage," which aims to soften our reaction to killing of civilians in the course of military action. The term "bycatch" is similar, referring to the foreseeable killing of non-targeted marine wildlife during efforts to capture and kill profitable species. "Bycatch" may be as high as 40 percent by weight of all life killed (Davies et al. 2009). It's easy to understand why those who fish use such a word, but why don't biologists use a more straightforward term?

"Harvest" is common and in wide use in conservation biology as well among those who study forests, fish, and other wildlife with the goal of maximizing exploitation and economic benefits. And it illustrates the history of the adoption of this and similar terms in conservation. Harvest is an ancient term and generally refers to "gathering in a crop," usually of grains, fruits, or vegetables planted or tended deliberately as human food. "Wildlife managers" in the twentieth century borrowed the term from agriculture (Leopold 1986 [1933]: 3–4), ironically the principal threat to wildlife and wild places for the last twelve millennia.

Although Leopold later changed his thinking on this topic, his initial conceptualization regarded wildlife management as producing crops of wild game, while maintaining maximum yield via human interventions in the landscape, interventions which included targeting other species such as predators to maintain the yield of the desired species. Several of these agricultural terms seeped into various biology disciplines by way of Leopold before his understanding changed.

"Harvest" is used to describe killing part or all of the individuals of a wild species for food or other purposes: because a species is inconvenient to some humans, for fun, or because humans have degraded habitat; or ecosystems are said to be "out of balance" and need to be righted. Interestingly the killing of domestic animals for food and sometimes other purposes is referred to as slaughter, a harsher term. Even "killing" can obscure the grim details: poisoning, shooting, leg-hold trapping, snaring, drowning, suffocating, chasing down with machines.

"Harvest" preempts acknowledgement of qualities that may be possessed by those creatures being killed:

- Sentience
- Uniqueness
- Place in social and family structure
- Desire to avoid death
- Fear

"Harvest" does not evoke caring and empathy, outrage at loss of life, but instead distances and objectifies.

It does not evoke the moral purpose of conservation but the notion of wildlife as crops owned by humans. It implies the human right to inflict injury and even impose death to balance the "books" we have brought disorder to. It conveys the idea that the killing is an orderly process intended to benefit people, and that such benefit is presumptively justified; it may also presume that the species being killed benefits along with the ecosystem of which it is a part.

Wild plants are also subject to the term "harvest." It is sometimes used to describe the destruction of complex living systems such as forests and their replacement by tree farms, domesticated monocultures, or subdivisions.

There are many other euphemisms that attempt to sanitize human violence toward the natural world:

- "Collect" is to kill for the sake of human knowledge without considering the knowledge lost by killing. Sometimes "sacrifice" is used as if we are priests.
- "Working lands" is a favorite, calling to mind the laziness of wilderness. In fact the lands referred to as working are domesticated and usually degraded. A common example is rangeland heavily grazed by cattle, sheep, and other domestic animals. Such lands are occupied lands, with human activities displacing other species. In many countries, such rangelands receive massive public subsidies: tax forgiveness or reductions, road construction, free water, and subsidized energy.
- "Fire destroys, blackens, and is catastrophic" ignores the essential role of fire in many systems and the serious and lasting damage of fire suppression. Using the term "fuels" instead of dead wood in a fire-adapted forest tends to distance foresters from seeing vegetation and its important role in such forests. It allows foresters to ignore their own role in creating an ecosystem prone to massive fires through fire suppression and logging.
- "Silvicultural treatment" usually includes the application of toxic chemicals that poison soil and water, or the use of heavy equipment that compacts or otherwise disturbs soils.

Tag, administrative removal, incidental "take," and bag limits are others that come to mind.

The conceptual grandparent of so many euphemisms might be "natural resources." It reduces all the world to narrow utilitarian human uses.

These terms disconnect us from the consequences of our actions. They diminish or preclude emotion. Yet it is emotion that connects us to each other, to other creatures, to the wider world that made us. Without emotion we would be hollow and lonely indeed. We would not be conservationists.

One more term deserves mention in this brief survey: cull.

Cull is a term that can obscure the cause of conservation problems. US agencies have killed, are killing, and plan to kill sea lions and cormorants in the Columbia River because they eat salmon that are endangered. Yes salmon are endangered, but why? Because of dams, water temperature increases in spawning streams, logging, livestock grazing, and road building. Not because of sea lions and cormorants.

The term cull makes the destruction of the largest double-crested cormorant colony in the world, at the mouth of the Columbia River, seem a difficult necessity rather than a case of scapegoating that rationalizes the violent destruction of life. By invoking the implication of unfortunate necessity, the real, human causes of wild salmon decline are off the table: massive hydro dams, logging which destroys spawning streams, grazing, and pollution. The difficult problem of changing human behavior and weaning ourselves off cheap hydropower (because the costs of this "green" energy are externalized) does not then have to be dealt with.

What are conservationists to do? They have an obligation to:

- Accurately describe how biodiversity works in the real world and to advocate for the importance and intrinsic value of biodiversity – not to make people comfortable.
- Explore more accurate language for how plants and animals are treated by humans, including conservation scientists and others. Maybe a simple place to start is to give animals names. Cecil the lion had a name and his execution generated outrage and an important discussion about the value of life.
- Use language that evokes our moral purpose.

Euphemism is not part of the solution, it is part of the problem. It is up to all of us to invent a new and better language.

REFERENCES

American College Heritage Dictionary, The. 1993. 3rd edn. Houghton Mifflin. Boston, MA.

Coffey, Brian. 2016. Unpacking the Politics of Natural Capital and Economic Metaphors in Environmental Policy Discourse. 25 *Environmental Politics* 2: 203–22.

Davies, R., S. Cripps, A. Nickson, and G. Porter. 2009. Defining and Estimating Global Marine Fisheries Bycatch. 33 *Marine Policy* 4: 661–72 (July). doi: 10.1016/ j.marpol.2009.01.003.

Ehhrenfield, David. 1979. *Arrogance of Humanism.* Oxford University Press. New York.

Goldstein, Paul Z. 1999. Functional Ecosystems and Biodiversity Buzzwords. 13 *Conservation Biology* 2: 247–55.

Leopold, Aldo. 1986 (1933). *Game Management.* University of Wisconsin Press. Madison, WI.

Orwell, George. 1968 (1946). Politics and the English Language. Pp. 127–39 in *Collected Essays, Journalism and Letters. Volume 4: In Front of Your Nose.* Harcourt, Brace and World. New York.

Oxford English Dictionary, Compact. 1971. (2 vols.) Oxford University Press. New York.

Society for Conservation Biology. 2016. Strategic Plan 2016–2020. http://conbio .org/images/content_about_scb/SCB_Strategic_Plan_2016-2020_Final.pdf (accessed October 7, 2016).

Soulé, Michael. 1985. What is Conservation Biology? 35 *BioScience* 11: 727–34.

14 Restoring Story and Myth

Humans understand and navigate the world mostly with story. Stories are especially important in conveying moral lessons and the most important and fundamental purposes which guide societies. Myths – stories about these most basic meanings and purposes, i.e. the sacred – establish the framework for group and individual stories. To make conservation a higher priority among those who are key audiences requires myths and stories about general principles and day-to-day behavior, i.e. lower order stories, that make other species and the wild moral objects – part of the community. Such stories must be compelling if they are to replace existing stories.

There are many elements critical to compelling stories which conservationists often ignore: drama; characters whom audiences can strongly identify with and are imbued with a clear sense of fairness that can be incorporated into the target audience's identities; characters that give reasons for participation and action; coherence; direction (beginning, middle, and end) to provide guidance through life's transitions and conflicts; memorable and vivid scenes conveyed with powerful symbols and that evoke bodily experience, and that provide answers to emerging questions which existing stories cannot provide; adaptability to a variety of media and time frames, from soundbites, songs and short films to full-length films, theater, art, comics and books; and the right messenger and channels. Stories must suit the venue – a courtroom is not a demonstration (Polletta 2006). Amidst contentious political circumstances effective stories are about threats, vengeance, redemption, wrongs righted, and final triumph.

There is no substitute for charismatic storytellers, but the elements of story can be mastered by others. This chapter discusses the primary elements of story, why they are important, and how they lead to action. The relation of story to other elements of mobilization is also noted.

Most conservationists have come to recognize that stories are the most effective vehicle for communicating conservation goals and their importance to audiences. They know that stories must appeal to audiences' needs, emotions, and cognitive categories. But conservationists have shied away from myth: not recognizing its importance, they do not seek to create new stories or to change existing ones. It's not even clear they understand the structure of stories. They seem perpetually caught in consciousness-raising (the cognitive) and fundraising and pay little heed to activism and how it is generated. They forget that action often precedes consciousness and creates emotional commitment (Aronson 1993). Many NGOs, of course, want checkwriters not activists and have no place for activism in their organizations.

Storytelling, and communication more generally, are not ends in themselves, though many conservationists behave as if they are, as evidenced by the lack of follow through. Stories are part of mobilization that harnesses resources to create a political force that can change institutional behavior so it is compatible with biodiversity. There is no substitute for organizing. Stopping the sixth great extinction and restoring healthy populations of species and functional ecosystems requires collective, organized action. Because stories help generate and guide action they have a central place in conservation.

There are two hierarchies to story hinted at above that are best made explicit. The first involves the relationship of group stories to each other. Nations, groups within nations, families, and individuals have stories they live by. Transnational groups often share common stories: Abrahamic stories, Hindu stories, Native American stories. These stories form a nested hierarchy: individual stories are situated within family stories, family stories within group stories, and so on.

There is also a hierarchy in the function of story. As noted, myths answer the why questions for a culture, the purposes and meaning of life. Their content is unquestioned – or sacred – and usually untestable, though over time myths prove adaptive or not. Myths are considered unchanging by those who believe in them. Myths legitimate lower order stories and bind a group to a particular worldview in the face of the many alternatives that exist and could exist, thus providing the emotional and mental basis for social cooperation far beyond kin groups (Rappaport 1999). There are at least three levels of story that myth legitimates.

The first are stories that embody beliefs or knowledge about how the physical and social world works in broad terms. These stories tell people about causes and effects, to what entities they ought to attribute volition (Deborah Keleman [1999] says we are prewired for this; it may not be literally true that entities other than animals have purposes, but to think so is useful in interacting with them); whether the universe is gendered; how to gain knowledge of the world; what can be changed; and they identify dualities such as nature and culture, and so on. General beliefs about how the world works (cosmological axioms, to use Rappaport's term) can and do change, generally without bringing into question the justifying myth. Such change for much of human history has been slow, but the enormous growth of knowledge has pushed aside not just beliefs but entire paradigms. Sometimes, however, because beliefs about purposes and beliefs about how the world works are closely entwined, there is significant resistance to change because fundamental beliefs are not supposed to change. For knowledge (information derived from observation or experiment) to replace belief (something based on faith or habit or unexamined experience) the ties of belief about the world's workings must be severed from myth.

The second category consists of stories derived from cosmological axioms, that give guidance about the rules governing day-to-day life. How should we go about interacting with others? what do we owe each other? who ought we to trust or not? who is it okay to eat and subjugate? are a few questions these stories answer. In recent millennia, laws have sought to provide direction, but still depend heavily on what has been internalized via story which in turn embodies experience and custom.

Elites have usually found it is cheaper to rule with legitimacy (story) than by force, so custom remains important. Rules for day-to-day behavior, then, include which laws we ought to obey, and which are accepted grudgingly, or skirted as much as possible (e.g. Scott 1990), or ignored. Among these rules are how people should treat other creatures: are humans lords and masters, deciding what creatures are varmint and can be persecuted, or do humans have a duty of compassion to all living things? Which approach dominates may be traced back to whether non-human others are considered enspirited or have lost that quality.

Finally there are stories embodying rules about how to respond to events in the world. What is the appropriate response to species' population declines? When are there too many humans and how should we respond to such circumstances? What should be done about institutions committed to endless growth and their plans to destroy more habitat? As with the two previous categories, the rules embodied in these stories change and they can change without necessarily calling into question higher order stories. Some groups, however, regard all levels of story as sacred and therefore unchanging. Such groups are usually marked by a high need for certainty – the purposes and meaning important to them represent the one truth. Alternative truths represent a threat, as do elements of reality that call their myths, axioms, and other rules into question. Fundamentalists, then, are not just literalists but take all rules and stories to be sacred and unchanging. These groups are most likely to cling ever more tightly to stories that are not working, rather than being open to new stories that work better. Both responses – openness and clinging – are responses to the need for myth and the sacred to anchor a culture.

Whether religious or secular, myths and the culture anchored in them satisfy the group need for particular rules in the face of almost infinite possibilities. They bind people to a group while also dividing groups. Culture satisfies the individual need for belonging. Few are disposed to "live in the question" or find their own way. Acceptance of myth and other cultural rules is based on socialization/enculturation, emotional investment, and ritual, and these are strong bonds.

But radical changes in reality and slower erosion of the reality that gave rise to certain stories in the first place makes change possible.

Myth, then, is the grand narrative which subsumes and legitimates lesser stories and tells individuals, groups, nations, and civilizations who they are, why they live, what is good and evil, moral, just, and possible, how to live and avoid disorder (= other orders), what kind of world is desired, what or who is in the way (the villains or devils). Myth gives each person adopting it the chance to be a hero by enabling them to find themselves in the story, be part of something bigger, and feel worthy. Myth answers the question all cultures must answer: "Why this way of living?" "Why cooperate and follow the rules?" These answers are created. Almost all groups deny they do this; for almost all believers the grand story comes from the gods, from the beginning of time, or adheres in the universe's order. Indeed, a function of culture is to make what is human-created seem not to be a matter of choice but something found or discovered; natural, in other words (Rappaport 1999). The answer myth gives to "why this way?" guides people through life's transitions and ideally encourages maturation – choices which are better for the long term and the group, in the face of short-term, individual advantages.

A conservation mythology makes safeguarding and restoring the natural world among the highest purposes of human society, if not the highest. A new myth won't overthrow on its own the existing societal order founded on endless growth, hierarchy, and destruction of the natural world. *But without a new myth, embracing biodiversity, calling on people to act on its behalf, and recognizing human limits,* the current lethal course will continue.

Some religions are moving in a more environment- and conservation-conscious direction, tweaking interpretation of their myth and adjusting their lower order rules for interacting with other species. The Creation Care movement is one example; they point to Genesis and other evidence that "God saw that it [the life he created] was good" (Genesis 1:12, 1:21). To love the Creator requires that one loves Creation and therefore cares for it (Kruger 2002). Pope Francis

(2015) has issued an encyclical, *Laudato Si*, calling on all Catholics to care for the Earth after the long history of abuse and plunder the Earth has suffered. Action will come from bishops or orders, however, rather than from the Vatican. Nonetheless, this represents a shift in how elements of myth are interpreted – stewardship rather than domin-ion – as well as in day-to-day rules.

In Protestant Christianity much depends on individual congre-gations and some see analogies with the US civil rights movement in this regard (McDuff 2010). Most churches, however, seem focused on environmental issues such as making their buildings more energy efficient, rather than conservation.

Islamic writing on conservation comes mostly from the developed world rather than predominantly Muslim areas, and much mainstream Islamic thought appears still wedded to the great chain of being. Those within the Islamic tradition have found efforts to create a conservation ethic and successfully propagate it an uphill battle, especially in the face of development challenges (Foltz 2006).

Buddhists, who teach compassion for all life, have been active in efforts to limit the ivory trade, and have had some success. But neither Buddhism nor Hinduism – religions which have long recognized the kinship of all life, the goodness of non-harming and not causing suffering – have been particularly successful at addressing the real destroyers of life: human population growth, industrialization, and growth in conversion of the Earth into commodities (Dwivedi 2006; Kaza 2006). Both emphasize individual behavior rather than collective political action, as is the case with many religions. But major elem-ents of both mythologies are remarkably supportive of a conservation ethos, more so than the Abrahamic myths whose origins lie with pastoralism and human domination. Indeed, according to Taylor et al.'s (2016) metastudy, Creation Care has not generated widespread action and a majority of those identifying were not even aware of it. Traditional and the New Confucianism are overwhelmingly focused on harmony in the human realm – though they are usually not con-sidered "antinature" according to Dwivedi (2006: 249); Shapiro (2001) disagrees, arguing that Confucianism seeks to order and regulate the environment for human use. Environmental disasters are now impinging on the capacity for harmony and, as with religions elsewhere, there is a search for "scripture" which might serve as the basis for a modern ecological sensibility (Berthrong 2006).

There are many other mythic traditions. Daoism (the philosophy of Lao Tzu rather than the later religious stories) and varieties of animism are probably the most Earth-friendly (Taylor et al. 2016). They have limited influence, though they remain in the repertoire of human stories that can be drawn upon. It's also important to note that the major religious traditions comprise many sects with often major theological/ideological differences. In much of the world the poor and those who exploit them embrace fundamentalist sects that reproduce poverty, high birth rates, and self-defeating politics (Norris and Inglehart 2004).

Any conservation mythology must go beyond trying to graft mild concern with biodiversity to a story that at root seeks to address the suffering and alienation brought about in the transition from foraging to larger-scale society. A new mythology must reconnect people to the wild and other species or it will fail to safeguard biodiversity or enable people to transcend their alienation; a healthy Earth requires something more than addressing human dysfunction. It must steer humans toward biodiversity and wildlands-compatible behaviors. It requires more than a new dogma but must help foster new experiences of the wild and other species.

As conservationists seek to fashion and propagate a new myth, continuing work to make existing theologies and ideologies more conservation friendly will be important. This is primarily work for religious conservationists who must lead from within their institutions to push them toward conservation action and beyond mere environmentalism. This is the legitimate work of culture change, as is the role of secular conservationists to work with religious colleagues. New stories, including myths, are never made out of whole cloth, but combine new elements with rearranged old elements, while jettisoning other elements.

Some conservationists possess many of the elements of a new myth and at least a rudimentary understanding of how myth works. They just need other conservationists to catch up with them and recognize the importance of this work. Sachs (2012) has pointed out in market-speak the elements of the hero's journey described in many of its variations by Joseph Campbell, a pre-eminent scholar of comparative mythology:

- The world is broken (conservationists know in what way, how it happened);
- Heroes are impelled to fix the world but are full of self-doubt;
- They have an epiphany or are guided by a mentor to act despite doubts;
- The hero embarks on the journey to fix things, to slay the devils, dragons, demons, and villains who are the causes of the problem (the causes are understood by many but not all);
- The hero defeats the villains and/or steals their secrets and sets out for home to bring that which will fix things;
- Before reaching home there is a final obstacle and crisis in which the hero triumphs over great odds and finally offers the secrets to their group so the world may be healed.

In a conservation mythology, salvation is not other-worldly, nor just about the human world; it is *this-worldly, in which humans grow up and find their place among the rest of life*. It is about the Earth.

Barlow (1997) and Wilson (2006) offered early outlines of such a story. Much more recently Butler (2015: unpaginated) outlined it in some detail in *Lord Man*:[1]

A Parable:

In the beginning, the world was whole, and beauty prevailed ...

Life begetting life, until the waters,

then the lands, were filled with creatures.

Myriad were their languages, from the nearly imperceptible song of moss to the bugling of elk.

---

[1] "Lord Man" is an allusion to John Muir's (1916: 343) statement that "if a war of races should occur between the wild beasts and Lord Man I would be tempted to sympathize with the bears."

Whales performed their symphonies in the deep. The sounds of life were everywhere. Life pulsed and contracted and flourished through the ages.

Eventually, a being appeared who learned to speak and count. For millennia he lived well among his wild kin.

But as his cleverness grew, so did his ambitions, until the day he declared himself ruler of all.

Believing the self-deception that his kind was sovereign over the others, he taught his children that the Earth had been made for Man's use and profit.

He no longer recognized his neighbors in the community of life, instead calling them "natural resources."

His work he named "progress."

The old religions, which had long tied the human tribe to the other creatures in a circle of reciprocity, were forgotten.

Feigning himself Lord Man, he grew ever-more clever. He learned to gather and burn fossil fuels made by ancient geological forces.

Praise was sung incessantly to the new god, Growth.

His numbers became multitudes.

As the multitudes spread across the face of the Earth, the songs of the other creatures grew fewer and fainter.

Many voices went permanently quiet, replaced by the sounds of machines – digging, churning, scarring the land, driving the whales crazy with the noise.

Every day the Earth became poorer. Bit by bit, it was transformed by Lord Man's numbers and actions.

The seas were emptied of fish and filled with garbage.

The trees were replaced by bleeding stumps.

The prairies were transformed into feeding factories for the ever-expanding human masses.

Smokestacks darkened the skies.

No place was sacred, no landscape safe from the insatiable creature's thirst for more energy to serve his God of Growth.

Lord Man tamed rivers, split atoms, decapitated mountains, and
stabbed the Earth everywhere he thought she might offer a vein of
fuel.

When the feverish Earth cried out, sending furies to communicate
her distress,

Lord Man ignored her sickness until it could no longer be denied.

Slowly, the scales began to fall from his eyes when he saw famine
ravage the land.

When he saw precious sources of freshwater disappear.

When the longing that gnawed on his spirit made him recall so
many creatures that had passed into oblivion.

Seeing the effects of his hubris, he began to wonder if his empire
was secure.

His delusion weakened just enough to reveal the choice before him:

Two paths, one leading to abundant Earth, filled with birdsong;

the other – the way of Growth – offered riches for some, misery for
many, and ultimate destruction for all his tribe.

Would he restrain his numbers and rejoin the community of life as
plain member and citizen?

Or attempt to engineer all the Earth to his will, heeding only the
call of *More*?

Lord Man: Parable Redux

Facing the stark choice to continue his futile quest to bend the
Earth to his will ...

or to rejoin the community of life, Lord Man renounced the goal of
empire, and was no more.

People around the globe began to remember the old ways, before
humans behaved as if the Earth was merely a storehouse of
resources for them.

The people looked to the landscapes around them to inform their
culture and shape their ways of living.

They valued the other members in the land community, giving
them space enough to flourish in their own ways.

Knowledge and tools for family planning were universally shared.

People began to restrain their numbers, with smaller families becoming a key to societal well-being.

Children were allowed to be children, not forced into marriages with adults.

All the children were loved, and all were encouraged to follow their dreams.

Development priorities began to shift from *more* to *better*.

Economic objectives shifted toward sustainability, sufficiency, and resilience.

Actions were judged ethical or not by whether they helped sustain beauty, biodiversity, and health.

The people chose lives of quality, with sufficient time for the activities and relationships that gave them joy.

Eventually the people forgot the dark days when they'd sought to rule, and they honored their new relationship with the Earth.

Whales, unmolested, sang in the deep.

The sounds of leaves rustling and children laughing settled over the land, and the tree of life grew toward the sky.

An effective conservation myth, like all myths, must have drama. The story must be told through the actions of human and other characters that are recognizable and that grapple with real-life problems. In a conservation mythology non-human species and natural processes must have major roles in the narrative. Humans are not in this alone. Nor are they at the center of the universe. The drama must challenge humans to recognize limits in order to ensure the health of the community of life. The human characters in the story must show what happens to people who are moral (they accept limits, embrace the wild and "the others," and are rewarded for their caring) and what happens to those who are immoral (bad things happen to them and their group for inflicting injury and death) and those who backslide (redemption is still possible, but takes work). The situations must be vivid and evoke strong emotion (love, anger, compassion, determination, exaltation, and awe), and speak to basic human needs to belong, to understand the world; characters must be as sharply drawn as the situations and choices they face so that people can identify with them and enter into the story.

Myth, it was noted above, is anchored through socialization/ enculturation; it's no mystery why myths are taught to the very young who lack critical faculties. Individuals and groups emotionally invest in the myths they have been socialized to, deepening their binding force – myths become what we see with to order and make sense of the world (Bennett 1980). It's one reason why rapid and major change in the dominant myth is difficult (Wallace 1970a; Rambo 1993). Conservationists spend little time, especially compared with opponents, on inculcating a conservation ethos and mythology. If this continues, conservation will slip. A conservation mythology will not arise or be internalized on its own – especially with children spending less and less time outside (Louv 2006).

Myth is constantly reinforced with ritual: codified collective action in which people publicly embrace a myth and related beliefs or knowledge (Rappaport 1999). Examples include ceremonial oath-taking, bearing witness, and certain aspects of public celebrations. Rituals may or may not be specified in myth itself. Public acceptance of myths by ritual binds people more strongly than private acceptance or mere words and provides peer-reinforcement. (Turner 1977; Kertzer 1988; Rappaport 1999). When people "keep together in time" through song, dance, or marching it binds them to the grand narrative and to each other (Kertzer 1988; McNeill 1995; Barker 2001; Lucero 2003; Smidchens 2014). It's difficult to think of any successful movement that is not rich in ritual, from the US civil rights and Vietnam anti-war movements, to Solidarity and pro-democracy movements such as the Estonian singing revolution. We need only think of the ability of song and music to stir emotion to recognize the deep basis of its role in social life generally, not just politics. Ritual has a very limited presence in conservation work but is essential if the movement is to build a committed political force that will take risks and resist repression.

Ritual can play a role in changing mythology as well, as when elites sought to replace delayed gratification as a positive value with endless shopping to fuel production after World War I (Sachs 2012). Shopping became a ritual that supported endless growth as a central human purpose; it generated personal pleasure and was reinforced by the actions of others. In Marcuse's (1964) now classic work on social control, he argues that elite control of others is much easier with pleasure than with denial of gratification; domination effected by indulging desire. Consumption also seems to assuage anxiety about human mortality (Solomon et al. 2004). Thus, after the Al Qaeda attacks on the US in 2001, US President George Bush encouraged Americans to carry on as usual: go shopping (Bacevich 2008). The well-organized material interests and cultural rationalizations behind the endless growth worldview are very powerful – and incompatible with a healthy natural world. For conservationists to move people toward embracing life will require a similar creative invention of ritual.

Propagation of a new myth is an enormous challenge, but there are striking opportunities. Although the cultural world is a very noisy place, slight shifts in myth and lower order stories seem possible – and certainly easier to achieve than a direct assault on the centers of power – but still present many obstacles. Old myths do not die just because they fail to explain what's going on, but it does make them vulnerable. Sometimes the keepers of myth, in an effort to keep them appealing, incorporate changes in interpretation or gloss, such as *Laudato Si*. The same Church at first ignored Darwin and then incorporated aspects of evolution, but in an earlier era it clung to the geocentric universe in the face of Galileo's challenge. Throughout much of the overdeveloped world the dominant religious myths have lost much of their hold, just as Marxism has in China. Since the early 1960s, starting with Rachel Carson's *Silent Spring* (1962), ecological reality has slowly undermined the faith in endless growth and technological cure-alls. Many hunger for something more than marketers can deliver – a deeper meaning and purpose than allegiance to this or that soft-drink or car (Sachs 2012).

The sacralization of lower order stories (fundamentalism) – embracing them as unchanging just as the sacred is unchanging – feeds the failure of a belief system to explain; cultural rigidity is usually maladaptive (Barnett 1953). If this failure is experienced as one more threat, in addition to material threats, resistance to change is often strengthened. Outdated stories feel like a refuge and not just to people in poor countries. Inequality can generate the same high need for certainty that childhood poverty does (Norris and Inglehart 2004). In the US, with relatively high inequality and a poor safety net, about 31 percent of the population adheres to a literalist Christianity (Gallup 2011). Self-reporting on religiosity (and textual literalism) is inversely related to income and educational level (Norris and Inglehart 2004; Gallup-International 2017). In countries across the Americas, Asia, and parts of Africa fundamentalist views have reasserted themselves; in India fundamentalist Hinduism has become politically powerful. In Iran, Saudi Arabia, and parts of Syria and Iraq they play powerful roles. In other countries such as Indonesia, they are less powerful, though overwhelmingly people are believers. One measure of fundamentalism is self-reporting on "how important religion is in people's lives." The US, at 53 percent in 2014, is closer to many poorer countries than to other developed countries (Pew Research Center 2015), though China is the least religious country in the world. In more religious countries conservation can be difficult if not dangerous; people may not be hostile to nature but feel challenged in their beliefs that god has given them dominion over the natural world if growth is excluded as a religion. Commercial interests, such as palm planters in Borneo and Sumatra, are a direct threat to biodiversity along with a rapidly growing population wanting agricultural land and that sees anything Western, from capital to conservation, as a threat (Dabelco 2009).

More specifically opportunities to influence myth change in three circumstances: in the contentious struggles that crises generate; as an element of intergenerational change; and in the day-in, day-out cultural conflicts over issues.

Let's start with crisis situations that sometimes result in replacement of old myths by new ones in a short time period, i.e. less than a human generation. Mostly change is slow. Conversion to Christianity in the Roman Empire was slow going until Constantine made it the official religion because he thought he owed the Christian god for helping him win a battle; even then the Roman church was still fighting to Christianize pagans and heathens centuries later. When old myths cannot explain a crisis or help navigate the disorder that has come to the world, people are left disoriented (Seeger and Sellnow 2016); new myths may be adopted if they offer better guidance or are imposed by conquerors. Many Native Americans reacted to conquest and massive death from disease by thinking their gods had failed them; they looked to more powerful gods – the conquerors' god (Wallace 1970a, 1970b; Rambo 1993). Their very identities were shaken. Conversion to a new myth usually involves many factors, not one big event such as a colonial invasion. Groups may resist imposition from outside and adopt a new myth fashioned from within, as was the case with the Seneca Iroquois and Handsome Lake's reweaving of tradition and a changed world (Wallace 1970b). Often a new mythology or religion may result in a marriage of sorts, with converts keeping elements of the old story and ritual in a new framework, just as Christian churches were built on top of Mayan and Aztec pyramids and local gods were incorporated into the Catholic pantheon. In addition to conquest, invasion, and overwhelming defeat in war and occupation are devastating epidemics, extended drought, and other catastrophes that cannot be explained. Einstein and Oppenheimer believed that the advent of nuclear weapons that could destroy civilization could only be understood with a new mythology or adapting existing myth; it was not simply a technological matter (Sachs 2012).

Climate change and looming resource limits in the context of the global economy rather than local economies have the likelihood of generating major crises that will require new understandings of how the world works and shake faith in traditional notions of progress, the ability of institutions to solve problems, and people's ability to make sense of the world. Resource wars and terrorism may not existentially threaten more powerful societies – though greater inequality within them might (Klare 2012) – but significant ongoing insecurity can erode confidence and commitment to the dominant story and the social order. Growth and exploitation of poorer countries has enabled elites in richer countries to maintain control by buying off other non-elite groups in their societies without diminishing elite wealth (Biel 2000; Tucker 2007). Countries such as China, which have broken out of subjugation and have themselves become subjugators, worry that if their growth engine falters the system's legitimacy could be undermined. The mythology of communism, replaced by "getting rich is glorious" more than a generation ago, is on life support. If the quality-of-life costs of growth become too high and growth slows what will take its place? In poorer societies a significant deterioration in standard of living and well-being can be expected and will likely be destabilizing as shrinkages in the span of control of economic and political centers occur. Regardless of the precise nature and consequences of crises, they invariably generate uncertainty and disorientation.

To ensure that crises are opportunities, conservationists will have to be ready with new stories in place and available to people. Propagating alternative stories prior to a crisis, as part of organizing and more broadly via film, music, and other mass means is essential groundwork. The biggest challenge for conservation is increasing its capacity for propagation. It's unlikely conservationists will have the means to saturate societies with their message, so careful targeting of the most important groups and of culture leaders is key. There is also a major material element to culture change in crisis: the development of alternative institutions that demonstrate that biodiversity-compatible livelihoods are possible and desirable. That can't be done initially at a large scale, but as some anti-colonial struggles have shown, starting place by place lends itself as a foundation for the large scale (Scott 1990). In the US mutual aid groups laid the foundation for ethnically integrated institutions (Skocpol et al. 2006).

Generational change lies at the cusp of incremental change and crises. Socialization and enculturation of each new generation is a mix of intentional efforts to inculcate beliefs by care-givers and institutions, "slippage" or poor transmission, and the different life experiences of the objects of inculcation. The more significant the background societal change, the more likely beliefs being passed on will not be accepted without a significant gloss or reinterpretation from the new generation. To the degree that beliefs are internalized and also in conflict with reality, there will exist internal tension that can generate denial or efforts to resolve the tension through change.

There are many types of societal change that can cause the failure to accept proffered knowledge and beliefs via enculturation and socialization. Perceived hypocrisy in the messenger (scandals involving cultural or political figures) or growing awareness of the failure of dominant institutions to deliver on their promises or representations (fair administration of justice; hard work results in success; equal access to education) undercut legitimacy. Technological changes resulting in ease of travel (cheap air fares) and communications (television, Internet) can, among other things, make people newly aware of alternative worldviews. Changes in production (automation) or energy sources can generate economic insecurity or require less consumption; solutions to problems create new ones (the Green Revolution included centralized control of seeds, the need for fertilizers and pesticides, and rapid growth in insect resistance). And the unexpected death or fall of authoritarian rulers (e.g. Tito, Hussein) can alter faith in the predictability of events and personal safety. Wars lend themselves not just to acute crises or to the hardships imposed on combatants (Grossman 2009), but have lasting multigenerational impacts as with the North American Indian wars, US Civil War, or British missteps in southwest Asia after World War I. Victories in anti-colonial struggles usually usher in a new dominant ideology, but this ideology may be at odds with elements of established worldviews used to mobilize people to fight the anti-colonial struggle (Fanon 1963; Geertz 1963). Such tensions, individual and societal, present opportunities for mobilization.

Events affecting a particular generation often have major unintended consequences. The US Central Intelligence Agency's experimentation with mind-altering drugs such as LSD was not intended to fuel a cultural revolution among college students, but it did. The Chinese Cultural Revolution did not cement the power of Maoists but ultimately led to a powerful rejection of their vision for the future and set China on the path of rapid economic development. At the same time this development, which half a century ago would have been regarded as approaching an economic miracle, is an ecological disaster with global consequences. Short of crises, Chinese road building at home and around the world, similar to post World War II road building in North America and the world, can make people ripe for mobilization.

Most changes in stories at all levels and the rules they embody are incremental. The substance of stories may change or different aspects may be emphasized or deemphasized. Institutions responsible for keeping stories gain and lose influence. Subgroups in societies wax and wane in their influence, which includes stories contending for influence across the entire culture (Hobsbawm 1984b). Class, ethnic and gender-based stories vie with each other to frame particular issues and broader questions about the social order and the human relationship with the rest of the world. Much of the "competition" is not the result of deliberate efforts to propagate stories and their meaning, but the result of diffusion. Stories don't just work to guide after all, but they appeal to pleasure and aesthetics. They warm and stimulate – or leave people bored and indifferent. Changes accumulate slowly, as with the demographic transition in Europe or urbanization in the eighteenth and nineteenth centuries. Cultural changes often express themselves in punctuated equilibrium – when a critical mass of people adopt them, it appears as if change was overnight, e.g. views on gay marriage in the developed countries which went from 35 percent approval in 2000 to 62 percent in 2017 (Pew Research Center 2017).

Day-to-day politics is mostly fought out in the cultural arena – usually not by trying to change stories so much as by using existing stories to gain support or opposition for particular policies. US churches took opposite sides on abolition, segregation and civil rights and sought to justify support for divergent politics based on the same mythology by stressing different aspects of scripture and relying on different lower order stories. The conservation movement is much conflicted over whether to anchor appeals in existing beliefs, mostly anthropocentric, or in new, ecocentric beliefs. The tension is real because existing beliefs probably will not support the major societal changes needed to reverse the extinction crisis and conversion to ecocentrism, if it ever happens, will take a long time. It is also true that once people are mobilized based on their existing beliefs, action can change beliefs (Cox 2006).

These cultural battles depend much on material resources – who owns or controls the media, how concentrated the media is, and so on, but much also depends on the quality of storytelling, the ability to connect with audiences, the calculus of taking action which is partly based on position in the social structure. Victories and losses in these struggles are incorporated into stories, changing them – delegitimizing aspects, reinforcing other aspects. Public health extended life for many, reduced infant mortality and in some places created more security while in other places it led to more material uncertainly due to rapid population growth; in the former case secular stories replaced religious ones; in the latter case fundamentalist approaches to religious myths were strengthened (Norris and Inglehart 2004; Floud et al. 2011).

Over recent decades concern with "the environment" has increased among many religions and secular mythologies. Human activity now threatens serious blow back and people expect moral as well as pragmatic guidance on how to deal with what are increasingly seen as major problems, just as changing weather was for early agriculturalists (Kirk 1970). Myth has always been important to the major task of ordering society and making sense of the world, especially death. Religious myths in particular have provided solace and a sense of certainty; secular myths are less good at that because they are recognized as human-created (Reynolds and Tanner 1995). Absent a strong sense of community (some go to church primarily to be part of a community) the weakening of religious myth has left people with a weaker sense of identity and freedom.

These three categories of story (and broader cultural) change are not so discrete as presented; they blend into each other. The point of drawing attention to differences in how change occurs is to better enable recognition of opportunities to influence change. In most all cases of seizing opportunities for change conservationists will have fewer resources than opponents – or those simply peddling a product (e.g. Tye 1998). Three advantages those who would safeguard biodiversity may enjoy are widely shared emotions such as biophilia – unfortunately a weak predisposition (Wilson 1984) – a good understanding of opportunities and a willingness to act on them, and a repertoire of compelling new stories and the means of dissemination.

Conservationists generally do a much poorer job of transmitting norms and behavior to the next generation than their opponents – perhaps out of respect for children's autonomy (Lakoff 1995). Those who lack such respect for children's autonomy are often quite effective at passing on belief systems that are not in the interests of the children or the natural world – but as Alice Miller (1983) says, are "for their own good." The socialization/enculturation process leaves large numbers of people with great difficulties forming personal and social bonds and bonds with the natural world because they are without access to their real feelings (e.g. Dinnerstein 1976; Miller 2007). In all but the simplest societies the sources of socialization and enculturation are not just reinforcing dominant institutions such as state, schools, commercial interests, and most religions, but also competing with subaltern groups such as critical NGOs, some schools, and so on. As children spend less and less time outside and with other species in spontaneous interaction they are more and more susceptible to human efforts to influence them and to human noise. In addition to propagating a conservation mythology and other stories, finding new ways to immerse children in the natural world will have to be tended to.

Efforts to understand and change or otherwise influence stories benefits from an understanding of neurobiology. Lakoff (1995), for example, has contributed much to understanding the salient features of stories internalized by different personality types in a society which can be very helpful in speaking to them. But story is not simply a cognitive phenomenon – it is profoundly emotional and need-based. Story lives in the body (Gebhard et al. 2003) and the many ways it is anchored there are not typically conscious, nor can they be easily made conscious. But emotions and needs powerfully shape the stories that resonate with individuals and groups, influencing those they adopt; emotions and needs also strongly influence openness to change and what type of change (Erikson 1968; Damasio 1993, 1994; Forgas 2001; Jost and Amodio 2012).

Conservation not only requires a new myth and better ways to utilize existing myths to safeguard biodiversity, but as a movement it fails to effectively utilize many of the tools of mobilization. Conservation has a limited narrative literature. It lacks the songs and music that were essential, for example, to the US civil rights movement – these songs "fortified and galvanized" participants, making them feel "safe and strong" in the face of official terror (*Freedom Summer* 2014); song was important to Solidarity in Poland, the "Singing Revolution" in Estonia, and the anti-Vietnam War movement in the US. Some Creation Care groups, like the US civil rights movement, have religiously based hymns (McDuff 2010). Conservation produces some very moving wildlife documentaries (watched by the same 2–3 percent of the population) but has no broad-based presence in the cinema, one of the most powerful media for myth transmission (Moyers and Lucas 1999); there is no conservation *Star Wars* – a cosmic-scale morality tale not unlike the US Western of the 1950s. Better use is made of television and radio *in some countries* by groups such as the Population Media Center; using the methods developed and successfully employed by Miguel Sabido in the 1970s (Nariman 1993), has created several 1–2 year long soap operas, well-researched, with credible characters and settings that evoke involvement; at the center are characters struggling with serious problems of population, STDs, sexual violence, staying in school and they have changed behavior (Ryerson 2013; Wang and Singhal 2016). There has been discussion of using this tool to reduce China's ivory consumption and protect tigers in India but no wider use thus far. There is no conservation theater. No conservation *Riverdance*. There are precious few conservation traditions or holidays; they need to be invented to help create and reinforce identities in which biophilic behavior is encouraged and reinforced in institutions and individuals (Hobsbawm 1984a). Thanksgiving in the US is not a longstanding ritual created in the seventeenth century, but was invented in the mid-nineteenth century (Muir 2004). (There is debate about whether such "private" rituals, even if widely shared, reinforce only family or group solidarity or broader societal solidarity.) Public monuments and holidays can perform the same functions of establishing loyalty and identity and provide opportunities for celebrations and ritual (Hobsbawm 1984b; Etzioni 2004). It's not just a matter of inventing something new but using existing holidays, such as Columbus Day in the US; Native American protests of this holiday gathered momentum over time, gain support from churches, students and others (Polletta 2004); Chinese students used the funeral of a party reformer to call massive demonstrations against repression.

Such aspects of culture are only part of mobilization, of course. The arena of myth is not self-contained. Painstaking grassroots organizing and NGOs that those organized can become part of are essential.

When myth informs or structures the content of media – or constitutes their content – action is more likely to be generated. Action arises from organizing based on the deep feelings myth can evoke, its collective character, and its strong and clear moral message. The expression of myth in ritual and other collective performances such as demonstrations, sit-ins, and so on, taps into the power of "keeping together in time" (McNeill 1995). There also remains no substitute in sustaining mobilization for connection with those parts of the natural world that remain unbroken. They offer a vision for a different future than the course humans are on. They offer a glimpse of our real home. Action itself is a source of story change – it is the raw material of new stories about shared experience.

Much of the world is ready for a new story, if for various reasons. Consumption in the wealthier parts of the world has lost the ability to enthrall the large mass of people as it once did (Lane 2000). Fundamentalisms have been used to justify cultural rigidity which at best is maladaptive and at worst justifies sometimes violent clinging to the past. A grand narrative story is needed by conservation to mobilize and guide human behavior toward societies which embrace the natural world while satisfying the hunger for a meaningful purpose.

REFERENCES

Aronson, H. 1993. "Becoming an Environmental Activist." 21 *Journal of Political and Military Sociology* 63–80 (Summer).

Bacevich, Andrew. 2008. He Told Us to Go Shopping. Now the Bill Is Due. *Washington Post.* www.washingtonpost.com/wp-dyn/content/article/2008/10/03/AR2008100301977.html (accessed February 4, 2017).

Barker, Colin. 2001. Fear, Laughter, and Collective Power: The Making of Solidarity at the Lenin Shipyard in Gdansk, Poland, August 1980. Pp. 175–94 in Jeff Goodwin, James M. Jasper, and Francesca Polletta (eds.). *Passionate Politics.* University of Chicago Press. Chicago, IL.

Barlow, Connie. 1997. *Green Space, Green Time.* Copernicus. New York.

Barnett, Homer. 1953. *Innovation, the Basis of Cultural Change.* McGraw-Hill. New York.

Bennett, W. Lance. 1980. Myth, Ritual and Political Control. 30 *Journal of Communications* 4: 166–79 (Autumn).

Berthrong. John. 2006. Motifs for a New Confucian Ecological Vision. Pp. 236–58 in Roger S. Gottlieb (ed.). *Oxford Handbook of Religion and Ecology.* Oxford University Press. New York.

Biel, Robert. 2000. *The New Imperialism.* Zed Books. London.

Butler, Tom (ed.). 2015. *Overdevelopment, Overpopulation, Overshoot.* Goff Books. San Francisco.

Cox, Robert. 2006. *Environmental Communication and the Public Sphere.* Sage. Thousand Oaks, CA.

Dabelco, Geoffrey. 2009. Environment and Energy. Pp. 65–82 in Neyla Arnas (ed.). *Fighting Chance*. National Defense University Press/Potomac Books. Washington DC.

Damasio, Antonio. 1993. *Looking for Spinoza*. Harcourt. New York.

Damasio, Antonio. 1994. *Descartes Error*. Grosset/Putnam. New York.

Dinnerstein, Dorothy. 1976. *The Mermaid and the Minotaur*. Harper and Row. New York.

Dwivedi, O. P. 2006. Hindu Religion and Environmental Well-Being. Pp. 160–83 in Roger S. Gottlieb (ed.). *Oxford Handbook of Religion and Ecology*. Oxford University Press. New York.

Erikson, Erik H. 1968. *Identity, Youth and Crisis*. Norton. New York.

Etzioni, Amitai. 2004. Holidays and Rituals. Pp. 3–40 in Amitai Etzioni and Jared Bloom (eds.). *We Are What We Celebrate*. New York University Press. New York.

Fanon, Frantz. 1963. *The Wretched of the Earth*. Grove Press. New York.

Floud, Roderick, Robert W. Fogel, Bernard Harris, and Sok Chul Hong. 2011. *The Changing Body*. Cambridge University Press. Cambridge.

Foltz, Richard C. 2006. Islam. Pp. 207–19 in Roger S. Gottlieb (ed.). *Oxford Handbook of Religion and Ecology*. Oxford University Press. New York.

Forgas, Joseph P. (ed.). 2001. *Feeling and Thinking*. Cambridge University Press. Cambridge.

Francis, Pope. 2014. *Laudato Si*. www.ewtn.com/library/encyc/f1LaudatoSi.pdf (accessed January 27, 2017).

Freedom Summer. 2014. Firelight Films/WGBH. Boston, MA.

Gallup (Jeffrey Jones). 2011. *In US 3 in 10 Say They Take the Bible Literally*. www.news.Gallup.com/poll/148427/Say-Bible-Literally.aspx. (July 8, 2011) (accessed January 25, 2018).

Gallup International. 2017. *Religion Prevails in the World*. www.gallup-international .bg/en/Publications/2017/373-Religion-prevails-in-the-world (accessed January 25, 2018)

Gebhard, Ulrich, Patricia Nevers, and Elfriede Billmann-Mahecha. 2003. Moralizing Trees: Anthropomorphism and Identity in Children's Relationships to Native. Pp. 91–111 in Susan Clayton and Susan Opotow (eds.). *Identity and the Natural Environment*. MIT Press. Cambridge, MA.

Geertz, Clifford (ed.). 1963. *Old Societies and New States*. Free Press. New York.

Grossman, David. 2009. *On Killing*. 2nd edn. Little, Brown. New York.

Hobsbawm, Eric. 1984a. Introduction: Inventing Traditions. Pp. 1–14 in Eric Hobsbawm and Terence Ranger (eds.). *The Invention of Tradition*. Cambridge University Press. Cambridge.

Hobsbawm, Eric. 1984b. Mass Producing Traditions: Europe, 1870–1914. Pp. 263–307 in Eric Hobsbawm and Terence Ranger (eds.). *The Invention of Tradition*. Cambridge University Press. Cambridge.

Jost, John T. and David M. Amodio. 2012. Political Ideology as Motivated Social Cognition: Behavioral and Neuroscientific Evidence. 36 *Motive and Emotion* 1: 55–64 (March).

Kaza, Stephanie. 2006. The Greening of Buddhism: Promise and Perils. Pp. 184–206 in Roger S. Gottlieb (ed.). *Oxford Handbook of Religion and Ecology*. Oxford University Press. New York.

Keleman, Deborah. 1999. Beliefs about Purpose: On the Origins of Teleological Thought. Pp. 278–94 in Michael C. Corballis and Stephen E. G. Lea (eds.). *The Descent of Mind*. Oxford University Press. Oxford.

Kertzer, David I. 1988. *Ritual, Politics and Power*. Yale University Press. New Haven, CT.

Kirk, G. S. 1970. *Myth, Its Meaning and Functions in Ancient and Other Cultures*. University of California Press. Berkeley, CA.

Klare, Michael T. 2012. *The Race for What's Left*. Metropolitan Books. New York.

Kruger. Frederick. 2002. *A Nature Trail through the Bible*. The Religious Campaign for Forest Conservation. Santa Rosa, CA.

Lakoff, George. 1995. *Moral Politics*. University of Chicago Press. Chicago, IL.

Lane, Robert E. 2000. *Loss of Happiness in the Market Democracies*. Yale University Press. New Haven, CT.

Louv, Richard. 2006. *Last Child in the Woods*. Algonquin Books. Chapel Hill, NC.

Lucero, Lisa J. 2003. The Politics of Ritual. 44 *Current Anthropology* 4: 523–58 (August).

Marcuse, Herbert. 1964. *One Dimensional Man*. Beacon Press. Boston, MA.

McDuff, Mallory. 2010. *Natural Saints*. Oxford University Press. New York.

McNeill, William H. 1995. *Keeping Together in Time*. Harvard University Press. Cambridge, MA.

Miller, Alice. 1983. *For Your Own Good*. Farrar, Strauss & Giroux. New York.

Miller, Alice. 2007. *The Drama of the Gifted Child*. 3rd edn. Basic Books. New York.

Moyer, Bill. 1999. *Free Speech for Sale*. Public Affairs TV/PBS. New York.

Moyer, Bill and George Lucas. 1999. *The Mythology of Star Wars*. http://billmoyers.com/content/mythology-of-star-wars-george-lucas/ (accessed February 1, 2017).

Muir, Diana. 2004. Proclaiming Thanksgiving throughout the Land. Pp. 194–212 in Amitai Etzioni and Jared Bloom (eds.). *We Are What We Celebrate*. New York University Press. New York.

Muir, John. 1916. A Thousand Mile Walk to the Gulf. Pp. 231–416 in *The Story of My Boyhood and Youth*. Houghton-Mifflin. Boston, MA.

Nariman, Heidi Noel. 1993. *Soap Operas for Social Change*. Praeger. Westport, CT.

Norris, Pippa and Ronald Inglehart. 2004. *Sacred and Secular*. Cambridge University Press. Cambridge.

Pew Research Center (Angelina E. Theodorou). 2015. Americans Are in the Middle of the Pack Globally When it Comes to Importance of Religion. www.pewresearch.org/fact-tank/2015/12/23/americans-are-in-the-middle-of-the-pack-globally-when-it-comes-to-importance-of-religion. (December 23, 2015) (accessed January 25, 2018).

Pew Research Center. 2017. Public Opinion on Same-sex Marriage. www.pewforum.org/fact-sheet/changing-attitudes-on-gay-marriage/ (June 26, 2017) (accessed January 25, 2018).

Polletta, Francesca. 2004. Can You Celebrate Dissent? Pp. 151–77 in Amitai Etzioni and Jared Bloom (eds.). *We Are What We Celebrate*. New York University Press. New York.

Polletta, Francesca. 2006. *It Was Like a Fever*. University of Chicago Press. Chicago, IL.

Rambo, Lewis R. 1993. *Understanding Religious Conversion*. Yale University Press. New Haven, CT.

Rappaport, Roy A. 1999. *Ritual and Religion in the Making of Humanity*. Cambridge University Press. Cambridge.

Reynolds, Vernon and Ralph Tanner. 1995. *The Social Ecology of Religion*. (2nd edn of *The Biology of Religion* 1983.) Oxford University Press. New York.

Ryerson, William N. 2013. *The Effectiveness of Entertainment Mass Media in Changing Behavior*. Population Media Center. Shelburne, VT.

Sachs, Jonah. 2012. *Winning the Story Wars*. Harvard Business Review Press. Boston, MA.

Scott, James C. 1990. *Domination and the Arts of Resistance*. Yale University Press. New Haven, CT.

Seeger, Matthew W. and Timothy L. Sellnow. 2016. *Narratives of Crisis*. Stanford Business Books. Stanford, CA.

Shapiro, Judith. 2001. *Mao's War on Nature*. Cambridge University Press. Cambridge.

Skocpol, Theda, Ariane Liazos, and Marshall Ganz. 2006. *What a Mighty Power We Can Be*. Princeton University Press. Princeton, NJ.

Smidchens, Guntis. 2014. *The Power of Song*. University of Washington Press. Seattle.

Solomon, Sheldon, Jeffrey L. Greenberg, and Thomas A. Pyszczynski. 2004. Lethal Consumption: Death-Denying Materialism. Pp. 127–46 in Tim Kasser and Allen D. Kanner (eds.). *Psychology and Consumer Culture*. American Psychological Association. Washington DC.

Taylor, Bron, Gretel Van Wieren, and Bernard Daley Zaleha. 2016. Lynn White Jr. and the Greening-of-Religion Hypothesis. 30 *Conservation Biology* 5: 1000–9 (October).

Tucker, Richard P. 2007. *Insatiable Appetite*. Concise rev. edn. Rowman & Littlefield. Lanham, MD.

Turner, Victor. 1977. Variations on a Theme of Liminality. Pp. 36–52 in Sally Falk Moore and Barbara G. Myerhoff (eds.). *Secular Ritual*. Van Gorcum. Assen.

Tye, Larry. 1998. *The Master of Spin*. Crown. New York.

Wallace, Anthony F. C. 1970a. *Culture and Personality*. 2nd edn. Random House. New York.

Wallace, Anthony F. C. 1970b. *Death and Rebirth of the Seneca*. Knopf. New York.

Wang, Hua and Arvind Singhal. 2016. East Los High: Transmedia Edutainment to Promote the Sexual and Reproductive Health of Young Latina/o Americans. 106 *American Journal of Public Health* 6: 1002–10.

Wilson, Edward O. 1984. *Biophilia*. Harvard University Press. Cambridge, MA.

Wilson, Edward O. 2006. *The Creation*. Norton. New York.

15 Conservation's Moral Imperative: The Human Obligation to the Wild

> Putting the needs of one species (humans) above those of all other species combined, as exemplified by the sustainable development theme, is one of the most pernicious trends in modern conservation.
>
> Reed Noss 1992: 13

For millennia an ethos of control and conquest of the non-human world has dominated human societies and accompanied pervasive efforts to remake the world in the image of humans. But not everyone lost their way. In the last century or more the many threads from different cultures that have embraced life and spontaneity, rejected control, and resisted inertia have become entwined. That these threads bear striking similarities is not due to an undiscovered correspondence between Lao Tzu and Ovid. Nor is there evidence that Harold Searles, the twentieth-century US psychiatrist who influenced Paul Shepard ever read Ovid, though he easily might have if his education included the classics. Instead these threads arise from the experience of hearts grounded in the Earth and not limited to the narrowness of the human world. The real connective tissue for the moralities that value the natural world rather than just our own kind or our kind's gods or sovereigns is not bibliography. It is the felt experience of sharing the world with other life; experience of the wild within and without, an experience the modern world makes more and more difficult to find in any form, let alone with great and life-changing intensity. Such grounding can result from emotional traditions, but it emerges afresh from the potential in each human to be touched by the natural world.

Today many North American conservationists can quote not only Thoreau and Muir but those from other cultures and from the distant past. Many religious scholars are seeking to recover a central role for caring about the natural world in their traditions and texts, notwithstanding what seem very long periods of dormancy.

A feature of these nature-grounded moralities is their warning about hubris and alienation from the Earth and the danger they present to life. For Searles (1960), we are inoculated against our alienation by recognizing that all life is made of the same stuff and suffers the same fate. For John Muir (1916) it was the recognition that the world was not made for us – if it was, why would there be mosquitoes and alligators; this was affirmed for him by immersion in self-willed places and experiencing "the forces of nature." As growing human numbers and human insatiability push other species to the edge, wilderness (self-willed land or the place of self-willed animals [Vest 1985]) is harder to find, and keeping places wild and rewilding are contentious issues. For many conservationists putting large, mostly intact areas into strictly protected areas is most likely to ensure the long-term health of the land and non-human species (Foreman 2004). Wild places are absolutely necessary to protect the world – and humanity – from the consequences of typically short-sighted human behavior. Not that humans can't injure such places or creatures from afar; edge effects and climate change demonstrate otherwise. But without wild places it would be open season on the Earth.

Strictly protected wild places are also contentious because economic opponents have helped to nurture critics who claim that either such places do not exist because the Earth is nowhere pristine (see Wuerthner et al. 2014); or that conservation needs to first and foremost consider equity among humans in all its actions, never mind equity among all species. It is OK for people to come to a place and make their homes by taking the homes of other species by converting or destroying them, even driving others to local extirpation. To defend other species' homes or seek to recover them, however, sparks outrage as a violation of human rights or property rights.

The fight over safeguarding wild places and biodiversity is about containing human behavior – behavior that affects not just human material circumstances but the flesh and blood of millions of other species and the communities their interactions generate. It is about which species and individuals will live and survive and which will be extinguished from the Earth, sometimes forever. It is a deeply moral fight about what is considered good and valuable and right and just by the single species whose killing power outweighs that of other species.

Appeals to human self-interest – that we need the wild or it has monetary value for medicines undiscovered, clean water, or recreation – have a role in reaching many people. But there is a cost. Such appeals often reinforce the very aspects of human personalities and institutions that are only capable of calculation and self-aggrandizement (Kasser and Crompton 2011; Bolderdijk et al. 2013). The use of economic terminology and metaphor – other species and ecosystems as natural capital, as natural assets, as ecosystem services, and even ecological debt – reduces the world to the value it has to a particular economic system of one species (Coffee 2016; Johns and DellaSala 2017). It is not simply reductionist but ignores that much of the natural world may never have any economic value, or enough value to generate action or cause humans to refrain from plundering a place or its species. It also reflects a morality anchored in emotional poverty. When people feel poor they must have more and more, as Thoreau observed in *Walden* (a person is wealthy in proportion to what they can leave alone [1964 {1854}: 335]). Stomachs are full but souls are hollow.

Though a very strong if partial case can be made that the societal machinery that converts so much of the world into commodities for one species – and disproportionately for a few millions at the very top of social hierarchies – is maladaptive and unhealthy for humans, it has not persuaded enough people to organize effectively enough to seriously challenge the destruction of the non-human world. Human vision is clouded because consumption operates like a drug – we feel good in the present consuming more and more, even though it's a poor substitute for connection with the wild and other losses, and we don't think about tomorrow (Dinnerstein 1976; Solomon et al. 2004). Appeals to self -interest alone can't break through such a dense fog. But appeals to justice can *and have* (Goodwin et al. 2001; Araiza 2014).

Securing biodiversity and wildlands depends on bringing about major changes in human behavior: institutional and systemic, individual and intermediate between them. Great changes in institutional and individual behavior have always been the result of action based on moral outrage at the transgression of justice and the abrogation of responsibility. It is not narrow self-interest that causes a critical mass of people to take risks to set things right, often on behalf of others they do not know. Although the golden rule is certainly at work (not the one about those with the gold making the rules, but the other one), action for justice against great odds is about self-transcendence. About being part of a bigger good that is felt personally but is not just about the personal. Such belonging is a deeply felt need, unmet in most people. Change is also motivated by a deep emotional bond forged in empathy and expressed in a powerful myth conservationists have yet to create: all life is made of the same stuff and suffers the same fate (Searles 1960) and caring for it is the highest calling.

Although the struggle over the future of wilderness and biodiversity depends in the largest part on mobilizing material resources, mobilizing those resources depends on motivating people's morality and sense of justice; they become material forces when adopted by people. The world is divided between a generous vision that embraces all life and a narrow one in which only humans or some humans count. The outcome will partly depend on events outside of human control such as drought (which will be exacerbated in some places as a result of climate change) and on the unintended consequences of human action; it will depend on which side is taken by those with the political-economic leverage. But it mostly will depend on who can be mobilized into the more effective political force based on a moral vision (Liu 2015).

It is unlikely that most humans will embrace bio- or ecocentrism. The biophilic flame in the human heart seems perpetually about to be extinguished like a candle wick by a pool of melted wax. It barely keeps from being smothered. *But short of bio centrism people might come to feel an obligation to live as if they were biocentric* – to avoid inflicting harm because it is the right thing to do. Behavior is guided in part by ritual – by public acceptance and commitment to a belief system (Kertzer 1988; Rappaport 1999); it becomes part of the social glue.

James Lovelock (1979: 145) wrote years ago that "[A]ll attempts to rationalize a subjugated biosphere with man in charge are as doomed to failure as the similar concept of benevolent colonialism." Colonialism and non-colonial imperial domination were of course about exploitation, almost invariably imposed by extreme violence (Fanon 1963). Colonialism was once considered quite natural, part of the civilizing mission of "advanced" countries. Human slavery was also considered natural. Views have changed, however. That humans are part of Nature does not and cannot, in a post-colonial view, justify humans' ever-growing footprint. Rationalizing Nature's colonization does not hide the ugly realities. Remaking the Earth in the human image is violent: forests and grasslands are transformed into tree farms, pasture, subdivisions, and endless corn and soybean fields or rice paddies. Inconvenient species are persecuted or destroyed en masse. Ecosystems are altered for the benefit of one species, and the biological community as a whole is discounted. Colonization diminishes the capacity of lands and waters to support diversity, replacing many species with a few or a diverse ecosystem with a monoculture. Colonization means human numbers grow and their consumption increases at the expense of other species' numbers, range, diversity, and even existence. The tiger is caged or dead and the oxen bred to plod endlessly before the plow. The beneficence of colonialism is a fantasy in the minds of the colonizers. It is certainly among the biggest feelgood lies perpetrated in the entire long and sordid history of politics, and human affairs more generally.

Colonialism, like slavery, is doomed because it rests on a flawed morality and understanding of how the world works. It morally cripples the colonial masters by alienating them from the world they depend on and requires they rationalize the relationships that produce that alienation as right and just. Humans need to feel they are just but it is a constant battle to believe exploitation is just, even when socially reinforced. Empathy must be repressed which generates inner conflict (Shepard 1982). Control and love are mutually exclusive, leaving emotions truncated. Colonial relationships – relationships of control and exploitation – also require those on top to chronically misread and distort reality, to oversimplify and mechanize their understanding of the world (Scott 1998).

Dismantling colonial relationships usually has required violence because of the resistance of those who want to perpetuate it. Despite popular belief that India's decolonization was achieved without violence, that was not the case (Heehs 1993).

Lovelock is not alone in disparaging colonialism and its boosters (Rodman 1977; Ehrenfeld 1978; Wuerthner et al. 2014). Brand's (1968) infamous statement, stolen from a British MP (Leach, 1968) without attribution, that we are "godlike" and should get good at it, and Marris's (2011) view that we can be competent gardeners – never mind that the Earth is not a garden – are just more examples of the same hubris that generates extinction, ocean dead zones, dust bowls, desertification and depleted soils, superfund sites, climate chaos, and nuclear power plants built in tsunami zones. We are about as godlike as a *drunken* bull in a china shop (Wright 2004).

Even in human terms the colonial worldview of nature is maladaptive. The dominant morality that human societies can do with the world what they please is deeply embedded in the structure of societies and is not just a matter of limited wisdom. Organized around endless growth, like a pyramid scheme, the natural world is turned into human artifacts at an ever increasing rate, thanks to an energy bubble: the human capacity to alter the Earth is magnified by the caloric subsidies currently at their disposal. The few thousands of decision makers at the head of government and business institutions are heavily invested in the current order and generally resist changes that could undermine their positions of power; so, halting the injury inflicted on others is off the table (Dye 2013). Their awareness is also constrained by the insulation that technology and hierarchy provide from the consequences of their actions (Harris 1977; Jackson 1987; Johnson and Earle 2000). Problem identification, formulation, and the range of acceptable solutions are heavily shaped by their hands (Lindblom 1977; Guber and Bosso 2007; Layzer 2007). They also control the machinery of repression: laws, police, armies, prisons (e.g. Klare 2002; Singer 2007).

Moving beyond the impasse over safeguarding wild places and biodiversity lies in recognizing what the wild has to teach humans about connection and what humans owe the Earth and the other humans they share the world with. Many, however, do not recognize this.

Many progressive critics argue that capitalism is *the* problem, causing all environmental harm. They are correct that capitalism is the most productive form of social organization in human history and therefore simultaneously the most destructive of life on Earth because of its capacity to transform everything into commodities (Kovel 2002; Environment-Ecology 2016; International Ecosocialist Conference 2016). Included in this criticism are capitalism's many variations from state capitalism and state socialism to "free-market" military dictatorships. The destructive attributes they describe, however, are not restricted capitalism, but are attributes of all civilized societies (e.g. Johnson and Earle 2000; Wright 2004). Hierarchy, unequal division of labor, patriarchy, alienation, plant and animal domestication, deforestation, depletion of soil, armies, prisons, certain infectious diseases, extinction, wholesale destruction of wildlife, and large-scale war are all attributes of civilization generally, though capitalism is certainly the most unrestrained in converting living systems into "resources" for humans – or some humans.

Capitalism is only the most recent form of "the problem" (Harris 1977; Chew 2001; Essl et al. 2011; Lenzen et al. 2012).

One proposed progressive solution to capitalist destructiveness is to replace it with ecosocialism, a system in which people will not be driven to destroy nature and meeting human needs will replace the drive to constantly accumulate profits (e.g. Kovel 2002; Johns 2003b). Hierarchy will fade. Putting aside what would likely be a long and non-linear struggle, it's unclear exactly how ecosocialism will stem biodiversity loss. There are many progressive critics of the status quo – bioregionalism, green economics, deep ecology, social ecology – but the focus here on ecosocialism is due to its effort comprehensively to reduce the "ecological crisis" to a form of social organization that cannot, by itself, explain that crisis, nor if abolished, solve that crisis.

Despite the comprehensive approach, ecosocialism leaves much unclear and even mysterious (Johns 2003a). How will meeting the "human needs" of 7–10 billion people reduce the pressure on the Earth's biodiversity and ecosystems? There is no discussion of the relationship of "scarcity" to democracy – the end of scarcity being the basis for the "realm of freedom" on which equality is supposed to rest – or how humanity will transcend scarcity without continued acceleration of biodiversity loss. Humans already take, use, or destroy 40 percent of terrestrial net primary product. There is no discussion of human population reduction, only the intimation that on the whole humans will consume less under ecosocialism, except for the poor. Nothing about shrinking the human footprint, though the limits of the Earth are recognized by the 3rd Ecosocialist Manifesto (International Ecosocialist Conference 2016) and implied in the initial manifesto (Kovel and Löwy 2002).

It's also unclear how ecosocialism will address the problems of hierarchy, which long pre-dates capitalism. With some few exceptions humans haven't lived in egalitarian societies since agriculture emerged (Boehm 1999; Johnson and Earle 2000; Flannery and Marcus 2017). The 99 percent have never been successful at ridding themselves of the 1 percent since the 1 percent came into being. The best the majority have been able to do is trade in on a new 1 percent. Can 7.5 billion people even be organized without hierarchy given the complexity of the society necessary to support such huge numbers? It appears the 1 percent will disappear by definition, much as the state was supposed to wither for Lenin. Or perhaps hierarchy not in the service of profit is not real hierarchy (Kovel 2002)? And should ecosocialists successfully usher in something like popular democracy on a mass scale, it appears to be only for humans. Equity is also only for humans, as is access to "decent and autonomous living conditions" (International Ecosocialist Conference 2016: Declaration 5). How are the interests of non-humans to be represented and enforced? There are no criteria for resolving conflicts between human demands and the needs of other species.

"Habitat" is used once in the First Ecosocialist Manifesto. "Biodiversity" is mentioned once in the Third Ecosocialist Manifesto. "Conservation" is not used in either, nor is "wild" or "wilderness," i.e. self-willed lands. "Ecological," used thirteen and five times respectively, usually modifies terms such as crisis, harmony, costs, production, framework, and destabilization, but never *integrity*. The concerns of conservation are reduced to one *human* interest among many. Kovel (2002) grants intrinsic value to nature but in light of the foregoing and the human "need to garden" and engage nature by transforming it through "production," it's not clear what that means. It does not explicitly challenge the human propensity to destroy what they can never create.

I critically discuss ecosocialism not because it is a powerful force – quite the opposite – but because it genuinely attempts to offer a solution to environmental problems, while most do not even bother and are content to apologize for things as they are (Kareiva and Marvier 2007) or to treat symptoms within the existing societal framework (most NGOs and many natural scientists).

One can endlessly debate whether animals or ecosystems have rights – it gets complicated legally and philosophically. It is easier and more direct to say *humans do not have a right* to destroy biodiversity and wildlands. They do not have a right to break the laws of community as described in the novel *Ishmael* (Quinn 1992): humans belong to the world (not the other way around), take only what is needed, and do not destroy others or their food. We have an obligation to care, to do justice. Sometimes we do. We have set aside tens of millions of acres in protected areas. But that does not mean we have done enough or have carte blanche to behave as colonial masters over the rest. As cultural animals humans are behaviorally flexible, able to limit reproduction and consumption.

To merely stop thinking in terms of the wilderness/civilization dichotomy cannot heal the material separation resulting from our day-to-day efforts at domination. To say a change of perspective in and of itself alters the violent reality is at best thin pretense. It obscures reality. And it obscures human alienation: living in our heads and regarding our ideas as something more precious than actual living creatures. Our frontal lobes are thin gruel and cannot substitute for deep emotional connections (Ehrenfeld 1978; Damasio 1994, 1999; Forgas 2000; Pinard 2011).

The rationalizations for human dominion are no different than the doctrines of discovery and conquest: a legalistic version of *might makes right*. Such rationalizations are feeble attempts to obscure the death warrants of large, intact areas and of the species dependent on them. If humans have not solved the problem of poverty in their long history of commandeering so much of the Earth, they are obviously on the wrong track. To try to solve human intra-species problems on the backs of other species is no different than one country transferring wealth from another to buy some domestic peace, e.g. imperial Britain's reshaping of the Indian economy to serve British rather than Indian interests. The examples are endless (Rodman 1977; Chase-Dunn and Hall 1997; Chase-Dunn and Anderson 2005; Goudie 2013; Smil 2013).

Wilderness and biodiversity stand as the antidote to the machinery of control. Absent them humans are left with the experience of their own hierarchies as the only model of order in the world (Shepard 1982). Alienation wins by default because devaluing and distancing from what is conquered and exploited is a psychological necessity (Fromm 1964; Grossman 2009) and leaves us afraid; our species makes bad decisions because we only see a narrow range of choices. The ability to love depends on connection, yet connections are frayed, if not completely destroyed, in colonial situations. In separating from the world by trying to control it humans have created a hunger that things can never fill, though we keep trying. We are wounded in our souls and our capacity for empathy and love diminished (Dinnerstein 1976). "This is what is the matter with us," D. H. Lawrence wrote (1968 [1930]: 504), "we are bleeding at the roots, because we are cut off from the earth and sun and stars, and love is a grinning mockery, because, poor blossom, we plucked it from its stem on the tree of life, and expected it to keep on blooming in our civilized vase on the table."

This is the great sacrifice humanity has made and it need not be. If destruction feeds on itself, so does healing (Maniates and Meyer 2010). Keeping large parts of the Earth free from colonization and restoring much of what we have lost to colonization is not a sacrifice. Our estrangement from the world is the great unmentioned and invisible sacrifice we are making. It is unnecessary. Humans can recover their wholeness.

It is not the advocates of placing some lands and waters off limits to human exploitation who have separated humans from the rest of the world. Agriculture and civilization did that (Searles 1960; Harris 1977; Shepard 1982; Berman 1989; Lancy 2008). Orwellian terms such as "interdependence" cannot mask that reality.

In the end it all does come back on humanity, though not in some immediate and simple sense found in fairy-tales. What we do to others we do to ourselves. What we do to nature out there, we do to nature in us.

Having initiated the divorce – it was not bears or birds or rivers – we are belatedly realizing how high the price is. In seeking to conquer the natural world, our societies have set themselves at odds with other life just as the slave-master did with the slave and the colonizer with the colonized (Fanon 1963; Jordan 1968).

Marginalizing wilderness and biodiversity protection negates the best insurance we have against our immaturity. Gardening can neither replace wilderness nor heal the self-inflicted wound of estrangement, any more than turning to an opium-laced nineteenth-century patent medicine to heal a life-threatening disease.

A moral vision cannot, on its own, safeguard and recover biodiversity and wildlands. As has been argued throughout, only grassroots organizing and resulting mass mobilization have been able to counter the powerful and change the dominant order of things – bringing down apartheid and segregation, winning women's rights and labor rights. Only such mobilization can halt and dismantle human domination of life on Earth. The motivation for such mobilization lies in empathy for and feelings of connection with other life.

REFERENCES

Araiza, Lauren. 2014. *To March for Others*. Pennsylvania State University Press. Philadelphia.

Berman, Morris. 1989. *Coming to Our Senses*. Simon and Schuster. New York.

Boehm, Christopher. 1999. *Hierarchy in the Forest*. Harvard University Press. Cambridge, MA.

Bolderdijk, J. W., L. Steg, E. S. Geller, P. K. Lehman and T. Postmes. 2013. Comparing the Effectiveness of Monetary versus Moral Motives in Environmental Campaigning. 3 *Nature Climate Change* 413–16.

Brand, Stewart. 1968. *Whole Earth Catalog* (Fall).

Chase-Dunn, Christopher and E. N. Anderson (eds.). 2005. *The Historical Evolution of World Systems*. Palgrave Macmillan. New York.

Chase-Dunn, Christopher and Thomas D. Hall. 1997. *Rise and Demise*. Westview Press. Boulder, CO.

Chew, Sing C. 2001. *World Ecological Degradation*. Alta Mira Press. Walnut Creek, CA.

Coffee, Brian. 2016. Unpacking the Politics of Natural Capital and Economic Metaphors in Environmental Policy Discourse. 25 *Environmental Politics* 2: 203–22.

Damasio, Antonio. 1994. *Descartes' Error*. 1994. Grosset/Dunlap. New York.

Damasio, Antonio. 1999. *The Feeling of What Happens*. Harcourt, Brace & Co. New York.

Dinnerstein, Dorothy. 1976. *The Mermaid and the Minotaur*. Harper & Row. New York.

Dye, Thomas A. 2013. *Who's Running America?* 8th edn. Paradigm. Boulder, CO.

Ehrenfeld, David. 1978. *The Arrogance of Humanism*. Oxford University Press. New York.

Essl, Franz, Marten Winter, and Petr Pyšek. 2011. Trade Threat Could Even Be More Dire. 487 *Nature* 39 (July 5).

Fanon, Franz. 1963. *The Wretched of the Earth*. Grove Press. New York.

Flannery, Kent and Joyce Marcus. 2017. *The Creation of Inequality*. Harvard University Press. Cambridge, MA.

Foreman, Dave. 2004. *Rewilding North America*. Island Press. Washington DC.

Forgas, Joseph P. 2000. Feeling and Thinking Summary and Integration. Pp. 387–406 in Joseph P. Forgas, (ed.). *Feeling and Thinking*. Cambridge University Press. Cambridge.

Fromm, Erich. 1964. *The Heart of Man*. Harper and Row. New York.

Goodwin, Jeff, James M. Jasper, and Francesca Polletta (eds.). 2001. *Passionate Politics*. University of Chicago Press. Chicago, IL.

Goudie, Andrew. 2013. *The Human Impact on the Natural Environment*. 7th edn. Wiley-Blackwell. Chichester.

Grossman, David. 2009. *On Killing*. 2nd edn. Little, Brown. New York.

Guber, Deborah Lynn and Christopher J. Bosso. 2007. Framing ANWR. Pp. 35–59 in Michael E. Kraft and Sheldon Kamieniecki (eds.). *Business and Environmental Policy*. MIT Press. Cambridge, MA.

Harris, Marvin. 1977. *Cannibals and Kings*. Random House. New York.

Heehs, Peter. 1993. Terrorism in India during the Freedom Struggle. 55 *The Historian* 3: 469–82 (Spring).

International Ecosocialist Conference, Third. 2016. Final Manifesto. http://alterecosoc.org/wp-content/uploads/2016/10/manifiesto-inglesez.pdf. (accessed January 19, 2017).

Jackson, Wes. 1987. *Altars of Unhewn Stone*. North Point Press. San Francisco.

Johns, David. 2003a. Has Eco-socialism Passed on the Tough Questions? 14 *Capitalism Nature Socialism* 2: 120–3.

Johns, David. 2003b. Review of Joel Kovel, The Enemy of Nature: The End of Capitalism or the End of the World. 25 *New Political Science* 1: 134–8.

Johns, David and Dominick DellaSala. 2017. Caring, Killing, Euphemism and George Orwell: How Language Choice Undercuts Our Mission. 211 *Biological Conservation* 174–6 (July).

Johnson, Allen W. and Timothy Earle 2000. *The Evolution of Human Society*. 2nd edn. Stanford University Press. Stanford, CA.

Jordan, Winthrop. 1968. *White over Black*. University of North Carolina Press. Chapel Hill.

Kareiva, Peter and Michelle Marvier. 2007. Conservation for the People. 297 *Scientific American* 4: 50–7 (October).

Kareiva, Peter, Robert Lalasz, and Michelle Marvier. 2011. Conservation in the Anthropocene: Beyond Solitude and Fragility. *Breakthrough Journal* 2: 29–37 (Fall).

Kasser, Tim and Tom Crompton. 2011. Limitations of Environmental Campaigning Based on Values for Money, Image, and Status. www.valuesandframes .org/resources/CCF_briefing_limitations_of_environmental_campaigning.pdf (accessed November 18, 2014).

Kertzer, David I. 1988. *Ritual, Politics and Power*. Yale University Press. New Haven, CT.

Klare, Michael. 2002. *Resource Wars*. Metropolitan/Owl Books. New York.

Kovel, Joel. 2002. *The Enemy of Nature: The End of Capitalism or the End of the World?* Fernwood. Halifax, Nova Scotia.

Kovel, Joel and Michael Löwy. 2002. An Ecosocialist Manifesto. 13 *Capitalism Nature Socialism* 1: 1–2, 155–7 (March).

Lancy, David F. 2008. *The Anthropology of Childhood*. Cambridge University Press. Cambridge.

Lawrence, D. H. 1968 [1930]. A Propos of Lady Chatterley's Lover. Pp. 487–515 in *Phoenix II*. Heinemann. London.

Layzer, Judith. 2007. Deep Freeze: How Business Has Shaped the Global Warming Debate in Congress. Pp. 93–125 in Michael E. Kraft and Sheldon Kamieniecki (eds.). *Business and Environmental Policy*. MIT Press. Cambridge, MA.

Leach, Edmund. 1968. *A Runaway World?* Oxford University Press. Oxford.

Lenzen, M., D. Moran, K. Kanemoto, B. Foran, L. Lobefaro, and A. Geschke1. 2012. International Trade Drives Biodiversity Threats in Developing Nations. 486 *Nature* 109–12 (June 7).

Lindblom, Charles. 1977. *Politics and Markets*. Basic Books. New York.

Liu, Hwa-Jen. 2015. *Leverage of the Weak*. University of Minnesota Press. Minneapolis, MN.

Lovelock, James. 1979. *Gaia: A New Look at Life on Earth*. Oxford University Press. Oxford.

Maniates, Michael and John M. Meyer (eds.). 2010. *The Environmental Politics of Sacrifice*. MIT Press. Cambridge, MA.

Marris, Emma. 2011. *Rambunctious Garden*. Bloomsbury. New York.

Noss, Reed. 1992. The Wildlands Project Land Conservation Strategy. *Wild Earth* Special Issue 1: 10–25.

Pinard, Maurice. 2011. *Motivational Dimensions in Social Movements and Contentious Collective Action*. McGill-Queens University Press. Montreal.

Quinn, Daniel. 1992. *Ishmael*. Bantam Books. New York.

Rappaport, Roy A. 1999. *Ritual and Religion in the Making of Humanity*. Cambridge University Press. Cambridge.

Rodman, John. 1977. The Liberation of Nature? 20 *Inquiry* 83–131.

Scott, James C. 1998. *Seeing Like a State*. Yale University Press. New Haven, CT.

Searles, Harold F. 1960. *The Non-human Environment in Normal Development and in Schizophrenia*. International Universities Press. New York.

Shepard, Paul. 1982. *Nature and Madness*. Sierra Club Books. San Francisco.

Singer, P. W. 2007. *Corporate Warriors*. 2nd edn. Cornell University Press. Ithaca, NY.

Smil, Vaclav. 2013. *Harvesting the Biosphere*. MIT Press. Cambridge, MA.

Solomon, Sheldon, Jeffrey L. Greenberg, and Thomas A. Pyszczynski. 2004. Lethal Consumption: Death-Denying Materialism. Pp. 127–46 in Tim Kasser and Allen D. Kanner (eds.). *Psychology and Consumer Culture*. American Psychological Association. Washington, DC.

Thoreau, Henry David. 1964 [1854]. *Walden*. Pp. 258–572 in Carl Bode (ed.). *The Portable Thoreau*. Viking Press. New York.

Vest, Jay Hansford C. 1985. Will-of-the-Land. 9 *Environmental Review* 4: 321–9 (Winter).

Wright, Ronald. 2004. *A Short History of Progress*. Anansi. Toronto.

Wuerthner, George, Eileen Crist, and Tom Butler (eds.). 2014. *Keeping the Wild*. Island Press. Washington DC.

Conclusion

We want no straddlers. For in the past far too much good wilderness has been lost by those whose first instinct is to compromise.

Bob Marshall (1934)

... [M]an claimed the earth was made for him ... [but] venomous beasts, thorny plants, and deadly diseases ... prove that the whole world was not made for him.

John Muir (1916: 358)

This book addresses why conservation is failing and what can be done to improve its efficacy. The situation of wildlife and wild places is dire. Only in novels can wildlife conspire to rebel in self-defense against human invaders. Absent that, it is up to some humans to contain the entire species' destructiveness, attempts at colonial domination and violence. This book suggests some tools that have been effective at various times for a broad range of social movements, including conservation.

The main obstacles to conservation are political, not difficult-to-solve scientific problems. The US congressional removal of protection from wolves in the US northern Rocky Mountains was a political decision and conservationists were too politically weak to prevent it. The failure of governments to reach Millennium Biodiversity goals and to make much progress on the Achi goals is political. The weakness of the Paris Climate Accord is due to a failure of political will.

At a broad level there exists among conservationists with vision a strong sense that half the Earth must be set aside for other species and their communities and that the other half of the Earth – for people – must not be allowed to degrade the former. Typically many areas set aside for non-humans are the least productive; determining which other areas, including highly productive areas, are needed to secure and restore biodiversity so that it can thrive on land, in the streams and lakes and oceans is not the challenge. The challenge is how to get there. What is the strategy?

To develop a strategy, specific goals must be set, decision makers identified, the elements of a coalition that can sway the decision makers determined, and those elements mobilized for collective political action. Mobilization involves not only coalition building but bringing new people directly into conservation organizations where they are available for action to bring pressure on decision makers or to replace them. It will require, among other things, that conservation goals become a high priority for a sufficient number of people to "make decision makers do the right thing" with regard to the goal.

Conservationists find themselves seeking direct protection of places but also doing battle with the causes of biological decline: growth in human population and consumption. The two are entwined, but as a practical matter it won't be one big conflict but many linked conflicts. As conservationists succeed with protection they will more and more come up against the obstacle of growth in individual fights. And protected areas will be threatened, as they are around the world, by the pressure of people seeking land and enterprises seeking "resources."

To prevail in safeguarding half of the Earth conservation will have to address the causes of biological decline and how to reorder human societies to make them compatible with wild places and creatures. Struggles over creation of protected areas can be framed as serving people increasingly sequestered in urban areas and needing places they can retreat to, but eventually those retreats and the growing human footprint will clash and require social changes so that PAs can be secured. Individual PA struggles will need to be linked with other PA struggles and linked to struggles over social change which are likely to occur on the national or multinational stage. Both types of linkages, for strategic reasons, may be stressed or played down.

Powerful countries will intervene in weaker countries and across the globe, as they always have, and their domestic politics will necessarily become an important arena of conflict for weaker countries and international regimes. Resources still flow from the global south to the global north and rich countries won't sit by while their interests are threatened.

Nothing like the effort to stop growth and its destructiveness has ever been attempted. Creating a PA is not a wholesale house cleaning. A wholesale political house cleaning is not the same as toppling a system and replacing it with another. Toppling a system and replacing it with another is not the same as dismantling a form of social organization with 10,000 years of inertia behind it and a leadership that will stop at nothing to preserve its interests.

Extinction is not just the enemy, biological decline is the enemy. Human societies have been eroding biodiversity and ecological health for a long, long time by taking, degrading, and transforming habitat (the homes of others) to exploit it for human uses. Humans have also directly persecuted other species. In the last 200 years human population and consumption have grown exponentially. In the twentieth century alone, human population more than tripled, from 1.6 billion to 6.1 billion. Consumption doubled between 1900 and 1950, then quadrupled between 1950 and 1992 and continues to grow.

Conservation is engaged in many asymmetric conflicts. The fight for wolves in the US Rockies was lost because those who sought to ensure re-election of a US senator were not convinced conservationists could deliver the organizing necessary to win the election. Indeed, they were not organizing in Montana. A mostly insider approach was not convincing to decision makers. Conservationists could have prevailed but in this case let themselves be run over.

The strategic failure of conservationists to protect wolves from the political party that nominally supported them does not bode well for causal issues in which prevailing is truly an uphill fight. Yet since the end of World War II the weaker party has prevailed in asymmetric conflicts against the stronger slightly more than half the time by pursuing strategies that the strong were not prepared for. So it is not just a matter of conservation being weaker or stronger in the classic sense of the term – being able to *force* certain actions from decision makers – but being able to get the desired decisions by virtue of strategy, leadership, resolve, and sometimes luck. Force does play and will play a role in some parts of the world and conservation can be dangerous work; there are too many dead park rangers and activists, let alone elephants, orangutans, lions, and millions of other species, to deny that defensive measures are important in places such as the Amazon and the Congo. Independent movements are not tolerated in places like China or Iran, and even in so-called democracies repression is common when powerful interests are challenged. The US abolitionist Frederick Douglass was not the firebrand John Brown was, but he understood that people with power did not give it up without a fight.

International morality and increasingly international law recognize the right of insurgency against colonization. The subjugation of other species and the natural world is not recognized, but action has always preceded rule changes. Rights are taken, not granted.

Efforts at fundamental social change have often failed or created worse outcomes than planned. But there are reasons to think fundamental change is possible. It will be contentious, but climate change, crises from oppressive structures, breakdown of increasingly (and pointlessly) complex economic arrangements, and emotional estrangement generate opportunities for change. Crises often mean elite unity breaks down and this provides opportunities as well, in part because elite factions need non-elite allies and are forced to bargain. Biodiversity-compatible human societies won't come about automatically: conservationists will have to jettison their timidity and push hard, as activists did against apartheid, Pinochet and other grim circumstances. To prevail requires organizing, organizing, and more organizing. There is no substitute for mobilizing political resources for collective political action to pressure, resist, take direct

action, and build alternative institutions. Organizing includes mobilizing people into conservation NGOs that make good use of their
activism, and forging alliances.

Alliance partners can be recruited on the basis of common
concerns, if less often on the basis of common interests. Humans are
often at odds with wildlife because they want more for themselves.
On a finite Earth, that clashes with conservation. But on specific goals
Nimby groups, religious and animal groups, cultural leaders (film,
music), some business entities, nationalist groups that take pride in
wildlife and that harbor anti-colonial feelings, youth, public health
groups, some legal groups, some women's groups, some labor groups,
and pro-democracy groups do support conservation.

The experience of efforts at large-scale conservation and restoration offers several lessons. The larger vision must be brought to
ground – the specifics of scale, place, and species are necessary to
guide action toward attaining goals. Scientific findings, scientific
judgment, and the precautionary principle are important elements,
but decisions often must be made without all the desired information.
The behavior of people and the timing of decision making will drive
the process.

In some geographic regions such as Costa Rica, Gorongosa, or
Patagonia, it is possible to achieve goals through insider approaches
and with the cooperation of top decision makers. In other cases, such
as the US forest wars, road building, and deforestation in the Amazon,
Congo, Indonesia, and elsewhere, or illegal fishing, and whaling, outsider approaches are important. To shy away from contentious politics is to miss opportunities to mobilize people and strengthen
organization. To shy away from contentious politics is to accept the
wholesale destruction of wildlife, the murder of rangers and activists.
To shy away from contentious politics is to ignore the responsibility
of conservationists to fight back and come to the aid of those working
in especially oppressive places. To shy away from contentious politics
is to undermine the moral and legal claims of the right to fight against
the infliction of bodily harm. To shy away from contentious politics is

to ignore the problem of weak states and corrupt states and the need to act against the destruction of wildlife when governments cannot. Enforcement is critical to making protected areas and other laws work, including when governments are violating the law.

The more financially self-sufficient NGOs can be, the more autonomy they have to act. Professionalization has raised the cost of running organizations, but even with grassroots organizations of low-paid activists funding is necessary for land purchases and restoration, for communications and other campaign expenses, and for independent enforcement where it is needed.

It is difficult for conservationists to stay ahead of the assault on wildlife and wild places, whether work is prioritized based on threats or opportunities. This whole book is in some sense about getting ahead of the curve: it is better biologically to conserve than to have to restore. What can help with ramping up conservation in addition to what we have discussed so far in this concluding summary? Systematically documenting campaigns and their lessons could help enormously as would restricting circulation of lessons to conservation NGOs. A greater sense of urgency among conservationists would help increase capacity to take on more projects and chip away at how far behind the curve protection efforts are. The loss of biodiversity calls upon conservationists to achieve the levels of mobilization achieved by some countries in the most extreme emergencies. It may also help to focus on expanding existing protected areas rather than distinct new ones.

To protect enough of the Earth to safeguard and recover species, ecosystem types, and disturbance regimes will require very large-scale ecological restoration rather than meliorative restoration, i.e. recreating those aspects of the world humans favor. The wild Earth is not "open space," nor a garden or a farm. Agricultural euphemisms and similar must be dispensed with: terms like harvest (wildlife are not crops), take, collect, cull, and resources all sanitize and mask human activity which is violent and ugly. Effective restoration requires clear goals; a clear legal structure that encourages local support – including identifying who is local and shares in the benefits of protection, such as ecotourism and other compatible economic activity that supports local well-being (not "development"); clear, enforced boundaries for protected areas, connections and human use zones; effective leadership; compelling stories that capture people's imagination and dispel fear; and an end to injuries to the lands and oceans caused by pollution, bottom trawling, industrial fishing, roads, dams, and livestock. Because the oceans are invisible to most humans, building support for their restoration depends on charismatic species.

Over the last few decades conservationists have talked much about needing good stories, but there is little evidence they understand the relationship between stories about day-to-day behavior, stories about how the world works at large (cause and effect) and stories about meaning and purpose, especially the most fundamental purposes of a culture: myth. Myths are stories about the sacred and they legitimate the stories about cause and effect and that guide day-to-day behavior. The world needs a new sacred: to care for the Earth and all its creatures. Conservation, if it is to achieve its goals, needs the world to embrace a new sacred story: humans have broken the world and now must heal it. They must act to overcome and stop those that persist in causing the world injury. At the same time systematic propagation of this new sacred to the coming generations is necessary as is its propagation to all others through ritual, music, song, cinema, theater, dance, holidays, and new institutions which foster basic human well-being without diminishing other species.

Conservationists have the basics of a new sacred story but it is in the form of a fable and incomplete; it awaits the characters and drama that make myth and other stories satisfying.

Just as owning human beings came to be seen as wrong and just as colonialism came to be seen as wrong, and just as these changed views gave justification to struggles to end slavery and colonial domination, so the domination of the natural world must come to an end. The struggles against slavery and colonialism – and more subtle forms of human-on-human domination – were extraordinarily difficult. Those with material and emotional vested interests in domination did not give up easily, they had to be pushed to the wall. And all along they sought to justify these ugly and violent relationships as just and natural. Moral outrage eventually prevailed if at a high cost.

Now some conservationists and others are challenging as never before the limits of what humans consider community. It is not a matter of toppling this or that 1 percent, only to have another elite replace it. Nor is it a matter of replacing one system with another if it continues to be based on the domination of the natural world, as most societies have been for a dozen millennia. Equity among humans does not mean equity among species, as should be all too clear when one listens to most humans debate matters of justice. The history of human societies has been destructive of the natural world even before the Neolithic, when such destructiveness became institutionalized. Now those institutions must be dismantled and the behavior of all humanity reconstructed.

As long as the domination of the natural world inheres in any form of human society, humans will be forced to live the lives of slaveholders – divided against themselves, afraid that the violence they do unto others will be done unto them, and alienated from the Earth that produced them. Love and domination are opposites. To try to ignore this tension or to make believe the domination is not real because it is out of sight – the messy work, as always, left to those who have no choice but to work in the "slaughterhouse" – leaves people alienated from that which is dominated, and managing that alienation is exhausting. Humans may never face the rebellion William Kotzwinkle imagines in *Doctor Rat* – and if we do it will likely be a virus, not mammals. But we do face the trauma of continually "bleeding at the roots" (Lawrence 1968 [1930]: 504). What we do to the world "out there" we do to ourselves. Having to numb ourselves to the pain we cause by our violence leaves us less than half alive.

REFERENCES

Lawrence, D. H. 1968 [1930]. A Propos of Lady Chatterley's Lover. Pp. 487–515 in *Phoenix II*. Heinemann. London.

Marshall, Robert. 1934. Letter to Harold Anderson, October 24. Robert Marshall Papers. Bancroft Library, University of California, Berkeley.

Muir, John. 1916. A Thousand Mile Walk to the Gulf. Pp. 231–416 in *The Story of My Boyhood and Youth*. Houghton-Mifflin. Boston, MA.

Index